W. JEROME D. SPENCE.

A HISTORY

OF

HICKMAN COUNTY

TENNESSEE

BY
W. JEROME D. SPENCE AND
DAVID L. SPENCE

"Some said, Print it; others said, Not so;
Some said, It might do good; others said, No."

NASHVILLE, TENN.
GOSPEL ADVOCATE PUBLISHING COMPANY
1900

Southern Historical Press
%The Rev. S. Emmett Lucas, Jr.
P. O. Box 738
Easley, South Carolina   29640

ISBN   0-89308-242-2

TO THE MEMORY OF

THE PIONEERS OF HICKMAN COUNTY

AND TO OUR FRIENDS WHEREVER FOUND

THIS BOOK IS DEDICATED BY

THE AUTHORS

PREFACE.

In this Preface to that which is perhaps a History, the authors desire to make some explanations, that those who would criticise may, after reading them, be just to themselves by not being unjust to us.

In the preparation of this book our source of information has been largely oral tradition, with but little documentary testimony at our disposal as to names and dates. Often statements made to us by different parties as to the same facts have differed radically. In many cases we have possibly accepted the wrong version. After an investigation of several years we are of opinion, however, that the things herein stated are in the main true. Where misstatements and errors occur we, in advance, express our regrets. To many Hickman County families we have not given the space which we desired to give them, solely on account of our inability to procure from these families the full information which we desired. We have used the most strenuous efforts in an attempt to secure a perfect list of Hickman County's soldiers, especially a correct list of those who wore the gray. In this we have been partially successful; and if those who read this knew how difficult it is, even after the lapse of a few years, to procure a correct and complete list of

Hickman County's Confederate soldiers, they would realize that in the list which we publish alone they have a full return for the price of this book. We hope those who are about to criticise will hesitate for a moment, and then conclude that, as this is the only History of Hickman County ever published, it is, after all, the best.

CONTENTS.

A HISTORY OF
HICKMAN COUNTY, TENN.

CHAPTER I.

EARLY HISTORY OF TENNESSEE.

IN 1540, forty-eight years after the discovery of
America by Columbus, Ferdinand De Soto, a Spanish explorer, after fighting his way with disastrous loss
through successive Indian tribes from the shores of
Florida through Georgia, Alabama, and Mississippi,
crossed with his army the Mississippi River at the
Indian village of Chisca, which stood upon the present site of Memphis. These were the first white men
who trod upon the soil which is now Tennessee. It
has been claimed that De Soto, in his wanderings,
traversed a portion of East Tennessee. This conten-
tion, however, is not supported by authentic proof.
De Soto found a burial place in the Father of
Waters nearer its mouth, and until 1682, when Robert
Cavelier Sieur de La Salle built the French fort of
Prud'homme, on Chickasaw Bluffs, now Memphis, the
savages held undisputed control of what is now Tennessee. In 1714 M. Charleville, a French trader, came
from Crozat's colony, at New Orleans, and built a

store " on a mound on the west side of the Cumberland River, near French Lick, in the Shawnee country." While the exact location of this store is not known, it was within the present corporate limits of the city of Nashville. The presence of Charleville and other French traders gave to the salt lick " on the west side of the Cumberland River " the name of " French Lick."

Despite the fact that English possessions in America were not recognized by Spain till 1670, Sir Humphrey Gilbert and others petitioned Queen Elizabeth, in the spring of 1574, " to allow of an enterprise for the discovery of sundry rich and unknown lands fatally reserved for England, and for the honor of your Majestie." In 1578 Queen Elizabeth complied by granting to Sir Humphrey Gilbert a patent " to undertake the discovery of the northern parts of America." Gilbert lost his life in 1583, and during the following year his grant was renewed to his half-brother, Sir Walter Raleigh. Raleigh's grant included the present State of Tennessee. The failure of the attempt to plant a colony on Roanoke Island; the birth of Virginia Dare, the first English child born in America; the final fate of the gallant, yet unfortunate, Raleigh ; and the story of what Spencer called " the fruitfulest Virginia " are all too well known to be further referred to here. No successful attempts were made by Raleigh to explore the interior, and his attempts at American colonization were fruitless, save that it was he who introduced tobacco and the Irish potato into England. Others less worthy than he profited by his mistakes and succeeded where he had failed.

In 1665 Charles II., King of England, granted land in America to Edward, Earl of Clarendon; Monk, Lord Craven, Lord Ashley Cooper, Sir John Colleton, Lord John Berkeley, Sir George Carteret, and Sir William Berkeley. Tennessee was included in this grant, it being until 1790 a part of North Carolina. The Lords Proprietors, as Clarendon and his associates were called, employed the celebrated philosopher, John Locke, to prepare a Fundamental Constitution. The " Grand Model " which Locke produced, providing for an intricate system of government by landgraves, caziques, and barons, was not suited for the swamps and poor and scattered people, and was therefore never more than a theory. A partial attempt to put it into execution completely failed after a trial of twenty-two years. North Carolina became a royal province in 1729, it having been ruled by a governor until that time.

In 1748 Dr. Thomas Walker, of Virginia, and a party of explorers penetrated Tennessee and gave the name of Cumberland to the mountains and river of that name, they being named in honor of the Duke of Cumberland.

In the granting of lands in America by the sovereigns of England, the claims of the Indians to these lands had been ignored. In 1756 a treaty was made with the Cherokees by Governor Dobbs, of North Carolina, which allowed the establishment of forts on

Indian lands. As a result, Fort Dobbs, in Rowan County, North Carolina, was built this year. In the following year Fort Loudoun (Loudon) was built at the junction of the Tellico and Little Tennessee Rivers by the English under Gen. Andrew Lewis. "This was the first fort built by the English-speaking people on Tennessee soil," and was named in honor of John Campbell, Earl of Loudoun. This fort remained in the hands of the English until 1760, when the Cherokees, enraged by an unfortunate collision with Virginians, attacked it and massacred the entire garrison with the exception of one " messenger of defeat," who escaped. This was avenged by Colonel Grant, who, in the following year, burned the Indian town of Etchoe. In this campaign against the Indians Gen. Francis Marion saw his first service. He was a lieutenant in the company commanded by Capt. William Moultrie.

The following inscription may yet be seen on a beech on Boone's Creek, near Jonesboro: " D. Boon cilled A BAR on tree in The year 1760." In this year Timote de Mont Breun (Timothy Demonbreun), a French soldier who had served under Montcalm in Canada, came to the French Lick, on the Cumberland. He was the first white settler of Nashville, and has hundreds of descendants in Tennessee.

The Treaty of Paris in 1763 gave to England the sovereignty of that region of the United States east of the Mississippi, a portion of which, including Tennessee, having hitherto been claimed by France.

In 1768 the treaty of Stanwix with the Six Nations

gave Tennessee to the King of England. This treaty was probably ratified by a few Cherokees who were present, but its conditions were never complied with by them.

In 1766 Colonel James, Joshua Horton, Uriah Stone, and William Baker, of Carlisle, Pa., with a negro slave belonging to Horton, explored the country around Nashville and named Stone's River after Uriah Stone. Three years later William Bean built a cabin at the junction of Watauga River and Boone's Creek. His son, Russell Bean, was the first white child born in Tennessee. During the same year (1769) Abraham Bledsoe, Casper Mansker, and others came from Virginia to where Nashville now stands. They found immense herds of buffalo and other game in abundance. In 1770 James Robertson, "the father of Tennessee," settled on the Watauga River, in East Tennessee. During this year Colonel James Knox and a party of hunters and explorers went as far west as the mouth of the Cumberland River. In the following year Casper Mansker established a station on Station Camp Creek, in what is now Sumner County.

In 1772 the settlements in East Tennessee combined under the name of the Watauga Association. This desire upon the part of the early settlers of what is now Tennessee for local self-government finally gave rise in 1784 to the establishment of the State of Franklin. The story of the State of Franklin and of its Governor, John Sevier, the idolized "Nolachucky Jack" of the mountaineers, is one of the most interesting to be found in the pages of Tennessee history. In 1774 Tennessee made its début as the "Volunteer State," when Capt. Evan Shelby and his company of fifty men participated in the battle of Kanawha, or Point Pleasant. The trouble between England and the colonies was now coming on. The North Carolina "Regulators" had, several years before this (1771), resisted British tyranny, the battle of Alamance being the result. Numbers of the defeated "Regulators" sought freedom over the mountains in what is now Tennessee. Now, when they saw that the struggle was surely coming on, they acted with the same promptness that had characterized their actions when they were called upon to resist Governor Tryon's tyranny.

On May 20, 1775, the patriots of Mecklenburg County, N. C., met and adopted resolutions which have passed into history under the name of the "Mecklenburg Resolutions." This was over a year before Jefferson wrote the Declaration of Independence, and some of the very phrases found in the "Mecklenburg Resolutions" are embodied in the Declaration of Independence. Later—April 4, 1776—the Provincial Congress of North Carolina, having among its members men from what is now Tennessee, passed resolutions favoring the United Colonies declaring independence. Tennessee now had a population of 600. The Whigs had a sufficient majority to enable them to force the Tories of the Nolachucky settlement to take an oath of allegiance to the Revolutionary cause. To-day there are many families in Hickman County who can give the names of ancestors who fought for American liberty during the Revolutionary War. The first white man to raise a crop in Middle Tennessee was Thomas Sharpe Spencer—erroneously called by Phelan "James Spencer"—who came to Bledsoe's Lick, now Castalian Springs, in 1776. He was a very large man, but lived during his stay at the Lick in a hollow sycamore tree. Many are the stories that have been handed down to us regarding the gigantic Spencer. That he was as generous as he was brave is exemplified in the story that when his comrade, Holliday, became faint-hearted and desired to return, Spencer broke his own knife and gave one of the pieces to Holliday, who had no knife. It is related that one of Captain Demonbreun's hunters, seeing one of Spencer's large footprints and not knowing that Spencer was in the vicinity, deserted his cabin and fled in terror to the French settlements on the Wabash, thinking that he had wandered into a land of giants. Notwithstanding his great strength, Spencer was for peace. Upon one occasion, in order to pacify a belligerent backwoodsman, he picked him up and tossed him over a ten-rail fence. Spencer was one of the first settlers at Nashville, and there had several bloody encounters with, and hair-breadth escapes from, the Indians. It was from their hands, however, that he finally received his death wound. This occurred in a mountain pass, near the present site of Crossville, in what is now Cumberland County. One of his peculiarities was that he would always go several yards either behind or in front of his party. This peculiarity, doubtless, cost him his life. Riding several yards in advance of his party, he was killed from ambush by Indians. The place where he fell has since that day been called "Spencer's Hill." This occurred in 1794. Spencer, the county site of Van Buren County, is named for this "big-foot hunter." Jonesboro, the first town in the State, was established by an Act of the North Carolina Legislature in 1778, being named for Willie Jones, of that State. In 1779 Tidence Lane organized the first Baptist Church in the State and commenced to preach regularly to the congregation. This church was on Buffalo Ridge, in what is now East Tennessee. Seven years before this Charles Cummins, a Presbyterian preacher, had established a church at the Watauga settlement, the location of the church being, however, within the present limits of the State of Virginia. The Baptist Church was therefore the pioneer church of Tennessee. Samuel Doak, the celebrated Presbyterian, commenced to preach to the people in Washington and Sullivan Counties a short time after Lane made his appearance on Buffalo Ridge.

During the winter of 1779-80 James Robertson, Mark Robertson, Zachariah White, and others came through Southern Kentucky from East Tennessee to the French Lick, on the Cumberland. New arrivals soon increased the number to about 300. This was the beginning of the permanent settlement of what afterwards became Nashville. On December 22, 1779, John Donelson started " in the good boat Adventure from Fort Patrick Henry, on Holston River, to the French Salt Spring, on Cumberland River." Donelson's party was composed of the families and friends of those who had gone with Robertson's company. After going down the Tennessee River to the Ohio River, up the Ohio to the Cumberland, and up the Cumberland to French Lick, the voyage ended on April 24, 1780. Of this expedition, it has been said: " It has no parallel in modern history." The winter of 1779-80 was one of unusual severity. The settlement at the Bluffs, near French Lick, was called " Nashborough," in honor of Gen. Francis Nash, a North Carolinian who had fallen in the battle of Brandywine. The fort of the settlement was situated on what is now Front street, Nashville, between the southeast corner of the Public Square and Church street (formerly called Spring street), near where the Davidson County jail now stands. Here the "battle of the Bluffs " was fought on April 2, 1781. The condition of these pioneers was very precarious until the close of the Revolutionary War, in 1782, and the advent of the commissioners appointed by North Carolina to run the Continental Line, which is referred to elsewhere. These commissioners were accompanied by a strong guard. From that time the permanency of the settlement on the Cumberland was assured, although the dangers and the hardships were far from being all removed.

Before the close of the Revolutionary War (October 7, 1780), 440 East Tennesseans, under Cols. John Sevier and Isaac Shelby, gave Great Britain a sample of what she afterwards received at New Orleans, by assisting in the defeat of Ferguson at King's Mountain. King's Mountain has been called "the turning point of the Revolution." In this engagement the American loss in killed and wounded was 88; the British lost 505 killed and wounded, and 600 captured.

James Robertson (1783) was Davidson County's first representative in the North Carolina Legislature. This year, Rev. Jeremiah Lambert came to the Holston Circuit, he being the first Methodist to preach in Tennessee. The following year a town was established at the Bluffs on the Cumberland by the North Carolina Legislature, the old name of Nashborough giving way to the present name of Nashville.

In 1789 the North Carolina Legislature passed the Act ceding to the United States territory embracing the present State of Tennessee. In the following year a deed was made, and on April 2, 1790, the territory was accepted by Act of Congress. William Blount was appointed Governor of this Territory, "the Territory South of the Ohio River." The Territory was divided into two districts—Washington and Miro. The latter embraced the counties of Davidson, Sumner, and Tennessee; and, therefore, included a large portion of the present county of Hickman. The name of this district is spelled " M-E-R-O " in all of the old records, but the name was given in honor of Don Estevan Miro (pronounced " Mero "), the Spanish Governor of New Orleans. This was done upon the suggestion of James Robertson, who was desirous of keeping on friendly terms with the Spanish, who then had control of the Mississippi River. James Robertson was appointed brigadier general of this district by President George Washington. In February of the following year (1791) he was made a major general in the United States Army. A few months later he was with Edwin Hickman, in what is now Hickman County, being present at the time of the Indians' attack upon the party near the present site of Centerville.

The following year (June 26, 1792) Zeigler's Station, in Sumner County, was captured and burned by Creek Indians. September 30 was the date of the attack on Buchanan's Station, four miles south of Nashville. The Indians were 700 strong, but were defeated by the fort's fifteen gallant defenders.

On June 1, 1796, Tennessee was admitted into the Union. Previous to this (January 11) a Constitutional Convention convened at Knoxville, and, upon the suggestion of Andrew Jackson, a delegate from Davidson County, the name " Tennessee " was given to the State. On November 12 he was commissioned as the first Representative in Congress from the new State. The winter of 1796-7 is said to have been the coldest in the history of the State.

CHAPTER II.

SOME PIONEER HISTORY.

IN the preceding chapter is given an outline of the early history of Tennessee in general and of the Cumberland settlement in particular. All of this is indirectly connected with the history of Hickman County. In this chapter those incidents more directly connected with its history will be referred to. A large number, if not all, of the early explorers of what is now Hickman County came from the Cumberland settlements.

In May, 1780, a few months after the commencement of the settlement at the Bluffs (now Nashville), Indians made a raid around Freeland's Station and captured a number of horses, loaded with meat, from Thomas Sharpe Spencer, who was returning to the Bluffs from a hunting tour. A pursuing party, headed by James Robertson, was organized. The party was composed of about twenty men, but the names of only three others are known—Alexander Buchanan, John Brock, and William Mann. Buchanan had come to the Bluffs from South Carolina, together with John Buchanan, Sampson Williams, Thomas Thompson, and others. He was one of the number killed by the Indians during the battle of the Bluffs on April 2, 1781. ' This pursuing party followed the Indians to a point near the old Lick, on Lick Creek, in the Fourth

District.   Here they came within hearing distance of
the pursued, who were building their camp fires.   The
whites dismounted and marched upon the Indians,
who deserted their camp and escaped.   The stolen
property was recovered and returned to the Bluffs.
This expedition was the first that went from Nashville
against the Indians.

At the close of the Revolutionary War, North Carolina had no money with which to pay her disbanded
soldiers.   It was decided to give them, in payment for
their services, land in the western portion of the State,
in what is now Tennessee.

By an Act of the North Carolina Legislature, in
1782, Anthony Bledsoe, Absalom Tatum, and Isaac
Shelby were appointed commissioners to lay off lands
to be allotted to the soldiers of the Continental Line.
They were to have guards not exceeding one hundred
in number.   In February, 1783, the commissioners
went from Nashville to Latitude Hill, in Giles County,
and, after having located the southern boundary of
the State, they went fifty-five miles to the north and
ran parallel to this southern boundary a line known
as the " Commissioners' Line."   This was to mark the
boundary of the land to be given to the Continental
soldiers.   This party at the same time laid off the
25,000 acres of land given by North Carolina to Gen.
Nathaniel Greene, they locating it in what is now
Maury County.   The Commissioners' Line ran
through Hickman County, passing near the present
site of Vernon, and some of those who went this way

in surveying and marking it were: James Robertson, Anthony Bledsoe, Daniel Smith, Isaac Bledsoe, Casper Mansker, Philamon Thomas, Elijah Robertson, Frederick Stump, Thomas Call, Andrew Casselman, William Davidson, William Loggins, Andrew Boyd, Patrick McCutchin, Samuel McCutchin, James McCutchin, James Hollis, Turner Williams, Sampson Williams, James Clendenning, David Frazier, Samuel Barton, Robert Branks, Ephraim McClain, Jr., Julius Sanders, William Collinsworth, David Hay, James Todd, Thomas Spencer, Edward Cox, William Bradshaw, Nathaniel McClure, Absalom Tatum, two men named Shelley, and three McMurrays. Many of these are names which often occur in the early annals of Tennessee. No marks of this line, however, can now be found in Hickman County. It immediately ceased to be a line of notoriety and is not mentioned in any of the early grants. The reason is this: The officers and soldiers of North Carolina were not satisfied with the allotment of lands made by the commissioners, and the North Carolina Legislature immediately passed an Act fixing the boundaries of the Continental Reservation as follows: " Beginning on the Virginia [Kentucky] line, where the Cumberland River intersects the same; thence south fifty-five miles; thence west to the Tennessee River; thence down the Tennessee River to the Virginia [Kentucky] line; thence with the said Virginia line to the beginning." General Rutherford was selected to supervise the running of this line, and, in February, 1784, he and party began on the Virginia (now the Kentucky) line and ran what they supposed to be fifty-five miles to the south to Mount Pisgah. Here the party divided, one portion going east to the Caney Fork River, and the other portion going west to the Tennessee River. The party which went east became confused in the snow, found that they were declining too far to the north, changed compasses, but continued confused. The surveyors of the party went as far east as Powell's River. Having failed to commence at the starting point provided for by the Act when they commenced their measurements to the south, the eastern boundary of the reservation was never run by North Carolina. This was done in 1807, by William Christmas, surveyor of the First District of Tennessee. The southern boundary, although run several miles too far to the south, was recognized as the true Continental Line, and was so called; the other being known as the Commissioners' Line. The surveyor, John Davis, who knew the location of the two lines, said that the Continental Line (the line of 1784) was seven or eight miles south of the Commissioners' Line (the line of 1783). The close proximity of these two lines—the one, legal; the other, not—caused much confusion, which was often worse confounded by designing land speculators, and the courts were often called upon to settle disputes as to land titles where the Continental Line was called for. Judge Parry W. Humphreys, in May, 1808, said: " The line run in February, 1784, is the true Continental Line and no person can be permitted to dispute it." The party which went west from Mount Pisgah ran the line, which is yet found to be plainly marked, through Hickman County. There were about sixty in this party, but the names of only the following have been preserved: Thomas Wright, John Hardin, —— Frazier, Henry Rutherford, John Tate (chain carrier), William Polk, Ezekiel Polk, Ephraim McClain, Sr., —— Bradley, and John Hibbets. Ezekiel Polk was the grandfather of President James K. Polk. Mount Pisgah, where the party divided, was twelve miles east of where the line crossed Carter's Creek, in Maury County. By some of this party this creek was known as " Hardin's Creek," named for John Hardin, who was one of the old men of the party. The name by which it finally came to be known was in honor of Capt. Benjamin Carter, for whom William Polk made an entry here. This line was marked by mile trees, and its course through Hickman County is as follows: Running west from Maury County, the first marked tree in Hickman County is on the ridge south of Leatherwood Creek and near the head of this creek. Another marked tree is on the farm of Dallas Johnson, near Jones' Valley. This tree is a beech. The line crosses Leatherwood Creek between the store at Jones' Valley and the Meadors place, crosses Duck River below the mouth of Leatherwood Creek, and runs into Anderson's Bend, where it was marked by a tree which stood in the yard where the pioneer, Robert Anderson, once lived. It leaves Anderson's Bend at the lower end.

Here a marked poplar tree on the Clifford Smith place, just above the mouth of Robertson's Creek, is still standing. After crossing the river at the lower end of Anderson's Bend it runs through the O. A. Jones farm and again crosses Duck River, running through the southern portion of Totty's Bend, near the phosphate mines. It crosses Swan Creek, near the river, and runs between Duck River and the Centerville and Columbia road, until it crosses this road south of Centerville. Crossing Indian Creek and Duck River, it runs through Shipp's Bend, near the place owned by the late John Thompson, and crosses Duck River above the Huddleston Bridge. It crosses Beaver Dam at the Jack Malugin place, and Sulphur Fork of Beaver Dam at the Jim Malugin place. Crossing the head of Cow Hollow, it continues west, crossing Buffalo River between Beardstown and Lobelville. It strikes the Tennessee River near Denson's Landing, in Perry County, the marked tree at this point being a sycamore. This line is well known from the point where it crosses Duck River, near the mouth of Leatherwood Creek, to its end on the bank of the Tennessee River in Perry County, this portion of the line being a portion of the Congressional Reservation Line of 1806. The purpose of the latter line is explained in following pages. In addition to the persons named above, Gen. Griffith Rutherford, Anthony Bledsoe, and Captain Looney were with the party which ran the line west from Mount Pisgah. Capt. John Rains was probably a member of this party, he having been a hunter for one of the parties. After reaching the Tennessee River they spent several days in camp, and members of the party made numerous entries along the Tennessee River and Buffalo River. These entries were made for themselves and friends, and a list of those in whose names entries were made in this section would not necessarily be a list of the names of the surveying party. Entries were made on Duck River; "Swan River, a branch of Duck River;" and " Cane Creek, a branch of Buffalo River," as the party went on its way to the Tennessee River, and by individual members on their return. The party divided into several small parties, who returned by different routes to Nashville. On April 29, 1784, an entry was made in the name of George Wilson between the twentieth and twenty-first mile trees—nine miles west of where the line crossed Carter's Creek. This entry was transferred to William Polk. On April 30 an entry in the name of "Thomas Polk, son of Ezekiel Polk," was made on Cane Creek, " beginning at the place where Ezekiel Polk, Captain Looney, and others camped on their return from the Tennessee River in 1784, after having run the west line." Entries near this were made on the same day in the names of Samuel Polk, William Polk, and John Polk. Samuel Polk was the father of President James K. Polk. On the same day an entry in the name of Thomas Sprot was made " where the line struck Duck River the second time "—that is, in Anderson's Bend. Other entries were: April 30—Robert McCree, on east side of " Swan River," beginning at the thirty-second mile tree; George Wilson, at the mouth of Cane Creek; Adlai Osborn, two and a half miles above the mouth of Cane Creek; Adlai Osborn, " on Duck River, one-half mile below where the west line of 1784 crossed the third time; " Adlai Osborn, " on Swan River, a fork of Duck River, four miles above where the west line crosses it; " David McRee, on " Swan River," two and a half miles above this line; Samuel McLea, on " Swan River; " George Oliver, on " Buck Creek," two miles above this line; and Samuel McLea, on Cane Creek. Several of these entries were transferred to members of the Polk family. On May 7 this entry was made in the name of James Lindsey: " In Greene County, on the south side of Duck River, joining the line run in 1784 and including the place where the commissioners and guards camped on the south side of said river in 1784." On May 10 an entry in the name of John McFarland was made as follows: " On the south side of Duck River, above the red bank, including General Rutherford's encampment and a large Indian encampment." On May 15 an entry in the name of Nicholas Long was made on both sides of Duck River where the line crosses the first time. On May 22 this entry was made: " Thomas Norris—On the north side of Duck River where the west line crosses the first time, including a small branch and a spring, a tree marked J. R." On the same date is this entry: " Griffith Rutherford, Sr.—On the north side of Duck River, opposite a small creek that empties into the river on the south side, joining Rutherford's Ford and the camp where General Rutherford camped in March, 1784." On May 24 the following entries were made: " Abraham McLealen—On the north side of Duck River and south of the line run by Rutherford and Bledsoe, beginning at the twenty-first mile tree; " "Archibald Lytle—On Swan River three or four miles above where west line crosses; " " G. Kerr—On the north side of Duck River opposite the red bank, where line crosses the fifth time." On May 25 an entry in the name of Samuel Clenny was made on Swan River three miles above the line; and in the name of Thomas R. Sharpe, " on the south side of Duck River, beginning at the mouth of the first creek that runs into said river on the south side above the line of 1784."

In 1787 the Indians shot down and scalped a son of William Montgomery, on Drake's Creek, and killed a number of others throughout the Cumberland settlements. The act, however, which caused retribution to quickly follow was the killing of Mark Robertson. Clayton's " History of Davidson County " says: " In May, Mark Robertson, a brother of the Colonel, had been killed, after a desperate defense, near the latter's residence." Ramsey says: " In May the Indians came to Richland Creek, and in daylight killed Mark Robertson near the place where Robertson's mill was since erected. He was a brother of Colonel Robertson, and was returning from his house." James Robertson, writing to Governor Caswell, of North Carolina, a justification of the Coldwater expedition, says, under date of July 2, 1787: " My brother, Mark Robertson, being killed near my house, I, by the advice of the officers, civil and military, raised about one hundred and thirty men, and followed their tracks." As James Robertson then lived near the present site of West Nashville, these accounts would fix the place of Mark Robertson's death within the present limits of Davidson County. However, local tradition is to the effect that John Gordon, the pioneer scout and Indian fighter, repeatedly stated that Mark Robertson was killed at a spring on Robertson's Creek, in the Fifteenth District of Hickman County. The late Bolling Gordon, a man of prominence and veracity, is authority for the statement that his father, John Gordon, made this statement to him, pointed out the place where Robertson fell, and said that it was from this that the creek took its name. The historical accounts of the death of Mark Robertson were doubtless taken from the letter of James Robertson, and the historians quoted above easily construed the expression, " near my house," as meaning only a short distance away; when, in fact, forty miles, as compared with the distance to the capital of North Carolina, was " near my house." Mark Robertson was, at the time of his death, in the Indian country, and in justification of the Coldwater expedition James Robertson suppressed some of the facts and made the vague statement of " near my house." Haywood and Ramsey, after the lapse of years, accepted this statement as being literally true. If the Indians came to Nashville and killed Mark Robertson, James Robertson could have more easily defended his action in going on the expedition against them than he could if he admitted that, in fact, Mark Robertson was, at the time of his death, surveying in the Indian country and a trespasser on their territory. James Robertson, who followed the dictates of a brother's love, did right in going on this expedition; and when it was all over, he palliated Governor Caswell, who was far away from danger, and, therefore, prone to criticise, by the perhaps misleading statement of " near my house."

The duty of making expeditions against the Indians had been assigned to Evans' battalion by an Act of the North Carolina Legislature, but the delay occasioned by the recruiting and equipping of this battalion was so great that Colonel Robertson determined to organize an expedition upon his own responsibility. He accordingly called for volunteers from the several settlements. One hundred and thirty men responded to this call and assembled at his house. Of these he took command. He was assisted by Lieut. Cols. Robert Hays and James Ford. "Among the number was Capt. John Rains' company of spies or scouts, a body which for efficiency in border warfare was never surpassed." Other members of the party whose names have been preserved were: Joshua Thomas, Edmond Jennings, Benjamin Castleman, William Loggins,

William Steele, Martin (or Morton) Duncan, John Buchanan, Jonathan Denton, Benjamin Drake, John Eskridge, and Moses Eskridge.

Lieutenant Colonel Hays was a brother-in-law of Andrew Jackson, he marrying a daughter of John Donelson. In 1792 he was a colonel of cavalry. He, Castleman, Loggins, Duncan, Buchanan, and Drake were in 1787 taxpayers in Davidson County, and were twenty-three years of age or over. Lieut. Col. James Ford " was over six feet high, rather fleshy, and of commanding appearance." He became colonel in the Davidson County militia, and participated in the Nickajack Expedition. From 1793 to 1796 he represented Tennessee County, which embraced the larger part of Hickman County, in the Territorial Legislature. In 1796 he represented this county in the Constitutional Convention. He was afterwards in the State Legislature. A more extended sketch of Captain Rains will be found in the following pages. Joshua Thomas and Edmond Jennings were for years almost inseparable companions on the hunt and scout, sharing together the many hardships and few pleasures of frontier life. Thomas was killed during the Nickajack Expedition in 1794, he failing to heed Jennings' advice to " take a tree." Benjamin Castleman was one of the fighting Castlemans, one of the most fearless of the pioneer families of the Cumberland. In the tax list of 1787 the name " William Loggans " appears. In the list of participators in the Coldwater Expedition the name appears as " William Loggins."

John Buchanan, founder of Buchanan's Station and ancestor of the Governor of that name, was probably with this expedition. That his famous fowling piece was along is a certainty, as Edmond Jennings with it killed three Indians at one fire. Benjamin Drake was one of a family of early explorers. He was one of the signers of the Cumberland Compact; but as the tax list of 1787 shows two persons of this name, it is impossible to say which one participated in this expedition.

In the early part of June the men left Nashville, well armed and provided with dried meat and parched corn. They were accompanied by the Chief Toka and another Chickasaw, who, aware of the location of the camp of the recent marauders, had come to Nashville for the purpose of acting as guides. The route they pursued is given by Haywood as follows: " They crossed the mouth of South Harpeth; thence they went a direct course to the mouth of Turnbull's Creek; thence up the same to the head, and thence to Lick Creek of Duck River; thence down the creek seven or eight miles, leaving the creek to the right hand; thence to an old lick as large as a cornfield; thence to Duck River where the Old Chickasaw [Trace] crossed it; thence, leaving the trace to the right hand, they went to the head of Swan Creek, on the south side of Duck River; thence to a creek running into the Tennessee River, which the troops called Blue Water, and which ran into the Tennessee about a mile and a half above the lower end of the Muscle Shoals. They

left this creek on the left hand." A discussion of the
route through Hickman County may be found in the
following pages. Reaching the Tennessee, they remained in hiding, sending Captain Rains and a small
party out to reconnoiter. When night came on,
Thomas and Jennings swam the Tennessee, a mile
wide at this place, and brought over a very leaky canoe. Forty persons attempted to cross by standing
in the canoe and swimming by its side. In this they
were unsuccessful. The canoe was again brought to
the north side and patched up, after which a small
party crossed and took position in the woods. It now
being daylight, the remainder plunged their horses
into the stream and swam over without accident. Advancing about eight miles, they came upon the Indian
village, which they charged. The savages were
routed, and fled to their canoes, which were moored
upon the banks of Coldwater Creek. Here they were
met by a destructive fire from a party under the command of Captain Rains. Twenty-six warriors, together with three Frenchmen and a white woman,
were slain. The houses of the village were burned
and several French traders captured. Their goods
were put into the canoes of the Indians and placed in
charge of a detachment of whites, who proceeded down
the river to what has since been known as Colbert's
Ferry. Here the prisoners were released, their sugar
and coffee was divided among the troops, and their dry
goods carried by the boats to Eaton's Station, near
Nashville, and sold. From this point the troops

marched north until they struck the path leading to the Old Chickasaw Crossing, where they had crossed as they went out. From this point they returned as they had come, and reached Nashville after an absence of nineteen days. None of the party had been killed or wounded.

An expedition by water, which had started at the same time with the view of coöperating with the land force, was not so fortunate. Going down the Cumberland and up the Tennessee to the mouth of Duck River, they had met with no resistance. At this place a canoe was noticed tied a short distance up Duck River. Capt. Moses Shelby's boat went up to investigate, when it was fired upon by Indians concealed in the cane. Josiah Renfroe, one of the ill-fated family of Renfroes, a number of whom were killed by Indians, was shot through the head, and died almost instantly. Hugh Rogan and John Topp were shot through the body; Edward Hogan, through the arm; and five others were slightly wounded. This brought to a close this expedition, which was commanded by David Hay. The wounded were conveyed overland to Nashville, about seventy-five miles away. Rogan, who was an Irishman, carried his gun the entire distance, although he was shot through one lung. Captain Shelby, referred to above, had settled in what is now Montgomery County in 1783, and afterwards became a colonel of militia.

The troops under the immediate command of Captain Rains had several engagements with the Indians in 1787 before they went out with the Coldwater Expedition. In April, Curtis Williams and Thomas Fletcher had been killed by the Indians near the mouth of Harpeth. Colonel Robertson ordered Captain Rains to raise sixty men and pursue. Referring to Colonel Robertson's selecting Captain Rains for the performance of this duty, Haywood says: " He was led to this choice by the entire confidence he had learned by experience to place in his diligence and prowess. He very often selected Captain Rains and gave him his orders, which were uniformly, punctually, and promptly executed, and with a degree of bravery which could not be exceeded." They failed to overtake the Indians, and were on their return to Nashville, when, near Latitude Hill, in what is now Giles County, they came upon the deserted camp of Indians on their way to attack the settlers on the Cumberland. They followed the savages, and came up with them and defeated them on Rutherford Creek, on the north side of Duck River, six miles from the mouth of Globe and Fountain Creeks, in what is now Maury County.

About a month later Captain Rains' troops went out the Chickasaw path, crossed Duck River and Swan Creek, and came upon a party of Indians composed of five men and a boy. Four of the men were killed and the boy captured. He was carried to Nashville by Captain Rains and named John Rains. He was soon afterwards exchanged and sent back to his tribe dressed in the garb of the whites. When he came to visit Captain Rains the following year, he bore no marks of the attempt to civilize him, but was a typical savage— dirty and scantily clad.

Immediately after the Coldwater Expedition the Indians commenced to come across the Tennessee River in small parties for the purpose of striking the outlying settlements. One of these parties, led by Big Foot, was followed to the Tennessee by Captain Shannon's company. The whites reached them as they were preparing to cross. Abraham Castleman, called by the Indians, on account of his reckless bravery, "The Fool Warrior," killed one. Big Foot, being the stronger, had almost succeeded in taking Luke Anderson's gun from him, when William Pillow sprang to the rescue and tomahawked the burly chief. Pillow was the uncle of Gen. Gideon J. Pillow, of the Mexican and Civil Wars.

In September, 1787, Captain Rains' company, reinforced by Captain Shannon's company, again went against the Indians. They crossed Duck River near Greene's Lick. On Elk River, Captain Shannon, leading the advance, passed over an Indian trail, which was detected by the veteran Rains. They came upon the Indians, and, during the fight which followed, John Rains, Jr., captured an Indian boy. He was carried to Nashville, and later to Washington City, where a white girl fell desperately in love with him. He was finally released, and this attempt at the civilization of an Indian was no more successful than the one mentioned above. He joined the Creeks, and was wounded in the battle of Talladega in 1813 while fighting against the whites.

In the following year—1788—the Indians in the daytime went to the house of William Montgomery, on Drake's Creek, and killed the boy whom they had scalped and left for dead the previous year. They also killed two of his brothers, this occurring at the spring, one hundred yards from the house. On December 23, 1793, Montgomery himself was badly wounded by the Indians, he receiving a bullet in the thigh. Another broke his arm.

On the night of July 20, 1788, Col. Anthony Bledsoe, one of the commissioners who ran the line of 1783, was shot by the Indians at Bledsoe's Lick, now Castalian Springs, Sumner County. It was seen that he could not live till morning. He had eight daughters; and, according to the laws of North Carolina, if he died without a will, they would receive no part of his property. There was no light in the house; but Hugh Rogan, who was wounded at the mouth of Duck River a year before this, went to the house of Katie Shavers, several hundred yards away, and returned with a torch. The Indians did not offer to molest him, they probably being dumfounded at such an exhibition of bravery. The will was completed before Colonel Bledsoe died. Phelan was referring to just such deeds as this when he said: " The marvelous tales of Cooper sink into commonplace when compared with the wonderful feats and adventures of Spencer and Jennings and Castleman and Rains and Mansker."

In 1789 the Indians made a raid upon Robertson's Station and shot Colonel Robertson in the foot. Capt. Sampson Williams, who was with the commissioners who ran the line of 1783, went in pursuit, and defeated the Indians on the south side of Duck River. Andrew Jackson accompanied this expedition as a private.

In April, 1791, occurred that event which gave to Hickman County its name. James Robertson, Edwin Hickman, Robert Weakley, John Garner, J. Smith, and Richard Shaffer left the Cumberland settlements for the purpose of surveying some lands on Piney River. The party, which had been out about two weeks, had commenced at the head of Piney, and had surveyed to its mouth and up Duck River to near the present site of Centerville, where they encamped for the night. Robertson and Hickman were up before daylight, and had made a large fire, when just at dawn they heard a cracking noise in the cane. An investigation developing nothing, they concluded that the noise was made by their horses, which had been hobbled and turned loose to graze. Robertson was sitting by the fire mending his moccasins, when Hickman, repriming his gun, remarked to the others, who were still lying down: " Come, boys; let's be going. I think the yellow militia are about, for I had a very bad dream last night." He had not completed the narration of his dream, when the Indians fired upon them. Hickman fell dead, and Robertson was wounded in the hand. The others, seeing Hickman fall and finding that they were outnumbered, ran in different directions. Weakley took the direct course for home, and, by traveling all of that day and the ensuing night, reached Jocelyn's Fort early on Saturday morning. The fort of Jocelyn was several miles out from Nashville, on the Charlotte Pike. When he reached the fort, he found the women milking, guarded by the men. He had considerable difficulty in reaching them without being shot, they mistaking him for an Indian spy. That night Robertson, Garner, and Shaffer reached Robertson's Fort, near the present site of West Nashville. Smith, being a poor woodsman, did not arrive till several days afterwards. The death of Hickman cast a gloom over the entire settlement, where he had been universally popular. A party composed of about twenty persons, led by Captain Gillespie, left Nashville on Sunday morning for the purpose of burying Hickman's body. They reached the place where Hickman fell on Monday at sunset. His body was nude, with the exception of his belt, which had not been removed, and it was so near the fire that the lower extremities were completely baked. The proximity of the fire had, however, kept the wolves at a distance, and the body had not been molested by them. The party hastily did that which they had come to do by laying the body beside a large log and placing small logs, chunks, and brush upon it. This was the usual mode of disposing of the bodies of those who fell far from home. While carrying the body to the log, William Pillow, who supported the head, observed that the Indians, contrary to their usual custom, had not scalped Hickman. The party did not tarry long in this dangerous locality, and immediately started on their return to Nashville, which place they reached on Wednesday. Their attempt to protect the body of Hickman from the wolves was futile, as they reached the body and left the bones to bleach in the forest wilds for years. They were afterwards buried, as stated in the sketch of the First District. It is said that during the return trip to Nashville a singular incident occurred. Upon leaving their camp on Tuesday morning, John Davis and William Ewing found that they had more bread than they would need. They half-jokingly proposed that they leave two pones in the fork of a low dogwood for Smith, who was supposed to be still lost in the woods. This they did, and the half-famished Smith, wandering aimlessly through the woods, came upon their trail a short distance from the camp, followed it, and found the bread. This gave him additional strength; and, following their trail, he finally reached Nashville. This party surveyed lands lying on " Pine River of Duck River " near the mouth of Spring Creek. These lands had been entered in the name of Elizabeth Robertson, a daughter of Elijah Robertson. They probably surveyed the lands granted to John Dickens. These lands lie in the Seventh District and are known as the Jessee James lands, now owned by F. P. Tidwell. Smith and Garner were chain carriers for the party.

Edwin Hickman was born in North Carolina in
1760.   He served in the Revolutionary War as a soldier in a North Carolina regiment.   After the close
of hostilities, he married Miss Elizabeth Pryor, of Virginia, the result of this union being two sons—Edwin
Hickman, who died a bachelor, and John Pryor Hickman.   In 1788 he was commissioned as a surveyor by
the State of North Carolina and sent west to survey
the Miro District.   John Pryor Hickman married
Narcissa, a daughter of Col. Robert Weakley, they
having only one child, Edwin Weakley Hickman, who
was the father of John P. Hickman, of Nashville,
from whom these facts were obtained.   The particu-
lars of Hickman's death and of the expedition which
went out to bury him are taken from a copy of the old
Nashville Orthopolitan.   This version of the affair is
regarded by Capt. John P. Hickman as being authentic.   Both Haywood and Ramsay state that Hickman
was killed in 1785, they confusing his death with the
attack made by Indians in 1785 on Peyton and others
on Defeated Creek, in Smith County.   The account
as published here is the version which the pioneer surveyor, John Davis, who was with the party that buried
Hickman, claimed to be true.

In June, 1791, three travelers were found dead on
the Chickasaw Trace, near Duck River.   There were
eight in the party, and only two arrived at Nashville,
leaving the fate of the other three unknown.

On April 20, 1793, Richard Shaffer, who was with
Hickman at the time of the latter's death, was killed

by Indians. On July 19 of this year Smith was also killed by the Indians.

On May 12, 1793, Captains Rains and Gordon, with a cavalry detachment of one hundred men, were ordered out on a scouting tour to Duck River and south of it, with instructions to guard the several paths and crossing places at rivers and creeks. They succeeded in giving the Indians much trouble, as it was difficult to pass Rains' vigilant scouts and reach the Cumberland settlements.

The immediate cause of this expedition was the killing of Nathaniel Teal, mail carrier between Natchez and Nashville. He was killed by Indians who had been hunting on Cathey's Creek. They were overtaken on the Tennessee River below the mouth of the Elk, they having stopped for dinner. Rains' men advanced on the right of the Indians, Gordon's on the left. Gordon's men came to a high bluff, down which they could not ride; but their gallant captain leaped from his horse, pursued the Indians, and killed one of them. Rains' men killed five and captured a boy. As to whether Captain Rains made any further experiments in the direction of civilizing Indians, using this boy as a subject, we are not informed.

About August 5, 1793, the Indians made a raid around Jocelyn's Station, and killed Samuel Miller. Captains Rains and Gordon headed a pursuing party, which came upon them after they had passed Duck River seven miles, and killed several of them.

CHAPTER III.

HICKMAN COUNTY.

WASHINGTON COUNTY, North Carolina, embraced all the territory contained in the present State of. Tennessee; Greene County, North Carolina, established later, embraced the territory within the present limits of Hickman County; Davidson County, established in 1783, was bounded on the north by the Virginia (Kentucky) line and on the east by the Cumberland Mountains. On the south it was bounded by the Continental Line, run in the following year, to the point where it crossed Duck River, near the mouth of Leatherwood Creek, in the present county of Hickman; then Duck River to its mouth was the southern boundary. It was bounded on the west by the Tennessee River. In 1788 Tennessee County, embracing within its limits Hickman County north of Duck River, was formed from the western portion of Davidson County. When Tennessee became a State in 1796, Tennessee County was divided into Montgomery and Robertson Counties, Montgomery County including the territory now embraced in Hickman County north of Duck River. In 1799 Williamson County, south of Davidson County, was established, a portion of its western boundary being the line which now marks the eastern boundary of Hickman County. In 1803 Stewart County,

bounded on the north by the northern boundary of
the State and on the south by the southern boundary,
was established.   It was bounded on the west by the
Tennessee River, while its eastern boundary was a
north and south line running thirteen miles west of
Clarksville.   Stewart County, as then established, included all of the present counties of Houston, Humphreys, Perry, and Wayne west of this line and all of
Hardin County east of the Tennessee River.   During
this year the Legislature established Dickson County,
bounded on the north by Montgomery and Robertson,
on the east by Davidson and Williamson, on the south
by Alabama, and on the west by Stewart County.
Therefore, Dickson County, as established, included
a portion of Cheatham County, all of Hickman, a portion of Humphreys and Perry, all of Lewis, a portion
of Maury, the larger portion of Lawrence, and a large
portion of Wayne.   On December 3, 1807, Hickman
County was established, being formed from the southern portion of Dickson.   It was bounded on the north
by Dickson, on the east by Williamson and Maury
(the latter being also established in 1807), on the south
by Alabama, and on the west by Stewart County.
This placed within the original limits of Hickman
County a small portion of Humphreys and Perry and
the larger portion of Lewis, Lawrence, and Wayne.
The erection of Humphreys County in 1809, Lawrence and Wayne in 1817, Perry in 1819, and Lewis
in 1843, together with minor changes in the county
line from time to time, reduced Hickman County to its

present limits. In the establishment of the counties of Williamson, Stewart, and Dickson, Tennessee ignored the claims of the Indians, but the early settler could not so easily ignore the savage himself. Therefore that portion of Dickson County embraced in Hickman county north of Duck River was not permanently settled until after the treaties made by the United States in 1805 and 1806, and that portion of Hickman County south of Duck River was not permanently settled until after the final treaty of 1818. So, while the territory now embraced in Hickman County was at various times included in Washington, Greene, Tennessee, Montgomery, and Dickson Counties, the real settlement of the county commenced but a short time before its establishment; and while the larger portions of Wayne and Lawrence were, prior to the treaty of 1818, included in Hickman, they were organized as counties as soon as they were settled; and while they were created in 1817, they were not organized and settled until after 1818.

CHAPTER IV.

THE FIRST DISTRICT.

THE First District of Hickman County lies on either side of Duck River, near the center of the county, and embraces in its limits that portion of the river's fertile valley from Rocky Branch, below Centerville, to the line of the Second District near Totty's Bend, above. It includes Council's Bend, Mayberry's Bend, Shipp's Bend, Bear Creek, Little Piney, Indian Creek, Mill Hollow, Defeated Creek, Haley's Creek, Gray's Bend, Eason's Bend, and a portion of Swan Creek. The general boundaries are: On the north, by the Seventh District; east, by the Fourteenth and Second Districts; south, by the Eleventh and Twelfth Districts; and west, by the Ninth, Eleventh, and Seventh Districts. This district has a greater population than any other district of the county, Centerville, the county seat, being within its limits. Centerville is situated on the south side of Duck River near the center of this district. It is also near the center of the county.

Shipp's Bend, just below Centerville and on the north side of Duck River, was regarded by many as the most suitable place for the county seat, and a strong influence was brought to bear in favor of locating the town there; but the influence in favor of the south side prevailed, and placed Centerville on the hill instead of in the level country of Shipp's Bend. This bend was first settled by a man of English parentage, Josiah Shipp, for whom the bend was named. His wife, prior to her marriage, was Esther Joyce. He settled here in 1806 with his family, consisting of three sons and three daughters. His eldest son, William, was then but ten years old. The other sons were Josiah and "Zid." The three daughters were Polly, Sally, and Esther, two of whom married Cothams. This bend was then a dense wilderness, abounding in game, while the streams contained large numbers of fish. All of this suited the fancy of this hardy pioneer and great lover of sport. Shipp located at the place where John P. Broome now lives. In 1822 he killed an elk near where David Huddleston now lives. This was an animal that was seldom seen here, even then. In addition to his being a lover of hunting and fishing, he was also an industrious farmer and a sportsman of the higher order. He was a breeder of fine horses, and tradition has it that he was not averse to giving all comers a race for their money. That he might engage in this to the full extent of his desires, he, with the help of his slaves, of which he had a number, opened and established a straight mile track in the bend, one end of which was near where the railroad trestle now is—near where Robert Griner, Sr., once lived. Griner owned the upper end of the bend in after years. After many years of hunting, fishing, working, and horse racing, Shipp divided the larger portion of his property among his children and removed to Mississippi, leaving behind him evidences that a man of spirit and energy had once resided here. He died in Mississippi. The lands of Shipp were divided among his sons, his daughters receiving as their portion his slaves. Thus the lands of Josiah Shipp passed into the hands of William and " Zid " Shipp, their brother, Josiah, having sold his interest to them. The middle portion of this valuable bend became the property of these two brothers, who were quite different in disposition. So different were they that there was no point of similarity, save that of " family favor." Yet both were good citizens and prosperous farmers, who were noted for the hospitality of their homes. William Shipp, born in 1796, married Bethenia, the daughter of Robert Griner, Sr., and was the father of Josiah Horton Shipp, of the Seventh District, and Dr. John E. Shipp, of Buffalo, Humphreys County. Other sons were Ira, Albert, Robert, and Moore, all of whom are dead. Dr. John E. Shipp, who is a successful physician and farmer, was the eldest son, being born in 1823. Josiah H. Shipp was born on April 18, 1827. The daughters of William Shipp were Emeline, Martha, and Tera Ann. The last-named is yet living, near Little Lot, and is the wife of J. W. Shouse, a farmer of that neighborhood. Josiah Shipp, brother of William and " Zid," married Eliza Griner, daughter of Robert Griner, Sr. He removed with his father to Mississippi, where he died. " Zid " Shipp, unlike his brother William, was of a fun-loving disposition and was much given to jesting. He was never better pleased than when perpetrating some practical joke at the expense of his brother William—a quiet man, who seldom engaged in merriment or jesting. He married Peggy Kimmins, and was the father of Frank Shipp, who now lives in Obion County, and of Joseph and James Shipp, who gave their lives for the " Lost Cause." Joseph died in a Northern prison; James, a gallant boy, died at his post of duty on the field of battle. His daughters were Caroline, Ann Jane, Margaret, Elizabeth, and Mary. Ann Jane, who married Josiah Scott, of Humphreys County, and is now a widow, lives on a portion of the old Josiah Shipp lands. William and " Zid " lived each to a good old age within a few hundred yards of each other, and died on the lands settled by their father when this bend was the home of the deer, the wolf, the panther, and the bear, and when he could stand in the door of his lone cabin and see the camp fires of Indians across the river. It was from this cabin that William Shipp, at the age of nineteen, shouldering his flintlock rifle and carrying the blessings of his pioneer father and mother, went with other Hickman Countians to New Orleans, where he took part in the preliminary skirmishes as well as in the final fight of January 8, 1815.

About 1807 the upper end of the bend was settled by Robert Griner, Sr., near the west end of the railroad trestle. He obtained water from the " blowing

spring " near the ford of the river. The next year
he moved out on the Natchez Trace, and had an inn
near where the Lewis monument now stands. This
was then in Hickman County, but is now in Lewis
County, named for Meriwether Lewis, who committed suicide here in 1809. Lewis, who was a Virginian, was one of the leaders of the Lewis and Clarke
expedition which three years before this had returned
from an exploration of the great Northwest, during
which the source of the Missouri River was discovered, the Rocky Mountains crossed, and the Columbia River explored to its mouth. From 1801 to 1803
Lewis had been the private secretary of President
Thomas Jefferson, and after his return from the
Northwest he was appointed by President Jefferson
Governor of the Territory of Louisiana. The regu-
larity of some of Lewis' official transactions was
being questioned, and he was hastening along the
Natchez Trace en route to Washington City for the
purpose of demanding an investigation, when one
night in 1809 he came to Griner's Stand, accompanied by two servants, one white and one black. One
of these was named Perney. When Lewis reached
the stand he had been drinking and was in such a
highly excited state that his servants feared him and
would not sleep in the room with him. During the
night three shots were heard, and when Lewis' room
was entered he was found lying near the door, beg-
ging for water. He lived until noon of the following
day, and was buried near by, where a monument to

his memory was erected by the State. This account of Lewis' death is substantiated by a statement made in 1879 by 'Linda, a negro woman, who was born in 1797. She was a slave of Robert Griner, Sr., and was present on the night of Lewis' death, and saw him before and after his death. A few years later Griner returned to the north side of Duck River and settled where he had first located. While an innkeeper on the Natchez Trace, Griner often sold whisky to the Indians. Their love for " fire water," as they called it, was so great that they would allow themselves to be bitten by snakes in order to get whisky. This method resulted disastrously to one, who, after surviving several bites, finally died from the effects of one. The sons of Robert Griner, Sr., were William, John, Albert, Robert, Jr., and the twin brothers, Hulett and Noble. Albert and Noble, in fits of insanity, committed suicide by hanging—Noble, near the old camp ground at the John Thompson place in 1855; and Albert, below the mouth of Indian Creek in 1850.

About 1830 Rev. Samuel Whitson lived in Shipp's Bend, and was one of the principal property holders of the bend. He was at one time Trustee of the county. He was the father of Rev. William E. Whitson, who was murdered by jayhawkers on Indian Creek, in Wayne County, in 1863. This inoffensive man was dragged away from his wife and little children, and shot to death within their hearing and in sight of his home. Jane, a daughter of Samuel Whitson, was the mother of Thetis W. Sims, who is at present Representative in Congress from the Eighth District of Tennessee. The Whitsons of Hickman County are related to the celebrated Vance family, of the Carolinas.

About the year 1810 Robert Wright located in Shipp's Bend near where Simpson Prince now lives, and kept a ferry at the place where the metal landing was afterwards established by operators of Ætna Furnace. Robert Wright was the father of Levin D., John, Robert, and Thomas Wright, the former being the only one who married. The wife of Levin D. Wright was the daughter of Frederick Mayberry. Two sons of Levin D. Wright are now living in this county. Another son is Dr. Levin D. Wright, of Dickson. A daughter of Robert Wright, Sr., married Maj. William P. Whitson.

In 1830 John Hulett lived at the place where David Huddleston now lives. He was a school-teacher, and was a man of intelligence and well educated for that time. As was the custom then, he kept his gun with him at the schoolhouse, frequently killing game while on his way to and from school. He was probably the first merchant of Vernon. He at one time possessed considerable property and was one of the moneyed men of the county. He was the owner of several slaves, but became involved in trouble. He was charged with the killing of John Gainer, which caused the sacrifice of most of his property. He afterwards engaged in school-teaching. Gainer was a fine-looking young man, and was present at the batrtle of New Orleans. He had many friends. His slayer was never known, but suspicion pointed to Hulett, who was justified by many, as the compromising conduct and the place where Gainer was when killed caused many to say that Hulett was right, even if he did kill him. It was never proven that Hulett was guilty. Gainer was killed at night by a shot fired through a window. The house where Gainer was killed was the most noted in the bend, as it had been the blockhouse, or fort, of the settlement. Its location was well adapted to the purpose, being near the center of the settlement on a high bluff overhanging the river. It gave a view of the Indian country south of the river, as well as a view of the neighboring whites on the north. The ground sloped gently to the west and north into the bend, where lived the whites, while an almost perpendicular bluff dropped several hundred feet from the fort to the river, this bluff preventing an attack from two sides. The Bear Creek country can be seen from this eminence, and a view may be had of Centerville, five miles away. From 1810 to 1812 a spirit of anxiety and suspense prevailed among the frontiersmen, as the Indians were encouraged by foreign emissaries to commit depredations. Bands of hunters and those not engaged in agricultural pursuits frequently organized as guards for the frontier. They made their headquarters at this and other blockhouses, where they were always welcome visitors, they bringing venison

and turkeys with them.   Here they deposited their
furs before starting with packs to the general mar-
kets.   These parties patrolled Duck River from
Shipp's Bend to the blockhouse at the mouth of
King's Branch in Brown's Bend, and from Shipp's
Bend up the river to the blockhouse on Leatherwood
Creek, near the old Chickasaw crossing.

Near the John Thompson farm in 1842 there was a
camp meeting held by the Methodists and Presbyterians.   William Ervin, father of Rev. Wesley Ervin,
of Maury County, lived there at this time.   The late
Abram Burchard was present, and remembered hearing a preacher named Moore sing a song in which
were these lines:

" I think I've heard some children say:
' I never heard my parents pray.' "

In 1830 William Shipp killed two bears and
wounded a third near the creek on the south side of
the river nearly opposite the old blockhouse.   From
this incident the creek took its name—Bear Creek.

In 1825 John W. Huddleston lived in the lower end
of Shipp's Bend.   He was the father of Benjamin
Huddleston, Howell Huddleston, and Jack Huddleston (who was sheriff of Hickman County in 1842).
He settled on the hill where A. V. (Tine) Burchard
now lives.   Near this point is the northeast corner of
a large survey, or entry, in the name of William J.
Council, which contained about 12,000 acres, and was
made about 1812.   This entry includes the fertile

lands near the bridge at present known as the Huddle-ston Bridge, on the south side of the river.

. This entry also includes the bend just below, which received its name—Council's Bend—from the man who first obtained a legal claim to it.   Council's entry extended down Duck River on both sides, including the W. P. Whitson land, on the south of the river, and that on the north side to the Old Mound Fields, near the mouth of Pine River, in the Seventh District.   In the extreme lower portion of the First District, north of the river, are the Young Mayberry lands, which were settled by James McClanahan in 1830.   He afterwards removed to Kentucky.   These lands lie north of the Council lands.   Council's Bend contains about 1,000 acres of good farming lands, and a portion was once occupied by George Whitfield, a brother of Gen. Jeff. Whitfield, Gen. John W. Whitfield, and Monroe Whitfield.   Whitfield sold to Abraham Dansby, he to Maxwell, and he to Samuel Williams.   This portion of the bend was at the time of his death the property of Gabriel Fowlkes.   The other, which consists of about 500 acres of farming land, was for many years the property and home of Capt. Robert Whitson.   It is now the property of John M. Graham.   G. Fowlkes, referred to above, overcame many early disadvantages, and at the time of his death, in 1898, had amassed a fortune of several thousand dollars.   He was constable of the Seventh District at the breaking out of the Civil War.   He became a soldier in the Confederate Army, and as such was faithful.

He was for several years a justice of the peace of this district, and was chairman of the County Court at the time of his death.

A history of that portion of the district lying southwest of Centerville would be incomplete were the names of the school-teachers omitted. Of these, Hulett, referred to in the preceding pages, was among the first and best. Others were: Thomas McClanahan, Albert Wilson, John Fowlkes, Dr. John E. Shipp, Dr. Reveaux Raymond; Mrs. Emily Cash, one of the best teachers who ever taught in the district; and her no less talented daughter, Mrs. Mary Shouse. Mrs. Cash was the mother of Dr. T. W. Cash. Her daughter, Mary, married Howell Shouse, who was an extensive live-stock dealer and raiser. He was at one time a deputy sheriff. Another daughter, Emma, married Frank Hornbeak; and another, Jennie, married Jacob Shouse and then Hon. N. R. Sugg, who at one time represented Dickson County in the Legislature. Mrs. Cash was a descendant of the celebrated Outlaw family, a family which derives its name from the fact that it is descended from Eadgar the Atheling, king of England, deposed in 1071 by his conqueror, William I.

One of the bloody tragedies of the Civil War was the death of William Carlisle, which occurred at a point near the public road between the places where A. V. Burchard and William Moore now live. Carlisle had been arrested by order of Col. Alonzo Napier at the stillhouse of Martin Gray, in Perry County, upon the charge of taking without orders a pistol and shotgun from Mrs. Susan Lomax, of Lowe's Bend. Carlisle claimed to be a member of Captain Lewis' company, then encamped near Lobelville. Captain Lewis disclaimed him, and started him under guard to General Forrest at Columbia. After crossing Duck River at Huddleston's Ford, Carlisle and his guards had proceeded about one-half mile, when Carlisle was shot and killed by C. B. Dotson, who, with the prisoner, was some distance in advance of the detachment. Dotson said his prisoner attempted to escape. He was buried near by on the place now owned by Burchard.

Near what has for many years been known as Huddleston's Ford there is now a bridge, erected by the county at a cost of about $6,000. There are five other bridges across Duck River in Hickman County. Near this bridge, on the south side of the river, are the lands of Robert and Newton McClanahan, sons of Absalom McClanahan, whose father, William McClanahan, came from North Carolina to Davidson County and from there to Council's Bend about 1835. Newton McClanahan was born in Davidson County on August 6, 1833. These facts are given in connection with the fact that the McClanahans have had much to do with the building of several of Hickman County's bridges. The first bridge erected was at Centerville, before the railroad had reached this place. Columbia, the nearest shipping point, was thirty-one miles away. The committee, whose duty it was to arrange for the delivery of the material for the bridge, employed Robert and Newton McClanahan and John T.

Fowlkes, a son-in-law of the latter. They, together
with Dr. T. W. Cash, agreed for $300 to deliver the
material at the point selected for the bridge. This
they did, bringing it by flatboats down Duck River.
The material for the Beaverdam Bridge, weighing, exclusive of the cement, forty tons, was carried by
wagons a distance of thirteen miles from Nunnelly
Station for $360, Newton McClanahan and John T.
Fowlkes being the contractors. The material for the
Totty's Bend Bridge, hauled fourteen miles by wagon,
was delivered for $330 by the same contractors.

Northwest from Centerville and across the river is
Mill Hollow, once known as Moore's Hollow, as a man
of that name lived there in 1825. He built a mill and
sold it in 1830 to William McCutcheon, who built a
carding factory at that place. McCutcheon in 1836
raised troops for the Seminole War. A man once
lived in this hollow whose name was Wigman, called
"Diggy" Wigman. The road leading up the hollow
toward Vernon was called the "Diggy" Wigman
road. A young man, William Poore, came to the
mill one Sunday morning for meal. His horse ran
away, threw him, and killed him one-fourth of a mile
south of the mill on the ridge. James Lawson was
miller here in 1840.

North of Centerville, on the opposite side of Duck
River, is Defeated Creek, which takes its name from
the fact that near its mouth Edwin Hickman was slain
by Indians, as narrated in a previous chapter. It is
there told how a party came from Nashville and

buried in an imperfect manner the remains of Hickman. Later a party of explorers found his bones and
interred them. When Allan Walker laid his land
warrant here in 1815, he found the grave of Hickman, and marked it by leaving a hackberry tree at
one end of the grave, and a poplar at the other.
So to-day one may visit and look upon the spot where
rest the remains of the man whose name the county
bears.

William Satterfield lived on Defeated Creek in
1832, and erected a mill near where Reeves Pace now
lives. He sold to Robert Griner, Jr. Satterfield removed to Missouri with his son-in-law, Elisha Dotson,
in 1840.

Allan Walker, who entered the land east of and adjoining Defeated Creek, added to the original amount
of lands until he owned about 900 acres of valuable
lands on both sides of the river. He established
Walker's Ferry, one mile above Centerville. He
reared a large family, which became prominent in the
development of the county. His sons were: Joel,
William, Allan, James, Pleasant, and Elijah. Dr.
Joel Walker went to Williamson County, where he
became prominent in business and political circles.
Pleasant Walker represented Hickman County several
terms in the Legislature, and was sheriff of the county
four years. Elijah Walker became one of the best
judges that ever presided in a Tennessee courthouse.
He was a good judge of law—not an eloquent speaker,
but a profound thinker. He was honest in his deci-

sions, and, as a lawyer, would refuse a fee when his would-be client was in the wrong.

William Arnold, Jesse Ratliff, Timothy Suggs, Shadrach Lawson, and Vanderford were early settlers on Haley's Creek.   Lawson was the father of John, Thomas, and S. S. (Dock) Lawson, and was, in the full meaning of the term, an honest man.

Persimmon Branch comes next above Haley's Creek, and is included in Gray's Bend.   The early settlers of this branch were: John Wilson, Aaron Wilson, and Elijah Cantrell, Sr. (the father of Elijah, Jr., Brown, and Pinkney).   Pinkney Cantrell emigrated to Texas in 1868.   Elijah, Jr., recently died on this branch at the age of seventy-six.   Elijah Cantrell, Sr., came here about 1810.

Peanut, a little village on this branch, was for years one of the polling places for the First District.   It was here that Skelt Rodgers killed Jackson King in a fist fight.   He caught King by the hair, jerked him forward, and dealt him a heavy blow with his fist on the neck, which was broken.   King fell dead, and Rodgers escaped.   He afterwards wrote back that he was dead, and the people thought he ought to know as to this. Thus the matter ended.

Alexander Gray, for whom the bend was named, lived in the bend as early as 1810.   He was the father of James, John, Sherrod, Alexander, Jr., and G. W. Gray.   His neighbors were Thomas Easley and Stuart Warren.   Thomas Easley was the father of James D., Warham, Thomas, Jr., Robin, Stephen, Edward, and William Easley. His daughter was Sally Easley. James D. Easley was County Court Clerk for twenty-four years. Gray came from North Carolina, and Easley from South Carolina.

Ned Nunnellee, who came from Virginia about 1806 to the Fifth District, came to Gray's Bend about 1810, and died here. He was the father of Washington, Mark, and Timothy Nunnellee. His daughter, Jane, was the first wife of Jesse R. Eason. Nunnellee was buried on the John V. Gray place. Anderson Nunnelly lived in Gray's Bend in 1818. These names are the same in pronunçiation, but are spelled differently.

There was a "big camp meeting" held in this bend by the Methodists in 1831. Rev. James Erwin, a fluent speaker, preached at this meeting. Britton Garner was a Primitive Baptist, who preached in the bend in 1831.

In 1830 a cotton gin was operated in the bend by Alexander Gray. Above Gray's Bend is Dry Creek, and higher up is Morgan's Creek, named for Morgan, who located here in 1815. Near the mouth of this Creek Aaron Wilson built an overshot mill in 1825. His wife was a Creole. George Foster laid his land warrant on Morgan's Creek in 1815. Later he became owner of the Wilson mill and of a fine body of land between Morgan Creek and Dry Creek, now known as the Foster lands. William Foster, his son, settled upon it, and, with the assistance of his slaves, opened a fine farm. William Foster married Sally,

the daughter of Anderson Nunnelly. Though a somewhat eccentric man, " Billie " Foster, as he was exten-
sively and favorably known, amassed a fortune of considerable proportions—this by industry and economy.

In 1818 Jackson Stanfill located on Swan Creek
about one mile south of the river. Here he opened a·
fine farm, and, by farming and stock raising, became
a prominent and wealthy citizen of the county. He
married Lamira Canady, of Maury County. His sons
were: Irving, Jackson, Jr., George, and Van; his
daughters were: Martha and Betsy. The latter married Sherrod Gray. Stanfill built a mill here about
1845.

In 1835 Thompson Fowlkes came to Swan Creek
from Bedford County and located near Stanfill. He
was the father of Johenry and Wilkins Whitfield
Whitman Fowlkes.

Above Stanfill on the creek was John McGill.
Ephraim Alexander lived near by in 1830. James
Spradling lived half a mile up a hollow on the " trail "
to Gordon's Ferry, now the road to Shady Grove.
Edmund Jones bought the lands of Spradling, who
emigrated to Illinois in 1832. Edmund Jones was
the son of Alston Jones, Sr. Edmund Jones married
Mary, the daughter of Gabriel Fowlkes. Gabriel
Fowlkes was born on April 21, 1777, in Virginia. He
married Jincy Hyde, who was born on July 11, 1792,
in North Carolina. She was the daughter of Hartwell Hyde. Thompson Fowlkes, father of Gabriel,
was a Revolutionary soldier. Gabriel Fowlkes came

to the Fifth District of Hickman County in 1806 and
to the First District in 1831. He located below the
mouth of Swan Creek near Joseph Jones Eason. He
was the father of Henry, Blount, Thompson, Washington, John, Richard, Mark, and James Fowlkes.
His daughters were: Mary, Nancy, Elizabeth, Lucy,
Sallie, and Martha. He was Hickman County's second sheriff, and served eight years, resigning to accept
a seat in the State Legislature. From his family
sprang some of the county's most successful financiers.
While Fowlkes was sheriff, he publicly whipped two
white men upon their bare backs, giving to each
thirty-nine lashes. This was done in 1830 by order of
the court, the men having been convicted—the one,
on the charge of stealing money; the other, on the
charge of forgery.

Joseph Jones Eason, who was of English parentage,
came from North Carolina to this district in 1819, and
settled on lands adjoining Gabriel Fowlkes, where he
spent the remainder of his life, and was buried in the
front yard of the place where Jesse Ross Eason now
lives. Joseph Eason believed that the land lying between the lands of Fowlkes and Allan Walker was
yet vacant. He asked John Davis, the pioneer surveyor, whose name appears in a previous chapter in
connection with the death of Edwin Hickman, as to
whether his theory was correct. Davis, although he
desired the land himself, was a friend of Eason, and
withal an honest man; and he immediately told Eason
that the land was vacant, whereupon Eason proceeded

to enter it.   It proved to be a good selection, and provided a valuable home for himself and children.
After the death of Joseph Eason's first wife, he married the widow of a man named Elliott, her maiden
name having been Kinney.   She was a native of Georgia.   She was the mother of Mills Eason, Jesse R.
Eason, and of a daughter, Mary Jane, who married
Hulett Griner.   The children of Eason's first marriage were: James, Joseph, Carter, Calvin, and Mills.
The latter died before his father's second marriage.
There was also a daughter, Susan.

It was the second Mills Eason who engaged with
William Holt in the most terrible fistic encounter that
ever occurred in the county.   This took place at Vernon.   Eason, it is said, tried to avoid the fight, which
was forced upon him by Holt, who was a pugilist of
renown in the early days of the county.   In the fight
Eason pulled the eye of Holt from its socket, yet Holt
refused to say, "Enough!" which was the signal for
friends to interfere.   This fight left Holt with but
one eye, and cost Eason what property he had accumu-
lated, in addition to trouble to himself and friends.
Eason would not leave the country, although advised
to do so by friends, until legal proceedings were at an
end.   He then removed to Texas in 1850.   He died
in Cherokee County, of that State, two years later.

Jesse Ross Eason, the youngest son of Joseph Eason,
was born on February 5, 1822, at the place where he
now lives, which is opposite the mouth of Haley's
Creek.   His first wife was a daughter of Ned Nun-

nellee; his second wife, Elizabeth Ann, whom he married over fifty years ago, is a daughter of Gabriel Fowlkes. She was born on November 22, 1822. The children of Eason's second marriage were: John F., Anna, Henry, Martha, Sallie, and Richard M. Jesse Eason has for years been one of Hickman County's most prominent men. At one time he was State Senator, and served his constituents in an acceptable manner.

In 1852 Jesse Eason loaded a flatboat with about four hundred barrels of corn in the ear and started from near the mouth of Swan Creek down Duck River for New Orleans. He went no farther than Memphis, where he sold his corn and boat. He returned to Nashville by steamboat. While on the boat he met a negro trader, from whom he bought a negro woman and child, he paying for them $650. He stayed overnight with John Davis, the surveyor, who lived five or six miles from Nashville, between the Charlotte and Hardin turnpikes. Davis, who was a genial gentleman, and who had partaken of Eason's hospitality, assisted him on his way homeward. This incident is here given not on account of its intrinsic historic value, but on account of its showing the lack of traveling and shipping facilities and the insight it gives into the customs of " the good old days."

In 1840 Thomas McClanahan bought the lands of Mills Eason, which were adjoining to those of Jesse Eason. McClanahan married a sister of Jack and Howell Huddleston. The children of this union were: L. B., Mortimer, Lycurgus, Dee, "Dock," William; Josie, who married Kinzer; Xantippe, who married Burton Anderson; and Nellie. The sons of Thomas McClanahan, under the firm name of Mc-Clanahan Brothers, operated a cotton gin, tanyard, stillhouse, and sawmill south of the Columbia and Centerville road, near the Stanfill old mill, about 1868. Thomas Harbison, who came from North Carolina in 1832, lived near McClanahan.

A flatboat loaded with cotton bales struck a snag in Duck River near the mouth of Swan Creek in 1835. The boat sprung a leak, and the cotton, in a damaged condition, was taken to Centerville in wagons. It was there rebaled at the gin of Henry Nixon. Near this part of the river Pemberton, a slave of Washington Gray, was drowned by the upsetting of a canoe. A short distance above Centerville is a ford known as the "Negro Ford," from the fact that about 1825 a negro man was at this point accidentally knocked from a flatboat and drowned. Local tradition is to the effect that at an early date Asa Shute, a pioneer land locator, was shot from ambush while crossing at this ford.

In 1829, in Gray's Bend, Henry Nunnelly, a negro, outraged and murdered a white girl, Tampay Carlisle. He went to the home of the girl, who was alone, and attempted to force an entrance into the house. The girl closed the doors and escaped through a window. She was pursued in her flight toward a neighbor's house, and was overtaken at a fence, dragged to the bushes near by, and murdered. He attempted to conceal her body by covering it with a heap of stones; but the crime was discovered, dogs procured, and a pursuit instituted, which resulted in the finding of Henry concealed under a barn. He was carried to Centerville, and there tried, convicted, and hanged. The hanging, which was public, was the first in the county's history, it taking place in 1830, while Gabriel Fowlkes was sheriff. The negro was hanged in the level near where A. W. Warren now resides and within one hundred yards of where the Christian church now stands. The entire country was aroused, but lynch law was then almost unknown, and the negro had the benefit of a trial by jury. He then paid the penalty which law and public sentiment said he unquestionably owed. In 1861 Carter Nunnelly, brother to Henry, murdered Jackson B. Nunnelly, a white man, this crime being also committed in Gray's Bend. The negro went to the house where his victim was living, and, with an ax, murdered him in a most brutal manner. For this and the murder of a white woman he was arrested, and, after trial and conviction, was hanged near the present site of the colored church, one mile east of the Public Square of Centerville. These brothers were the only persons ever legally hanged within the present limits of the county. The first man sent from Hickman County to the penitentiary was Treadway, who stole a horse from William Phillips, of Pine River. The first inmates of the county asylum for the poor, then located on Defeated Creek, were Mary and Mittie Williams.

We now come to a class upon whose virtues we love to dwell—the teachers of the old-time schools—good men and true, who were heroes no less than those that assisted " Old Hickory " in rebuking the haughty Briton at New Orleans. Robert Cooper taught in Gray's Bend in 1821. The following year he taught on Indian Creek. Dr. Kinkead taught on Swan Creek in 1835. He was a good teacher, who had been educated for the Presbyterian ministry. An uncontrollable desire for intoxicants had hurled him from his high estate, and he became a country school-teacher—the first in the county, however, who commanded a salary of $40 per month. On the same creek Samuel Aydelott and William Twilly taught in 1835 and 1836. Hayden Church, who also taught on this creek, was a typical old-time schoolmaster, who spoiled no child by sparing the rod. James D. Easley taught in Centerville, on Swan Creek, in Gray's Bend, and on Indian Creek.

Another class of heroes of the early days is that composed of pioneer preachers, who came into the wilderness bearing aloft the cross, and who kept unfurled to the breeze the banner of Israel's King. Through the darkness of the pioneer period shone the light of the gospel, which served to guide and direct the footsteps of our fathers as they penetrated the wilderness in search of homes and happiness. Soldiers of the cross, faithful and brave, while your earthly deeds are being recorded, you possess the crowns promised to those who are faithful to the end. The pioneer preachers of the kind here described were not confined to the First District; their names appear in the sketches of the several districts of the county. But the names of some just as Christlike, just as faithful, are not mentioned here; their names are written in the imperishable records of heaven. The pioneer preacher—

"Remote from towns, he ran his godly race,
Nor e'er had changed, nor wish'd to change, his pace.
Unskillful he to fawn or seek for power
By doctrines fashion'd to the varying hour;
Far other aims his heart had learned to prize,
More bent to raise the wretched than to rise.

.   . .   .

To relieve the wretched was his pride,
And e'en his failings leaned to virtue's side;
But in his duty, prompt at every call,
He watch'd and wept, he prayed and felt for all;
And, as a bird each fond endearment tries
To tempt its new-fledged offspring to the skies,
He tried each art, reproved each dull delay,
Allured to brighter worlds, and led the way.

.   .   .   .

Truth from his lips prevailed with double sway,
And fools who came to scoff remained to pray.

.   .   .   .

To them his heart, his love, his griefs were giv'n;
But all his serious thoughts had rest in heav'n.
As some tall cliff that lifts its awful form,
Swells from the vale, and midway leaves the storm,
Though round its breast the rolling clouds are spread,
Eternal sunshine settles on its head."

Prior to 1830 Benjamin Lancaster, a Primitive
Baptist, preached in this district, as did also Samuel
Whitson, who preached at Centerville. In 1834
Womack and Sorry preached at a camp meeting in
Shipp's Bend. One of the songs sung by Sorry, the
words of which are recalled by a hearer over sixty
years later, contained these lines:

> " Come, humble sinner, in whose breast
>   A thousand thoughts revolve."

In 1820 the county seat was still Vernon, on Piney
River; while the lands where Centerville now stands
were the property of McLemore, who lived at Nashville and was an extensive landowner. He donated
about twenty acres to the county for a site for the proposed new county seat. This land, after setting apart
enough for a public square, was divided into lots and
sold in 1821. Then the building of the town was be-
gun. Eli B. Hornbeak, a citizen of Vernon, erected
on the south side of the Public Square a double log
house, afterwards occupied by him as dwelling and
storehouse. Peter Morgan's house was the first house
completed in Centerville. It was a round log cabin,
and with him boarded the men engaged in building
the houses of the town. Peter Headstream built the
first hotel, which was of hewn logs. In 1822 Maj.
Eli B. Hornbeak entered into the mercantile business
here in copartnership with Robert Sheegog, who also
came from Vernon. Sheegog soon returned to his
former home, selling his interest in the business to

James Weatherspoon. In 1823 the county records were removed from Vernon to Centerville. The courthouse at Vernon, which was of large hewn poplar logs, was torn down and hauled by wagons to the new county seat, eight miles away. The jail building was not removed from Vernon, the commissioners, after their experience with the moving of the courthouse, deeming it less expensive to build a new one. It, like the old one, was made of logs. Garrett Lane was one of those who superintended the removal of the court-house. Samuel Bean, a very large man, was the first jailer here.

One of the first settlers at Centerville was William Bird, mentioned in the sketch of the Seventh District. He came here from Bird's Creek in 1823. He was a typical pioneer. At the time of his marriage he could not read and write, these arts being taught him by his wife. John G. Easley succeeded Headstream as ho-tel keeper, and he was succeeded by Maj. John Bul-lock, the father of Lee Bullock. Major Bullock ran a hotel here from 1842 to 1845. He was also at one time a merchant here. John Phillips and E. W. Dale were merchants at Centerville in 1830.

Archibald, Samuel, and Joshua Williams were merchants here during the decade from 1850 to 1860. The partnership between William George Clagett and Horatio Clagett, merchants, has extended over a pe-riod of more than fifty years, harmoniously and profitably. The late William G. Clagett was born in Maryland on December 7, 1813. Horatio Clagett is a younger brother. Their father was Horatio Clagett, who came to Hickman County and located on Lick Creek, where J. W. Shouse now lives, in 1816. W. G. Clagett married Theodocia, the daughter of Wilkins Whitfield, a Virginian, on July 21, 1835. Clagett, after the death of his first wife, married Elizabeth, daughter of Eli B. Hornbeak, on February 10, 1842. He died in 1898, his wife dying during the same year. She was born at Vernon on February 18, 1818. William G. Clagett, so long prominent in the business circles of Centerville, was a man who never deceived his fellow-man. His statements were plain and to the point. Eli B. Hornbeak, mentioned above, married Sallie Combs, of East Tennessee. His son, Pleasant, was the father of Eli, John, Samuel, Frank, and Pleasant Hornbeak.

Centerville's first lawyer was Henry Nixon, father of Orville A., John, Henry, and a daughter, who became the wife of Samuel Williams. He was twice married, each time to a sister of Stephen C. Pavatt, of Humphreys County, who was several times a member of Congress. Nixon, in addition to his legal business, engaged largely in land speculations, extending into adjoining counties. He operated a cotton gin here from 1830 to 1833. He did much toward the development of the town from 1821 to May, 1833, the date of his death.

Elijah Walker, one of the early lawyers, was prominent as a lawyer on account of both his legal learning and extreme candor in expressing himself as to points of law and equity. Among the lawyers here at a later date were: John W. Hornbeak, James D. Easley, John H. Moore, and William Moore, natives of Hickman County; and Josiah Hubbard, Thomas P. Bateman, J. J. Williams, Alexander H. Vaughan, Will. M. Edwards, James L. Sloan, Richard Lyle, and —— Jobson, who were natives of other counties. Among the eminent lawyers from other portions of the State who practiced in the courts of Hickman were: A. O. P. Nicholson, L. D. Myers, David Campbell, George Gaunt, James H. Thomas, Jacob Leech, W. C. Whitthorne, N. N. Cox, and Jo. C. Guild. The members of the bar at present are: J. Alonzo Bates, John H. Clagett, —— Beasley, W. L. Pinkerton, W. P. Clark, W. V. Flowers, W. A. Knight, John H. Cunningham, and Henry Nixon, the latter a grandson of Centerville's first lawyer. E. W. Easley, of the Seventh District, and R. L. Peery, of the Twelfth District, are also members of the Centerville bar. Among the early judges were: Parry W. Humphreys, West H. Humphreys, Edmund Dillahunty, and Stephen C. Pavatt.

The first physician to locate at Centerville was Samuel Sebastian, who came here from Vernon. Other physicians of the early days of Centerville were: Samuel B. Moore, Bird Moore, Reveaux Raymond, Rodney Raymond, W. B. Douglass, John Sebastian, and John C. Ward. The last named, Dr. John Cofield Ward, son of David Cofield Ward, is yet

living in Centerville.   David Cofieald Ward, born on
March 2, 1802, on White's Creek, Davidson County,
married Mary Bowen Moore, a near relative of Gov.
William Bowen Campbell.   She was born in Smith
County on May 2, 1800.   Dr. Ward was born in
Smith County on February 26, 1828, and came in
1843 to his uncle, Dr. Samuel Bowen Moore, at Centerville.   In 1846, at the age of eighteen, he enlisted
under John W. Whitfield, captain of Company A,
First Tennessee Regiment.   This was the famous
" Bloody First " of the Mexican War, commanded by
Col. William B. Campbell, who was afterwards Governor.   Dr. Ward was one of the regiment's surgeons,
was present at the capture of Monterey, and, after this,
was detailed for duty in the hospitals at Tampico.
From Tampico he returned to Centerville, where he
has since almost constantly resided, and where he has
practiced his profession for over fifty years.   Dr.
Ward married Sarah Casandra Charter, daughter of
Robert Charter, one of the pioneer merchants of Centerville.   After the death of his first wife, he married
Kate McMurray, of Humphreys County.   Dr. Ward
is justly proud of his ancestral line, which goes back
to the English house of Cofieald.

Dr. Samuel Bowen Moore, who came from Smith
County to Centerville, was for years one of the most
prominent physicians in the county.   He did a very
extensive practice, visiting almost every section of the
county even after physicians became more numerous
than when he commenced to practice here.   He was

the young practitioner's friend, meeting him often in consultation without any exhibition of a desire to overwhelm him with his greatness. He preserved the dignity of the profession which he, as a member, adorned—a man of brains and a man of honor, whose hospitality was proverbial. Dr. Moore represented Hickman County several times in the General Assembly of the State, and, as a public servant, sustained the character for honesty and uprightness which he had established as a private citizen. Being popular with his associates in the Legislature, his influence was often sought, but given only to worthy causes. That vacancy made in Hickman County by the death of Dr. Samuel B. Moore, although years have rolled by and others have come and gone, has never yet been filled.

" His life was gentle, and the elements
  So mixed in him that Nature might stand up
  And say to all the world: ' This was a man.' "

Physicians here at a more recent date were: John W. Hornbeak, E. G. Thompson, —— Ragsdale, James L. Thompson, S. McE. Wilson, and J. A. Edwards. Dr. J. E. Shipp, a prominent physician of Humphreys County, practiced for a short time in Shipp's Bend. The physicians of Centerville at present are: J. C. Ward, J. T. Ward, K. I. Sutton, and J. N. Doyel. Dr. A. H. Grigsby, dentist, is now located at Centerville. Dr. J. H. Plummer, dentist, was for several years located here.

The First District has furnished a fair propor-

tion of the county's representatives in both houses of
the State Legislature—viz.: Gabriel Fowlkes, Jesse
Eason, S. B. Moore, Joel Walker, Pleasant Walker,
O. A. Nixon, E. G. Thompson, and J. A. Bates.
Judges Elijah Walker and T. P. Bateman were from
this district.

T. P. Bateman, Josiah R. Hubbard, J. J. Williams,
and Robert M. Whitson, captains in the Confederate
service, were from this district.   Bateman was promoted to lieutenant colonel; Williams and Hubbard
were each promoted to major.   Those who left this
district as captains are mentioned not because they
were better, truer, or braver men than those they led,
for from the ranks of these companies fell on many a
sanguine field some of Hickman County's best young
manhood during the days between 1861 and 1865.
Scarcely a home in the district was free from the
shadow thrown across its threshold by the death angel's wing; scarcely a home in which were not heard
the lamentations of some Southern Rachel, weeping
for the one who went away wearing the gray, but who
came not back again—weeping for one who gave his
life for Dixie, one who sung as he marched and said
while he fought:

> " The fairest and dearest land upon earth
>   Is Dixie, fair Dixie, the land of my birth."

Among the early magistrates of this district were
William Craig, John McGill, Alexander Gray, John
Gray, Washington Gray, and Troy S. Broome.   The

latter was born in North Carolina on February 22, 1806. He was a son of Jonathan Broome. In 1835 he married Mary E. Gannt, and after her death, he, in 1843, married Mary E. Sebastian, daughter of Dr. Samuel Sebastian. He was the father of John P. and Samuel T. Broome, and of a daughter, Sallie. One of the justly celebrated magistrates of this district was William G. Clagett, a man who never allowed his ideas of justice to be warped by any iron-clad rules of law. As a magistrate and as a man, he was stern, but just. James D. Easley, J. A. Bates, Henry Gray, John B. Gardner, E. A. Dean, G. Fowlkes, John P. Broome, and others have been magistrates in this district.

James Brown, R. C. Murrell, John F. Lawson, Van Buren Shouse, Howell Shouse, H. H. Walker, and John F. Dean are the names of a few men who have served as constable of this district. The latter, while in the discharge of his duty, shot and killed a negro in 1896.

Reeves Pace was deputy sheriff under Sheriff John Baker (1866-68). During the Civil War he was a lieutenant of cavalry. Van Buren Shouse, Howell Walker, and Howell Shouse were other deputy sheriffs furnished by this district.

Col. John H. (Jack) Moore, son of Dr. Samuel B. Moore, was at one time a prominent candidate for Congress, and, had he been opposed by any less popular man than W. C. Whitthorne, would have been successful. Colonel Moore was at West Point at the breaking out of the Civil War, but he immediately enlisted in the Seventh Tennessee Regiment, commanded by the gallant Robert Hatton, and served with distinction in the Virginia campaigns. Lavisa, Colonel Moore's only sister, married W. M. Johnson, who was for many years clerk and master of the Chancery Court at Centerville, where he shot and killed Martin Bentley, a desperate character of the town.

On October 29, 1863, Capt. John Nicks' company of the Twelfth Tennessee Cavalry, C. S. A., engaged a Federal regiment, commanded by Colonel Scully, at the ford west of Centerville. The premature discharge of a gun lost to the Confederates the advantage which would have attended a surprise, and almost the entire company was captured. J. Sharp, of Nicks' company, was killed.

Centerville was the scene of a considerable conflict in 1864 between the Federals, under the command of Colonel Murphy, and the Confederates, under Col. "Jake" Biffle. The Federals had been pursued for nearly two days from Buffalo to Centerville, a distance of forty miles. At the latter place they took refuge in the courthouse and other buildings, from which they checked the Confederate advance. Although the firing was for a time very brisk, the casualties were few. One Confederate, Jasper Springer, was killed by a shot from the courthouse. He fell on the point where Mrs. S. McE. Wilson now lives. During the running fight four Federals were killed near the Charter place, on Indian Creek. The Federals, after a short resistance, retreated rapidly in the direction of Nashville. Later the courthouse was burned by order of Capt. Henon Cross to prevent it being further used as a fort by the Federals, who had been operating in Hickman County from Centerville as a base. They had made portholes in the walls and had converted it into a fort, impervious to an attack from small arms. During the same year the Perry County Jayhawkers, under Capt. John Taylor, burned the business portion of the town, including a large number of private residences. They left the town in ruins, a smoking mass of coals and ashes over which Desolation reigned supreme.

In 1828, Ashley Hickman and his son-in-law, James Wofford, lived at the head spring of Indian Creek, three miles south of Centerville. They came from North Carolina in 1815 with Allan Walker, and preferred the healthy location at the spring to the cane-covered bottoms of Duck River, upon which they could have as easily placed their land warrants. Below Hickman, on the creek, was George Lovelace, who soon after erected a mill. He was the father of Lee Lovelace, who was a gunsmith, this being a very important trade in the early days. Peter Lovelace, another son, had but one eye, but was a fine marksman, and could see a bullet hole sixty yards. He often waged his money upon his skill as a marksman.

Tradition weaves around the name of Indian Creek a beautiful story of love, romance, and tragedy. It is said that before the beginning of the present cen-

tury a party of adventurous whites, after crossing
Duck River, came upon a lone wigwam on what is
now Indian Creek, and that this lone wigwam had
but a single occupant. From the Indian the whites
learned that he had been banished from the village of
his tribe, far to the south, on account of his attempt
to wed the daughter of his chief. He told them that
in a hollow not far away he had built a lodge, and that
he would some day steal back to the village and return
with the daughter of the chief. The whites returned
to the settlements, and by them this creek was called
" Indian Creek." Years after this, one of this party
came this way again, and found the place where the
lone wigwam had stood deserted. He investigated
further, and from some Indians learned that the ex-
iled Indian had carried into execution his designs.
With the assistance of another brave, he had been able
to steal the chief's daughter away from the village,
and together they had fled toward Duck River. They
were pursued to the river, where the trail was lost,
the last trace that the pursuers found being a dead
fish in the edge of the river. In this fish was an
arrowhead of the kind fashioned by their tribe.
They knew that the pursued had come this far, and,
supposing that they had crossed the river into the
country of the whites, the pursuit was no longer continued. Several years later a party of Indians from
this tribe gathered at Gordon & Colbert's ferry, and
there engaged in a drunken row. One of these, separated from the others, wandered down the river,

crossed Indian Creek, and in what is now called the Haunted Hollow of Little Piney he came by accident in sight of a lodge. Watching closely, he soon saw the missing daughter of his chief, her husband, and two little Indian boys. He immediately returned to his village with the news, and a few nights later a band from the village, headed by the chief, came here, burned the lodge, and killed the entire family. Here in this hollow yet grow numerous wild flowers, planted here, it is said, by the Indian girl. Here, too, tradition says, the pioneer hunters often saw a milk-white doe attended by two milk-white fawns. The most unerring marksmen failed to bring them down, and soon concluding that these were the spirits of the murdered Indians, they allowed them to roam the hills unmolested.

CHAPTER V.

THE SECOND DISTRICT.

THE Second District is bounded on the north by the Fifth District; on the east, by the Fourth and Thirteenth Districts; on the south, by the Fifteenth District; and on the west, by the First District. It lies on both sides of Duck River above the First District, to which it is adjoining. Within its limits are the fine lands of Totty's Bend, on the south side of Duck River, and the equally fine lands in the bend opposite to and above Totty's Bend on the north side of the river, where the village of Little Lot stands. This village is situated in one of the most beautiful valleys of the county. It is a short distance north of the mouth of Lick Creek, and is about one mile from Duck River. From Little Lot there extend roads up the river, down the river, up Lick Creek, and to the several valuable farms in the vicinity. One and a half miles below Little Lot is a bridge, located near the site of Baird's Ferry, which was operated for many years prior to the erection of the bridge. This bridge, which connects Totty's Bend with the Little Lot and Lick Creek sections of the Second District, was erected by the county at a cost of about $8,000, and was completed in 1895.

In the lower portion of the Second District is Onstot's Branch, now known as Greer's Branch, which received its name from a Dutch family, who came here in 1810, they being the first settlers. They came here about the time that Robert Totty, for whom the bend was named, settled on the opposite side. Robert Totty was a son of Francis Totty, who lived and died in Virginia. He came to Nashville in 1809, and lived one year on land belonging to James Robertson. In 1810 he came to the mouth of Morgan's Creek, where he encamped, living for a short time in his wagon. Then he lived in a tent until he could erect a house, the first on the present Foster farm. Morgan, for whom the Creek was named, lived farther up the creek. Totty, while living here, laid a soldier's warrant, in 1810, upon the land across the river, where Col. Lewis P. Totty lived and died, and where L. P. Totty, Jr., now lives. While Robert Totty lived near the mouth of Morgan's Creek, his two sons, Matthew and William, enlisted for the War of 1812, and were present at the battle of New Orleans. After their return they laid land warrants on lands now owned by John Cummins and Fletcher Harvill. They, being young and unmarried, lived with their father and assisted him in opening a farm in Totty's Bend, to which he removed with his family in 1815. Soon after both Matthew and William Totty died and were buried in the graveyard at the mouth of Morgan's Creek. Robert Totty, Jr., inherited the lands of his deceased brothers. Lewis Perkins Totty, another son of Robert Totty, Sr., inherited his father's lands. The name "Lewis Perkins" was given him by his father as an evidence of the high regard he had for a Virginia gentleman of that name for whom he had been overseer previous to his removal to Tennessee. Lewis P. Totty was born in Virginia in 1807, came to Nashville with his father at the age of two years, and to Hickman County at the age of three. He remembered traveling in a wagon, this being his only recollection of the journey. He grew to manhood in Totty's Bend, was highly esteemed by his neighbors, and was recognized by all who knew him as a prominent citizen of the county. He was second lieutenant in Company A, First Tennessee Regiment, during the war with Mexico, after which he was a colonel of Tennessee militia. He was a large man, being over six feet tall and weighing two hundred pounds. He possessed great muscular power, but, being of a kind and quiet disposition, he took no pride in an exhibition of this power, as many men of that day did, in fistic encounters. He was firm, but not a fanatic; brave, but not brutal; positive, but patient; determined, but not despotic; and was, therefore, very popular as colonel at the general and petit musters, which were frequently held on his premises, and at other times on the Killough place on Lick Creek, near the upper line of the district.

At the latter place, during one of the petit, or district, musters, Joe Arnold and Lemuel Smith had a fisticuff. Arnold was a son-in-law of David Killough, and Smith was a renter on Killough's farm. In the fight Arnold was getting the better of his antagonist, when a man named Hooten and one of Smith's brothers, Edmond Smith, " showed foul play," as it was termed, by assisting Smith. This resulted in a general fight between the friends of the combatants. At the time of the fight most of the men were on the muster field drilling. When it was discovered that a fight was in progress, Capt. " Lam " Kelly gave orders to break ranks, which order was obeyed with alacrity, and they double-quicked to the scene of the conflict. Upon arriving there, the Captain, upon learning of the foul play, deliberately pulled off his coat and hat, mounted a stump, and announced to the crowd that he could whip either of the men guilty of the act. The accuracy of this statement was not questioned. He then announced that he could whip any man who was not a friend to Joe Arnold and David Killough. The reception of this statement was of a kind that indicated that all present were the warm personal admirers of the gentlemen named. This is related as a typical incident of " the good old days."

In 1830 Neal Younger lived on Onstot's (or Greer's) Branch. He came from North Carolina. In the same year Harrison Totty lived where Ben. Arnold now lives. Robert Totty, Sr., owned this land, having bought it in 1815 from John Davis. Robert Totty, Jr., lived at the Fletcher Harvill place, from which he removed to Texas in 1840. Nancy, a sister of Col. Lewis P. Totty, married Col. William Reeves, who emigrated to Grayson County, Texas, about 1840. Matilda, another sister, married Albert

Griner, father of William and Lewis P. Griner.   Hill
Totty, who came to the bend at an early date, and who
is the ancestor of a majority of the Tottys who now
live in the bend, was distantly related to Robert Totty,
for whom the bend was named.   Robert Totty, who
located at the mouth of Morgan's Creek in 1810, was
a first cousin of William Totty, who located at the
mouth of Sugar Creek, in the Eighth District, in the
same year.   They came together from Nashville to
Turnbull Creek, where they separated, each going his
way.   John Davis entered a large tract of land in this
bend, and Joseph McLaughlin, one of his tenants,
lived at the place where the late Young J. Harvill
lived.   Other tenants of Davis were Alexander Nunnellee and Alexander Cathey, who lived in 1815 near
the John A. Jones place.   This land was entered by
Davis in 1810.   He was a generous man, kind to the
poor, and lenient with his many tenants.   A widow
named Clymer with a large family lived on a portion
of his lands several years rent free.   He gave to the
public a building site on which now stand a public
schoolhouse and church, free for all denominations.
His request was, however, that no Mormons be allowed
to hold services there.   Davis was a member of no
church, but was inclined to the Universalian doctrine,
claiming that God is too good to condemn any of his
creatures to eternal punishment.   He believed that
the disobedient would be punished here and hereafter,
but not eternally.   He often told of his nephew, who,
while acting as chain carrier on one of his surveying

tours, was accidentally shot. The wound was mortal, and while dying he told Davis that he would soon be at rest, and that he felt assured that he was going to eternal rest. This young man was not a member of any church, and this incident helped to confirm the faith of Davis. Many pleasing incidents and generous acts are connected with the history of this pioneer surveyor, who marked the way far in advance of permanent settlements in almost every part of Hickman County from 1790 to 1820. One of the many proofs of the high regard which those who dealt with him had for him is the fact that a granddaughter of the pioneer, William Totty, of Sugar Creek, was named Sophia Davis, this being the name of one of Davis' daughters who, in 1815, married Joseph W. Horton, of Davidson County. Davis was a tall, slender man, possessing wonderful powers of endurance. He could subsist for days on parched corn when out surveying. John Davis, son of Frederick Davis and Fannie (Grieves) Davis, was born in North Carolina on July 30, 1770. He came to Davidson County in 1788; in 1791 he was with the party that buried Edwin Hickman; in February, 1794, he was out under Capt. Thomas Murray in an expedition against the Indians near Muscle Shoals, and later in the year was with the Nickajack expedition. His last service against the Indians was in January, 1795, when he was out with a detachment of mounted infantry. In 1798 he married Dorcas Gleaves and became the father of ten children. His wife died in 1851, and he, at the age of eighty-three, died suddenly and peacefully in 1853. He was not ill, and was lying down waiting for breakfast when the summons came. He lived and died in Davidson County, but there are few districts in Hickman County where his name is not met with in connection with its early history.

Another pioneer surveyor, whose name appears in the land papers of the county, was McLemore, from whom Maj. Edwin Baird bought lands in 1820. Edwin Baird was a son of Samuel McClearen Baird, who was born in Buncombe County, N. C., and came to this district in 1811. Edwin Baird was born in Lincoln County, N. C., on March 1, 1799. His wife was Jane Clampitt, who was born in Wilson County, Tenn., in April, 1802, and who was married on July 20, 1820. Other sons of Samuel McClearen Baird were Albert, Joseph, Samuel, Jr., and James P., who a few years ago died in Arkansas. The daughters of Samuel McClearen Baird were Matilda and Roena. Matilda married Jacob Fite, and was the mother of John, Leonard B., and Samuel Fite, of Nashville. Roena married William Anderson, of the Fifteenth District. Edwin Baird, after his marriage to Jane Clampitt, removed from his father's place, near Little Lot, to Totty's Bend, where he opened up a farm, and where he and his wife lived to a ripe old age. Their children were the late W. Campbell Baird and James Perry Baird, who now lives in Nashville. James P. Baird married Parmelia Williams, of Maury County, He was born on September 11, 1822.

Edwin Baird was known as a man of honor, true to what he conceived to be right, discreet in all things, industrious in his habits, correct in his calculations, just in his judgments, true to his friends, and reasonably lenient with those from whom he differed in opinion. Col. Alfred Darden once lived on lands adjoining those of Edwin Baird.

In 1845 Neal Brown, a very remarkable man, came to Totty's Bend. He lived at the place where Mrs. Hendricks now lives, near the church. He came from Turnbull Creek, in Williamson County. After coming to Totty's Bend he commenced the manufacture of whisky and brandy, which he sold, but did not drink. When a young man, he had, while intoxicated, been beaten in a rough-and-tumble fight, during which one of his eyes had been pulled from its socket. The eye was replaced, the sight not being seriously impaired; but Brown, as the story goes, was never again intoxicated. He, however, was at all times ready for a fight, being willing to fight any man in order to settle the momentous question as to which was the better man. During the few years he resided in the bend a man frequently came down Duck River on flatboats, who, like Brown, was "much of a man." Consequently a rivalry sprang up between them. Banterings and challenges followed. The boatman finally agreed that upon his next trip down the river he would land his boat and settle the question in dispute. The time came and the boat landed. Brown was there, and he and his rival greeted each

other cordially, each understanding the purpose of the
meeting. Little time was lost in preliminary arrangements, and soon the principals were stripped
of hats, coats, and shirts. They then proceeded to
fight in the most approved fashion of that day.
Standing erect at first, they proceeded to strike each
other with their fists; then they clinched and fell
to the ground. Brown, being an expert wrestler,
threw his antagonist, who, being larger and more
powerful, turned him. But the wary wrestler would
not remain underneath, and was soon on top of his
more powerful antagonist. Thus the contest was
waged, the victory being still in doubt. Brown was
"long-winded" and "game;" but the boatman, equally " game " and more powerful, finally partially tri-
umphed. He and Brown were both satisfied, and
neither insisted on a further discussion of the point at
issue. And this was a characteristic incident of " the
good old days." Brown lived during his latter days
at the mouth of Defeated Creek, where, with accumu-
lated money, he bought the lands upon which his son,
D. L. Brown, now lives. He was the father of Mrs.
Hendricks, of Totty's Bend, and of James A. Brown,
of Centerville.

Samuel McClearen Baird located in 1811 where
Mrs. Suggs now lives. In the following year he established Baird's Ferry, one of the first established in the
county. Henry Truett, who married Sallie Clampitt,
a sister of the wife of Edwin Baird, lived near Baird's
Ferry in 1812. Benjamin Greer and James McCa-

leb lived near Baird's Ferry in 1811. They owned
the lands upon which the western portion of Little Lot
now stands. McCaleb had a cotton gin here in 1820.
He was a Primitive Baptist preacher, and preached
here as early as 1815. There is a record of his having
preached at the house of Henry Truett in 1820. He
was a man of energy, and cleared much of the land
between the present site of Little Lot and Baird's
Ferry. He was the owner of several slaves, and, with
their help, operated his gin and also engaged in the
raising of cotton. His neighbors also cultivated cotton, which he ginned for them, thereby encouraging
the culture of this plant here at an early date. He
was buried at the McCaleb (or " old peach orchard ")
graveyard, near the place where now lives Zebulon
Hassell the Third.

Zebulon Hassell the Second was born on October
18, 1804, in North Carolina, and came to the Lambert
place, on Hassell's Creek, with his father, Zebulon
Hassell the First. Here he lived with his father until
April 5, 1827, at which time he married Mary Mc-
Caleb, who was born on June 27, 1810. Soon after
his marriage he lived near Little Lot, where, in 1846,
he enlisted in Whitfield's company, First Tennessee
Regiment, and served in the war with Mexico. His
neighbor, Alfred Darden, enlisted in the same company. They returned to Hickman County in 1847.
After serving as comrades in the army, they bought
adjoining farms, Darden buying the Gill Anderson
place, and Hassell buying the place where his son,

Zebulon Hassell the Third, now lives. They bought from Joseph Anderson, Hassell paying $3,000, and Darden paying $3,500. Artin Hassell, who was killed at Shady Grove by Griff. Nichols, was the oldest son of Zebulon Hassell the Second. Other sons were Joseph and James. The latter removed to Texas, where he died. A daughter, Nancy, married William Suggs, deceased. Zebulon Hassell the Third married a daughter of Col. Lewis P. Totty, and she takes pleasure in telling the many stories of pioneer life told her, when a child, by her parents.

Joseph Anderson, from whom Darden and Hassell bought lands as above stated, married a daughter of Benjamin Greer, from whom he inherited these lands. Greer, together with James McCaleb, owned the larger portion, if not all, of the land from Little Lot to Baird's Ferry.

In 1835, George Martin, father of Washington Martin, owned the brick house, at Little Lot, now the property of John A. Jones. This house was built by Hugh McCabe, who came here in 1810 from Maryland. McCabe entered the land on which Little Lot stands, or bought it from Asa Shute, who was here also at that date. McCabe was a wealthy man, possessed of slaves and money. He owned a half section of land. McCabe, in 1815, at the solicitation of neighbors, who had concluded that they needed a church and schoolhouse, gave them a site upon which to build. Out of his hundreds of acres he made the princely donation of one-fourth of an acre. When the neighbors assembled to haul the logs and build the house, one of them suggested that all other churches had names, and that one should be provided for this. Parker Tyler, the Lick Creek wag, replied: "It is such a d—n little lot, we can't give it a big name." The people concluded that Tyler was right, and from its size it took its name, Little Lot. This is how Little Lot was named almost a hundred years ago.

Parker Tyler was a brother of Wat Tyler. He was much given to frivolities and was somewhat dissipated, while his brother was a sober citizen and a leading church member. Their father lived a few miles from Little Lot on Lick Creek, and was the owner of a number of slaves and of much other property. One of the negroes was a carpenter, and Parker had him make a coffin, in which he kept his tobacco, giving as his reason that the negroes would not dare to approach the coffin in the night to steal his tobacco. He added: "Then I may need it later for another purpose." This is a characteristic anecdote told of the thoughtless, but generally esteemed, Parker Tyler.

In 1829 Robert Bratton, Sr., came from North Carolina and located at the Rochell place, on Swan Creek. In 1835 he removed to the Second District, settling near Little Lot, where he bought two hundred and fifty-five acres of land for $1,600. His sons were Claiborne, William, Robert, Jr., George, James, J. J., and Samuel H. William Bratton married a daughter of John Griffith, uncle of J. O. Griffith, at one time a prominent newspaper man of Nashville. Bratton was a member of the firm of Bratton, Fowlkes, & Stoddard, who at one time operated Oakland Furnace, in the Seventh District. Claiborne Bratton was the firm's bookkeeper, and was retained in this position by Carothers & Easley, who afterwards owned and operated this furnace. The wife of Robert Bratton, Sr., was Matilda Hull, of Williamson County.

In 1845 William Spence lived where William Stanfill now lives. He was born in North Carolina in 1792, and came to Harpeth, near the Newsom place, in 1810. He was a poor boy without education, and worked here as a hireling for ten years. At the age of twenty-eight he married Phœbe Forehand. John Davis, who lived in that neighborhood, induced him to visit Hickman County, where Davis owned land. The result was he purchased from Davis four hundred and fifty acres south of, and adjoining, Little Lot. He settled on this land in 1845. His sons were Miles, Mark, and John; his daughters, Narcissa, who married Robert Bratton, Jr.; Rebecca, who married Gill Anderson; Nancy, who married Robert Dean; and Tennessee, who married James Harrington. Gill Anderson's father was John Anderson, of the Fifteenth District. Gill Anderson was born on June 11, 1827, in the Kettle Bend of Duck River, in Maury County. His father was born on February 25, 1805, in North Carolina.

Ferdinand B. Russell was the first to establish a general store at Little Lot, which he did in 1853. William Gary was one of his clerks. The first physi-

SECOND DISTRICT. 95

cian to establish himself here was either Francis Easley or Clagett Sothern, in 1850. Physicians here at a later date were Dawson, Hall, James T. Ward, A. N. Doyel, Bryant, and Dennis W. Flowers, a grandson of William Flowers, one of the pioneers of the Ninth District. He is a son of the late Rev. Gideon Flowers.

Two miles south of Little Lot, below the mouth of Lick Creek, O. A. Jones now lives on a tract of land once owned by Lawson Harrison Nunnelly. Jones came to this place from the Fourth District, above John Groves' mill on Jones' Branch of Lick Creek. O. A. Jones' father was also named Alston Jones. He has one son, John A. Jones, a prominent business man of this section.

Lawson H. Nunnelly, who once lived here, was born in North Carolina in 1801. He came to this county in 1810. He afterwards removed to Davidson County, but returned to this county in 1830. While he lived here there occurred an incident of which he spoke in after years with much merriment. This was his fight with Fowler.

In 1830 Jeff., a valuable slave of Robert Totty, was drowned at the ford above Baird's Ferry. In the following year his funeral was preached by Champion Anderson, a negro preacher, at Baird's Ferry. Zebulon Hassell the Second lost two slaves by drowning near the Jones place. They had been allowed the customary Saturday night and Sunday liberty to visit their wives, who lived in Anderson's Bend. They were returning on Monday morning before daybreak in order to be at their quarters ready for work. The river had risen since they crossed, but they were not aware of it. They drifted from the mule they were riding, it swimming to the shore. Their bodies were recovered near where the bridge now is.

In 1864, at the house of J. C. Bradley on the hill near Little Lot and near the mouth of Lick Creek, was committed the most cowardly and brutal murder in the history of the county. This was the killing of the young men, Pointer and Buford, by a company of Federals under the immediate command of the notorious Creasy, who bore, and disgraced upon numerous occasions, a captain's commission. The young men, who were from Williamson County, stopped here for breakfast, which they were just preparing to eat when the presence of fifty Federals at the gate was announced by members of the family. There were only two doors to the room in which the young men were. To pass through one was to come face to face with the approaching Federals; to pass through the other was to enter a small bedroom from which there was no other means of exit. They retreated through the latter and awaited the advancing Federals and their own approaching doom. Creasy came to the door of the room and demanded their surrender. Young Pointer gave the Masonic sign of distress, and replied, " We surrender; " whereupon Creasy commenced firing, and did not cease until his victims lay dead at his feet, murdered after having surrendered to odds of twenty-five to one. These young men, who were members of prominent families, were guilty of no offense, save that of their sympathy for the rebellion. They had left home to avoid being arrested and carried to Northern prisons, and were probably preparing to enter the Confederate Army. Creasy was the brute who, while acting in the capacity of captain of a negro company, upon more than one occasion insulted good women and brave, though powerless, men throughout the county.

Below the bridge, north of the river and opposite Totty's Bend, is Gerry's Branch, named from the fact that a man named Gerry entered and owned a large tract of land, including the branch and adjacent hills. He lived on this land as early as 1830. In these hills are some of the finest surface indications of iron ore to be found in Hickman County. Gerry's Branch lies between Little Lot and Morgan's Creek. On this branch, in 1863 and 1864, was Tarkington's still-house. In 1864, near this place, after a chase of nearly three miles, David Miller shot and killed a Federal soldier, who was fleeing from the scene of the engagement near Baird's Ferry, described elsewhere.

Panther Branch comes into Duck River a short distance above Gerry's Branch. On this branch is Panther Cave, which has never been explored sufficiently to justify a statement as to its dimensions. In early days panthers were supposed to rear their young here, as they and numerous wolves came from these hills and committed depredations upon flocks of geese, calves, and sheep belonging to early settlers on Lick Creek and in the valley of Duck River near Little Lot.

Drury Harrington was born in Chatham County, N. C., in 1788, came to Tennessee in 1809, and settled near the large spring about one mile north of Little Lot. His wife was Mary Mattocks, of Chatham County, N. C., who was born in 1790. He died on August 10, 1844. The children of Drury Harrington were Jane, who married William Malugin; James, who was born in 1811; Miles, Calvin; Sallie, who married Meredith Gossett, of Mill Creek; Fannie, who married William Worley; and Philip, who married Martha, the daughter of Benjamin Wilson, of Leatherwood Creek. The late Philip Harrington was born on March 27, 1814. At the age of eighty-four he was still strong and healthy, and lived at the place where his father settled ninety years ago. He remembered when all around Little Lot was a swampy wilderness through which wolves and panthers roamed. He recalled the fact that the first clock he ever heard strike was the property of Hugh McCabe. The clock was one of the old-fashioned kind that stood on the floor and reached to the ceiling overhead. Drury Harrington's brothers, who came here about 1809, were Dempsey, Robert, and William. They were great hunters and trappers. They built wolf pens on the head of Mill Creek, and one on Morgan's Creek. In the latter they caught a large wolf one Sunday morning in 1835. Several men of the neighborhood gathered for the purpose of visiting the pens, carrying with them their guns and dogs. The Mill Creek pens were found to be empty, but when they reached the Morgan's Creek pen they found a large, fierce wolf safely entrapped, despite its desperate efforts to escape. It was killed in the pen and its body carried back to the settlement.

Thus the pioneer days were frequently enlivened by the chase, the hunt, and other pastimes and pleasures of a kind unknown to the present generation. One of the popular sports engaged in by our forefathers was the shooting match—legalized betting upon their skill as marksmen. This form of gambling was legalized for the purpose of training the early settlers in the use of firearms. To the training obtained at these early shooting matches was largely due the deadly skill with which the Tennesseans handled their rifles at New Orleans, where they gave an exhibition of marksmanship which not only astonished the British, but the entire world. At these shooting matches the procedure was about as follows: Each participant contributed a dollar to what was called " the pony purse," taking in exchange five chances, or shots. He then took a board and burned it until one side was blackened. Upon this blackened surface he placed a cross, indicating its position by placing upon the cross a small bit of white paper. Placing this board sixty, and sometimes a hundred, yards away, he lay down, and, resting his gun upon a " chunk," fired at the " spot." When all had done this, the judges, previously appointed, compared the boards and gave the

" pony purse " to the contestant who had placed three bullets within a smaller radius than had any other. If there was a tie, it was decided by allowing the contestants three shots, the nearest two winning. Sometimes a " beef," worth five or ten dollars, took the place of the " pony purse." In this case the " hide and tallow " was called the " first choice," and went to the marksman who made the highest average. The heaviest " hind quarter " was called the " second choice; " the other " hind quarter," " third choice; " the heaviest " fore quarter," " fourth choice; " the other " fore quarter," " fifth choice." By this arrangement there were always five partially successful contestants, the " choices " going to the best five marksmen. However, the contests did not always end here, the " choices " sometimes being " staked " one against the other. This often resulted in the " beef " being driven home alive by some successful marksman. While these meetings were for amusement, they did not always pass off pleasantly, but occasionally ended in a general fight, in which case all guns were laid aside and a thought of bringing them into the fight was never entertained. George Martin, father of Armistead Martin, was one of the early marksmen of this district. At a distance of sixty or one hundred yards, it was no unusual occurrence for the cross or " center " to be " knocked out " or " drove " by expert riflemen. The shooting match was a characteristic incident of " the good old days."

Up to the time of the Civil War guns with " percussion locks," now almost entirely obsolete, were considered as luxuries obtainable only by the wealthier class. The guns used by a large majority of the people were the old flintlock rifles. After the close of the Mexican War a number of flintlock muskets were to be found throughout the county. These were called " British muskets." At the breaking out of the Civil War these muskets were collected by the Confederate authorities and provided with percussion locks, generally known as " cap locks." This was the gun with which Confederate soldiers were principally provided during the first year of the war. Flintlock rifles were made by local gunsmiths. A steel octagon, about four feet in length, was bored out and rifled, this constituting the barrel, which was incased in a wooden stock, which ran the entire length of the barrel. Near the " breech pin " and in the side of the barrel was the " touchhole," which opened into the " pan," which was attached to the lock just beneath. When powder was placed in the barrel, a portion would drop into the pan, constituting the " priming." The pan was covered by a lid, to which was attached a piece of smooth-faced steel, against which the flint would strike. The flint was fastened by a clamp in the hammer. There were two triggers; the rear one " sprung the trigger," the front one caused the hammer to fall. The flint striking the face of the steel piece over the pan caused a spark to drop into it, the lid falling forward. The powder ignited in the pan communicated instantaneously with that in the barrel. The rifle was loaded with powder measured accurately in a charger made of a piece of cane or the tip of a deer's antler. This charger was attached to the strap by which the shot pouch was suspended from the shoulder. In this shot pouch were carried bullet molds, lead, bullets, and " patching." The " patching " was cloth, which was placed over the muzzle of the gun, into which the bullet was forced to a level with the muzzle. The patching was then clipped with the hunting knife, which was carried in a scabbard attached to the shoulder strap of the shot pouch. Then bullet and patching were " rammed home " with a " ramrod " made of hickory and carried in the stock of the gun beneath the barrel. A flint after much use would become so dull and smooth that it would not emit a spark, and this would necessitate its being " picked." Sometimes the powder in the pan would fail to ignite that in the barrel, and this was called " a flash in the pan." This imperfect description of the pioneer's most trusted friend will perhaps be of no particular interest to many now living; but in these days of long-range Krag-Jorgensen and Mauser rifles and smokeless powder, the old flintlock rifle and musket will soon be forgotten, along with the sickle, the bar-share plow, the metal mortars in which grain was pounded into meal, the hand loom, and the spinning wheel; yet these were the guns that were used at King's Mountain and New Orleans.

On Lick Creek at the mouth of Hassell's Creek, in 1810, lived David Killough, who came from Pennsyl-

vania and bought a half section of land from Asa
Shute. This land lay at the mouth of Hassell's
Creek and on both sides of Lick Creek, including the
mouth of Fort Cooper hollow. His place was near
the road leading to Leatherwood, Williamsport, and
Columbia; also, near the roads leading to Charlotte, Reynoldsburg, Vernon, Franklin, and Nashville. This caused the Killough place to be one of
note, at which were held elections, musters, and other
public meetings.

A near-by neighbor was Dr. Smoot, who was the
father of twins, Betsy and Polly. Betsy married
Frank, a son of David Killough.

Farther down the creek, from 1812 to 1815, at
what was afterwards known as the "Jack Tarkington
place," lived Elizabeth Berry, the widow of Humphrey Bybon Berry, who died in Maryland. She
came here with her father, William Tyler, father of
Wat and Parker Tyler. Her sons were William
Tyler Berry and Ferdinand Berry. The former went
to Nashville, where he became a prominent citizen;
the latter, to Memphis, where he attained equal prominence. Mrs. Berry married John I. Webb, of Williamsport, at which place they both died. They were
buried in the graveyard on the "Jack Tarkington
place." The name of the wife of William Tyler was
Stoddard. She was a relative of William Henry
Harrison. At the death of her husband she became
the sole owner of his extensive property, which she
in turn gave to her son, George Parker Tyler, who

named Little Lot.   Mrs. Berry had in her possession silver spoons upon which were engraved the name of Humphrey Bybon Berry.   These spoons were among the first of the kind brought to the county.

In 1816 Horatio Clagett, father of William and Horatio Clagett, so long prominent business men of Centerville, lived at the place where J. W. Shouse now lives.

In this neighborhood were a number of families who came from Maryland, among whom were the Tylers, Berrys, Primms, Smoots, Clagetts, Gannts, and Smiths.   They were refined, wealthy, and well educated, and brought with them physicians, lawyers, and school-teachers.

In this neighborhood, at a later date, lived Col. "Jack" Tarkington, who bought the Tyler lands.   He was a prominent trader and stock raiser, carrying large droves of hogs and mules to Alabama and Mississippi markets.   His stallions and jacks were the best in the county, and, as a trader, he removed the surplus stock of the county, and, in exchange, put into circulation large sums of money.   He was the father of George and J. H. C. Tarkington.

Henry Tucker lived near Baird's Ferry in 1815. William Mattocks, in 1809, lived near his brother-in-law, Drury Harrington.   He emigrated to Arkansas, where he committed suicide by hanging.

In 1825 Britton Garner, the Primitive Baptist preacher, preached at Little Lot and in Totty's Bend. Epps Bishop, of the same church, preached here about the same time. In 1897 the wife of the latter was still living at Lyles Station, drawing a pension on account of her husband's service in the War of 1812. The names of a few of the preachers who have preached in this district at a more recent date are: H. O. Moore and A. N. Doyle, of the Methodist Church; and John and James Morton, of the Christian Church. Of the preachers of this district, local and visiting, no one is entitled to more prominent mention than Elder Young James Harvill, of the Primitive Baptist Church, who was born in Cumberland County, N. C., on June 19, 1821, and came to Dunlap Creek, in the Third District, in 1826. His father was Moses Harvill; his grandfather, James Harvill. His mother was Mary Simms, whose father was Ambers Simms. All of these lived in North Carolina. He died in 1898, one of the most widely known and generally respected preachers who ever lived in Hickman County.

George Gannt, who came from Maryland, taught school near the Killough place in 1820. Wiley Harper taught school at Little Lot from 1820 to 1822. James D. Easley taught in Totty's Bend in 1835. Nathan Springer taught at Little Lot in 1840; —— Gibson, in 1836; and Robert Cooper, in 1830.

In 1864 David Miller—who then lived, as he does now, in Anderson's Bend—was at the head of a company of independent Southern scouts which operated in the upper portion of Hickman County and in the adjacent portions of Maury and Williamson Counties.

The Federals, who had possession of Columbia and of the Northwestern Railroad, were anxious to capture or kill Miller, and several unsuccessful expeditions had been made into the county for this purpose. In the lower portion of the county there was an organization similar to Miller's, commanded by Cross. One night in 1864 these two commanders met in Totty's Bend for the purpose of consulting as to the reception which should be given a Federal detachment then in the vicinity. A. J. (Jack) Sullivan, a well-known citizen of Mill Creek, was acting as guide for the Federals. Sullivan bore a captain's commission. The Federals had passed through Totty's Bend boasting of the horrible fate that would befall any "bushwhackers" that they might encounter. They had arrived at Little Lot, and on the following day twenty-four returned in the direction of Baird's Ferry. The Rebels, numbering eleven, including Miller, Cross, and McLaughlin, had crossed the river at Baird's Ford and concealed themselves in a skirt of timber near the road between Zebulon Hassell's and the river. Captain Cross went in the direction of Little Lot to reconnoiter, and, after passing Hassell's front gate, he discovered the Federals coming through a long lane. He wheeled his horse, and, taking his hat, waived defiance at his approaching foes. They started toward him at full speed, and he retreated rapidly in the direction of the river. A lively chase ensued, with Jack Sullivan leading the pursuers. No sooner had Cross passed the point where his comrades lay in ambush than he turned and fired into the Federals, who halted just as a volley came flashing from their right, fired by an unexpected and hidden foe. The pursuers now became the pursued, and back over the road they went, the clatter of horses' hoofs intermingled with the rapid reports of small arms. One-fourth of a mile east of his home, at the turn of the lane, Hassell and his neighbor, Colonel Darden, stood and watched this exciting chase. Near this point was a gate. When opposite this gate a horse turned to the right and entered it. Just inside the gate, near where now stands a large elm, its rider fell from its back, lifeless. The dead man was Jack Sullivan. Another horse came through the gate, and its rider fell dead near the chimney of a near-by house. A woman had crouched behind this chimney for protection from the flying bullets. The chase continued to Little Lot, and even farther. It was during this chase that David Miller killed the Federal near Tarkington's stillhouse in the vicinity of Gerry's Branch. In this affair were engaged twenty-four well-mounted, well-armed Federal cavalrymen and eleven Confederates whose courage sometimes became foolhardy. Of the Federals, eleven were slain; of the Confederates, not one was killed or wounded. The lucky thirteen that escaped reached their camp on the Northwestern Railroad that night, and, reinforced, returned on the following day under the leadership of the cur, Creasy, who came ready for that work in which he was most proficient—the burning of houses, the robbing of defenseless homes, and the insulting of unprotected women.   He came with the intention of burning the residence of Hassell, but loyal citizens of the neighborhood prevented this by their influence. One of Creasy's soldiers, who had been in the fight of the day before, argued against the burning of the house, saying: "Nobody is to blame but ourselves. They surprised us and whipped us, all of which is fair in war."

Since 1893 phosphate deposits in the upper end of Totty's Bend have been worked with varying degrees of success.   The output of the mines was at first carried to Centerville by wagons; later it was towed to Centerville in barges by a small steamer.   Finally, an arm of the Centerville branch of the Nashville, Chattanooga and St. Louis Railroad was run from Centerville to the mines.   This road runs along the valley of the river, crossing Swan Creek near its mouth, to the mouth of Onstot's Branch, and up the branch to its head, where the mines are located. These mines were for several years under the immediate management of the late W. B. Comer, formerly superintendent of the ore mines at Nunnelly.

CHAPTER VI.

THE THIRD DISTRICT.

THE Third District is bounded on the north by the Thirteenth District; on the east, by Maury County; on the south, by the Fourteenth District; and on the west, by the Fifteenth District. It includes that portion of Hickman County on the south side of Duck River and north of the Fourteenth District, extending from the Maury County line to Buck Branch. A small portion of the district is on the north side of Duck River near Gordon's Ferry. The section of country surrounding the quiet village of Shady Grove was the scene of some of the most important events of the pioneer days, a number of which are described at greater length in a previous chapter. Somewhere near Gordon's Ferry and the " Duck River licks," situated on Lick Creek, was the fight with the Indians in May, 1780. Over the line in Maury County were located Gen. Nathaniel Greene's 25,000 acres of land, laid off by Shelby, Bledsoe, and Tatum in 1783. Through the adjoining districts, the Thirteenth and Fifteenth, ran the Continental Line of 1784. Through these districts ran also the old Chickasaw Trace, or path, which was, prior to the opening of the Natchez Trace, the road from Nashville to Natchez and the Chickasaw country. It was over a portion of this trace that the Coldwater Expedition went in 1787 to avenge the death of Mark Robertson, who had been killed on Robertson's Creek, in the Fifteenth District, up which the trace ran. It was over this trace that the desperately daring bands of scouts under Capt. "Jack" (John) Gordon and Capt. John "Golong" Rains marched often over a hundred years ago. It was over this trace that, in 1795, the old Col. Casper Mansker went with a detachment of men from Nashville to the assistance of the Chickasaws, who were sorely pressed by the Creeks. In January of this year the Chickasaws, who were in the main friendly toward the whites, had come upon a body of Creeks on Duck River, somewhere in this vicinity, and had taken five scalps. These were sent to Nashville, with the explanation that the Creeks at the time of the attack were on their way to attack the whites. A war ensued, and the Chickasaws called for assistance, which was furnished under the leadership of the veteran, Mansker. Piomingo, of the Chickasaws, in his appeal for help, stated that if it did not soon arrive, " You shall soon hear that I died like a man."

The most prominent of the early settlers of this section was Capt. John Gordon, remembered by a few old citizens of the county as " Old Capt. Jack Gordon." He had a reputation as a fighter from Nashville to New Orleans. Here, as early as 1804, he, in partnership with General Colbert, one of the famous Chickasaw chiefs of that name, had a trading post. He did not bring his family here until two or three years later. At this time he kept a tavern in Nashville, on the west side of Market street, near the Public Square. At this trading post Thomas H. Benton, " Old Bullion," afterwards United States Senator from Missouri, was a clerk. He also taught school on Duck River somewhere in this section. John Gordon had married Dollie Cross, sister of Richard Cross, and prior to 1805 Gordon and Cross located on the north side of the river near Gordon's Ferry, which was then established, Gordon and the Indian, Colbert, running it in partnership. Up to this time the whites had no legal treaty right to any lands within the present limits of Hickman County. This territory belonged to the Chickasaws. It was also claimed by the Cherokees, who alleged that they had assisted in the expulsion of the Shawnees. They made this claim the excuse for their numerous inroads into Tennessee. The most persistent of the Indians in their attacks upon the whites were the Creeks, who never even attempted to excuse themselves by claiming any of this territory. The reservation by North Carolina of lands for her soldiers, the southern boundary of which was marked by the Line of 1784, included much of Hickman County, but it must be understood that North Carolina obtained her title from England at the close of the Revolutionary War. England had obtained her title from the Six Nations by the treaty of Stanwix in 1768. The Six Nations held by the right of conquest, and after this relinquishment to the whites the Southern Indians reasserted their claims.

Adventurous surveyors, holding military warrants, made locations in Hickman County after the running of the Line of 1784; but few, if any, attempts were made to settle upon these lands prior to the treaties of 1805, which will be referred to in the following pages. From this it will be seen that the running of the Continental Line of 1784, locally known as the Military Line, had no connection with any treaty with the Indians. Captain Gordon, in running the trading post in connection with the Chickasaw chief, General Colbert, had only a trader's rights in this territory, but it enabled him to make a good selection of lands, which he soon afterwards occupied. Local tradition says he had permanently settled here before 1805. If so, it was because his business connections with the influential Colbert family made him safe from molestation.

In 1801 a treaty was made at the Chickasaw Bluffs which gave permission to the United States to lay out and cut a wagon road between Nashville and Natchez. The Chickasaws were to be paid $700 for furnishing guides and other assistance. This work was commenced immediately under the direction of United States troops commanded by Capt. Robert Butler and Lieut. E. Pendleton Gaines. This trace came by the way of Kinderhook, Maury County, crossed Duck River at Gordon's Ferry, passed between the head of Dunlap Creek and Jackson's Branch on the east, ran along the ridge between Cathey's Creek, of Maury and Lewis Counties, and Swan Creek, of Hickman

County, crossing the latter creek at the point known as Johnson's Stand, below the Kittrell place. It was on this trace at Griner's Stand, in Lewis County, that Meriwether Lewis met his death. While this trace was being opened, Benjamin Smith, uncle of the late Daniel Smith, lived at Kinderhook, as did also Squire Kearsey, father of Rev. John Kearsey, who at one time lived in the Eighth District. Squire Kearsey is said to have been the original of the following time-honored story: While magistrate, application was made to him for à search warrant for a broadax. A careful perusal of his well-worn form book failed to discover a form for a search warrant for a broadax, the nearest approach being a form in which a turkey hen was mentioned. This form was accordingly copied, and the applicant was instructed by His Honor to take it along and "keep an eye out for the broadax."

John Willey, who afterwards lived in the Fifteenth District, was one of the party that opened the Natchez Trace, known locally as the "Notchy" Trace. Some time was spent in digging the banks of the river at the mouth of Fatty Bread Branch, on the north side, and the banks on the south side near where Joseph Bond now lives. While this was being done the party camped at the large spring at the foot of the hill where Samuel Cochran now lives. This spring is on Dunlap Creek, and directly on the trace one mile west of where it crosses Duck River near Gordon's Ferry. The spring is one and a half miles south of Shady Grove, and was well suited for a place of encampment.

The party remained here for several weeks, after which the camp was moved to Swan Creek in what is now the Twelfth District.

On July 23, 1805, a treaty was concluded between the Chickasaws and James Robertson and Silas Dinsmore, representing the United States, by which the Indians ceded land in Tennessee to the whites. A portion of the boundary agreed upon was as follows: "Up the main channel of the Tennessee River to the mouth of Duck River; thence up the left bank of Duck River to the road leading from Nashville to Natchez; thence along said road to the ridge dividing the waters running into Duck River from those running into Buffalo River." On October 25 of this year the Cherokees, by treaty, relinquished all claims to lands north of Duck River, and in the following January Sour Mush, Turtle at Home, John Jolly, Red Bird, and other Cherokee chiefs ceded to the United States all lands north of the Tennessee River. These treaties placed the dangerous Cherokees far to the south, and made Duck River throughout the county, and the Natchez Trace at one corner, the boundary between the whites and the comparatively peaceable and honorable Chickasaws. This date marks the commencement of the permanent settlement of Hickman County on the north side of the river. The permanent settlement of that section of the county lying south of Duck River followed the treaty of October 19, 1818, by which the Chickasaws relinquished all claims to Tennessee soil. Isaac

Shelby and Andrew Jackson represented the United States. One of the considerations was that the United States pay Capt. John Gordon $1,115 due him from the Chickasaws. This was probably the amount of the bad debts left on his old trading-post books. The forty-five Tennesseans who had in 1795 gone to assist the Chickasaws against the Creeks, referred to above, were paid $2,000 by the United States. Maj. James Colbert had, while on a visit to Baltimore two years before this, lost $1,089 at a theater. This was refunded by the government, and as to whether the gallant Chickasaw, Colbert, was at the time of the loss overcome by force of numbers or by that enemy of his race, John Barleycorn, is left to the imagination of the reader. That accomplished villain and prince of traitors, William McGillivray, received $150, as did also Iskarweuttaba and Immartoibarmicco. Despite the superior length of their names, Hopoyeabaummer, Immauklusharhopoyea, and Hopoyeabaummer, Jr., received only $100 each. These were some of the minor considerations, the terms of the treaty being in general unusually favorable to the Chickasaws.

Following the treaties of 1805 and 1806 came the congressional reservation line, described in an Act of Congress, approved April 18, 1806. As this line is in local tradition confused with the line established between the whites and Indians, the events leading up to its establishment are here referred to. The location of the Third District of Hickman County makes it a place par excellence for the illustrating of the confusion attending the perfecting of titles to land in Tennessee from 1796 to 1806. North Carolina, relying upon the title obtained from the Six Nations, in matters of legislation studiously ignored the claims of the Chickasaws and Cherokees. This is made evident by the erection in 1777 of Washington County, N. C., which embraced all of the present State of Tennessee. At the time of the cession of this territory to the United States in December, 1789, there were unperfected titles to lands in Tennessee founded on military service in the Revolutionary War; on entries in John Armstrong's office; on service in Evans' battalion; on services rendered in laying off the military reservation—that is, running the lines of 1783 and 1784; on grants to particular persons, like that to General Greene; and on settlements made on public lands—preëmption rights. By the terms of the Act of cession North Carolina retained the right to perfect these titles. After the admission of Tennessee into the Union, this State declined to recognize the right of North Carolina to perfect these titles, and the opening of entry taker's offices bade fair to cover the State with a new series of entries. The matter was happily arranged as between the two States by North Carolina's transferring to Tennessee the right to perfect these titles, reserving for herself the right to issue warrants to be laid in the military reservation. This was assented to by the United States, with the additional conditions set out in the Act providing for the " Congressional Reservation Line." This line is described as follows: " Beginning at the place where the eastern or main branch of Elk River intersects the boundary of the State; thence due north to the northern or main branch of Duck River; thence down the waters of Duck River to the military boundary line; thence with said line west to the Tennessee River; thence down the Tennessee to the northern boundary of the State." Tennessee surrendered all her right to the land south and west of this line, the United States in turn surrendering her right to the land north and east of it. So the United States, while recognizing the Chickasaws' title to the land as far north as Duck River, also recognized Tennessee's title to the land as far south as the Military Line, or Line of 1784. The general belief that the Military Line was the true boundary between the whites and Chickasaws, and Duck River the recognized boundary, is, therefore, erroneous. Tennessee could perfect titles as far south of Duck River as the Military Line; but the well-founded fear that the Chickasaws would enforce with the tomahawk that treaty which made Duck River the boundary prevented any attempts at permanent settlements on the south side prior to 1818. Possible exceptions to this general rule are to be found in the Third District. Here the Chickasaw line turned to the south along the Natchez Trace, and the settler who encroached upon this corner of the reservation risked not as much as he who encroached farther down the river. Here were doubtless made permanent settlements on the south side of the river and on the Indian side of the trace. The early settler on the north or east side of the river, like Capt. John Gordon, obtained his title from North Carolina through Tennessee; the early settler on the opposite bank of the river and on the east side of the trace obtained his title from the United States; the early settler on this side of the river and on the west side of the trace was a " squatter."

Immediately after the treaty of 1805 a man named McIntosh commenced a " clearing " on the place where the late Joseph Bond lived. Tradition says that this was the first " clearing " in the county. A detachment of soldiers patrolled the trace after the treaty in order to restrain the " squatters," which term, as applied to some of the most daring of the early settlers of the county, is certainly used here in no offensive sense. On the ridge, near where Samuel G. Baker's residence now is, there had been erected a round-pole schoolhouse. The teacher was George Peery, Hickman County's first surveyor, who afterwards became one of the most prominent pioneers of the Twelfth District. He owned land on the other side of the river, near the Gordon place. One day his school was interrupted by the sound of horses' feet, and a troop of government rangers turned out of the trace and rode up to the schoolhouse. He was told that the house was on the Indian side, and, after ordering him and his pupils out, the building was torn down. He was ordered to rebuild on the other side or not at all. The house was not rebuilt, and this ended the school. While the party at work on the trace were encamped at the spring at the Cochran place, they cleared away much of the cane and underbrush around the spring. Later John Pruett, in looking for a desirable place to settle, fixed upon this on account of the good spring and surrounding partial clearing. He accordingly erected a dwelling house on one side of the trace, and a corncrib and stables on the other. As the party which had encamped here had partially opened up land on either side of the trace, he naturally did this. In addition to this, he fenced land on both sides. The government rangers, on one of their tours, told him to remove his crib and stables from Indian territory. He replied with great emphasis and some profanity that he would build wherever he pleased. The rangers at once set fire to his buildings and fences on the Indian side, and told him that if he rebuilt on that side they would the next time destroy the buildings on both sides. Robert Dunlap, from whom Dunlap Creek took its name, settled at this spring in 1810,

Capt. John Gordon was a man whose prominence has given him a place in Tennessee history, and he is certainly entitled to a prominent place in a history of the county in which he lived during his latter days, and with the early settlement and development of which he and his family had much to do. Captain Gordon was born in Virginia, and, tradition says, was a descendant of Pocahontas, as was also his wife, Dollie Cross, whom he married in Davidson County.

He came to Nashville between 1780 and 1790, and died in Hickman County prior to 1823, as Judge Haywood, writing at this time, said: " Captain Gordon was a brave and active officer, distinguished through life for a never-failing presence of mind, as well as for the purest integrity and independence of principle. He had much energy, both of mind and body, and was in all, or nearly all, the expeditions from Tennessee which were carried on against the Indians or other enemies of the country, and in all of them was conspicuous for these qualities. He now sleeps with the men of other times, but his repose is guarded by the affectionate recollections of all who knew him." One of his expeditions against the Indians, not already mentioned, started from Nashville on June 11, 1794. He followed a party of Indians, who had killed Mrs. Gear, nearly a hundred miles before he overtook them. Later in this year he was out with the Nickajack Expedition, which resulted in the destruction of the upper Cherokee towns. Before crossing the Tennessee River, Colonel Orr, who was the nominal commander of this expedition, called a council of war, in which were Colonel Mansker, John Rains, John Gordon, and other veteran Indian fighters. Captain Gordon was among the first to swim the river on this September morning before daylight, and he stood on the bank and counted the whites as they reached the bank and fell into line preparatory to making the attack. In this expedition were Joseph Brown and William and Gideon Pillow, ancestors of prominent Maury County families. Gordon's future commander, Andrew Jackson, served as a private in this expedition. In 1796 he was a justice of the peace in Davidson County, and was Nashville's first postmaster, serving from April 1, 1796, to October 1, 1797. Following this came his trading-post venture near what is now Gordon's Ferry, and his removal to Hickman County, which became his home. Here he evidently hoped to end in peace an eventful life, satisfying his love for adventure by an occasional trip to New Orleans on a flatboat. Before he came to Duck River he had made at least one trip to New Orleans. He had a loaded flatboat tied up at Nashville. He and one of his negroes, while attempting to fasten it more securely, allowed it to drift from its moorings and out into the current of the Cumberland River. They had provisions already on board, and, without attempting to again bring it to the shore, these two set out for New Orleans, a thousand miles away. They reached this point after a voyage of many days, and when, as was the custom, an offer was made to assist them in landing, Gordon replied: " Ned and I have brought this boat from Nashville, and I think we are able to land it." And they were.

Whatever may have been his dreams of peace, they were rudely interrupted in September, 1813, by the news of the horrible massacre at Fort Mimms, Alabama, of five hundred whites by Creek Indians. He was now advanced in age, and nearly a score of years had passed since he had last heard the vengeful crack of a Tennessee rifle followed by the death cry of a savage; yet the feelings of indignation with which he heard the horrible news rolled back the tide of the years, and the hero of 1794 became the hero of 1813. His ancestors in old Scotland never rallied around the bearer of the cross of fire with more alacrity than did " Old Captain Jack " Gordon answer the call to arms. He reported for duty and was made captain of a company of scouts, or spies, which rendered such service in the war which followed that the name of Gordon became inseparably linked with those of Jackson, Carroll, and Coffee. On November 16, 1813, after the battles of Tallushatchee and Talladega, the troops, worn out by fatigue and weakened by lack of food, demanded that General Jackson lead them back home. He was on the point of acceding to this demand and abandoning Fort Strother, when, thinking how much the desertion of the fort would encourage the Indians, he declared that he would remain at the post if only two men would bear him company. Captain Gordon was the first to volunteer, and, moved by his example, over a hundred agreed to remain. Later, when Jackson's command was reduced by desertion in the face of the enemy to about 800 men, Gordon's spy company was " faithful among the faithless found." At Enotachopco Creek, on December 24, 1813, when the Indians made a spirited and unexpected attack upon the rear guard, Captain Gordon, who had command of the advance guard, recrossed the creek and assisted in changing what bade fair to be a disastrous defeat into a complete victory. Referring to this affair, one historian calls him " the famous spy captain of Duck River, Gordon;" another refers to him as " Capt. John Gordon, an old pioneer hero." In August, 1814, after a treaty had been concluded with the Creeks, Gordon was called upon to perform one of the most hazardous duties of his whole career. Clayton, referring to this, says: " General Jackson, being anxious to make sure of the fruits of his important victories, now sought to make the Spanish Governor of Pensacola a party, as it were, to the treaty with the Indians, so as to hold him to a stricter responsibility for his future conduct. But to reach him it was necessary for the bearer of his messages to traverse a long stretch of tropical wilderness, unmarked by road or path, and rendered doubly difficult of penetration by reason of numerous swamps, lagoons, and rivers. The bearer of the dispatches was Capt. John Gordon, who, with a single companion, undertook the dangerous and seemingly desperate mission. At the end of the first day's journey the companion of Captain Gordon became so much appalled by the prospects ahead that the Captain drove him back and continued his mission alone. After many difficulties and dangers from hostile Creeks, he reached Pensacola. On his arrival he was surrounded by a large body of Indians, and it was only by the greatest presence of mind that he escaped instant death and reached the protection of the commandant. His mission being ended, he returned as he came, and reached General Jackson in safety." The information obtained by Gordon resulted in General Jackson's marching against Pensacola, attacking it, and bringing the Spaniards to terms. As to whether Gordon participated in the fights around New Orleans, we do not know, but later in the year 1815 we find him engaged in operating a cotton gin, which was located on Dunlap Creek between Duck River and Shady Grove. Eight years later Judge Haywood refers to him as one who is no more.

Captain Gordon's brother-in-law, Richard Cross, was a very wealthy man. On his land in what is now South Nashville was the first race course in the vicinity of Nashville. Here General Jackson ran some of his noted horses. Cross owned the valuable lands on the Natchez Trace adjoining the Gordon place. He dying without issue, these lands were inherited by the children of his sister, Mrs. Gordon. These children were Bolling, Powhattan, Fielding, Andrew, Richard, John, Mary, Dollie, and Louisa.

At Gordon's old ferry Duck River is now spanned by a good bridge, built by the counties of Maury and Hickman at a cost of $10,000. Fatty Bread Branch, which flows into Duck River here, is for a short distance near its mouth the line between Maury and Hickman Counties. The large, white house among the cedars on the hill near by was the residence of Maj. Bolling Gordon, who for years was, politically, Hickman County's most prominent citizen. The large number of surrounding buildings were the quarters of his numerous slaves. All of these buildings show plainly the marks left upon them by Time in his flight. The brown brick building with the severely straight walls which stands in the valley south of Bolling Gordon's old residence was the home of Capt. John Gordon. This much-dilapidated and out-of-date building was for years the most elegant home in Hickman County. Here lived the most aristocratic family of the county. The name of Gordon, once so prominent in the county, is now no longer to be found here, and it is doubtful if even a relative can be found in the county. The old home is almost in ruins, and where once was grandeur, gloom now is. And the waters of the near-by branch with the peculiar name seem to murmur:

> Men may come and men may go,
> But I go on forever.

Bolling Gordon married Mary Watkins, of Virginia. He was a member of the General Assembly of the State from 1828 to 1836, sometimes as Senator, sometimes as a member of the Lower House. He was a member of the Constitutional Convention of 1834, and also of the Constitutional Convention of 1870, being one of the few men of the State who enjoyed the distinction of being a member of two constitutional conventions. When the convention convened at Nashville on January 10, 1870, Bolling Gordon, on motion of A. O. P. Nicholson, was made temporary president of the convention. Major Gordon, on taking the chair, referred to the fact that he was the only one present who had been a member of the other convention, which had met " almost on this identical spot thirty-five years ago." He referred to some of those with whom he was then associated, naming the venerable Blount, the upright Walton, and the brilliant Francis B. Fogg. In closing, he said: " May I not invoke this convention, in which I see so many gray heads and so many distinguished men, to aid in making a constitutional government which shall answer all the ends designed? May I not invoke you to discharge all the duties of the occasion with credit to yourselves and with benefit to the State?" Later, when the president of the convention, John C. Brown, was absent, Major Gordon was, upon motion of John F. House, again called to the chair. During the convention he served with distinction as a member of the Committee on Elections. As chairman of the Committee on Common Schools, he left his impress upon that portion of the Constitution providing for Tennessee's present public school system. Major Gordon died about 1880.

On September 24, 1835, in the brown brick building above referred to as the home of John Gordon, Louisa Pocahontas Gordon was married to Felix K. Zollicoffer, who, while leading a Confederate brigade, was killed at the battle of Mill Springs, Ky., on September 19, 1862. Zollicoffer, who was a Whig, edited the old Nashville Banner, was Comptroller of Tennessee, and was at one time a member of Congress.

No braver man ever wore either the blue or the gray.

Powhattan Gordon married Caroline Coleman, of Maury County, who was a sister of William and Rufus Coleman. Rufus Coleman was the best fiddler to be found in Hickman County in the early days. He clerked for William Coleman and Powhattan Gordon, who, about 1830, had a store near where the late Joseph Bond lived. This store was on the Dr. Greenfield Smith place, and was situated on the south bank of Duck River near the old ferry landing. Dr. Smith, who was a cousin of Dr. Greenfield, of Greenfield's Bend, lived here in 1825. He afterwards lived on Lick Creek. He was one of the colony which had come from Maryland to Tennessee. The Colemans probably also came to Tennessee with this colony. They were, at least, related to some of its members, the Tylers. Near Gordon & Coleman's store Ben. Wilson, of Leatherwood, sold whisky; and just above, on the lands of George Church, were two race courses, one a half mile in length, the other a mile. This section bore the suggestive name of " Pluck-'em-in," and was the scene of many a revel in the twenties and thirties. In 1825 John Skipper had a stillhouse on Jackson's Branch. Richard Smith was probably the first to sell whisky in the village of Shady Grove, but this was long after the notorious " Pluck-'em-in " had gone out of existence. George Grimes had a saloon at Shady Grove in 1854. The laws were not then so stringent, and men, while under the influence of

whisky, seemed to have less of the brute in their
nature than has the average drunken man of the present day. Men did not then fill up on mean whisky
in order to prepare themselves to make murderous
assaults upon their fellow-men as they do in this day
of higher civilization.

During the existence of " Pluck-'em-in," one of its
frequenters was Robert White, a noted gambler. One
day there came to George Church's race course a
stranger riding an ugly, " slab-sided," bobtailed bay
horse, with mane roached, like a mule. The stranger
was shabbily dressed, and the questions he asked about
the horses and horse racing showed him to be entirely unfamiliar with the sport then in progress. He
drank some and was very anxious to buy cattle, of
which he was in search. He learned that there would
be in a few days a big horse race on Josiah Shipp's
track near Centerville. By going there he could see
cattle owners from all over the county, and, in addition to this, he was told that he could see a very lively
horse race. For this latter he did not care, but, although an additional twenty miles' ride would be
rather hard on his horse, he concluded to go on to Centerville in order to buy cattle, of which he was in great
need. He went to Centerville the night before the
day on which the races were to be run. The next
morning he was one of the large crowd at the track;
but by the demon, Drink, the quiet, inoffensive cattle
buyer had been transformed into a swaggering drunkard, who wanted to bet on the race money which his

appearance showed he could ill afford to lose. His condition was such that he could scarcely walk, and his faculties were so overclouded that he did not care which horse he backed. He just wanted to bet. He had seen other people bet at Church's track, and, so he said, he had as much money as anybody. His own old horse was hitched near by, and, mounting it, he, continuing his boasting, announced that it could beat anything on the ground. Remonstrances were in vain, and he, continuing to wave his money, soon found takers. He was, in race-course parlance, " an easy thing," and soon there was a mad rush for his money. Having come for the purpose of buying cattle, he had money to cover all money offered him, and, in addition to this, was soon betting money against watches, pistols, overcoats, etc. When the horses lined up for the start, some of the more observant noticed that the stranger seemed to have become strangely sober in a short time. When three-fourths of the track had been gone over and the stranger and his horse were still well up in the bunch, it was remembered that nobody had seen him take a drink. When the stranger's horse won with ease, beating Griner's horse, the pride of Hickman County, it gradually dawned upon those who had bet with the stranger that they had been victimized. The stranger was Shilo True, the trickiest trickster of them all, and the missionary work that he did that day produced lasting good. Many saw the error of their way and never bet again. Many who that day bet with the professional gambler, Shilo True, afterwards became the most prominent citizens of the county. Two of his converts were Emmons Church and his father, Abram Church, who, riding back to Shady Grove without their overcoats, agreed that they would gamble no more. For years, whenever people saw the appearance of fraud, a cheat, or a swindle, or when they wanted to halloo, " Enough! " they simply said, " Shilo! " and were understood.

On the old " Pluck-'em-in " grounds lived the late Joseph McRea Bond, a progressive and well-to-do farmer, who was born in Maury County on February 14, 1833. He came to the Eleventh District, near Ætna, in September, 1851, but soon afterwards removed to the Fourteenth District, where he was for many years a magistrate. He came to the Third District a few years ago, and until his death owned this valuable land along the Natchez Trace. It was here that McIntosh felled the first timber in the county preparatory to making a clearing. The first corn raised in the county, however, was on the place now owned by Thomas Field, in the Seventh District, where the cane was cut away and corn raised in 1806.

From 1813 to 1815 many troops passed over the Natchez Trace going to and returning from the South. Jackson's army in the Creek War, in the operations against Pensacola, and in the fights around New Orleans, was composed of Tennessee militia. His soldiers, who are entitled to the name solely on account of their fighting qualities, were unused to military service and seemed to be controlled by the idea that they could serve until they became tired, then quit. It was Jackson's ability to hold enough of these together to win every fight in which he engaged that showed he was a great general. During these two years squads of neighbors would form, go and attach themselves to some command in Jackson's army, serve until they became hungry and tired, and then return home. The prospects of an immediate fight would more nearly serve to keep them together than any army regulations. So the general statement to be found in local tradition that General Jackson marched his army over the " Notchy " Trace to New Orleans is misleading. At the time the British fleet bore down on New Orleans, Jackson was at Pensacola. Coffee was also there, and marched his men through to New Orleans. Carroll, who had the immediate command of the 2,500 Tennessee hunters who practically fought and won the final battle of New Orleans on January 8, 1815, carried his men to New Orleans by boats, starting at Nashville on November 19, 1814. In January, 1813, Coffee, with 650 cavalrymen, had gone over the trace to Natchez. However, the larger portion, if not all of the Tennessee portion, of Jackson's army returned from New Orleans by the way of Natchez, and over the Natchez Trace to Nashville. It is said that the soldiers from this section of the State were discharged on the Natchez Trace near where the Lewis monument now stands, the parting between General Carroll and his soldiers being an

affecting scene.   So, while Jackson's army did not in
a body go over the trace to New Orleans, it returned
this way, and during the Creek War many straggling
detachments went and returned this way. ' A story of
the return trip from New Orleans was told to the late
Daniel Smith by William Grimmitt, who lived on
Smith's land on Dunlap Creek, and is yet remembered
by many citizens of the Third District.   Grimmitt,
in connection with the story, pointed out a hollow tree
on a hillside near the trace.   Grimmitt, when he
enlisted, lived in Dickson County.   On the return
from New Orleans in the spring of 1815, a former
neighbor of his became seriously sick before they came
to the Tennessee River, and he was detailed to drop
out of ranks and care for his sick friend.   Owing to
the sick man's condition, they traveled very slowly.
Other Dickson County soldiers, reaching home, told
Grimmitt's father that his son was in company with
the sick man somewhere on the Natchez Trace this
side of the Tennessee River.   The father proceeded
to find the trace and follow it in search of his son.
When Grimmitt and his sick companion were near the
tree pointed out, a rain came up, and his companion
sought shelter in this hollow tree and remained until
the rain ceased.   They then continued on their journey, but, after crossing Duck River, the sick soldier
became much worse, and, lying down by the side
of the trace, soon expired.   Securing assistance, the
body was carried to the Dr. Long place, now known
as the Rufe Puckett place.   Jack Charter, of Leather-

wood, made the coffin. Charter was the father of
Cave Charter, a well-informed citizen of the Thirteenth District. The dead soldier was buried on the
Long place, and soon after friends or relatives came
from Dickson County and placed a rock wall around
his grave. On the day of the burial Grimmitt's father arrived with horses, and they returned together
to Dickson County. This is the story of the rock-
walled grave of the unknown soldier on the Rufe
Puckett place. Grimmitt, while he lived in Hickman
County, drew a pension as a soldier of the War of
1812, and a part of his pension money was used to
pay his burial expenses. He was buried in the
old Presbyterian churchyard on Cathey's Creek in
Maury County. Soon, perhaps, his grave, too, will
be marked "Unknown," as no stone with epitaph
marks the last resting place of this old soldier of the
War of 1812.

> He has fought his last fight,
> He sleeps his last sleep;
> No sound can awake him
>   To glory again.

From the late Daniel Smith much information was
obtained concerning the history of the Third District.
His father, George Smith, was born in Georgia in
1779, and came to Nashville in 1797. From Nashville he went to Dickson County. He came to Hickman County in 1825 and settled on the lands owned
by the late Joseph Bond, locating within two hundred

yards of Gordon's Ferry. Here he and several members of his family are buried. Near McConnico's Church, on South Harpeth, he married Nellie Baker, daughter of Absalom Baker. She was born in Virginia in 1794. Their children were: Daniel, James, Benjamin, George, Lindsey, Collins, Catherine, Mary, Rebecca, and Emeline.

Daniel Dansby Smith was born on Jones' Creek, in Dickson County, on May 13, 1813. He died on Dunlap Creek in 1898. The names of his children are: R. J., J. H., Erastus, Daniel L., George E., Francis, and Ellen. R. J. Smith was killed during the Civil War by Federals near Charlotte. After the Thirteenth District was detached from this, about 1848, Daniel Smith was elected constable of the Third District. The election was held at Shady Grove, which then became the polling place, and there was a general fight on the day of the election. Later he was one of this district's magistrates for six years, and in 1862 was elected sheriff, receiving every vote cast in this district, save one.

Prior to the adoption of the Constitution of 1834 justices of the peace were elected by the Legislature, the basis being not more than two for each militia company in the county, with the exception of the one which embraced the county town; for this one, not more than three. In 1834 civil districts were first established, they becoming the basis of representation as they are now. After this the justices of the peace were elected by the people. Previous to this the people sometimes made their selections, communicating their wishes to their Representative. This was done here in 1827, when Samuel A. Baker and Granville M. Johnson were selected as the choice of this section. The selection was made by the friends of the several candidates lining up by the side of their choice. The men in the several lines were then counted and the result declared by tellers. For some time after 1834 the larger portion, if not all, of the present Third, Thirteenth, and Fifteenth Districts were in one civil district. The voting place was at the place where William McEwen now lives, William Weems living there then. Johnson lived on Leatherwood Creek. Baker was the father of John Baker, the first sheriff of the county after the Civil War. He was a magistrate from 1827 to the time of his death in 1862. He was succeeded by James Nelson Bingham, who served eighteen years. Bingham was born on March 25, 1808, in North Carolina, and died on January 16, 1876. He married Rebecca Smith, a sister of Daniel Smith. She was born in Dickson County on December 13, 1811, and died on·April 15, 1885. James N. Bingham was a son of Robert Bingham, and came to Hickman County in 1830. The first constable of the district was John H. Davis, who was not related to the surveyor, John Davis. He lived at the George Mayberry place, north of Gordon's Ferry. He could neither read nor write, and the magistrates did his writing for him. He was, however, a faithful officer. Josiah S. Wheat, son of Wyley Wheat, was born on

March 7, 1840.   He was constable of this district
for twelve years, and was deputy sheriff under Sheriff
John V. Stephenson.   Phil. Hoover, of this district,
was at one time a deputy sheriff, and William J. Mc-
Ewen made one of the most popular and efficient
sheriffs the county ever had.

Shady Grove, situated on Dunlap Creek one mile
from Duck River, was given its name by Henry
(Harry) Nichols, who was the first merchant here.
The name is still an appropriate one.   Shady Grove
is noted for its churches and schools.   The Christian
Church has a membership of one hundred and twenty-
five, and the Methodist Church has a membership of
about fifty.   In the upper story of the Methodist
Church is the lodge-room of Trinity Lodge, No. 501,
F. and A. M.   This lodge was organized in 1871, and
was for years the only working lodge in the county.
John R. Bates was its first Worshipful Master.   In
1897 some of the officers were: George McGahee, W.
M.; J. R. Bates, S. W.; G. W. Adkisson, J. W.; P.
P. Anderson, Treasurer; D. W. Flowers, S. D.

From 1800 to 1805 was the time of the " Great
Revival," an era of great religious excitement throughout Southern Kentucky and Northern Tennessee.   It
was during this time that " the jerks " prevailed and
camp meetings originated.   Barton Warren Stone
was pastor of a Presbyterian Church in Bourbon
County, Ky., and, hearing of " the jerks " or " epi-
demic epilepsy " which prevailed at the camp meetings which were now becoming numerous, he attended

one. This hitherto staid Presbyterian was so impressed with what he saw that he wrote a book describing it. A writer, referring to this, says: " Elder Stone has been described as a man of respectable bearing, of spotless character and childlike simplicity, and easily attracted to the strange and marvelous. His judgment was somewhat under the dominion of his imagination." A further extract from the same author is given without comment: "About the same time (1804) other sects sprang up, known by the respective names of ' Stoneites,' or ' New Lights; ' ' Marshallites,' ' Schismatics,' etc. By these ' heresies ' the Synod of Kentucky lost eight members. The ' Stoneites,' or ' New Lights,' were a body formed mainly through the efforts of Elder Stone after he had decided to abandon Presbyterianism altogether. This new body was called by its adherents the ' Christian Church,' while by outsiders it was called by the name ' New Lights.' They held many of the views which afterwards characterized the Campbell reformation, especially the famous dogma of ' baptism for the remission of sins,' and Elder Stone intimates in his book pretty plainly that in adopting it the ' Disciples of Christ ' or ' Campbellites,' as the followers of Alexander Campbell were originally called, had stolen his thunder. When the Campbell reformation reached Kentucky, Elders Stone and Purviance united with the reformers, and thus the Southern branch of the old ' Christian Church ' disappeared. Since then the name ' Disciples,' or ' Campbellites,' has been exchanged for the old name, the ' Christian Church.' " Without discussing the appropriateness or inappropriateness of any of these names, the simple statement is here made that this church has for nearly eighty years been one of the leading churches in this section of the county, and from its starting point here has spread to nearly every other neighborhood in the county. Here near Shady Grove, at what is known as " The Stand," this church was first established in Hickman County about 1820, and here was held their last camp meeting in 1834. In addition to its being the first in the county, it was among the first in the State. Barton W. Stone preached here during the twenties, and the celebrated Tolbert Fanning preached here at a later date. Nathaniel Kellum, William Nicks, and John Hooten, of this church, preached here as early as 1825. John Hooten was a son of Elijah Hooten, who, as a soldier in the American army, was present at the surrender of Cornwallis at Yorktown. He came from Virginia to Tennessee about 1811. He was one of ten children, and was the father of eleven. He married Mary Reeves. His son, William R. Hooten, was also a preacher, having been ordained in this district in 1829. John Hooten had but one eye, and could not read or write. However, he is said to have been a good preacher, and his memory was so good that he gave out his songs correctly, quoted his texts correctly, and told where they could be found. He died in Marshall County at the age of seventy-five. William

Nicks was the father of seventeen children, one of whom is the venerable Elder John Nicks, the well-known preacher, who now lives in the First District. John Nicks was born in the Third District on April 2, 1829.   Another Nicks who preached at "The Stand," at a later date, however, was Absalom Doak Nicks, Jr., son of Absalom Doak Nicks, Sr.   Absalom Nicks, Sr., was a brother of William Nicks, and was born in North Carolina on March 6, 1794, and died in Arkansas in 1848.   He married Hester Perry, who was born in South Carolina on October 8, 1788, and died at Williamsport, Maury County, in July, 1858.   Absalom Nicks, Jr., was born on Mill Creek, in the Fifth District, on July 19, 1826.   In 1845 he married Margaret Blocker, who was born near Williamsport on July 10, 1829.   His chances for obtaining an education were limited, but by home study he stored his active and retentive mind with much valuable information.   He was a close student of the Bible, and it is said that while at work in his blacksmith shop he had this first of all books so placed that he could read while at work.   He moved to Dickson County, and there made a record of which any man might feel proud.   At the close of the Civil War, when it became necessary to reorganize the State government, Governor Brownlow, in appointing Representatives from the disloyal counties, appointed Nicks, a conservative Union man, to represent Dickson County.   He accepted the appointment, which came without solicitation; but when he entered into the discharge of his duties, he voted as he pleased and according to his ideas of justice and honesty. This did not meet with the approval of his partisan associates, and they preferred charges of disloyalty against him and declared his seat vacant. The elective franchise having been restored to the people of Dickson County, they elected him to fill the vacancy. He so satisfied his people that he was tendered a reëlection. This he declined. He now lives in the Fourth District of Hickman County.

The first Methodist to preach at " The Stand " was Arthur Sherrod, who preached here as early as 1825. He was from Leiper's Creek, and had been a captain of militia before he commenced to preach. While the Presbyterian Church, weakened by the secession of the followers of Elder Stone and others, was finally rent asunder by the effects of the " Great Revival," the Methodist Church gained greatly by this religious awakening. In Tennessee, in 1796, there were 799 white Methodists and 77 colored; in 1803 there were 3,560 whites and 248 colored. Phelan tells the story of the advent of Methodism into Hickman County when he says: " Other denominations have followed in the wake of civilization; the Methodist circuit riders led it." The one church in Tennessee which neither gained nor lost by the " Great Revival " was the Baptist Church. Its members kept the even tenor of their way, looking upon their neighbors who had " the jerks " with feelings in which were blended pity and contempt. Occasionally at a camp meeting a

Baptist spectator would feel an attack of " the jerks " coming on, but by the exercise of will power he generally warded it off. As early as 1809 John Gill lived at the place where the late Daniel Smith last lived. The house in which Gill lived is still used as a residence. Here at an early date preached George Nixon, grandfather of the late Chancellor George H. Nixon. He was a Methodist, and Mrs. Gill was a member of this church. They having no church house at that time, services were held at the homes of the members. Mrs. Gill was an aunt of Richard A. Smith, of the Thirteenth District. A church was built on Dunlap Creek just below the Samuel Cochran place, but this was destroyed by a hurricane in 1830. In 1839 Wyley Ledbetter, father of Rev. Henry S. Ledbetter, of the Sixth District, preached at the home of Nehemiah Nichols. About the same time the funeral of Mrs. Weems was preached at the William McEwen place by Rev. —— Erwin. The Mormons have no organized church in the county, but in this district there are about thirty members of this church. When an elder preaches here, it is at the residence of some member. As to the doctrines of this church or their practices in Utah, we know nothing, but, as citizens of Hickman County, the Mormons of the Third District are hospitable and industrious.

At Shady Grove is located the finest, best, and most conveniently arranged school building in the county. It has many modern conveniences, and was erected at a cost of $2,000. Here in recent years have taught

Professors Salmon, Parrish, Carraway, and Marshall. About 1887 Elder R. W. Norwood, of the Christian Church, taught school at Shady Grove. Elsewhere an account is given of the closing of George Peery's pioneer school by government rangers. The first permanent schoolhouse in this section was built out on the ridge toward Buck Branch about 1820. It was an imposing structure for those days. It was built on government land, and was built of hewn logs. The seats were made of split logs, made smoother by a broadax. The legs were long wooden pegs driven into auger holes in the half logs. A writing desk was made by boring holes in the wall and driving long wooden pegs into these holes. On the pegs was placed a plank or board. Writing was done with goose-quill pens made with a penknife by the teacher or some of his " large scholars." Gold pens and steel pens were not then in existence. A good goose-quill pen would last well when proper care was taken of it, and did as well as a steel pen or a gold pen of the present day. Some of those who taught here were Nicholas P. Simms, John C. Kelley, James Winns, Dr. Joseph Shields, —— Branch, William Dickey, Samuel Baker, William Willey, and William Leiper. Simms was a Methodist preacher, and came here from Williamsport. Shields was an Irishman, and was educated at Edinburgh College. He was a fine mathematician and rigid disciplinarian. In punishing his pupils he used papaw bark, which he kept at the schoolhouse for the additional purpose of bottoming chairs at recess. He taught school at Columbia before coming here in 1831. Willey was the adopted son of John Willey, who helped to cut out the Natchez Trace, and who lived at the big spring on Dunlap Creek where Cochran now lives. John Willey was the father-in-law of Craig Anderson. William Leiper was a brother of the late Green D. Leiper, of the Tenth District, and married Amanda Nicks.

Beyond this schoolhouse from Shady Grove lived Archibald Ray, the father of Hal, "Hy," and "Dick" Ray. It was Ray who remarked, after the seventh baptism of Capt. "Lam" Kelly: "Next time we baptize 'Lam' we'll use warm tar, so that it will stick or make him stick." Hal Ray was killed by a negro at the Jewell place. In 1858, about three-fourths of a mile from Shady Grove on Buck Branch, William Brinkle stabbed and killed Elijah Deaton at the home of Deaton's daughter, who was a widow. Brinkle was never arrested. He, at the breaking out of the Civil War, enlisted in the Confederate Army, and after the close of the war he did not return to the county. In 1865 or 1866, at Henry G. Nichols' store in Shady Grove, Griff. Nichols stabbed and killed Artin Hassell. In 1897 Winfred Cotton, an old and respected citizen of Shady Grove, committed suicide.

Dr. Greenfield Smith was the pioneer physician of this section. Here at an early date was Dr. McPhail, who was a brother-in-law of John W. Whitfield, a man long prominent in the military and political affairs of the county. From 1830 to 1840, and for many years afterwards, Dr. Samuel B. Moore, of Centerville, was the family physician of many citizens of this district. Dr. John Reed was located here in 1847. Dr. D. B. Cliffe, of Franklin, was at one time a physician here. In 1897 the physicians of Shady Grove were Dr. Q. A. Dean and Dr. Charles Walters. Dr. Quintin Abel Dean was born in Centerville on March 23, 1847. He is a son of Ransom Dean, who came from Kentucky to what is now the Eleventh District prior to 1820, and for years lived with Squire Kimmins, of Beaverdam. In 1846 Ransom Dean went to Mexico as color bearer of Capt. John W. Whitfield's company.

In 1825 William Savage and Gilbert Nichols occupied lands on Dunlap Creek. In order to perfect their titles they were later forced to pay twelve and a half cents per acre for their land. The locations were made by a friend of Nichols, James Dobbins, a surveyor and land speculator. Elijah Emmons had located here, but, being unable to pay the required number of cents per acre, Dobbins paid it and took the land. Dobbins was the locator of other lands on Dunlap Creek, but the most valuable were the lands around Shady Grove, which he located for John Pruett, of Virginia. The land upon which Shady Grove now stands, and some lying on the present road from the village to the bridge at the site of Gordon's Ferry, was located for Johnson and James Miller. Gilbert Nichols was born in Maryland in 1768, and married Ellen Charter, of Pennsylvania. He came to Tennessee in 1819, and in 1825 settled at the place where his son, Christopher Nichols, now lives. This house, which is still a good one, was built in 1823 by Nimrod McIntosh, who was the champion rail splitter of that section. Christopher Nichols was born in Bedford County, Va., on September 10, 1812, and came with his father to this district. He married Prudence Manerva Nicks, one of the seventeen children of William Nicks. She was born on Mill Creek on December 1, 1816, and is the mother of nine children. James Miller, who located here about 1810, was the father of Simpson, Francis, and James Miller. The latter two are citizens of Shady Grove, and have had much to do with the building of this thriving little village.

On a portion of the original Miller tract of land now lives John Minor Anderson, who was born on March 17, 1848. He has been county surveyor since 1883, previous to which he taught school. He is a son of " Big Dick " Anderson. " Kettle Dick " Anderson, brother of Robert Anderson, who was the first settler of Anderson's Bend, was his maternal grandfather. David Anderson, who lived in Bedford County, was a brother of Robert and " Kettle Dick " Anderson, and was the father of " Big Dick " Anderson. The children of " Kettle Dick " Anderson, who lived in Maury County in the Kettle Bend of Duck River, were: John, who married Mary, daughter of John Gill, of Dunlap Creek; David, Henry; Craig, who married a daughter of John Willey; and Mary, or Polly, who married John Y. Smith, father of Richard A. Smith. After Smith's death she married her cousin, " Big Dick " Anderson, the father of John M. and David Henry Anderson. David H. Anderson was born on June 5, 1841. He has in his possession a powder gourd raised in North Carolina in 1773. It will hold about a pound of powder. It was brought to Tennessee by " Kettle Dick " Anderson, and was inherited by his nephew and son-in-law, " Big Dick " Anderson, at whose death it became the property of his son, David H. Anderson. The pioneer brothers, Richard and Robert, belonged to different political parties. Richard (" Kettle Dick ") was a Whig, and Robert was a Democrat.

In 1836 Simpson Miller had a wood shop where Shady Grove now is. He had a turning lathe, and made for the people of the surrounding country many bedsteads, bureaus, sugar chests, cupboards, sideboards, spinning wheels, reels, etc. Henry G. Nichols, the first merchant, commenced to sell goods here about 1844. Nichols was a deputy under Sheriff W. H. Carothers. In 1849 a man named Pruett had a shoe shop here. A few years ago T. B. Walker, now of Whitfield, and J. B. Walker, now cashier of the Centerville Bank, were merchants here. In 1897 the merchants here were J. D. Evans and J. H. Houser. D. H. Anderson had here at the same time a shoe, saddle, and harness shop; John Leek, a saddle and harness shop; and John Thornton and D. Chamberlain, blacksmith shops.

As early as 1815 Joel Pugh had located at the Grimes place, near Shady Grove. He was born in Kentucky, and came to Mill Creek in 1810. Here George Pugh was born on May 12, 1812. Other children were Sally (born on September 15, 1815), who married Henry Cummins; Jane (born on March 30, 1818), who married Joseph Webb, of the Seventh District; John W. (born on April 11, 1820); and Mary Melissa (born on May 12, 1825), who married M. H. Puckett, who was at one time County Court Clerk of this county. Henry Cummins was at one time a deputy sheriff, and was the father of Samuel and John Cummins, two of the county's substantial citizens. Samuel Cummins is now one of the magistrates of the Third District, and says what he thinks, and thinks what he says. The other magistrate is James Grimes, who is also a descendant of one of the pioneers of the Third District. Joel Pugh was a millwright and wood-workman, and cleared about the first land west of Shady Grove. Some of his early neighbors were: John Grimes, Samuel Montgomery; George Gannt, a lawyer; and George Harvill, an uncle of the late Elder Y. J. Harvill. Evans Shelby lived at the B. B. Bates place, near Buck Branch.

On the Natchez Trace, between Pruett's Spring and Duck River, Samuel Alderson Baker located in 1816. He was born in Virginia on June 16, 1792. His wife was Frances Walker, who was also born in Virginia. He located where his son, Samuel Giles Baker, now lives. Samuel G. Baker was born here on June 25,

1833.   He is the owner of his father's lands, through
which the Natchez Trace runs.   Samuel A. Baker
located 160 acres here, and afterwards bought 240
acres more.   The sons of Samuel Alderson Baker
were: John (born in 1823), who was sheriff of
Hickman County immediately after the Civil War;
Thomas, William, Samuel G., and James P.   Alice,
the wife of George Church, was his daughter.

CHAPTER VII.

THE FOURTH DISTRICT.

T HE Fourth District is bounded on the north by Dickson County; on the east, by Williamson and Maury Counties; south, by the Thirteenth District; and west, by the Second and Fifth Districts. It includes the valley of Lick Creek, from the mouth of Hassell's Creek up to the lines of Dickson and Williamson Counties, which lie beyond the head waters of the northwestern tributaries of this creek. The line of the Fourth District, however, does not cross Lick Creek until it reaches the mouth of Dog Creek, where it crosses and embraces in the Fourth District all of this creek, save a small tributary, Sugar Creek, which lies in the Thirteenth District.

Zebulon Hassell the First, from whom the creek took its name, settled at the Lambert place, on Hassell's Creek, a short time after the Indian treaties of 1805 and 1806. The next tributary of Lick Creek above Hassell's Creek is Morrison's Branch, named for a family which lived on it at an early day. Jesse Peeler, who died a few years ago in the Eleventh District, lived on this branch in 1836. Frank Killough lived here in 1835. A fork of Morrison's Branch is Jones' Branch, upon which John Groves now has a mill and dry goods store. It received its name from Alston Jones, father of O. A. Jones, who settled upon it about 1825. At its mouth Harvey Giles lived in 1835. Ned Carver, a noted gunsmith and blacksmith, had a mill at the Tatom place in 1835. Ferdinand B. Russell owned the Little Rock Mills, now owned by Groves, in 1858.

Above Morrison's Branch is Gin Branch, which received its name from the fact that Frank Worley had a gin here in 1825. Col. Alfred Darden lived here in 1836, and from this place he went, ten years later, to Mexico as a member of Whitfield's company. J. H. Nichols, of the Fourth District, was also in the Mexican War. On this branch, in 1846, lived William Jefferson Bond, who was born at Hillsboro, Williamson County, on July 26, 1826. He was a son of William Bond, of Virginia. He married Clara Mayberry, a daughter of Gabriel Mayberry, who was born in June, 1828. William J. Bond was the father of John T. Bond, who was born on January 9, 1851, and of Albert J. Bond, who was born on January 29, 1863. In 1867 a negro woman, Nancy Mayberry, was shot and killed by unknown parties in Gin Hollow. The shot was fired through a window one night. The gin has long since disappeared, and only the name recalls the fact that here the farmers of the upper portion of Lick Creek brought their cotton to have it ginned, preparatory to passing it into female hands to be, by the cards, the spinning wheel, the reel, and the loom, transformed into clothing for the family.

Just below the mouth of Gin Hollow (or Branch),

near a good spout spring, lives Jerome Reeves, one of
Hickman County's best citizens. He is a son of John
Reeves, who was born in Kentucky on August 13,
1800. John Reeves was a son of James Reeves, who
was born in Greene County, Tenn., in 1778, and who
married Peggy Ayres, of Kentucky. John Reeves
came with his father to Maury County in 1805. He
came to the Fourth District in 1836 and settled on
the John Overbey place, which he bought from Robert
Oakley, who had bought it from Henry Potts, who
had located here about 1815. Hugh Hill then owned
the place where Jerome Reeves now lives. Hill afterwards sold it to James Oliver, father of Captain Oliver, C. S. A. Sons of John Reeves were S. Jerome
Reeves (born on September 28, 1829), and Leonard
Reeves (born in 1839). His daughter, Cleander,
married William Dean, of Dog (or Cedar) Creek.
Ophelia Reeves married Joseph Holmes, who, while
a soldier in the Confederate Army, was killed at Ma-
rietta, Ga. Garrett Turman, Jr., lived at the W. T.
Warff place in 1836, and about the same date James
Anglin lived at the Blount Turman place. At what
is now known as Martin's shop, Phelps Martin lived
in the long ago, and his near-by neighbor was Benjamin Vaughan. Turman Parker lived on this, the Barren Fork, about 1835. George W. Hicks, who lives
at the mouth of the Barren Fork of Lick Creek, was
born on April 22, 1835, on Lick Creek. He is a son
of William M. Hicks, who was born in Virginia on
January 9, 1804, and who married Margaret, the

daughter of Josiah Davidson, who was a North Carolina soldier in the Revolutionary War. Margaret Davidson was born in Rutherford County, Tenn. The Hicks family came to Lick Creek in 1815. Jerre Ingram laid a soldier's warrant at the Hicks place in 1815. The land upon which W. T. Warff lives was granted to Butler, the grant embracing 640 acres. An adjoining grant of the same number of acres was to Grant. The Grant lands are on the Trace Fork, and have since been known as the Tidwell or Dean lands, and lie adjoining to the Ingram lands. The Butler lands, which were also for military service in the Revolutionary War, were located about 1810. The Tidwell above referred to was Eli Tidwell, father of the late Levi J. Tidwell, who was for many years one of the Fourth District's magistrates. Levi J. Tidwell was a man of determination, firm in his views upon all questions, whether personal, political, or religious. He was a Missionary Baptist, having joined that church at Union Hill, Henderson County, Tenn. In politics he was an unflinching Republican, and was at one time a candidate for Representative. He was beaten only eighty-four votes by Col. Vernon F. Bibb, who was considered the strongest Democrat in the county. Tidwell was born on March 14, 1825. He lived in what is called " The Barrens," above the head waters of Lick Creek, on the Tannehill entry, which was made in 1826. This entry embraced several thousand acres. A near-by entry was one made by John Stone in 1820. Alfred Tidwell, a son of

Levi J. Tidwell, was a deputy under Sheriff John V. Stephenson, and another son, Johnson Tidwell, is at present one of the magistrates of the Fourth District. The Tidwells came from North Carolina in 1843. There is a large family of them in the flat country along the county line, and they have built up a thrifty settlement, known as the "Tidwell Settlement."

At the Hicks place Lick Creek forks. The Barren Fork, already referred to, rises near Martin's Shop. The other fork, known as the Trace Fork, rises in Williamson County and runs about twelve miles before entering the Fourth District of Hickman County.

The first place on Lick Creek in Hickman County was settled by John Mayberry, who came from Virginia, near the Peaks of Otter. He was here as a hunter as early as 1800, and made a permanent settlement here about 1806, he being the first settler on Lick Creek in Hickman County. He was a farmer and blacksmith, and has hundreds of descendants throughout Hickman, Maury, and Williamson Counties. He was the father of a large family, all of whom were older than the present century. His sons were Mike, Job, John, George, and Gabriel. He was the grandfather of Walker and Sim Mayberry. A daughter of John Mayberry married a Kinzer; another married Alston Jones, and was the mother of O. A. Jones; and another married Pleasant Russell, and was the mother of Ferdinand B. and Washington B. Russell. Gabriel Mayberry, after the death of his father, lived at the old Mayberry place, where John T. Morton now lives. It is said that when an old man he kept as one of his most valued treasures a pair of trousers which his mother had made. These he kept folded carefully and laid away in an old-fashioned chest. Occasionally he would take them out, gaze on them reverently, and say: " Mother made these for me, and I want to be buried in them." When he died, friends granted his wish.

Farther down the creek, on the lands entered by Grant, Stockard settled at an early date. Hardin, a soldier of the Revolution, lived here a few years later. This is the place at which Tidwell and Dean later lived.

In 1807 Robert E. C. Dougherty settled on the creek below the Stockard place. He was a school-teacher and was one of the early magistrates of the county. In 1819 he resigned his seat in the State Legislature and removed to West Tennessee. At the place where Dougherty settled there now lives Garret Turman Overbey, who knows much of the history of the Fourth District.

Daniel Overbey, early in the present century, emigrated from North Carolina to Sumner County, Tenn., and in the autumn of 1814 he came to Hickman County, settling in the following spring at the head of one branch of the Barren Fork of Lick Creek. His wife was Emily Tyler, who was related to President John Tyler. Overbey and his wife both died in 1869. Daniel Overbey, Jr., a son of Daniel Overbey, Sr., on March 15, 1832, married Sarah Parker, and they became the parents of eight children. He died on February 2, 1865, his wife living until December 15, 1890. Sarah Parker was a daughter of Elisha and Rebecca Parker. Rebecca Parker was a daughter of Garret Turman, Sr., who was a soldier in the Revolutionary War, and who was at one time held a prisoner by the Indians for six months. This was during the Revolutionary War, when North Carolina and Georgia were overrun by the Tories and the frontiers devastated by the Indians. Garret Turman Overbey, a son of Daniel Overbey, Jr., was born on October 13, 1834, and, on December 23, 1858, married Emily J. Moss, who was born on September 11, 1837. He is the father of six children—John T., W. W., America L., James D., T. F., and Annie C. The wife of G. T. Overbey is a descendant of the Foote family, of Virginia, a member of which was at one time Governor of Mississippi.

No portion of Hickman County is more closely connected with the early history of Middle Tennessee than is the Lick Creek country. "Lick Creek of Duck River" was one of the first streams of Middle Tennessee to receive a name. It derives its name from the black sulphur spring on the south side of the creek, on the old Russell (and later Beale) place, now owned by John T. Overbey. Here buffaloes, deer, and other wild animals congregated in large numbers. Such places as this were called, in the pioneer days, "licks." The buffaloes coming from across Duck River to this lick crossed at the mouth of Leather-

wood Creek, and the path they made was used by the
Chickasaws when they came into the Cumberland settlements. According to the late Maj. Bolling Gordon, the route of the Chickasaw Trace, the path by
which the whites and Indians traveled to and from
the Chickasaw country, was as follows: " Up Trace
Creek in Lawrence County, down Swan Creek, and
across Blue Buck somewhere near the residence of
Jo. M. Bond; then over to the spring on Robertson's
Creek, where Mark Robertson was killed by Indians;
then over to Lick Creek, near Mrs. Beale's residence;
thence to Nashville by way of Johnson's Lick, on
Richland Creek near Charles Bosley's; then on to
French Lick, now Nashville." The Chickasaw Trace
ran for several miles up the Trace Fork of Lick Creek.
When James Robertson, in 1780, made the first expedition from the Bluffs against the Indians, he came
upon them near this lick on Lick Creek. When the
Coldwater Expedition went out from Nashville in
1787 to avenge the death of Mark Robertson, it went
west from Nashville to the mouth of Turnbull Creek,
and up that creek to its head. They then went to the
head of Lick Creek, and traveled several miles along
the ridge, leaving the creek to their right. They then,
turning into the creek valley, came down Trace Fork
to the lick on the John T. Overbey place, described
as " an old lick as large as a cornfield." They then
crossed Dog Creek, went up the Gee Hill, over to
Leatherwood Creek, and down this creek to its mouth,
where they crossed Duck River. Then leaving the

Chickasaw Trace, which ran up Robertson's Creek, to the right, they went to the head of Swan Creek. From this point they went the route described in preceding pages.

John Dean, father of William, Robert, Ephraim, and Mark Dean, came to Hickman County on March 24, 1844, and located at the T. J. Oakley place. Soon after locating here he commenced the manufacture of plug tobacco, the first industry of the kind ever operated in the county. The factory was near the Oakley place. The reputation of the "Dean Tobacco" as a high-grade tobacco is yet remembered by many, and this reputation was sustained by William Dean, who in 1857 erected a factory at the mouth of Dog (or Cedar) Creek. John Dean was born in East Tennessee on August 7, 1803, and in 1825 married Eliza Andrews, of Williamson County. Dean died at the T. J. Oakley place, and is there buried. His father was William Dean, who married Alice Woodward, of East Tennessee, from which place Dean came, in 1811, to Maury County. William Dean died in 1819 on his return from Missouri, where he had been to locate land. Robert A. Dean, son of John Dean, was thrown from a mule and killed near Little Lot on February 25, 1880.

In 1836 Josiah Davidson lived at the John W. Mayberry place. Here, during and after the Civil War, lived Joseph Bizwell, a hospitable man and a Christian gentleman. Before the war he was tax collector for Hickman County, and was at one time deputy sheriff.

At the John T. Overbey place, in 1835, lived the widow of Pleasant Russell, the father of F. B. and W. B. Russell. This place is frequently called the Beale place, as it was once owned by Capt. Charles Wesley Beale, who commanded a company in the Twenty-fourth Tennessee Infantry, and who died at Bowling Green, Ky., in the latter part of 1861. In 1836 Vincent Irwin lived where H. G. Primm now lives, and later sold the lands to F. B. Russell.

In 1830 John T. Primm, who was born in Maryland on September 22, 1790, located at the place so well known as the Primm place. Primm married Cecilia C. Gannt, also of Maryland, who was born on May 6, 1803. Other daughters of Mrs. Elizabeth Gannt married Alten Massey, Captain Clagett, and Rev. George Hicks. In 1834 Hicks went to Mississippi, where he died. Primm was a school-teacher, and taught here, as did also his brother-in-law, Gannt. He was also a merchant, and was one of the first to sell goods on the creek. This place, noted as one of the earliest settled in this vicinity, was first owned by William Lytle, who laid a soldier's warrant here in 1811. The Primms, Smoots, Smiths, Gannts, Clagetts, Tylers, and Berrys came here from Maryland at an early date and formed a Maryland colony near the lines of the Second, Fourth, and Thirteenth Districts, where they had schools of their own. They had two doctors, Smith and Smoot; two teachers, Gannt and Primm; and one merchant, Primm. They brought no preacher with them, but the eldest son of John T. Primm—Oliver Hazard Perry Primm, who was born on October 24, 1819—became a preacher. Another son is Hinson Groves Primm, who was born in August, 1839. There were nine other children. Hinson G. Primm, who married Emma V. Rooker, is also the father of eleven children. Another son, Clagett Primm, now lives on Hassell's Creek.

In 1825 a man named Cox lived on Dog (or Cedar) Creek, on a portion of the lands now owned by William Dean. He had no children, and he willed the lands to Stephen (or Jesse) Harper, a boy whom he had reared. At times Cox would become violently insane, and his neighbors would be forced to confine him. After he would recover he would take revenge upon those who had confined him by refusing to allow their children to have any apples out of his fine orchard. The other children of the neighborhood would be given access to the orchard. Finding that his fine flock of sheep was decreasing in numbers, he commenced to keep a close watch for wolves, which infested the hills near by. One day a large " dog wolf " pursued his sheep to within a few steps of his house. Snatching his rifle from the rack—two forked sticks nailed to the wall—he killed the wolf. The report of the killing of this pest spread throughout the neighborhood, and from the killing of the " dog wolf " the creek took its name—Dog Creek. Ac-

cording to William Dean, Edward Mahon, of Maury
County, bought land on the creek from Malugin and
erected a mill on it.   Mahon became tired of telling
his old neighbors in aristocratic Maury County that he
lived on Dog Creek; so, when Colonel Bibb was in
the Senate, Mahon had him to introduce a bill changing the name to " Cedar Creek."   This bill passed
both houses, was approved by the Governor, and became a law " from and after its passage, the public
welfare requiring it."

Primm's Springs are at the head of this creek.
These springs were almost unnoticed until 1831, when
Alten Massey, a brother-in-law of John T. Primm,
entered the land surrounding them.   He had married
a Miss Gannt, and, not having any children, he willed
the springs property to the children of Primm.   The
springs in 1836 were fitted up for visitors, and since
that time this has been a popular resort.   It is said
that Matilda, the wife of J. W. Stephenson, and an
aunt of William Dean, gained a pound a day while
staying here in 1837.   Primm's Springs are now
principally the property of Maury County parties.
Hickman Countians who have interests here are: O.
A. Jones, John A. Jones, and R. A. Smith.   These
springs, like almost all others of their character, were,
before they were fitted up for guests, considered public property, and hither in the early days resorted
hunters, trappers, and explorers.   They came when it
suited them, and departed when they pleased.

William Dean came to this creek from the Oakley

place in 1857 and erected a tobacco factory. The first plug of tobacco he made was at the Oakley place, on August 5, 1846. Here on Dog (or Cedar) Creek he had also a tanyard, which he operated, together with the tobacco factory, until 1861. The " Dean Tobacco," the trade being then unlimited by taxes or by laws, was carried in wagons and sold in either large or small lots throughout Middle Tennessee and portions of Mississippi and Alabama. Dean bought part of his lands from a man named Helms, who had bought from Asa Shute, a pioneer land locator. That Shute was here as early as 1811 is evidenced by the fact that a beech tree on the creek was marked: "Asa Shute, 1811." Another, which stood near by, was marked: "Asa Shute, Thomas Ingram, 1811." These trees stood about halfway between Primm's Springs and the mouth of the creek, about one-fourth of a mile above where Dean now lives, and near the foot of Gee's Hill. These inscriptions were cut in the bark of these beech trees, which, as they stood near the creek, have been washed away. They were once important landmarks. Gee's Hill takes its name from a man named Gee, who once lived here, and from whom the ford at the mouth of Dog (or Cedar) Creek and the road leading over to the head of Leatherwood Creek take their names—Gee's Ford and Gee's Road, respectively. This Gee was probably the one who killed so many deer while herding cattle in the Cow Hollow, in the Ninth District. On Dog (or Cedar) Creek a house built by John Irwin in 1809 is still used as a residence.   There is a hewn-log house on the place where G. W. Malugin now lives which was also built in 1809.   This place is known as the "Billy Malugin place."   There is yet another house built in 1809 on this creek.   This is situated on a tributary of the creek, and is within the limits of the Thirteenth District.   This house was built by —— Mattock, and from it John G. Malugin once ran in great fright to the home of Gee.   He ran down the creek valley and through a dense canebrake, thinking that Indians were in close pursuit.   His hasty arrival and the terrible news he brought caused Gee to also become frightened.   They made arrangements to resist the savages as best they could and to fight them to the last.   After hours of weary waiting and of suspense, they concluded that it was a false alarm, and such it was. Robert Dean, an uncle of William Dean and a brother of John Dean, located on Bell's Branch, in the Seventh District, in 1820, and taught school there.

As early as 1830, and probably earlier, Pleasant Russell lived at the John T. Overbey (or Beale) place. His son, the late Hon. W. B. Russell, was a great hunter.   In 1840, after a long chase, he lost the trail of a deer in the Dog (or Cedar) Creek bottoms.   A few hours later he went to the sulphur springs at the head of the creek for water, and there found the deer on a like errand.   The deer was slain.

During the Civil War this district furnished its quota of brave men for the Southern army.   They were led by Captains Beale, Oliver, and Campbell.

Capt. Thomas Campbell was badly wounded in the leg during the war. After the war he was elected tax collector, defeating Robert Green, a one-armed ex-Confederate. In another race for the same office Green defeated Campbell, and thus Hickman County gave this, the most responsible county office, to these two wounded heroes. The majority each time was very small, and it seemed that the voters wanted to elect both men.

Ferdinand B. Russell was at one time one of the leading mill men of the Fourth District. He lost his eyesight while blasting rock near his mill on Jones' Branch. His father was Pleasant Russell, who was born in Virginia. F. B. Russell was born in Williamson County on March 10, 1822.

Felix Cockrum was drowned at the mouth of Lick Creek, in the Second District, in 1851. His body was recovered at or near the O. A. Jones (or Nunnelly) place. At the Inkstand Point—so called on account of its peculiar shape—near the mouth of Lick Creek, the body of a man named Ashworth was recovered in 1887. He was drowned at Gordon's Ferry, and lived in Maury County. In Lick Creek, in the Fourth District, at what is called the Pine Bluff Hole, little Charlie Haley, of Maury County, was drowned in 1888. He was in bathing with other boys.

The early physicians here were Drs. Smoot and Smith, already mentioned. They lived near the mouth of Fort Cooper Hollow. Physicians here at a recent date were Drs. Daniel, Capps, and Shacklett.

On Jones' Branch Elder J. P. Litton lived in recent years. He by his upright course made many friends and gained the esteem of even those who differed from him on doctrinal points.

CHAPTER VIII.

THE FIFTH DISTRICT.

THE Fifth District is bounded on the north by Dickson County; on the east, by the Fourth District; on the south, by the Second District; and on the west, by the Sixth District. It includes that portion of Hickman County known since the first settlers came here as " The Barrens." It received this name on account of the lack of timber. Grass, however, was to be found here in abundance, and here grazed vast herds of deer, even for years after the first hunters came. This district includes the head waters of Mill Creek, Big Spring Creek, and Little Spring Creek; it also includes the larger portion of Bear Creek. All of these rise in the Fifth District and flow westward into Pine River. Mill Creek is in the southern part of the district, and Bear Creek in the northern part. The two Spring Creeks are in the west central part.

Near the head waters of Mill Creek, and on the edge of " The Barrens," the first hunters who came here found evidences of an Indian dancing ground and camping place. This was near the Daniel Cockrum (or A. J. Rodgers) spring at the head of the west branch of Mill Creek. For years numerous arrowheads were found here. Daniel Cockrum, who was born in Kentucky, settled at this spring in

1818. He bought the lands from A. J. Rodgers, who had settled here in 1810. Daniel Cockrum was the father of Henry and William Cockrum. The latter was born here on February 11, 1821. James Pickett, the father-in-law of Henry Cockrum, came from Kentucky about this time and settled on the creek below Cockrum. In 1815 Absalom Nicks, Sr., lived on the head waters of Mill Creek, as did also his brother, William Nicks, the preacher. They lived at the Lafayette Wynn place.

In 1814 a forge was built by Hardin Perkins on the McAllister place, five miles down the creek from the Cockrum place. Here iron was made from ore, which was melted, " puddled," and rolled into balls. Into these balls a bar of iron was inserted for a handle. The balls were then turned over and over, while a ponderous hammer struck the red-hot metal repeatedly. When by this process it had been converted into a good quality of iron, it was drawn into bars, which were conveyed from the forge by wagons, and sold throughout the country for ten cents a pound. This iron was by the blacksmiths of the county used in the construction of the primitive farming implements then in use. Much of the iron made here was sold in Kentucky, to which State it was hauled in wagons. Perkins built another forge, called the "Lower Forge," near the mouth of Mill Creek, in what is now the Seventh District. In 1825 Montgomery Bell came to Hickman County and bought these two forges from Perkins, who was his most formidable competitor in the manufacture of iron. Bell, who was a Pennsylvanian, owned and operated at that time Cumberland Furnace, on Barton's Creek, in Dickson County. This furnace he had bought from Gen. James Robertson prior to 1800, and here were cast all of the cannon balls used by General Jackson at New Orleans. The cannon balls were carried to the Cumberland River, eight miles away, and shipped to New Orleans in keel boats. Bell also operated a forge at the Narrows of Harpeth, in what is now Cheatham County. By his trade with Perkins he evidently intended to monopolize the entire iron trade of Middle Tennessee, West Tennessee, and portions of Kentucky, Mississippi, and Alabama. Bell made no attempt to operate the forges bought from Perkins, being satisfied with the removal of so formidable a competitor. Perkins, like Bell, was also looking alone to his own interest, and, gathering his slaves and employees, he in a short time erected two forges between those he had sold to Bell and commenced to operate them. Bell abandoned the field, and Perkins continued to operate his forges until 1835. In 1825, and for several years previous to this, David Duncan was manager for Perkins. He was succeeded by Daniel McCord. Duncan was the father of Thomas Duncan, of the Seventh District. Mill Creek received its name from the mill built near its mouth in the Seventh District, this being the first mill erected in the county.

In the valley of the upper portion of Mill Creek some of the first settlers of the county located. Nathaniel and Gabriel Fowlkes, who were brothers, located near where Taylor Jones now lives as early as 1806. They came from Virginia to Rutherford County, lived there a few years, removed to Williamson County, and came from the latter county to Mill Creek. Nathaniel married Lucy Wynn, daughter of James Wynn, who lived on the creek. He was twice married. His children were: James, Martha, Sally, Jane, Nancy, Edward, John, and Gabriel. The latter was the late Gabriel Fowlkes, of the First District, who was born on Mill Creek on January 27, 1833. Gabriel Fowlkes, the brother of Nathaniel Fowlkes, lived near the forks of the creek in 1828, and his daughter, Mrs. Jesse R. Eason, went to school to George Ingram, who taught school in a log schoolhouse which had no floor. Mrs. Eason was then seven years old, and, although seventy years have passed, she remembers the force with which her toe struck a small stump which stood in this little log schoolhouse which had a dirt floor. " Billie " Bates and Moses Thornton were school-teachers here in 1829 and 1830, respectively. William Nicks was a preacher in this neighborhood. He and his followers were called " Schismatics." They had " mourner's benches," called for " mourners," and had " shouting revivals." Nicks baptized Mrs. Hartzogg in Mill Creek in 1829. From this neighborhood, in 1828, William Cockrum went to a school three miles away. It was located near where A. Groves now lives. The teacher was named Thompson. Here Wesley Erwin taught in

1829. All schools then were subscription schools, this being long before the present free-school system was inaugurated. In 1836 the Methodists and Presbyterians held a camp meeting above the Upper Forge at the place where Alex. Gossett now lives. Preparing for this camp meeting, William Cockrum was trying to kill a pig, when the animal turned upon him and upon his left arm left a scar as a souvenir of this " big camp meeting." In 1840 Colonel Adair, the father of Joseph Adair, a " singing master " of to-day, " sung by note " at the Quilly Tidwell place. He used " the four-note system."

In 1820 James Wynn came from Virginia and settled on Mill Creek near where his son, Lafayette Wynn, now lives. Lafayette Wynn was born on December 26, 1840.

In 1823 Robert Bates came from Virginia and located at the Alex. Gossett place. He was born in Albemarle County, Va., in 1787. His sons were B. B. Bates (who died near Shady Grove a few years ago) and Samuel Richard Bates. Samuel R. Bates was born near Hillsboro, Williamson County, on January 22, 1814. He married Charlotte Suggs, a daughter of Timothy Suggs, who came from Bedford County to Mill Creek in 1833. Suggs bought land from Matthew and Alston Myatt, who came from North Carolina to this creek in 1820. They removed to Dickson County. In 1897 Samuel Bates, at the age of eighty-three years, lived with his son, Mac Bates, near Lyell Station. When Hardin Perkins operated the forges on Mill Creek, Bates chopped wood for him to pay for iron at ten cents a pound, with which he had made a bar-share plow. The work was done by John Malugin, a blacksmith, who lived near Little Lot. In 1834 Bates heard Rhoda Marlin, afterwards Mrs. Jones, " sing by note," she, too, using " the four-note system." She was the mother of Taylor Jones, a justice of the peace in this district. David Duncan and Josiah Thornton were magistrates here at an early date. Edward (" Ned ") Nunnellee, who came from Virginia to Bedford County, and from that county to this district, prior to 1810, was one of Hickman County's magistrates in 1817, this being after he had removed to what is now the First District. Gabriel Fowlkes was a magistrate in 1815. Fowlkes was sheriff while he lived on Mill Creek, and was also sheriff after he removed to the First District. In 1829 articles of impeachment were found against Judge Joshua Haskell. He was charged with having left the courthouse on several occasions during the progress of trials, going out to engage in conversation, business, and amusement. During this trial it developed that the judge had on one occasion escaped from the fleas which infested the courthouse, and from the lawyers who were arguing a case, and had gone outside to eat a watermelon with a member of the bar. During the trial of Judge Haskell, Gabriel Fowlkes testified that upon one occasion he was, during the progress of a trial, sent for the Judge, and that he found him either in the courthouse yard or at a show near by. While the Judge was absent from the court-room a dispute arose between the lawyers as to the admissibility of testimony. A disinterested attorney was called upon to decide, which he did, and the trial proceeded. Despite his watermelon-eating and flea-escaping proclivities, Judge Haskell was acquitted by the State Senate. The late J. A. Harvill was sheriff of the county for six years, and J. C. Yates, also of this district, is the present incumbent. Thomas Patton, who is personally acquainted with every voter in the county, served one term as tax assessor. He made a courteous and efficient official. Jo. Beasley was sheriff at one time, and John L. Griffin, in the days before the Civil War, was Circuit Court Clerk.

Taylor Jones, Sr., brother of Bart. Jones and father of Taylor Jones, Jr., lived on Mill Creek as early as 1820. He married Rhoda Marlin.

On the north branch of Mill Creek, on the lands where James Barnhill lived from 1810 to 1825, Warner Furnace was built in 1880—Barnhill lived at the spring above the furnace. Before being placed in the furnace, the ore was washed and crushed, a great improvement on the methods employed in the early days. The charcoal was burned in brick ovens, in which were placed cords of wood. This, too, was a great improvement on the primitive and tedious method of burning the wood in small heaps in the forest, covering the wood with dirt and leaves. This furnace was operated until 1893.

Where Quilly Tidwell now lives Joel Carroll lived

in 1825, he having located there in 1810.   He sold to
James McMinn.   At this place were the precinct and
muster grounds.   Here the people met to vote, to
muster, and, incidentally, to drink Abner Ponder's
whisky.   Fisticuffs often took place here.   Prominent participants in muster-day festivities were Robert Lyell, Sr., "Billie" Boothe, and Arch. Ponder and
his brothers.

In 1835 Jonathan P. Hardwick came from Dickson
County, bought 2,700 acres of land from his son, Dillard Hardwick, of Mississippi, and located about one
mile north of Bon Aqua Springs.   Here he erected
an inn for the entertainment of travelers who came
this way from Kentucky to the Southern States.   Dillard Hardwick bought this land from the heirs of
Abner Ponder.

The large amount of wild game to be found on this
Hickman County prairie, " The Barrens," caused
hunters to come here as early as 1790.   The first step
toward permanent settlement was, however, in 1800,
when Abner Ponder came from Georgia and laid
a land warrant for one acre around the large free-
stone spring one mile above the Bon Aqua Springs.
This spring was then over ten feet deep and forty feet
in diameter, and contained many fish.   This is the
head spring of Big Spring Creek.   Ponder returned
to Georgia, but revisited this spring in 1801.   Again
he came in 1804.   With him were George Hartzogg
and James Barnhill.   They were natives of Germany.   Hartzogg laid a land warrant on a branch of

Mill Creek about two miles from Ponder's location, and Barnhill laid one on the land around the spring above the present site of Warner Furnace. Ponder was born in Germany in 1755, and was a soldier in the Revolutionary War. He, during his short stay here in 1804, located other lands around his spring, and planted here a peach orchard of ten acres, having brought the seed with him from Georgia. He afterwards became an extensive landowner and a wealthy and prominent citizen of Hickman County. He, Hartzogg, and Barnhill returned to Georgia. Immediately after the Indian treaties of 1806, Ponder came with his family and made a permanent settlement here. He built a tavern here, and " Ponder's Inn " was a popular stopping place for those who went over this route from Kentucky to the Southern country, and for those who passed this way going to and from Duck River and the Tennessee River. This celebrated inn was made of small poles. The cracks were filled with stones, pieces of wood, and mud. The rooms were so large that a man of average height could very easily stand upright in them. Yet great was the comfort they afforded, compared with what would have been the traveler's lot had they not been there. Here stopped the various classes of men to be found on the borders of civilization; here stopped hunters, home seekers, and adventurers. Tradition says that an unknown man stopped to rest at this spring in 1799, and was slain. In 1807 a Kentuckian named Willis was killed two miles from Ponder's Inn on the road to Charlotte. Robbery was the motive, as he had $1,000 and had been South looking for investments. He had been followed for miles by his unknown murderers, who at last accomplished their purpose.

John A. Murrell, " The Great Western Land Pirate," often passed this way during the years between 1820 and 1834. Murrell came from a respectable Middle Tennessee family, but was a professional robber by the time he was twenty-one years of age. At first he operated singly; then he gathered around him a few confederates; then he became the chief of what he called a " noble band of valiant and lordly bandits; " and, finally, he emerged from the penitentiary an imbecile. The organization of this clan was almost perfect, and the crimes they committed are without parallel in the criminal history of the Southwest. The clan was governed by what was called the " Grand Council of the Mystic Clan," which held its meetings under a large cottonwood tree in Arkansas. The Council directed the operations of the individual members of the band, called " strikers." These were the small thieves and robbers, who, under the direction of Murrell and his immediate associates, caused a reign of terror throughout the entire Southwest. Lacking the intelligence and energy which Murrell unquestionably possessed, these " strikers " would, under the direction of this master mind, perform the most fiendish of crimes. While they did not hesitate to rob from the person, and then carry out their motto, " Dead men tell no tales," their operations were confined principally to horse stealing and negro running. The completeness with which stolen horses and runaway slaves disappeared convinced the sufferers that there was an organization of this kind; but the name of Murrell was not connected with it in the beginning, and of its very existence they were not certain. A suggestion that such an organization existed was laughed at by the " strikers " in every neighborhood, and by prominent men who had much at stake and feared to incur the enmity of an organization, the individual members of which they did not know. The completeness and secrecy of this band's work created a condition in which the law-abiding citizen knew not whom to trust. Murrell being inordinately vain, Virgil A. Stewart so successfully worked upon his vanity that Murrell told of his past life, of his clan, and of his future plans. Stewart betrayed him, and Murrell was sent to the penitentiary in 1834. Murrell then lived in Madison County. Murrell has been described as a man of pleasant address, possessed of much intelligence—as a man who could adapt himself to his surroundings, whether he stood in the midst of his Mystic Clan around the Arkansas cottonwood tree, or in the pulpit preaching to a God-fearing congregation. He could pose as an eminent lawyer or cut a throat; he could quote scripture and pass counterfeit money with equal ease. As a man, he is said to have been cool, possessed of good judgment, fearless, just in his dealings with his

" strikers," to whom he always gave a portion of what
they stole for him. As a husband, he was kind; as
a friend, faithful. Some of these attributes he may
have possessed, but the following extract from his confession shows the fiendishness which predominated in
his nature—a fiendishness which, had it been elimi-
nated, might have left a man of such parts that he
would have been an upright man and good citizen.
Murrell, in his confession, said: " While I was seated
on a log, looking down the road the way I had come,
a man came in sight riding a good-looking horse.
The very moment I saw him I determined to have his
horse, if he was in the garb of a traveler. I arose
from my seat and drew an elegant rifle-pistol on him
and ordered him to dismount. He did so, and I took
his horse by the bridle and pointed down the creek
and told him to walk before me. We went a few hundred yards and stopped. I hitched his horse, and
then made him undress himself, all to his shirt and
drawers, and ordered him to turn his back to me. He
said: ' If you are going to kill me, let me have time to
pray before I die.' I told him I had no time to hear
him pray. He turned around and dropped on his
knees, and I shot him in the back of the head. I
ripped open his belly and took out his entrails and
sunk him in the creek. I then searched his pockets
and found $401.37 and a number of papers that I did
not take time to examine. I sunk the pocketbook and
papers and his hat in the creek. His boots were
brand-new and fitted me genteelly, and I put them on

and sunk my old shoes in the creek to atone for them. I rolled up his clothes and put them into his portmanteau, as they were quite new cloth of the best quality. I mounted as fine a horse as I ever straddled, and directed my course to Natchez in much better style than I had been for the last five days." This story, in Murrell's own words, of the deliberate murder of a defenseless traveler is one of the many stories of the bandit, Murrell, which overshadow all of the good traits of character of which tradition says he was possessed. Tradition says that Murrell had friends along this route, and that a pretended friend— Peter Clifford, of Big Spring Creek—upon one occasion betrayed him. Clifford learned from Murrell that he had stolen a horse in Humphreys County, and was then on his way to Williamson County to sell it. Clifford followed him and had him arrested by Williamson County authorities. Murrell was punished by thirty-nine lashes upon his bare back. While confined in the Franklin stocks, he, it is said, wrote upon them a transfer of his interest in them to a citizen of Hickman County, giving as his reason that the citizen named should have that which was justly due him. These stories of Murrell and his clan are not intended as a reflection upon the law-abiding citizens of the Fifth District or upon their no less law-abiding ancestors. Bad men pass through all communities; bad men live in all communities.

Abner Ponder, the builder of Ponder's Inn, was the father of several children, some of whom were:

Madison, Archibald, Penn, Abner, and Clarissa. The latter was born on March 15, 1813. She married Leroy Perkins, the ceremony being performed by Daniel White, a Primitive Baptist, who preached often at the head of Bear Creek between 1825 and 1830. After the death of Perkins she married Joseph Webb, of the Seventh District. At the age of eighty-four her mind was still vigorous, and she talked entertainingly of how she and her little brother watched their father's sheep as they grazed upon the luxuriant grass of " The Barrens." She carried a tin horn, so that she could sound an alarm in case of an attack by wolves. In the event that she became lost, she was to sound this horn, so that her father could find her. She also told of how she gathered the wild flowers and strawberries which grew around her father's mill, built at his spring in 1820. That the fear of wolves was well founded is made evident by a wolf hunt engaged in by Joseph Weems and Arch. Ponder. Ponder, early one morning, went near the spring where Edney or McCord now lives, in search of his milch cows. He came upon a fawn, which he killed. He was preparing to lash it to his saddle, when the restlessness of his horse caused him to look toward the place where he had slain the deer. Near this place he saw a large black wolf, which he immediately fired upon. The wolf fell, rolled over and over, snapping and snarling. Then it sprang up and ran rapidly away. Ponder, knowing that the animal was wounded, went for Weems, who kept a large pack of hounds and a particularly ferocious cur. The chase went first in the direction of Turnbull Creek, then through the hills of upper Mill Creek, finally, after ten hours, coming to an exciting end in a hollow near Lick Creek. Here, when Ponder arrived, the wolf stood at bay. Dismounting, he again shot it. The wolf, however, again rose, and this time rushed at his pursuer. Not having time to reload, Ponder sprang behind a tree which had been struck by lightning. From this he jerked a large piece of wood and with it again brought the wolf to the ground. Weems arrived at this juncture. With him was his large cur, valueless during the chase, valuable at the finish. The already sorely wounded wolf was soon slain.

James Birden, who married a daughter of Abner Ponder, was in the American army at the battle of New Orleans. When the Tennessee soldiers returned home, Birden was not with them, and his fate was unknown. Late in the autumn of 1819 a stranger came to Ponder's and asked for lodging. He was dressed in plain, but good, clothing, and wore a heavy beard. When he entered the yard, a dog which had belonged to Birden commenced to leap about him, manifesting great joy. The stranger asked for Mrs. Birden, and when told that she had been dead two years his genuine grief disclosed his identity. It was James Birden, first recognized by his faithful dog. Soon after this he returned to his former home, Georgia, to which State his three children were afterwards carried by his brother-in-law, Penn Ponder.

Andrew Carothers, a Primitive Baptist, preached on the head of Bear Creek between 1820 and 1830, as did also Thomas Murrell, of the same church. In 1820 Jacob Tucker taught school about one and a half miles from Ponder's Spring. Here Mark Thornton and Doyal Beard also taught. Dr. Haley, who lived on Pine River, was one of the first physicians of this section.

Near Lyell Station lived the late William Lyell. During the Civil War he served for a time in Morgan's Cavalry. After the war he engaged in a hotly contested race for sheriff against E. A. Dean, Dean winning by a small majority. William Lyell had much to do with the building of Lyell Station, as did also John and Robert Lyell, who live near by. Lyell Station is located upon a portion of a large entry made by —— Stump, a member of a German family that were among the first settlers at " The Bluffs," now Nashville. Asa Shute, who was a pioneer land locator, was also a German. This family came to Nashville nearly twenty years after the Stump family came. One corner of this large entry is a white oak near the Blue Spring at the head of the west fork of Big Spring Creek, near where —— Fitz lives on the road from Pinewood to Nashville. Another corner is near the Wynn place at the head of Mill Creek. Matthew Thornton, who died a few years ago on Sugar Creek, in the Eighth District, was one of the chain carriers when this survey was made. Near the Blue Spring, above referred to, Richard Beach, of

Williamson County, was killed during the Civil War by a detachment of Federals. At Lyell Station there are now two stores—one conducted by Overbey Bros.; the other, by Lovell & Son. The senior member of the latter firm, James Anderson Lovell, was born on Pine River on January 12, 1826, and has lived near his present place of residence since 1845.

Near the head of Big Spring Creek is Brister's Branch, named for Brister, a negro, who lived on this branch. Brister had been the slave of Edward (Ned) Nunnellee, but had purchased his freedom. In a cave on Brister's Branch saltpeter dirt was found. This dirt was placed in hoppers made of boards. Upon it water was poured. The drippings were caught in vessels and boiled down. When sufficiently crystallized, the product was carried in large quantities to Nashville, where it was easily sold. It was one of the principal ingredients used in the manufacture of powder, and there was a great demand for it. Much of the salt used by the pioneers of Hickman County was taken from the earth in the above manner. Most of it, however, was bought at Nashville, saltpeter and pelts being exchanged for it. Nicholas Dudley, who was a prominent citizen, was engaged in the saltpeter business from 1812 to 1815. During the pioneer days he often acted as dentist, surgeon, and physician for his neighbors. He extracted teeth, set broken limbs, and kept on hand a collection of native herbs, the medicinal properties of which he understood.

Near Bon Aqua Station are the famous Bon Aqua Springs.   These springs did not particularly attract the early settlers of the county, and no particular attention was given them until William B. Ross became the owner, about 1823.   Even then there was nothing done, except to establish the ownership.   The lands around the springs remained unoccupied.   Ross located on the Tennessee River above where Johnsonville now stands, and established what has since 1835 been known as Ross' Ferry.   He ran the original line between Dickson and Hickman Counties.   While the springs and a small tract of the surrounding land belonged to Ross, there were no buildings or inclosures, and the hunter, the trapper, and the citizen were at liberty to camp there for whatever period they liked. In 1827 Jacob Humble, Millington Easley, and James D. Davis, of Pine River; Garrett Lane, of Vernon; and Gen. William D. Williams, of Maury County, together with their families, spent the summer in the valley just above the springs.   They occupied four little log cabins.   From this point they went forth to the deer chase or wolf hunt; from here they went out in the early morning and " gobbled up " turkeys; from here they went in search of wild strawberries and chinquapins, which grew in abundance on the surrounding lands.   In the near-by forest they could almost any day find a " bee tree," with its treasure of honey.   No violence is done the memories of these good citizens when the statement is made that here in the shade they often took a " drap," " peach and honey" and "mint juleps" being their favorite medicines. Later many others came, living during their stay in wagons, tents, rude shelters, and cabins.

William Loche Weems was the first to make of this a famous watering place and health resort. He was born in Prince George County, Md., on December 9, 1792. He married Elizabeth Taylor Birch, who was born in the same county on April 11, 1797. She was a cousin of Gen. Zachary Taylor. Weems came to Tennessee in 1825 and located on Lick Creek. In 1826 he lived near Vernon, on the W. F. Mays place; and in 1827 he moved to the William McEwen place, in the Third District, at which place he lived until 1839. In 1837 he bought the springs, which he named " Bon Aqua "—good water. He bought the springs and four hundred and six acres of land. He afterwards added to this until he owned about eighteen hundred acres. These lands were bought from McKenzie and Long and from Dickey and Long, who had grants from North Carolina. In 1839 Weems, having an idea of the true value of the springs, and believing that they could be made profitable to himself and beneficial to mankind in general, erected about fifteen cabins of hewn logs and began to advertise his springs as a health resort. From that date the name and fame of Weems' Springs went far and wide, and visitors from many places and many States came here from year to year. Weems also commenced to improve his farm, and, with the assistance of his slaves, which he owned to the number of

fifty, he opened about two hundred acres of farming
land. In 1840 the springs were managed by William
H. Deadman, who lived on Leatherwood Creek. He
was a native of Virginia. After this year Weems
assumed in person the management of the springs,
and continued as manager until his death, in 1852.
He was buried at the McEwen place, in the Third
District. After his death the springs and farming
land became the property of his youngest son, to whom
he had bequeathed them. This son was Philip Van
Horn Weems, the son of Weems' second wife, who
was Ann Elizabeth Burchett, of Virginia. Capt. P.
V. H. Weems enlisted in Bateman's company of the
Eleventh Tennessee Infantry in May, 1861. Of
this company he later became captain, and, while
acting as colonel of the regiment, he was mortally
wounded in front of Atlanta, Ga., on July 27, 1864.
He died on July 30. As a child, he had been the
idol of the home and the pet of every visitor to the
springs; as a friend, no man was ever truer; as a
soldier, no braver man ever donned a uniform or
waved a sword. Such was Capt. Philip Van Horn
Weems—brave, noble Van Weems—who sleeps beneath the soil of his native county, far from the
bloody field upon which he laid down his life. After
the close of the war the springs were bought by the
Bon Aqua Springs Association. This company placed
many expensive improvements here. Numerous nice
cottages took the place of the log cabins, and a large
hotel was erected at a cost of $40,000. Bon Aqua

took first place among the watering places of Tennessee, and for several years enjoyed an era of great prosperity. Here rested from their labors some of the most prominent men of Tennessee. In August, 1888, misfortune came. The large hotel burned, and has never been rebuilt. A small hotel and a number of neat cottages yet remain.

Nathaniel Weems, a son of William and Elizabeth (Birch) Weems, died several years ago in the Third District. He was a wealthy and prominent citizen.

Another son, Hon. Joseph Weems, represented this county in the Lower House of the Forty-fourth General Assembly. He was born in Prince George County, Md., on September 19, 1820, and was brought by his father to Hickman County in 1825. In 1846 he enlisted in Company A (Whitfield's company), First Tennessee Regiment. He returned from Mexico in 1847. Since that time he has been active in the public life of the county.

Ellen Weems, a daughter of William Weems, married Henry Cummins, and was the mother of John and Samuel Cummins.

Elizabeth Taylor Weems, another daughter, married Albert Wilson, who once owned the land upon which the village of Pinewood now stands. He moved to Texas, where he died.

This district, in addition to Captain Weems, furnished another brave officer to the Confederate Army —Lieut. John L. Griffin, of the Forty-eighth Tennessee Infantry—and from this district went a large number of private soldiers as brave as those who led them.   From this district a few saw fit to enlist in the Federal Army.   Some of these fought well under the flag they chose to follow, while others acted as guides for Federal detachments operating in Hickman County.

Ernest Harold was killed by a train near Lyell Station in 1894.   Joseph Lyell and a son of Thomas Yates were killed near Bon Aqua on July 4, 1893. Their slayer escaped.   A negro, Sowell, was burned to death by molten metal at Warner Furnace a few years ago.

On the branch just below Bon Aqua Springs, during the latter part of the Civil War, Perkins shot two men, Moore and Gracey.   Moore afterwards died from the wound inflicted.   The men had some trouble about a horse, and an attempt was made to arrest Perkins, who seemed inclined toward taking charge of the springs, despite the remonstrances of the manager, McMinn.   Constable Henry Cockrum and posse had Perkins in charge.   When opposite the place where Joseph Weems lives, Perkins dismounted and opened fire upon them.   The result is given above.   Perkins, who claimed to be from Kentucky, escaped.

Capt. Dick McCann, of Nashville, while encamped with his body of independent rangers near Bon Aqua Springs, was surprised and captured by a Federal company in 1863.   One of McCann's men was killed during the attack.   McCann explained to his captors that, while his capture might have an unpleasant result, as far as he was concerned, anything was pleasant to him, just so that it was a change.

During the latter part of the war Jesse K. McMinn was killed by Federal soldiers at his home near Bon Aqua Springs.

CHAPTER IX.

THE SIXTH DISTRICT.

THE Sixth District lies in the northeastern portion of the county, and includes that portion of Pine River between the mouth of Bear Creek and the line of the Seventh District which crosses the river between the residences of M. M. and H. T. Petty, one and a half miles below Pinewood. It is bounded on the north by Dickson County; on the east, by the Fifth and Seventh Districts; on the south, by the Seventh District; and on the west, by Humphreys County. Included in this district are Garner's Creek, Beaver Creek, and Plunder's Creek, all on the west side of Pine River. Flowing into Pine River from the east are Big Spring Creek, Little Spring Creek, and Bear Creek, which rise in the Fifth District; also, Key's Branch. Pine River, which flows through the Sixth and Seventh Districts, rises in Dickson County near the town of Dickson. It runs in a southern direction and empties into Duck River near the noted Indian mounds in the Seventh District.

Jesse Fuqua, the Primitive Baptist preacher, in 1827 located on Big Spring Creek, one and a half miles from its mouth, on lands then owned by Solomon Jones. R. R. Brown, the father of James, Robert, William T., and John Riley Brown, has lived on Big Spring Creek since 1836. He was born in Dickson County on November 26, 1828, and is a son of Spencer Brown, who came from North Carolina.

On the west side of Pine River, opposite the mouth of Big Spring Creek, lived Jacob Humble in 1825. In 1849 he donated to the Primitive Baptist Church the lands on which is now located Humble Church. James Weatherspoon taught school at the mouth of Beaver Creek in 1829. —— Hutchens taught at the head of Little Spring Creek in 1827, and James Crockett, a cripple on crutches, taught at the same place in 1828.

The following is the story that tradition tells of the origin of the name " Plunder's Creek: " Early in this century hunters came from Dickson County for a hunt on Pine River and its tributaries. With them was Lemuel Russell, who was the owner of a valuable dog, " Old Plunder," the first in a deer chase and the last to leave a bear fight. Here on Plunder's Creek human eyes last rested on " Old Plunder," who left his master's side in pursuit of a retreating bear. The hunters, in honor of their lost friend, named the creek " Plunder's Creek."

Tradition has it that at an early date a party were on Garner's Creek. One of them, Colonel Garner, in attempting to cross the creek, fell from the log on which he was attempting to walk, and from this incident the creek received its name. Col. William Garner settled near the head of the creek, in Dickson County, and in 1809 was killed by Indians, who crossed Duck River and came through Humphreys

County. Whether it was for him or for John Garner, who was a chain carrier for Edwin Hickman in 1791, when Hickman made his disastrous locating tour down Pine River and up Duck River, that this creek was named, is not known. It is known, however, that this party located land in this vicinity— at the mouth of " Spring Creek of Pine River."

Beaver Creek received its name from the large number of beavers which the pioneer hunters found there. Near the head of this creek, in 1840, Richard Hobbs operated a tannery and distillery, supplying the people with two articles—one a necessity, and the other, in that day, thought to be a necessity. Edmond Shumach and Cornelius D. White located on this creek about 1805. At an early date Oliver Smith laid a land warrant for 640 acres at the mouth of Beaver Creek. On this creek occurred the birth of the first white child born in Hickman County—Jane Wilson, sister of Ben. Wilson. In after years she became the second wife of Jared Curl. Before the erection of Humble Church there stood at the mouth of Beaver Creek a Primitive Baptist church. Here this church, whose membership exceeded in number that of all the others combined, flourished under the leadership of Andrew Carothers, Jesse Fuqua, and Claiborne Hobbs as ministers, and such men as Jacob Humble and Solomon Jones as members. Several years after the building of Humble Church the Methodists and Cumberland Presbyterians built Kedron Church, at the mouth of Garner's Creek. At this church have preached James Parrish, of Dickson County; John Reynolds, —— Nesbit, the Hinsons, Will. Allan Turner, —— Whitten, —— Moody, W. T. Dye, H. S. Ledbetter, R. R. Jones, George Coleman, W. D. Cherry, and others. After the erection of the cotton mills at Pinewood by Samuel Graham, a church was built here, with a Masonic hall overhead. Here a Christian Church was organized, and some of the preachers who have preached here are E. G. Sewell, Rufus Meeks, James and John Morton, and James P. Litton. After a suspension of twenty years, a Masonic lodge has recently been reorganized here. The officers of Pinewood Lodge, F. and A. M., are Rufus Sugg, W. M.; William McDonough, S. W.; T. D. Thompson, J. W.; J. C. Frazier, Secretary; Joel Errington, Treasurer.

John Gordon taught school on Garner's Creek in 1821, and one of his pupils was Emily Steel. Isaac Wright taught here in 1830, and about that time married Emily Steel. The widow, Elizabeth Steel, came to this creek in 1821. She was born in North Carolina on July 2, 1779. Her husband, Thomas Steel, was born in the same State on November 26, 1769, and died in Orange County, N. C. Elizabeth Steel came to Garner's Creek with her five children—three girls and two boys. The eldest daughter, Rebecca, married Lint Box, of Humphreys County; her second daughter, Rachel, married Jesse George; the third is Mrs. Emily Wright. William Alston Steel, the elder son, married Susan Stone, of Dickson

County, and lived in that county. The other son, Thomas Steel, was a deputy under Sheriff Solomon Jones George. The widow, Elizabeth Steel, was a half-sister of Solomon Jones. Mrs. Steel's mother was the widow Pollard, who married James Jones, the father of Solomon Jones. Solomon Jones married Chrissie Alston in North Carolina. He came to Tennessee in 1807, and settled at the mouth of Big Spring Creek. He exchanged his lands in North Carolina for military land warrants, and laid them here. Later he returned to North Carolina and induced his sister to come to Tennessee. Several of his brothers-in-law, the Alstons, came in 1810, and settled on Beaver Creek. His sons were Col. Dennis Jones, who married Martha Atkins, sister of Hon. J. D. C. Atkins, of Henry County; William Jones, who married Susan McNeilly; and James G. Jones, of Humphreys County, who married Elizabeth Griner. The mother of James G. Jones was the second wife of Solomon Jones. She, at the time of her marriage, was the widow of Daniel Murphree, one of the pioneers of the Eighth District. One of the daughters of Solomon Jones was the first wife of Millington Easley; another married John Stuthard.

Mrs. Emily Wright (*nee* Steel) was born on May 21, 1813. At the age of eighty-four she possessed a vigorous mind filled with memories of other days. She lives alone, save the companionship of her several pets. These pets are a milch cow, a calf, a mule thirty-five years old, ten cats, and a goose thirty-four

years old. Sixteen years ago the goose quit lay-
ing, and since then Mrs. Wright has not picked it.
Another and oft-consulted companion is her family
Bible.

Below where Mrs. Steel located, Bartlett and Andrew Stuart settled prior to 1815. They lived at the
present Freeman place.

At the old Christian place, Greenberry Leathers,
father of John, Thomas, and Fielding Leathers, located in 1806. He lived there at the time of the
earthquake of 1811, which rattled the dishes in his
cupboard. This cupboard is now the property of
Mrs. Emily Wright. Although over ninety years
old, it is well preserved. It was made by a negro
cabinet workman, who was the slave of James Davis.
Leathers lived on Garner's Creek at a time when
settlers gathered their families at certain places at
night for protection against the Indians. When
morning came each would return to his home for the
day's work, assembling again at night.

Joel Errington, from North Carolina, settled on
Garner's Creek, five miles from its mouth, in 1809.
His son, Jacob, who was born on April 17, 1821, is
now living at the old homestead. He has been mar-
ried three times. His last wife is the daughter of
Lemuel Russell, the pioneer hunter, for whose dog,
" Old Plunder," a creek was named.

In 1812, at what is now the Reeves place, lived
Thornton Perry, father of Dr. Eli Perry, of Humphreys County. Just below him on the creek lived

Aaron Potter. While Perry and Potter were running after a hog, Potter heard behind him a heavy fall and a groan. Turning, he found Perry lying dead on the ground. Potter lived to be about seventy years old. He was the father of Joel Potter.

At the Lytle Haley place, in 1812, a man named Ham erected a mill. In 1820 John Christian, father of George W. Christian, erected a mill, which has later been known as the Solomon George mill, the Stanfield Andrews mill, and the John Martin mill. Solomon J. George lived at, and owned, this mill in 1856, when he was elected sheriff. He sold to Andrews and moved to Centerville. George was a son of Daniel George, of North Carolina. Daniel George married Miss Pollard, a half-sister of Solomon Jones, for whom he named his son, Solomon Jones George.

At the place later called the "Aaron Caughran place," Daniel Martin, father of William Martin, lived in 1815. James Joslin lived near this place in 1809. In 1810 James Eason lived where Frank Scott now lives. Near by lived George Evans, who was a great pugilist, and who had, when he was a young man, lost a portion of one ear in a fight.

One of the early preachers on Garner's Creek was ——— Hale, a Primitive Baptist. In 1822 John ("Daddy") Brown preached at the home of Mrs. Steel, there then being no church house in this section. Mrs. Steel was a Baptist, and during Brown's sermon she several times interrupted him, calling attention to what she claimed were misstatements.

One of the first to locate on Plunder's Creek was Andrew Haley, who came from North Carolina in 1810. He was the father of the late Lytle Haley, of Garner's Creek.

Moulton Reeves, the father of Marvin and Albert Reeves, was a prominent farmer and citizen of Garner's Creek. Jacob Humble lived on Pine River below the mouth of Garner's Creek, and was one of the county's magistrates. Joel Errington, who later lived on Garner's Creek, was the first to settle the place opposite the mouth of the creek. Claiborne Hobbs lived here at a later date.

Indian Camp Hollow, named on account of its once having been the site of an Indian camp, runs into Garner's Creek near the Dickson and Hickman County line. Chimney Hollow is so named on account of the peculiar standing rock near its mouth. This rock bears a striking resemblance to a chimney. Gordon Hollow received its name from the pioneer school-teacher, John Gordon. Chalk Hollow is so named on account of a white clay deposit found in it. The Biter Hollow received its name on account of a family of that name who lived in the hollow. Cave Hollow is named for the cave near its mouth. This cave has been explored for over a mile. One of the curiosities to be found in this cave is a peculiar rock which, when struck, gives forth a bell-like sound. In the floor of the cave is a pool called " The Well."

In 1865, in the creek valley near where Samuel Errington now lives, Frank McCaslin, a Primitive Baptist, preached the funeral of G. Washington Christian. Christian was a member of Vernon Lodge, No. 217, F. and A. M.

Joel Fuqua, a son of Jesse Fuqua, was born on June 17, 1819, and married Rebecca Dudley on August 20, 1846. He located at his present place of residence in 1850. He assisted in the erection of the Plunder's Creek mill, which was built in 1862. Prior to this he had assisted in the building and rebuilding of the Pinewood mills. He possesses remarkable ingenuity as a worker in wood, iron, and leather. As a fifer, he, in 1846, played for Whitfield's company of volunteers at Vernon. Dorsey Weatherspoon was the drummer.

In 1810 James Davis lived on the hill where John McDonough now lives. Dr. Shelby boarded with him in 1829 and 1830. In 1832 Dr. Lewis boarded with him. Dr. Lewis married a Miss Bowen, and later lived at Vernon.

On the east side of Pine River, on Little Spring Creek one mile from its mouth, Andrew Clark located on April 22, 1822. His son, Thomas Clark, now lives near where his father first settled. Andrew Clark was born in North Carolina in 1778. He exchanged his lands in North Carolina for the lands on which the late John L. Temple lived. Here Clark died in 1852. These lands, before Clark traded for them, belonged to Solomon Jones, who had come from North Carolina several years before this. Some of those who came to Tennessee through the influence

of Jones were Andrew Clark, Jesse Fuqua, James
Alston, and Mrs. Steel. Jones bought these lands
from Billy White, who was probably the first individual owner. Sons of Andrew Clark were William
A. Clark and Joseph R. Clark. A daughter, Susan
H. Clark, married John Loyd Temple on April 26,
1849. Mr. Temple will again be mentioned in the
sketch of the Thirteenth District, where he was born
on April 18, 1825. In 1855 Mr. Temple, while
clearing land, found a terrapin. Carving the date
on its shell, he released it. In 1885 he again found
this terrapin—thirty years older, but going the same
old gait. Again he carved the date and again released it. On November 25 he covered a terrapin
with leaves and dirt and left it by a stump. In the
following February he raked away the covering and
found the terrapin alive, well, and with speed undi-
minished. On June 15 he found a terrapin on a
nest in which were five eggs. On September 15 he
removed the covering of the nest and found five little
terrapins. A terrapin was found on Mr. Temple's
farm with the following dates carved on it: 1862,
1868, 1873, 1878, and 1880. In 1896 it was carried
to Pinewood, the date and initials " H. H. G."
(Harry H. Graham) carved on it, and released. On
December 25, 1848, Mr. Temple, while crossing Pine
River at the mouth of Little Spring Creek, missed
the ford. While battling with the current the swimmer was encouraged by shouts from a negro, Bob
Davis, who stood on the bank. No white people

living near, Mr. Temple went to Bob's cabin, which stood where the brick storehouse of H. H. & T. H. Graham now stands, and dried his clothing. Bob had been the slave of James Davis, who owned the mill site here and the land on both sides of the river. Bob had been given his freedom and the land on which North Pinewood now stands. This was done on account of Bob's wife having become the mother of ten children. The land given to Bob was then timbered land.

James Davis had come to this place about 1810, and as early as 1820 had a gristmill and cotton gin here. Under Davis' control was a boy, Albert Wilson, who became the owner of this property after Davis' death. Wilson sold the mill site to William Lytle, who had married a sister of Samuel L. and Richard A. Graham. This sale to Lytle and the Graham brothers marked the beginning of a new era in the business of the district and entire county. Wilson, who sold the property, was a gentleman of the first order. He married Miss Weems, sister of Hon. Joseph Weems. Lytle was an Irishman, possessed of the noble characteristics of that race. He soon sold his interests here to his brothers-in-law, the Grahams, and bought property on Sugar Creek, in the Eighth District. A few years later he removed to West Tennessee. The Graham brothers, now having full control, began the building of Pinewood, to which they gave the name. The gristmill was improved, and in 1851 the cotton mills had about 1,200 spindles. Tenement houses were erected, and soon Pinewood, touched by the magic power of money, directed by the hand of industry and wise economy, came forth from the shades of obscurity into the full light and busy bustle of a live little town. In 1862 Richard A. Graham sold his interest in the Pinewood property to his brother, Samuel L. Graham, and removed to New York City, where, after several years of successful business, he died. He never married. After the departure of his brother, S. L. Graham took charge of the business, and, although it was during the dark days of the rebellion, he remained at his post. He suffered from raids by Federals and Confederates alike. Frequently parties unauthorized by either government raided his mills and factory and appropriated his goods to their individual use. After the din of war was hushed he continued to prosper, and in 1870 he formed a partnership with his son, John M. Graham. On July 15, 1871, the cotton mills were destroyed by fire, the result of spontaneous combustion. The loss was $60,000. This was a severe blow to S. L. Graham & Son and to the surrounding country, but the spirit which first planned and built was alive, and that energy which knew no failure began to remove the rubbish ere the smoldering ruins had cooled. Larger buildings soon took the place of those destroyed. At Pinewood there was little friction between employer and employee. Mr. Graham employed and discharged his men without taking the outside world into his confidence.

Under his management Pinewood was a model village, where industry and morality held uninterrupted sway. Mr. Graham was industrious and moral, the inhabitants of Pinewood were industrious and moral—a noble example wisely followed. After the death of Samuel L. Graham, John M. Graham built a large brick store and put improved machinery in the mills; but, in the division of the property, these improvements became the property of the other heirs, H. H. and T. H. Graham.

Between where Pinewood now stands and the mouth of Beaver Creek, Clem. Deshazo lived in 1828 and 1829, at what was later known as the " Howell Huddleston place." At this time the place was claimed by one Leftwick.

Howell Huddleston married Anna Easley, daughter of William Easley, who in 1820 lived where Dr. Thomas Cash now lives. William Easley was the father of William Easley, Jr., known as " Long-jaw Bill," so called to distinguish him from other William Easleys—" Texas Bill," " Red-eyed Bill," and " Russell Bill." A negro named William Easley was called " Proper Bill." William Easley, Sr., was born on May 8, 1761, and died on January 20, 1826. He was buried at the Easley graveyard, now known as the " Petty graveyard." One of his daughters married Robert Sheegog, the well-known Irish merchant of Vernon. A son, Millington Easley, settled where Hardy Petty lived for years, and where Rev. H. S. Ledbetter now lives. The Easleys owned most of the level bench land north of Key's Branch. On this land a circular race track a mile in length was situated, extending from near where M. M. Petty lives to near where the Graham Cemetery now is. Here, between 1825 and 1840, many dollars, horses, and slaves changed hands as the result of bets on the several horses that here contested. One of those who never hesitated to back with his money his favorite horse was Claiborne Hobbs, afterwards a faithful and zealous preacher in the Primitive Baptist Church. On these lands William Joslin lived in 1807. In his house were held the first courts of Hickman County prior to the erection of a courthouse at Vernon.

William Phillips once owned the lands north of the Easley lands and adjoining the James Davis lands. Upon them that portion of Pinewood south of the principal street now stands.

Hardy Petty, for several years a leading member of the Hickman County Court, lived for many years at the Millington Easley place, where he died on June 18, 1888. He was born in North Carolina on December 5, 1810. He married Susan Wrenn, of Virginia. She was born on April 15, 1815, and died on August 8, 1885. The sons of Hardy Petty are: George, John, Wyley, Milton, and H. T. (" Dock ") Petty. His daughters are: Mrs. Thomas Field and Mrs. H. S. Ledbetter.

Peter Wrenn (born on April 8, 1801; died on April 2, 1874) came to Tennessee from Virginia, and to Key's Branch, in 1852. Mr. Wrenn was a respected citizen, and when he and his brother-in-law, Hardy Petty, died, Hickman County lost two worthy citizens. Matthew and John Wrenn are the sons of Peter Wrenn.

Hardy Petty and wife and Peter Wrenn and wife are buried in the graveyard near where Milton M. Petty now lives. On a tombstone in this cemetery is this inscription: " B. B. Satterfield, born February 18, 1804; died July 2, 1885." Colonel Satterfield died near Burns, Dickson County, from the effects of a pistol shot. Whether this shot was suicidal or accidental, no one will ever know. Colonel Satterfield was a man of pride, but not haughty. He was at one time possessed of considerable property, which was swept away by the Civil War. He was a fine carpenter and cabinet workman, and, undaunted by misfortunes, he, in his old age, resumed the trade long before this abandoned. For many years he lived near Vernon, where his hospitable home was open to all. On his tombstone are the Masonic emblems, as he was a member of Vernon Lodge, No. 217, F. and A. M. Mrs. Satterfield died on December 8, 1849. On a near-by tombstone is this inscription: " William Satterfield, born November 7, 1837; died, 1858." On another: " S. J. Easley and M. R. Easley, 1835." Another: " Louisa Stephenson, born, 1809; died, 1861." Here in an unmarked grave lies Allan Ethridge, who for many years was machinist at Pinewood. Here Ethridge, his wife, seven children, and two grandchildren are buried side by side.

On a tombstone here is this inscription: " W. T. Easley, born October 4, 1838; died December 26, 1870." Emily Easley, his wife, was a daughter of Hardy Petty. She was born on November 25, 1843, and died on March 23, 1882. The tragic death of W. T. Easley is yet well remembered. On the day of his death he was the guest of Joseph Webb, who lived on Pine River below Vernon. With his uncles, J. T. and D. T. Webb, he was engaged in a deer chase. While they were galloping through the woods a limb struck D. T. Webb's gun, causing a discharge. The contents of the gun struck Easley, killing him. Easley was a son of Solomon Jones Easley, son of Millington Easley. Other sons of Millington Easley were Samuel, Dennis, and Frank. Dennis is buried at the Petty graveyard in an unmarked grave. Samuel went to California in 1849, was one of the famous " Forty-niners," and died in California a bachelor, possessed, it is said, of considerable wealth. In the spring of 1849 Easley, Ephraim Willey, and the late William C. Thompson entered into an agreement to go to California. If one of them failed to go, he was to forfeit one hundred dollars to the party or parties who did go. Easley alone went, but never demanded the payment of the forfeits.

At the Petty graveyard, in unmarked graves, are William Philips and his good wife, Susan, the universally beloved daughter of James McNeilly. Phillips was for three terms sheriff of Hickman County,

and for one term Representative of Hickman County.
He married Susan Jones, who was the widow of that
highly respected citizen, William Jones. Standing
in this graveyard is a large cedar tree which is said
to mark the grave of the first one buried here. However, nobody knows who this was.

The Sixth District has furnished a number of good
officials. William Phillips and W. B. Russell served
their constituents as members of the Lower House of
the State Legislature. John M. Graham is at present State Senator. This district has furnished the
following sheriffs: William Phillips, Solomon J.
George, and E. A. Dean. Under Sheriff George,
Thomas Steele was a deputy. Some of the magistrates of the district were: Jacob Humble, Hudson
Dudley, William Wilson, W. B. Russell, Hardy
Petty, W. P. Russell, Ed. Still, W. A. J. McDonough, and William Brown. One of the present
magistrates is John McDonough.

Where William Harbison now lives, on Big Spring
Creek, William Walker, aged eighty years, in a fit of
despondency, committed suicide by shooting. At
Pinewood a young man named Jones was drowned.
Here, too, Samuel, a son of S. L. Graham, was
drowned. A few years ago a sister of Mrs. S. L.
Graham was drowned in Pine River opposite the
Graham residence.

At Pinewood, during the Civil War, a man named
Buchanan, who was one of a raiding party, was seriously wounded by James M. Meacham. Buchanan

was attempting to enter Graham's store. Meacham was a clerk in the store. Another more serious shooting occurred at Pinewood during the Civil War. Jones Collins, who had just returned home after service in the Confederate Army, was employed as night watchman by Mr. Graham. A man named Parham came to Pinewood, and, while engaged in an attempt to assume charge of affairs there, was having an altercation with James M. Meacham, when Collins came up and took part. During the fight which followed Parham was killed by Collins. Here at Pinewood Calvin Ladd shot and seriously wounded Aaron Caughran.

A man named Cooper built and operated a spinning factory in 1830, just below where the present Pinewood Mills stand, and nearly opposite the residence of James Meacham.

Near the southern boundary of the Sixth District, on the west side of Pine River, is the Camp Ground Hollow, so called from the fact that in 1845 the Methodists and Presbyterians held their camp meeting here. These meetings were held here as late as 1850. Near the mouth of this branch were spent the boyhood days of Rev. Lee B. Thurman, the well-known preacher.

Near this branch, on the Millington Easley (or Hardy Petty) place, now lives that veteran soldier of the cross, Rev. Henry S. Ledbetter. He was born on August 18, 1831, and was licensed to preach on August 3, 1857. He preached his first sermon at

Enon Church, in Bedford County. His text was: " Go ye into all the world, and preach the gospel to every creature." Right well has he obeyed this command, and now, aged though he is, he is still strong in the faith. His grandfather was Rev. Charles Ledbetter, who came to Tennessee from Virginia in 1790. His father was Rev. Willie Ledbetter, who was born on July 31, 1803. Rev. Willie Ledbetter married Martha Knott, daughter of William and Elizabeth Knott, of North Carolina. She was born on August 22, 1802.

CHAPTER X.

THE SEVENTH DISTRICT.

THE Seventh District is bounded on the north by the Sixth District; on the east, by the First and Sixth Districts; on the South, by the First and Ninth Districts; and on the west, by the Eighth District and Humphreys County. It includes a portion of Pine River valley, Wilson's (or Pretty) Creek, Taylor's Creek, Bird's Creek, and a portion of Mill Creek. Pretty Creek, formerly called "Wilson's Creek," is about four miles long, flows from the west, and empties into Pine River near Vernon. John Wilburn settled near the head of this creek in 1815. He bought the lands on which he settled from Isaiah Green, who bought from Hugh Johnson, to whom a large tract had been granted by the State about 1810. Felix McGuire settled on the north fork of the creek near —— Snipes, who had settled there in 1806. Snipes was the first settler on the creek and one of the pioneers of the county. In 1813 Barney Donelson settled on what has later been known as the " Cates place." Merriman McGuire also located here. Lower down the creek Colonel Bailey located in 1807, on the place later owned by Jesse George, the first man who raised peanuts in Tennessee. The peanut crop was for years the " money crop " of the farmers of Hickman, Humphreys, and Perry Counties, there being more peanuts raised in these three counties than in all of the other counties of the State combined. From the place of its introduction on Pretty Creek, this crop spread to the surrounding districts and counties, so that in a few years almost every farmer in the above-named counties had a crop of " goobers," as peanuts were called. Tradition has it that upon one occasion George carried a load of badly mildewed peanuts to Nashville. The merchants there asked him to what particular variety these peanuts belonged. He looked innocent and informed them that they were " Big Brindles." The merchants thereupon bought from this unsophisticated countryman his peanuts for one dollar and forty cents per bushel. They probably received fifty cents per bushel for them.

At an early date John Wilburn had in his employ a man named John Phelps. When they came to settle Phelps claimed that Wilburn did not pay him all that was due him. He said that he would get even. Next morning Phelps was gone, as was also Wilburn's fine stallion. Traders carrying furs to Nashville took with them the news of Wilburn's loss, and told of the fifty dollars reward which he had offered. From this point the news spread to all of the Middle Tennessee settlements, and Phelps was soon apprehended, and he and the stallion were returned to Hickman County. The reward was paid by Wilburn, and Phelps paid the penalty of his crime. He was publicly whipped at Vernon, the county seat, by

Sheriff William Phillips the First, father of Sheriff William Phillips the Second, and grandfather of Sheriff William Phillips the Third, who now lives in Shipp's Bend.

James Barr, the pioneer Presbyterian preacher, at one time lived on Wilson's Creek. He built a gristmill near the forks of the creek, this mill being the only water mill ever operated on the creek. Evidences of this mill may yet be seen here. John H. Whitson operated a steam sawmill and gristmill on the farm of the late Col. John Parham from 1885 to 1890. Tradition says that Rev. James Barr, while he lived on Wilson's Creek, had several beautiful daughters. So beautiful were they that the creek on which they lived came to be called " Pretty Creek." The old name, " Wilson's Creek," is now seldom heard. One of the daughters of Rev. James Barr was the late Mrs. Cynthia Easley, of Gray's Bend, widow of Millington Easley; Mariah, another daughter, married William H. Carothers. Rev. James Barr was a finely educated divine, and one of the strictest of his sect. He married a sister of Charles Bowen, who was a near relative to the prominent Bowen family, of Smith County, and to Lieut. Reece Bowen, who was killed at King's Mountain.

Richard Parham, from South Carolina, located at the mouth of Pretty Creek, on the south side near a fine spring, in 1808.

On the north side of the creek, opposite Parham, Armistead Estes located. He was a peculiar character, though a prominent citizen and the owner of several slaves. One of these, Bob, is yet living at an advanced age. Bob, when a young negro, was considered one of the strongest men in the country. He was a swift runner and a good jumper. His fingers were never put to the ground under a hand-spike at the logrollings, which were then common. These logrollings were heavy tasks which the early settler had to perform in connection with the clearing of fields. After the trees were felled and cut into logs of convenient lengths, so that they could be handled by the expected force, an invitation was sent to neighbors for miles around to come on an appointed day and help " roll logs," as it was termed. At an early hour on the appointed day the settlers would commence to assemble at the appointed place. Then they would work all day long as if for wages, carrying the logs and laying them in heaps. These log heaps would later be burned. Every man did his best, knowing that all present would help him on like occasions to roll his logs. Logrollings were only one kind of pioneer reciprocity. There were quiltings and house raisings and corn shuckings, where the pioneer men and women assisted their fellows. When the day's work was over, a free-for-all dance was indulged in, and the " old Kentucky reel " was run from dark till dawn. He who could jump the highest, " sift sand " the longest, and " cut the pigeon's wing " with the most vigor was the lion of these occasions. Those were glorious, grand old days

—the days our ancestors knew. Despite the thorns of pioneer life, they gathered the wild roses that grew in the wilderness. Men were then just as gallant as now; women, just as fair. Pioneers—noble, grand, and brave—God bless their memory! They cleared the fields; we have only to till them. They penetrated the pathless wilderness; we enjoy broad highways. They kept watch at night for the savages.; we sleep in security and dream only dreams of peace.

Taylor's Creek is in the southwestern portion of the Seventh District, and flows into Duck River. It is about three miles long, and is noted for the bold spring about two and a half miles from the river. The water from this spring sinks a half mile below the spring and rises again before it reaches the river. As tradition has it, a man named Taylor came from North Carolina in 1792 and entered a large tract of land around the mouth of the creek, which was afterwards called "Taylor's Creek." Early in the present century Taylor returned from North Carolina to look after his interests here. He stopped overnight with a settler and was never again heard of. Those with whom he stopped claimed that he had returned to North Carolina. His friends in North Carolina sent fruitless inquiries here concerning him. The early settlers believed that he was slain by his host, and the dead body thrown into one of the near-by sink holes. The more superstitious claimed that Taylor's voice could be heard nightly resounding through these subterranean passages making appeals for help.

At the large spring above referred to, Henry and Andrew Stobaugh (or Stobuck) located about 1806. They were cousins of Mark Robertson Cockrill, of Davidson County. Andrew Stobaugh was a son-in-law of William Curl, who in 1806 settled on the flat lands east of Taylor's Creek, where Olinton post office was lately located. Curl was born in Chatham County, ,N. C., in 1767. He married Keziah Gamblin, who was born in North Carolina in 1770. He died in 1862, within a few steps of where he located. The house which he built eighty years ago is still standing, as is also a portion of a rock chimney built at the same time by "Black" John Warren, so called to distinguish him from another John Warren of fairer skin. When Curl first settled here the Indians from across Duck River were frequent visitors at his house. They were at all times friendly, and would bring wild honey which they would exchange for homemade soap. This they did not use in the orthodox way, but amused themselves by blowing soap bubbles. Curl, who was a saddler, sold them a fine saddle, which, mounted on a pole, they carried with them on all of their hunting and fishing expeditions. Mrs. Curl, who was always kind to them, was much loved by the savages. On one of their visits they found her seriously sick. They immediately, after the fashion of their tribe, commenced ceremonies to frighten away the evil spirits which annoyed her. With wild cries they marched around the house. Then, with deep sorrow depicted on their faces, they filed slowly through the house, each brave, as he passed, placing his hand on the sick woman's brow. Curl, in 1819, made a journey back to North Carolina on horseback to assist in the settlement of his deceased father's affairs. He left home in October and returned in the following February. William Curl was a prominent citizen of the county, and was one of the first magistrates of Hickman County, holding the position while Vernon was the county seat. When he had held this office as long as he wished, he was succeeded by Thompson Wright, the father of Bartlett and "Blue John" Wright. Jared Curl, a son of William Curl, was for many years a magistrate in the Seventh District. He lived to be more than one hundred years old, and died a few years ago in the Ninth District, at the home of his daughter, the widow of Dr. David D. Flowers. Jared Curl, together with Thomas Uslam, John Richardson, and others, enlisted under Captain Porter, of Vernon, and were present at the battle of New Orleans. With them went Dr. Schmitton, a German, who has descendants in neighboring counties. Local tradition makes him the hero of an oft-told story. It is said that his prayer in broken English just before the battle was: " Lord, if you are not for us, don't be against us; just stand aside and see one of the d—nest fights you ever saw." Keziah Curl, a daughter of William Curl, married Elijah Frazier, who came from Dickson County. She became the mother of Jared C. and William G. Fra-

zier.   Judge Curl, of Arkansas, is a descendant of
the pioneer, William Curl.

William and James Holmes located on Taylor's
Creek below Curl in 1808.   A young man named
Holmes fell dead at a dance on this creek in 1810.

One of the first schools, if not the first school, in
the Seventh District was taught by George Y. Peyton near William Curl's in 1812.

The early settlers in the Seventh and Eighth Districts would go in small companies with pack horses
and carry their corn to a mill on Yellow Creek, in
Dickson County, forty miles away.   They carried
their rifles as a precaution against robbers and wild
beasts as well as to provide themselves with food.
These hardy pioneers, after a trip of a week, would
return home with their corn ground into meal, and
bringing with them a good supply of turkeys and
venison, and frequently bear meat.   There was another way by which their corn was converted into
meal.   The shelled corn would be placed in a mortar
made by burning a hole in a stump or log.   A heavy
wooden pestle was then suspended over the mortar
and attached to a sweep.   By regular movements of
this sweep the corn was pounded into meal, the
coarser portions being used as hominy.

The mill near the mouth of Pine River, known
as " Montgomery's mill," was built in 1830 by an
ingenious workman, Hugh Johnson.   The money
necessary for the purchase of the machinery was fur-

nished by Vernon's Irish merchant, Robert Sheegog, who eventually became the owner of the mill. He sold it for $3,000 to John Montgomery, who came from Charlotte, Dickson County, in 1840. Montgomery was a lawyer, and was one of the pioneers of his profession at Charlotte. Hugh Johnson, in addition to being a millwright, was a clock maker. While operating this mill he made a number of clocks of the tall, old-fashioned kind. Montgomery's mill was erected near the face of a high bluff from which burst a stream of water which furnished the power. This stream is almost Pine River in its entirety, as most of its waters sink over a mile above and come through a subterranean passage to this point. That portion of the river which does not enter this underground channel flows southward. It abruptly strikes a towering bluff, changes its course from south to northwest, and flows almost parallel with Duck River for about two miles, until it reaches the point at which the waters of the two rivers are united. On the high strip of land lying between the rivers are located the celebrated mounds built by some prehistoric race. If these mounds were erected for defense, the location is an ideal one. On two sides are high bluffs which could not have been scaled by an attacking force, while the remaining sides are protected by earthworks. The great age of these mounds is made manifest by the large trees now growing upon them. Near the mounds are a number of graves. Near the base of the bluff on the Duck River side is a fine spring, reached from above by the " Winding Stairs," a series of roughly cut steps.

In 1806 Robert Bowen, father of Robert and Charles Bowen, located on Pine River. Charles Bowen bought a large tract of land near what is now known as the " Hassell place " from Mrs. Orlean Smith, in whose name 640 acres of land had been entered in 1806. Charles Bowen lived on the east side of the river; Robert Bowen, on the west, between the places where David and Thomas Webb now live. The heirs of Robert Bowen sold these lands to William H. Carothers, who in 1845 erected a cotton gin at the Thomas Webb place. Charles Bowen married Naomi Carothers, a sister of Andrew, Samuel, and William Carothers, and an aunt of William H. Carothers. Narcissa, a daughter of Charles Bowen, married a lawyer named Howry, who lived at Centerville, the ceremony being performed by Eli Hornbeak. About 1832 Charles Bowen sold his lands to John Hassell and moved to Mississippi, where his son-in-law, Howry, joined him a few years later. John Hassell was the father of Hardeman, Joseph, and Hiram Hassell.

In 1807 three brothers—Andrew, Samuel, and William Carothers, of Georgia—located on Pine River. Samuel Carothers bought the Montgomery place in 1810 from Charles Bowen. He married Naomi Brown. Andrew was a Primitive Baptist preacher, and later lived on Sugar Creek, in the Eighth District. He was the father of William

Howell Carothers, who was at the beginning of
the Civil War the largest slaveholder in Hickman
County. He was also a prosperous farmer, and
speculated largely in lands, hogs, and mules. He
carried large droves of hogs and mules overland to
Holly Springs and other Mississippi points. He
rendered great service to the farmers of the surrounding counties by making a market for their surplus
stock. He at one time, in copartnership with William Easley ("Long Jaw Bill"), owned and operated
Oakland Furnace, on Mill Creek. He was at one
time sheriff of Hickman County. At the close of
the Civil War, his slaves all free, and a stanch
friend of the Confederacy, having a large lot of
worthless Confederate currency, he found himself,
like a great many other Southern men, a financial
wreck. Undismayed by disaster, he emigrated to
Coryell County, Texas. He there bought a farm,
and by hard work paid for it. He died there in
1880. He served several years as tax collector for
Coryell County.

John Lowe, the father of Jesse and Maj. Lewis
Lowe, in 1815 located on Pine River above where the
Reynoldsburg road crosses it, and between the Hugh
Johnson and Orlean Smith lands. Jesse Lowe mar-
ried Jennie Carothers, a sister of William H. Ca-
rothers.

Joseph Webb, who was born in York County, S. C.,
in March, 1797, came to Cathey's Creek, in Maury
County, and then to Hickman County, where he mar-

ried Elizabeth Carothers, a sister of William H. Carothers. He settled on the Smith lands. His house being on the Reynoldsburg road, and he the most hospitable of hosts, his became one of the most popular of the wayside inns along this road. Here was the scene of a stirring incident in the winter of 1863. A troop of Federal cavalry was in the county capturing Confederate soldiers at home on furloughs. They pretended, however, to be in search of the guerrilla bands of Henon Cross, Duval McNairy, and James McLaughlin. On the day referred to they had captured Capt. John H. Coleman, Willis Turner, and others, and had stopped at " Uncle Joe " Webb's to spend the night. Just about dusk, and while the soldiers and their prisoners were scattered about the yard, the hurrying of hoofs was heard just down the road, and a lone horseman galloped to the front gate about thirty feet away. He called out a demand for an immediate surrender and fired his revolver rapidly into the crowd. Before the one hundred men had recovered from the disorder into which one man had thrown them, James McLaughlin, who had encountered odds of one hundred to one in an attempt to assist the prisoners to escape, had disappeared. Evidences of this daring dash may yet be seen in the form of bullets from McLaughlin's pistol embedded in the wall of the house. After McLaughlin had gone his way in safety, one of the gallant Federals retrieved the fortunes of the day by sending a musket ball through both the arms of

Captain Coleman, a defenseless prisoner, who was making no attempt to escape. From this same house, upon another occasion, eleven Federal cavalrymen went in pursuit of Duval McNairy. McNairy left the main road and ascended a steep, rough point. When he reached the top, he turned and discharged both barrels of his shotgun at his pursuers, wounding ten out of eleven. He, however, did not stop to learn the result of his shot.

On the east side of Pine River nearly opposite where the waters sink is a branch, called "Jacob's Pillow," so called on account of a large stone in the middle of the valley down which the stream runs. Near this rock the Presbyterians and Methodists held camp meetings in 1848, 1849, and 1850. In 1861 Nathan Hickman erected a tannery near this point.

Two miles above Jacob's Pillow, Bird's Creek flows into Pine River from the east. This creek is named for William Bird, who located near its mouth in 1807. Bird was in the battle of New Orleans, and during the engagement his rifle became useless. He immediately rolled over the breastworks and secured a gun from a prostrate enemy. After the battle he went out on the field over which the British had charged, and soon returned with a fine saddle, which was later identified as the property of Sir Edward Packenham, the dead leader of the English forces.

At the head of Bird's Creek, Stuart Warren settled in 1807. He owned the present site of Goodrich

Furnace. He was the father of John, Goodloe, and David B. Warren. The latter was at one time clerk of the County Court. Stuart Warren's three daughters married three prominent citizens of the county— Pleasant Walker, Jack Huddleston, and James D. Easley. The first-named was county judge and a member of the Legislature; the second was sheriff; and the third was for many years County Court clerk, and was also a member of the Legislature.

John Muirhead located at the forks of the creek where John H. Barr now lives, and erected a mill and distillery just below the forks of the creek.

Elisha Green located near the mouth of Bird's Creek in 1807. A near-by neighbor was a man named Dezell.

John Hulett taught school on Bird's Creek in 1836, and Harper taught here in 1838.

Dr. Samuel Sebastian at an early date lived in the Pine River valley below Vernon and above the mouth of Bird's Creek. He was one of the pioneer physicians of this district; another was Dr. Hailey. In after years were Drs. Lewis, Shenault, Douglass, Hunt, Hall, Puckett, William Montgomery, Thomas D. Thompson, and others.

At the Stuart Warren place, on Bird's Creek, in 1812, lived William Carter, a brother-in-law of Asa Thompson. Carter lived here until his death, in 1869. He was in the War of 1812, and was out in the first Seminole War (1819). After his death his heirs sold the lands to the Standard Charcoal Company, which company in 1882 erected Goodrich Furnace and wood alcohol works. These were later operated by the Warner Iron Company and the Southern Iron Company. They are now, after a period of several years' inactivity, being operated by the Tennessee Iron Company. The village, post office, and furnace are named for Levin D. Goodrich, a son-in-law of Dr. Bellefield Carter, who was once prominent in Middle Tennessee as the owner of several furnaces in Dickson and Hickman Counties. Before the Civil War, Goodrich was the manager of Ætna Furnace, in the Eleventh District. " Lev." Goodrich, as he was familiarly known, did more than any other man toward putting on foot the plans which in 1878 and 1879 resulted in the commencement of the building of the Nashville and Tuscaloosa Railroad, now the Centerville branch of the Nashville, Chattanooga and St. Louis Railway. Then, too, he did more than any other man in securing the rebuilding of old furnaces and the building of new ones in the county. When the first train was run over the Nashville and Tuscaloosa road to Centerville, Lev. Goodrich was seated on the cowcatcher in front of the engine. He has gone to his final reward, but he deserved a front seat on the first train, and deserves a prominent place in the history of Hickman County. About a mile north of Goodrich Furnace are the ore mines, formerly called the " Oakland ore banks," now the Nunnelly ore banks. These mines were operated during the same time as the enterprises at

Goodrich.   Operations were suspended at the same
time (1893), and are just now being resumed.

Near where the railroad crosses Mill Creek is a
small station—Graham Station.   Below the railroad
trestle is a large dam across Mill Creek.   From this
point water was formerly forced over a hill two hundred feet high, and carried in pipes to the ore washer
at the Nunnelly ore banks, one and a half miles away.
One-half mile below Graham Station may yet be seen
the ruins of the once-famous Oakland Furnace.
This furnace was built in 1854 by Felix Studdart,
Blount Fowlkes, and William H. Bratton.   This
furnace was erected at the place where before this
had stood the Lower Forge of Mill Creek.   The ore
for the furnace was taken from the Oakland ore
banks, now the Nunnelly ore banks, and conveyed by
wagons to the furnace.   The furnace and ore banks
gave employment to many citizens, and, in addition
to free labor, the operators hired from the neighboring slaveholders their surplus slaves for periods
ranging from one to twelve months.   The negro
slaves employed here were allowed to visit their families on Saturday nights and Sundays.   However,
there were instances where some of the slaves remained away from their families for the entire period of twelve months.

Near the site of this furnace, in 1806, a mill was
built by the united efforts of the settlers.   The erection of the mill was superintended by Charles Muirhead, of Bird's Creek, and it was operated under his

direction. Two years later William Hale, from East Tennessee, converted this temporary mill into a permanent one. A good dam was erected instead of the brush dam. This was the first mill built in Hickman County, and from it this creek took its name. Before its erection the temporary structure built by the settlers (the Muirhead mill) had not a sufficient output to supply the demands of the settlers, and they had been compelled to go to Yellow Creek, in Dickson County, as narrated in previous pages. Near the mouth of Mill Creek, near where T. D. Field now lives, Adam Wilson cultivated the first crop of corn cultivated by a white man within the present limits of Hickman County. This was in 1806, and Wilson made no clearing, save the cutting away of the cane.

At the mouth of Mill Creek, where Thomas D. Field now lives, William Holt in 1838 built a gristmill, sawmill, cotton gin, and spinning factory. Holt owned and lived on these lands, and was for years a prominent citizen of this section of the county. His daughter, Madaline, married Andrew Carothers, a brother of William H. Carothers, the ceremony being performed by Jesse Fuqua, the Primitive Baptist preacher. Andrew Carothers had lost one eye as a result of fever. He moved to Mississippi, where he died. A daughter, Elizabeth, married Dr. Elisha Green Thompson.

Thomas Thompson came in 1806 from York District, S. C., and settled one and a half miles south of Vernon and to the north of Bird's Creek. Thomas

Thompson was the father of Asa, William, John, James, and Elisha Thompson. His son, Asa Thompson, who was born in South Carolina in 1798, lived near the old homestead until his death, in 1877. Asa Thompson married Mary Carothers, a daughter of Andrew Carothers, the Baptist preacher. Two sons of Asa Thompson—Drs. Elisha Green Thompson and Thomas D. Thompson—have been prominent physicians of the county. Dr. E. G. Thompson was for two terms the deputy of Circuit Court Clerk William G. Clagett, and was for two terms Circuit Court Clerk. He was also at one time Clerk and Master of the Chancery Court at Centerville, and filled out the unexpired term of Dr. A. J. Lowe, who died while a member of the State Legislature. Dr. T. D. Thompson was aid-de-camp to Gen. James E. Raines, and served in that capacity until the death of General Raines, at Murfreesboro. William C. Thompson, another son of Asa Thompson, held several important district offices, and was at the time of his death a member of the County Court, of which body he had for years been a member. Another son, John B. Thompson, who saw service in the Civil War, although he was several years below the regulation age, is at present a prominent citizen of this district, as is also Dr. Thomas D. Thompson. Two other sons of Asa Thompson—Andrew and Stuart—lost their lives while soldiers in the Confederate Army. A son of the former, William D. Thompson, at present a citizen of Centerville, was twice elected register of the county, and by majorities among the largest ever given a candidate for office in Hickman County. Elizabeth Thompson, daughter of Asa Thompson, married Joseph Herndon, who died while in the Confederate Army. Their only child, Mollie Herndon, married James F. Martin, the founder of the Hickman Pioneer, established in 1878, at Centerville, the first paper published in Hickman County. Susan Thompson, daughter of Asa Thompson, married Rev. William Whitson. One of their sons, John H. Whitson, in connection with Horatio C. Thompson, a son of William C. Thompson, at one time published the Hickman Pioneer, succeeding S. L. Neely. Neely purchased the paper from Martin, who had successfully conducted it for a number of years. Whitson and Thompson sold the Pioneer to J. H. Russell, son of Ferdinand B. Russell. The Pioneer, a few years after this, suspended publication. About this time Horatio C. Thompson established the Hickman County News, which he published for several years. Thompson is now editor of the Savannah Courier. Thompson was succeeded as editor of the News by S. S. Speer, of Georgia, and he by W. P. Clark, who sold to Stockard & Ozment, the present publishers. Dr. W. T. Childress, of Terrell, Texas, married Catherine, a daughter of Asa Thompson. After her death he married her sister, Mrs. Elizabeth Herndon.

Richard Craig, the father of John, Solomon, and Elijah Craig, was one of the early settlers on Bird's

Creek.   John Craig married a daughter of Andrew
Carothers.

James Singleton taught school just below Vernon
in 1832.   At this point, one mile below Vernon, was
erected the first schoolhouse and church constructed
in the county.   It was erected by the Primitive Baptist preacher, Andrew Carothers.   The location of
this building is now marked by a walnut tree in the
graveyard below Vernon.   In this graveyard Andrew Carothers is buried near the scenes of his former labors.   The Primitive Baptist Church was the
strong church of early days, but among the prominent preachers of the pioneer days was James Barr,
the Presbyterian.   The Presbyterian Church has
never been a strong church in this district, but, supported by it, the Methodist Church has supplanted
the Baptist Church in the Seventh District.   The
Christian Church has in recent years become one of
the prominent churches of the district.   Rev. Lee
Thurman has in recent years preached the doctrine
of entire sanctification, and has made many converts
in this section of the county.

The date of the first permanent settlement at Vernon is not known.   The large spring at the foot of
the hill was, before the place was permanently settled, a stopping place for hunters and trappers.   In
1800 James Wilson and Joseph Lynn laid a land
warrant here, and a few years later they, together
with Garrett Lane, William Hale, and Dr. William
Brown, came from East Tennessee and permanent-

ly settled here. In 1808 Carey Pope settled here. In 1812 Samuel D. McLaughlin, who had been a schoolmate of Gov. William Carroll, lived at Vernon. When Garrett Lane and associates came here this territory was embraced in Dickson County. Joseph Lynn was Vernon's first hotel keeper, and John Hulett its first merchant. When Hickman County was created and Vernon made the county seat, a hewn-log jail and a hewn-log courthouse were erected. When the county seat was removed to Centerville, in 1823, the courthouse was torn down and removed to the new county seat. A new log jail was erected, and the old one was allowed to remain at Vernon. However, before these buildings were completed, the first court of the county was held on the third Monday in January, 1808, at the house of William Joslin, who lived near the present site of Pinewood. In 1809 the courthouse had not yet been completed, and the court met at the house of James Wilson, on whose lands Vernon was located. William Stone was then clerk of the court, and tradition has it that when he was once fined for contempt of court, he coolly refused to enter the fine and the incident was closed. Stone removed from Vernon to Jones' Creek, in Dickson County. After a lapse of ninety years, it is difficult to learn anything as to the proceedings of this pioneer court. The paper of which the following is a copy was found among the papers of the late William G. Clagett, and it is probably the only portion of the records of that court now in existence:

" State of Tennessee) To the Sheriff of Hickman
   Hickman County   )   County Greeting

Where as here to fore to wit at October Term of
the court of pleas and quarter Sessions for the county
of Hickman Richard Compton Sued out a writ of
capias ad respondendom against James Peery commanding the Sheriff of Hickman County to take the
Body of James Peery and have him before the court
of pleas and quarter sessions to be holden for the
county of Hickman at the House of William Joslin
on the third monday of January then to answer the
said plaintiff of a plea of covenant broken to his dam-
age one thousand Dollars &.C. upon which writ the
Sheriff made the following return to wit) not found
Signed William Phillips S H C. Where upon it is
ordered that a Judicial Attachment Issue against the
Estate of the Said Defendant according to act of
Assembly in that case made and provided—

These are therefore to command you, that you,
Attach the Estate of the said James Peery if to be
found in your county or so much there of repleviable
on Security as shall be of Value Sufficient to Satisfy
the said Damages according to the above complaint
and such Estate so attached in your hands to secure
or so to provide that the same may be Liable to further proceeding there on to be had at the court to be
held for the county of Hickman at house of William
Easleys on the third monday of July next so as to
compell the said James Peery to appear and answer
the above complaint of the said Richard Compton,

when and where you Shall make known to the said court how you have executed this writ Witness William Stone clerk of our said court at office this third monday of April in the year 1809 and the 33rd year of the American Independence—

William Stone C C."

On the back of this are the following entries:

" Richard Compton
            vs   } Judicial Attachment.
James Peery

To July Term 1809
Isd 23rd May 1809."

" Came to hand May the 24 1809 leved May the 27 1809 on 500 [Here " ten thousand " is written and a line drawn through it] acres of land where James Peery Senr and James Peery Junr now lives on Leatherwood Creek of Duck river

Wm. Phillips, shff hickman county."

All of the above is legibly written, and, considering the lack of educational facilities at that time, the number of mistakes in spelling and punctuation is surprisingly small. The William Easley at whose house the court met in July, 1809, is the William Easley referred to in the sketch of the Sixth District. He lived where Dr. Thomas Cash now lives, and represented Hickman County in the Legislature in 1815, 1817, and after the resignation of Robert E. C. Dougherty in 1819. The court met at the homes of citizens until the courthouse at Vernon was completed. Three of these citizens were William Joslin, James Wilson, and William Easley. After the establishment of circuit courts, in 1809, Judge Parry W. Humphreys held court at Vernon. Robert Estes was the first clerk of this court. James Wilson lived in what is now the Seventh District. After the erection of the public buildings and until the county seat was moved to Centerville, Vernon was a prosperous frontier town, rivaling in its magnificence Charlotte and Reynoldsburg. Among the prominent lawyers who attended court here were Felix Grundy, A. O. P. Nicholson, Cave Johnson, John Montgomery, and Elijah Walker. After the real court had adjourned, the moot court commenced its sessions, and much was the amusement furnished to judge, bar, and visitors. Parties were tried for all kinds and conditions of offenses, both real and imaginary, and the punishment was almost uniformly a fine of sufficient amount to buy liquid refreshments for judge and jury, lawyers, litigants, and spectators. When the docket had been cleared late at night, the moot court adjourned, if sober, which was not often the case; otherwise it scattered.

In 1817 Major Hornbeak lived near where J. H. Shipp now lives, and operated a stillhouse on the opposite side of the river. He supplied Vernon with whisky and brandy. He was the father of Pleasant Hornbeak, Mrs. William G. Clagett, and Mrs. Samuel B. Moore.

The pioneer, Garrett Lane, lived to a good old age,

and to the last retained his love for outdoor sports. In 1850 he was the promoter of a " gander pulling." A live gander was suspended by its feet, and the contestants, mounted on horseback and riding rapidly, tried to carry away in their hands the token of victory in the form of the gander's head. Jones Easley broke the gander's neck, but Claiborne B. Dotson wrenched off its head and won the prize of eighty dollars in gold. Old Vernon has been the scene of perhaps more " fist-and-skull," old-fashioned, rough-and-tumble fights than any place in Tennessee. The most serious of these was the fight, in 1847, between Mills Eason and William Holt, during which the latter lost an eye. Robert Sheegog sold goods in Vernon in 1836; Carothers & Easley, in 1845; William Balthrop and John Primm, in 1850; and Marable Reeves, in 1855. Robert Sheegog, who was born in Ireland, died in Texas in 1879. T. N. Carter ran a saloon here for a number of years, as did also Solomon George. George was a saddler and a good citizen. William Gravitt was a good saddle and harness maker. Among the good citizens of this place were Col. B. B. Satterfield and Andrew Walker. Colonel Satterfield was at one time a merchant here. Philip Maroney, Sanford Bros., A. I. Brown, Miles Mays, and W. S. Nunnelly have sold goods here at different times since the Civil War. Vernon was almost entirely destroyed by Federals in 1864, and the burned portions were never rebuilt; so it does not now appear as did Old Vernon when it was new.

In 1829 Hawkins Ward taught school at the mouth
of Taylor's Creek.   Ward was from North Carolina,
and was journeying westward.   He was coming down
Duck River in a canoe, and stopped overnight with
John Scott, who soon learned from his conversation
that he was a well-educated man.   Ward was employed to teach school, and continued teaching until
other emigrants from North Carolina brought the
news that Ward had a deserted wife in the Old State.
Ward immediately renewed his journey westward.
John and Thomas Thompson were teachers in this
district in the early days.   Bartlett Wright taught on
the ridge west of Pretty Creek and three miles west
of Vernon in 1855.   At Vernon many good teachers
have taught, several of whom were ladies.   Miss
Kate Guthrie taught near where W. S. Nunnelly now
lives.   Miss Bettie Osborn, in 1849, taught in Tem-
perance Hall at Vernon, and later in the valley south
of the village.   In this valley Mrs. Elizabeth Nunnelly taught school prior to her marriage to Lawson
H. Nunnelly.   She was of Irish parentage, refined,
intelligent, and well educated.   She lives to-day, far
beyond the allotted threescore years and ten; and
when she goes away, Hickman County will lose one
of its noblest women, one who has few equals and no
superiors.   Later Misses Emily and Mariah Sheegog
taught here.   The former taught at Vernon for many
years; the latter afterwards taught at Centerville,
and then went to Maury County.   In later years
Misses Nora Bly, Lula Crutcher, Genie Crutcher,

and Dollie George have taught here. Some of the men who taught at Vernon were James H. Fowlkes, Gabriel Fowlkes, and "Bunk" White. One of the best schools taught here was that taught by W. D. Askins in recent years.

Among the early magistrates of the district were Garrett Lane, William Curl, Thompson Wright, and Jared Curl. William Bird was chairman of the County Court from 1840 to 1846. Capt. E. W. Easley has held this position several times in recent years. Some of the magistrates of later years were William Gravitt, Jesse James, Solomon George, William C. Thompson, and J. T. Webb. The present incumbents are E. W. Easley and J. T. Duncan. Some of the constables of the district were William C. Thompson, W. D. Thompson, W. H. Stuart, and John F. Lawson. The present incumbent is W. H. Betty. W. D. Hedge, of Taylor's Creek, was a deputy under Sheriff J. A. Harvill.

There have been a number of violent deaths in this district. William Balthrop was drowned in Pine River, near Vernon, in 1850; a white man named Hodges was drowned above Vernon in 1866; and a negro, Adam Spence, was drowned below Vernon in 1895. In 1864 David Seymour and Howell Luten, a boy of about fifteen years, were murdered in their beds. These murders occurred on Pretty Creek, two miles west of Vernon, and the object was evidently robbery. Seymour was dead when found by neighbors, but the boy lived in an unconscious state for several days. They were killed with an ax. The murderer was never apprehended, and, amid the stirring events of that year, the murder was soon almost forgotten. In 1885 William ("Buck") Brown killed William T. Easley, at Graham. In 1886 Absalom Cathey was killed at Goodrich by his brother-in-law, Samuel Devault. About this time, and at the same place, Henry Warren killed "Buck" Brown. At Goodrich, in 1887, Alfred Dunn killed Walter Oliver. At Goodrich, in 1891, James Lawson killed two negroes, Anthony Lockridge and Henry Crutcher. About this time Samuel Phillips, a negro, killed Wade Carothers, another negro, near Nunnelly; and William Phillips, a negro, was killed at Vernon by Vernon Hedge.

During the Civil War the Seventh District was the scene of several thrilling incidents, in addition to those already mentioned. This district was much frequented by the band of independent scouts, or bushwhackers, under command of Henon Cross, a son of Professor Cross, of Nashville. Cross had associated with him Duval McNairy, of Nashville, and James McLaughlin, of Maryland. They first came as refugees to Hickman County, where their pleasant manners and gentlemanly deportment assured for them a hearty welcome. Soon tiring of inactivity, they gathered around them a band of adventurous spirits and proceeded to wage war against the prowling bands of Federals that often passed this way. In Cross' command were all kinds of men—

good, bad, and indifferent. Those whom they especially desired to fight were a similarly organized band of Federal sympathizers, the Perry County jayhawkers. In July, 1864, a company of these, encamped at Centerville, concluded to visit Pinewood Mills in search of booty. On their way to Pinewood they treated harshly a number of citizens whom they met. One of these was Lafayette Turbeville. They robbed him of his pocketknife and tobacco, and made by force an exchange of hats with him, in which Turbeville was badly beaten. Finally, adding insult to injury, they forced him to take the oath of allegiance. He went that night to the camp of Cross, who immediately commenced to take steps toward attacking them on their return from Pinewood on the following day. This he did in a hollow through which the old Centerville road passed one-half mile south of Vernon. Cross took them by surprise, firing upon their flank from his place of concealment in the bushes. At the same time Turbeville and McLaughlin charged from the rear, yelling and firing their pistols. This stampeded those who had not already been shot, and a wild chase ensued from there to Centerville, eight miles away. The jayhawkers lost eleven in killed and wounded, about a dozen horses and mules, and two wagons loaded with flour and other spoils gathered at Pinewood. Turbeville recovered his hat. Campbell Kimbrough, a citizen of Hickman County, who had joined the jayhawkers as a guide, was mortally wounded. He was taken to the home of Dorsey Weatherspoon, on Taylor's Creek, where he died. Cross' party sustained no loss.

In December, 1864, the Federal troops were being concentrated at Nashville. The Federal General, Cooper, was at Johnsonville, and, having had communication with Nashville cut off by a raid along the Northwestern Railroad by the Confederate General, Lyon, he marched to Nashville by the way of Centerville and Columbia. He came the Reynoldsburg road, and had met with no enemy when he reached Pine River and encamped for the night near H. H. Hassell's and Joseph Webb's. During the night Cross gathered his little band and determined to annoy them on their march to Centerville. Next morning, soon after the Federals had left the valley and had entered the woodlands on the ridge, they were attacked by Cross' men, who would fire and retreat, only to appear a few minutes later in an attack on the flank or the rear. During one of these attacks Brownlee Cross, a brother of Henon Cross, was seriously wounded. The Federal loss was one killed, several wounded, and fifteen captured.

In 1864 Captain Cross was captured by a detachment of Federals, piloted by Alex. Puckett, a citizen of Hickman County. At the time of his capture Cross was attending church at Briggs' Chapel, near the Montgomery Mills. Capture in this case meant death in a few hours, but Cross walked about seemingly unconcerned, closely guarded by his captors. Cross came close to where his horse stood hitched.

With one bound he mounted his horse, broke the limb
to which it was tied, leaned over to the opposite side
from his late captors, and escaped under a heavy fire,
his horse making its way with safety to itself and
rider up a steep hillside. It was this and other daring deeds by their leaders that made the people almost
forget some of the questionable acts of some of the
bushwhackers. Moses Wright, a slave, who was always faithful, was present on this occasion, wearing
a coat on which were a number of Confederate buttons. These buttons were cut off by the Federals.
For this act, Moses, so he said, gave Alex. Puckett
" a good cussin'." He, however, qualified his boast
by the statement that it was some hours after Puckett
and his Federals had gone before the vials of his profanity were uncorked.

CHAPTER XI.

THE EIGHTH DISTRICT.

T HE Eighth District is bounded on the north by Humphreys County; on the east, by the Seventh District; on the south, by the Ninth District; and on the west, by Humphreys and Perry Counties. This district lies in the extreme northwestern portion of the county, and includes a portion of the Duck River valley. Sugar Creek is the principal stream, which lies entirely in this district. It flows into Duck River from the east, and is about eight miles in length. It has several branches, one of which is known by any of the three names: the " Coleman Branch," the " Barren Fork," or the " South Fork." Through the valley of this fork of Sugar Creek runs one of the first roads opened in Hickman County— the Reynoldsburg road. This road ran from Reynoldsburg, which was in Humphreys County about two miles below the present site of Johnsonville, to Vernon, and later to Centerville. It entered Hickman County at the head of Ocmulgee Hollow, and ran down that hollow to where it intersects Sugar Creek, about one mile below the forks of the creek. It followed the valley of the creek, running in an easterly direction, until it reached Lee's Furnace, where it left the main valley of the creek and ran up the Coleman Branch to its head. Striking the ridge, it ran to Vernon. Later, when Centerville was built, the Reynoldsburg road forked at what is now called the " Rossen place," and the Centerville fork ran to Pine River, which it crossed between the Webb and Hassell places, and thence to Centerville, crossing Duck River at the Griner Ford. The place where it crossed Pine River is no longer a fording place, and the old Reynoldsburg road is now for miles no longer a public highway. The town which gave it its name is now only a memory. When Humphreys County, named for Judge Parry W. Humphreys, was organized, it included all of what is now Humphreys and Benton Counties. In 1812 the county seat was located on the Tennessee River below the present site of Johnsonville, and named " Reynoldsburg " in honor of Congressman James B. Reynolds, who lived at Clarksville. In 1836 Benton County, named for Thomas H. Benton, was established, and the county seat of Humphreys County was moved to near the center of the county. The new county seat was named " Waverly " by Hon. Stephen C. Pavatt, who was an admirer of Scott's " Waverly Novels." The decline of Reynoldsburg was swift and sure, and the thriving little town, situated on the Nashville and Memphis stage road, which at one time ranked with Vernon and Charlotte among the prominent towns of Middle Tennessee, is now indeed a " Deserted Village," whose almost-forgotten location is marked alone by its dilapidated brick courthouse, which for years has been used as a residence. So also has the glory departed from Grattan's Grove, at Clarksville, where lived the genial Irishman, James B. Reynolds, known as " Count Reynolds."

In 1808 Andrew Carothers, the Primitive Baptist preacher, located on the Coleman Branch of Sugar Creek, at what has for many years been known as the " Coleman place." Near where he located is a fine spring, at which the numerous travelers over the Reynoldsburg road stopped to quench their thirst. Jesse Sparks, father of James, Hale, Absalom, and Jesse Sparks, and grandfather of J. J. Sparks, for many years lived on the farm adjoining the Coleman place. Samuel Walker lived on Sugar Creek as early as 1807.

In the Wilkins Hollow, which runs into Duck River above the mouth of Sugar Creek, there lived the pioneer Baptist preacher, Jesse Fuqua, Sr., father of the Baptist preacher, Jesse Fuqua, Jr. He was loved best and honored most by those who knew him best. His faith was strong in his power to wield the " divining rod," with which he located underground streams of water. Wells, when dug, would always reveal the presence of water at the places he designated. Fuqua came to this county with Solomon Jones, and first located on Big Spring Creek, in the Sixth District.

Above Lee's Old Furnace, and on the main fork of Sugar Creek, William Thornton and William Forrester now live. The line between their farms divides one of the finest springs on this creek. Here at this spring was located one of the blockhouses to which the early settlers repaired for protection against roving bands of Indians. The farm on which this blockhouse was located was for many years the property of William Nicks, who settled there about 1830.

One mile above the blockhouse is the juncture of the north and middle forks of Sugar Creek. The creek was named " Sugar Creek " on account of the large number of sugar maples which grow in the valley of this stream, from its source to its mouth. The products of these sugar orchards were a source of revenue to the pioneers. A small basin was chopped in the trunk of the trees. This was called " tapping." From below, a small hole was bored into this basin and a cane inserted. Through this cane the sap of the tree would stream into a wooden trough two feet long. The sap—called " sugar water "— thus collected was carried in buckets and pails to the " sugar camp," where it was boiled down to sugar, which was placed in cups, saucers, and plates to cool. From these primitive molds it was taken ready for the market.

At the head of the Middle Fork of Sugar Creek, Leonard Claiborne, from South Carolina, settled in 1809. In 1820 Samuel Dunaway came from South Carolina and married Mariam Claiborne, a daughter of Leonard Claiborne. Their sons were Giles, Thomas, Benjamin, Mark, Hiram, and Daniel Dunaway. Giles Dunaway lived to be ninety years of age,

and died a bachelor. Samuel and Claiborne Dunaway, sons of Thomas Dunaway, now live on Sugar
Creek near where their ancestors settled.

The North Fork of Sugar Creek was settled by
Reeves and Forrester. Jonathan Reeves, Sr., was
a prominent citizen, and he and Obadiah Turner,
Sr., were the only slaveholders on the creek above
Lee's Furnace. Richard Forrester, from South Carolina, the father of Silas and Hezekiah Forrester, settled here in 1815. Silas Forrester was the father of
Madison, Carroll, and Silas, Jr. Isaiah Forrester
was the father of Alfred, Stephen, and Willie Forrester. Lucinda, a daughter of the pioneer, Richard Forrester, married William Turner, a brother
of Obadiah Turner, Sr. Alston Moppin, of South
Carolina, was one of the first settlers here.

In 1830 Samuel B. Lee and James Gould entered
and purchased several thousand acres of mineral and
timber lands in Hickman and Humphreys Counties.
On Sugar Creek, just below where it is entered by
Coleman's Branch, they located their furnace, the
old-fashioned stack standing there now. The charcoal for this furnace was burned in the old-fashioned
coal pits, and hundreds of laborers, white and black,
were employed in cutting wood in the adjacent for-
ests and burning it into charcoal. When the furnace
was being built here it was thought that in the hill
against which it stood there was a rich deposit of ore.
When they came to investigate it further, this was
found to be not so, and they were compelled to go

near Vernon for ore, which was found in abundance near Pretty Creek. They obtained their ore from two banks—one south of the Reynoldsburg road, one and a half miles from Vernon; the other on the north side of Pretty Creek, three-fourths of a mile from Vernon. The ore was taken from the earth with picks and shovels, placed in ox carts and horse wagons, and conveyed to the furnace, nine miles away. This was a slow method of mining and transporting, compared with the steam shovels and railways of the present day. The heavy expense which attached to these primitive methods, together with the heavy expense of transporting the products, soon caused the abandonment of this furnace. The pig-iron products of the old Oakland Furnace, on Mill Creek in the Seventh District, were carried overland to the boat landing at the lower end of the Young Mayberry lands, in the First District. From this point they were conveyed by flatboats down Duck River. From Lee & Gould's furnace, on Sugar Creek, the pig iron was carried by wagons to the mouth of the creek and placed on flatboats. These boats were flat-bottomed boats constructed by skilled designers. They were about sixty-five feet long and twenty-five feet wide, and would carry several tons. When a boat was loaded and ready to start on the voyage down to the Tennessee River, some trusty man of nerve, who was acquainted with the channel of the river, the nature and strength of the current, and the different and difficult points which must be passed on the voyage,

was selected as captain and pilot. He selected as
many men as he thought necessary, and after taking
on board a good cable, some bread, some jerked venison, dried beef, or a side of bacon, he started on his
journey and began his lookout for dangers ahead.
Sometimes they floated safely into the Tennessee
River and on to their destination; sometimes they
foundered at " The Hackle; " sometimes they sank
in the " White Horse Bend; " and sometimes the
treacherous sucks and whirls of the " Paint Rock
Bend " claimed the boat's cargo, which, once at the
bottom, was seldom recovered. When one of these
boats sprung a leak, the pumps were worked rapidly,
for the heavily laden boats filled quickly, and to be
on a sinking metal boat was hazardous in the extreme.
" Uncle Al." Lowe, an aged negro who is yet living,
on one of these trips years ago misunderstood the ex-
clamation, " Look out! " for the order, "Jump out! "
He obeyed with alacrity, jumped about twenty feet
from the boat, went to the bottom of the river, arose,
and saw with surprise that the boat was still floating
in safety and that he alone of all the crew had obeyed
the imaginary order. At the end of the voyages and
after the cargoes had been unloaded the boats were
sold.

The landing from which Lee & Gould's boats were
launched was a small bottom just below the mouth of
Sugar Creek. This was a portion of the land sold
to William Totty, Sr., on February 27, 1810, by Asa
Shute. B. G. Stuart was then register for Hick-

man County. Totty owned the lands adjacent to the mouth of Sugar Creek and on both sides of Duck River, and a portion of these lands are now owned by J. B. Pruett, a great-great-great-grandson of William Totty, the title to the land having remained in the family for ninety years. William Totty came with his cousin, Robert Totty, from Virginia to Davidson County in 1807, and then to Hickman County, as stated in the sketch of the Second District. He was the father of one son, William Totty, and the father of four daughters. Polly married Amsel Epperson, who came from Davidson County; Chanie married Henry Ammons; Sallie married Arthur Russell; and another daughter married James Singleton, the school-teacher, who at one time taught in the Seventh District. William Totty, Jr., was the father of one son, William Harrison, and one daughter, Sophia Davis, who married Dr. John L. Spence. Epperson lived on the south side of Sugar Creek about a mile from its mouth. He lived opposite the large hollow which bears his name. On the same side and farther down the creek, below a large spring, lived his brother-in-law, Arthur Russell, a well-educated Irishman, who taught school on the creek from 1818 to 1820. One morning Russell rushed into Epperson's house calling loudly in his Irish brogue for "Omsel." Epperson soon found from Russell's excited and almost unintelligible statements that Russell had a deer imprisoned in his stable at home. Epperson took his gun and went with Russell to kill

the " dom big beast." As he went he learned that
the deer, closely pursued by dogs, had come to a high,
heavy fence recently built by Russell, and had followed it to a corner near the stable, where it was surrounded by its pursuers. Russell discovered it, and,
rushing in, seized the untamed and desperately an-
gered animal by the horns and led it to the stable,
the door of which he closed with rails. He left his
wife to guard the door with a club while he went for
" Omsel." While putting the deer in the stable,
Russell was assisted by his wife, who had the deer by
the tail, guiding its course. Russell, while this was
going on, said: " Sally, hold tight to his tail or ye
moight lose ye mon." The deer was slain by Epperson.

Dr. John Lycurgus Spence, who in 1835 married
Sophia Davis Totty, a granddaughter of William
Totty, Sr., was born near Coopertown, Robertson
County, on August 13, 1810. He was the youngest
son of David Spence, who was a hatter. David
Spence was the son of Thomas and Sarah (Herri-
man) Spence. He was born in New Jersey, and at
the breaking out of the Revolutionary War he enlisted in Capt. Robert Wilkins' company in the Sixth
Pennsylvania Regiment. While a soldier in General Greene's army he was retreating through Surry
County, N. C., when he, a half-famished, ragged
Continental, was fed by Mary Ann McElyea, the
daughter of Lodwick McElyea. He told her that
if he lived through the war he would return to

North Carolina to see her. This he did, and they were married and moved to Robertson County, Tenn. From this county three of their sons—Thomas, Joseph, and Daniel—went with the Tennessee troops to New Orleans and participated in the battle there. David Spence died in Robertson County in 1839. His wife died at the home of her son, Dr. Spence, in Hickman County, at the advanced age of ninety-nine years, eight months, and twenty days. Dr. John L. Spence was educated in the common schools of Robertson County. One of his teachers was Jerome Loring. He studied medicine under Dr. Thomas, of Springfield, in 1831 and 1832. He went from Springfield to Reynoldsburg in 1833 to practice his profession, but in the following year he came to Lee & Gould's furnace, on Sugar Creek, where he boarded with James McNeilly. He practiced medicine on this creek and throughout the surrounding country for fifty-one years and until his death, which occurred on January 5, 1885. Soon after he came to Hickman County he was employed to teach school at the newly erected schoolhouse and church house in the Wilkins settlement. To this place he gave the name " Mount Zion," this being the name of a church which stood near the home of his childhood in Robertson County. New buildings have succeeded the old ones, but the name " Mount Zion " still remains. After the death of his first wife he married Mrs. Rachel Tennessee Patterson, widow of Mark R. Patterson, of Nashville. Before her marriage to Patterson she was Miss Boyd, of Nashville, a daughter of Col. Richard Boyd. Colonel Boyd was a son of John Boyd, who came to " The Bluffs " with Donelson's party in 1780. Colonel Boyd was born on one of the boats during the voyage. When the Mexican War came up, Dr. Spence volunteered as a member of Capt. Jefferson Whitfield's company; but this company was one of the many raised at this time in the Volunteer State, and its services were never needed by the government. In 1850 Dr. Spence and his wife established a boarding school near their home. It was called " Spring Mount Academy," and for several years it was a flourishing and well-patronized boarding school. This was for a time a flourishing locality, and here Dr. Spence engaged in the mercantile and milling business until the breaking out of the Civil War, which brought disaster to so many Southerners. Here was established the first post office of the Eighth District. It was named by Dr. Spence, the postmaster, "Dunnington," in honor of F. C. Dunnington, of the Nashville Union and American.

James McNeilly came from North Carolina in 1810, and located on Sugar Creek just below Lee's Old Furnace. He owned all the land on the creek from that point down to Totty's line, near the mouth. He was a man of intelligence, energy, and honesty. He had plenty of land and live stock, some money, a few slaves, and many friends. His home was on the Reynoldsburg road, and for years he conducted one of the most popular inns along the road. He married Mary Yates, daughter of John Yates, who was also from North Carolina. He died on February 3, 1835. His sons were William, Thomas, John, James, and Matthew McNeilly. The latter married Nancy, the daughter of Joseph Webb. Susan McNeilly, a daughter of James McNeilly, was born on September 16, 1814, and died on October 23, 1856. She married William A. Jones on December 24, 1833. William A. Jones was a son of Solomon Jones, and was born on September 23, 1812. He died on August 10, 1845. He was the father of Solomon and Dennis Jones. The former died while in the Confederate Army, and the latter is a prominent preacher of the Baptist Church. Mary, Martha, Nancy, Sophia, and Priscilla were daughters of William A. and Susan Jones. After the death of Mr. Jones, his widow married William Phillips. The result of this union was two sons, William H. and Jacob Phillips, and one daughter, Nellie, the wife of W. S. Nunnelly. William A. Jones was a brother of Dennis Jones, who lived and died at the mouth of Beaverdam Creek, in the Ninth District. William A. Jones was buried at his home on Duck River below the mouth of Beaverdam Creek. His wife was buried at the Millington Easley graveyard, near Pinewood.

Near his home on Sugar Creek, James McNeilly in 1829 erected a sawmill and gristmill. This gristmill supplied the citizens for miles around with meal, and later with flour, which was obtained by grinding the wheat, and then taking it from the box into which it fell and placing it in a hopper on top of the bolting chest. Through the bolting chest a fine cloth sieve extended. At one end of the chest was a crank attached to the sieve within. By turning the crank the ground wheat in the hopper was jostled into the sieve and the flour dropped into a chest; while the larger portion, the bran, was carried down the incline sieve and fell into a box at the other end of the bolting chest. The flour made in this way was rather dark, but, as everybody thought then, made good biscuits for Sunday mornings and when company came. Farmers then sowed but little wheat, which was reaped with reap hooks held in one hand. Each swath was caught by the hand and carefully laid in place. The sheaves were afterwards laid in a circular heap on the bare ground, and the grain trampled out by riding and leading horses over it. The heap was occasionally stirred to separate the straw from the wheat. After this the wheat and chaff in vessels were held at arm's length overhead and poured slowly on a sheet. If a wind was blowing at the time, the chaff was carried away and the wheat fell in a heap below; if there was no wind blowing, two men stood near by, and by the shaking of a sheet or quilt blew the chaff away. These facts considered, it is small wonder that the early settlers had biscuits only on Sunday mornings and when visitors came.

The old-fashioned ginger cakes sold on election days and muster days at McNeilly's mill were the best ever eaten, unless it were those eaten at other places in the county on muster days and election days. On these days, at McNeilly's mill, the entire male population of the Eighth District would meet to vote or muster. On muster days the ante-bellum militia captain would put his men through involutions and maneuvers of which the great Hardee never heard, and which he himself could not possibly have executed, had he tried. But these were good old days. We had the ginger cakes there; we had the cider there; we had the boys all there; we were " at peace with all the world and the rest of mankind."

Here at this mill was the voting place for the Eighth District, which, in addition to Sugar Creek, included Brown's Bend and Cude's Bend, on the north side of the river, and Blackwelltown, a settlement on the south side. The Sugar Creek vote about equaled the vote of the other three sections combined; hence, in the election of district officers, there was much rivalry between the sections. This culminated later in ill feeling, resulting from a race for constable. The contestants were Ben. F. Wills, of Sugar Creek, and Clement Wilkins, of the Brown's Bend section. Each faction loyally supported its champion, and Wills, on the face of the returns, received a majority. Wilkins, however, had positive assurances from a sufficient number of voters to justify the belief that he had been elected and that there had been a fraudulent count. He thereupon canvassed the district and received the positive statement of a majority of the

voters to the effect that they had voted for him.   Desiring to be assured of this fact before commencing a
contest, he secured the services of a magistrate and
went over the district taking the affidavits of those
who had voted for him.   Coming to Andrew J. Turner, whose vote was needed in the Wilkins column, the
usual oath was administered and the usual question
asked.   Turner replied: " Clem., I told you the other
day that I voted for you.   I am swearing now.   I
swear that I voted for your opponent, Wills."   The
contest was dropped.   Wilkins, though sincere himself, had been deceived.

Richard Wilkins, the father of Thomas, Clement,
John, and James Wilkins, located within one hundred
yards of the celebrated Mount Zion Spring in 1808.
He was known as " Little Dickey " Wilkins.   He
married Susan Epperson, a sister of Amsel Epperson.
His son, John Wilkins, married a daughter of Carey
Epperson and moved to Texas.   There he was slain
by a negro whom he was attempting to handcuff, the
negro striking him with a hammer.   The daughters
of Richard Wilkins were Nancy, Susan, Melinda,
and Lucinda.   The last two were twins, and married
brothers, William and Richard Brown.   Richard Wilkins was born in 1771, and died in February, 1863.
He was a son of Clement Wilkins, who emigrated
from Virginia to Georgia, and from Georgia to Yellow Creek, in Dickson County, in 1798.   Clement
Wilkins married Clarissa Dicker, of Virginia.   Richard Wilkins saw all phases of pioneer life.   When a

mill boy in Georgia, he was chased by Indians. His horse became entangled in a grapevine, and was extricated just as the foremost Indian was almost upon him. Here he lost his bag of meal. The Indian stopped, struck his tomahawk into the sack, poured out the meal, and then disappeared into the forest, carrying away in triumph the empty sack. Clement Wilkins ran a stillhouse in Georgia. This stillhouse was frequented by the Indians. One night, after a party had left, carrying with them a large supply of whisky, Wilkins and family were aroused by repeated knocks on the door. Wilkins, of course, refused to open the door, and demanded the names and business of the midnight intruders. After a muttered consultation on the outside, the spokesman of the party of visitors said: " Up, Wuckerson ! Up! Hal Tony be dead." This was the name of one of the day's visitors; and Wilkins, finally becoming satisfied that the Indians meant him no harm, went on the outside. There he found the valiant Hal Tony dead drunk. Hal Tony recovered and lived to lead many a band to battle against John Barleycorn. But Richard Wilkins' experience with the Indians did not end with his residence in Georgia. After he married he came to Hickman County. After erecting his cabin near the spring and making other preparations for a permanent settlement here, he locked his cabin, containing all of his worldly goods, and, together with his wife, returned to Yellow Creek. They went for the purpose of weaving cloth out of which to make their clothing, they having no loom at their new residence. When they returned they found a heap of ashes marking the place where their cabin had stood, the Indians, during their absence, having come from across the river and committed this and other depredations.

In 1809 a blockhouse was built near where Clement Wilkins had located, he having followed his son from Yellow Creek and located near the mouth of King's Branch. Mrs. Clarissa Wilkins was the second person buried in the graveyard at this place. The first buried here was Rhoda Pierpont, who was slain by Indians in 1810. She was in the blockhouse, surrounded by her children, when the Indians fired the fatal shot through the door. The next day Mrs. Wilson, who lived in what was later known as "Cude's Bend," heard of this killing, and, as her husband had gone to the Yellow Creek mill, in Dickson County, she was much frightened. She awaited his return until dark, and then, taking up her baby boy, she left her isolated cabin and commenced her journey to the Beaver Creek settlement, twenty miles away. From this settlement she had come six months before. The way was but imperfectly marked and the journey a perilous one, but all through the night she walked on, carrying her boy. Just before day she reached friends and kindred on Beaver Creek. The son of this heroic woman was William Wilson, who for many years was a magistrate of the Sixth District. He lived at the Russell place. In his honor was named Wilson

Lodge, F. and A. M., which met at the church house at Lee's Old Furnace.

The Mount Zion church house and schoolhouse was built in 1833. Here the Primitive Baptists have had an organized church since the days of Jesse Fuqua and Claiborne Hobbs. Since they went to their reward there have followed in their footsteps Jesse Fuqua, Jr., —— French, the three Edwardses, Young J. Harvill, David Thomas, Willis Bryant, Dennis Jones, and many others who have at times visited this sacred spot and made their sacramental meetings and May meetings events to be long remembered and well by the hundreds who have gathered here in the sweet long ago. Here many school-teachers have taught. The first was Dr. John L. Spence. Others were Albert Wilson, Robert S. Hudspeth, Clement Wilkins, Oscar Sutton, and Monroe Rodgers. These and others taught here before the Civil War. One of those who taught here since the war was Reveaux Raymond, who has since become a prominent preacher in the Methodist Church.

In 1858 Andrew J. Stanfield taught school on the Coleman Branch of Sugar Creek. He later taught at the Old Furnace, and still later at Centerville. He was one of the best school-teachers that ever taught in the county. He died a few years ago in Union City.

In 1845 Jonathan Reeves, Jr., had a small mill just above the old blockhouse farm, on Sugar Creek. It was a water mill, the only kind that existed in Hickman County then. In 1820 Willis Weatherspoon erected a mill in the southeastern portion of the district. It was located in the midst of a pine forest, and was a sawmill as well as a gristmill. From this mill the settlers procured planks, this being a considerable improvement over the whipsaw method of supplying lumber for the growing demand. In 1870 Thomas Spencer brought the first steam mill into the district. It was located in the Slate Stone Hollow, on the lower end of the William Jones place, now owned by J. J. Sparks and H. R. Carothers. Since then a number of steam mills have been operated in the district. Among the number was one run at Mount Zion by Dr. A. C. Wilkins, for years a prominent physician of this district. The post office at Mount Zion is now called " Only; " it was at one time called " Dreamer." In 1885 a steam mill was operated in Brown's Bend by Stephen Owens. Another steam mill in this district in recent years was run by Willis Weatherspoon, a grandson of the pioneer miller, Willis Weatherspoon. The Weatherspoon family is a family of mechanics. James E. Weatherspoon, the youngest son of the pioneer, Willis Weatherspoon, now lives at an advanced age upon the same land on which his father located in the early days of the county. He runs an overshot water mill, the ingeniously arranged machinery being the wonder of those who see it. This family has produced some of the best blacksmiths, wheelwrights, and coopers to be found in the county. Redden, Ruffin, and Calvin Weatherspoon were all good workmen, but James was the wheelwright and cooper of the family. Before the Civil War he made a very superior quality of cedar ware, equal in finish and superior in quality to that turned out from the workshops of the State prison at that time. Many washtubs, water buckets, churns, etc., are yet to be seen throughout the county, mute witnesses to his skill. There are also yet to be seen throughout the county Weatherspoon wagons, all displaying a superior quality of workmanship.

While the Primitive Baptists are largely in the majority in this district, other denominations are and have been represented here. In 1856 the Cumberland Presbyterians, under the leadership of Rev. B. B. Brown, established a church at Spring Mount Academy, on Sugar Creek. When Brown moved to West Tennessee, this church was gradually absorbed by the Methodists. It was, however, occasionally visited by the well-remembered and much-loved Rev. James Parrish, who lived in Dickson County. At Lee's Old Furnace, on Sugar Creek, the Methodists organized a church. Among the preachers who labored here were John Reynolds, Simon P. Whitten, Will Allan Turner, the Hinsons, —— Nesbitt, from Yellow Creek; —— Brooks, and —— Coleman. Here many great revivals were held. Among those who held out faithful to the end was Rev. James Johnson, who from early boyhood lived in this district, and who died here in 1895 at an advanced age. His voice in song and prayer was often heard in the revivals of the county. Not a brilliant man, not an educated man, a man in whose veins no blue blood ran, a man who perhaps had some of the frailties peculiar to humanity, he was a man who in his humble way served the Lord after his own manner and according to the dictates of his own conscience. The Christian Church has never been as strong, numerically, in this district as the others named above, but it had here one faithful preacher and representative, Elder David Jackson Blackwell, familiarly known as "Davy Jack." He was the son of Jesse Blackwell, who settled in Blackwell's Hollow (or Blackwelltown), on the south side of the river, in 1818, just as soon as it was abandoned by the Indians. Jesse Blackwell was a man of ability in business matters. He wrote title papers in land trades for his neighbors, was their legal adviser, and was considered by the early settlers as authority on questions of law. He erected a gristmill on the lower end of his fine body of land. It was located north of his residence, one mile. Near it stood a large, hollow sycamore tree, in which the horse of the mill boy was often stabled while waiting for the grinding of the grain by the slow process of that day. In recent years the Freewill Baptist preacher, Rufus Choate, of Humphreys County, has preached on Sugar Creek.

On a branch flowing from the southeast into the Barren Fork of Sugar Creek lived John Coleman, father of ex-County Court Clerk William P. Coleman. Above the mouth of this branch, on the Barren Fork, lived Robinson Coleman, father of Capt. B. F. Coleman, who gave his life for the "lost cause." He was also the father of Capt. John H. Coleman, who taught school for many years in this district, and who died recently in Texas. The father of John and Robinson Coleman was Benjamin Coleman, who died suddenly while out hunting. He was found on the hillside near his home, sitting by a tree, dead. A hollow running into the Dry Fork, below the Coleman place, is called the " Sand Quarry Hollow," from the fact that when Lee & Gould's furnace was being built, sandstone was quarried here for the hearth. At the head of the Middle Fork of Sugar Creek is Dead Man's Hollow, in which the skeleton of an unknown man was found in 1869. It is supposed that the man was some Federal soldier who had fallen into the hands of bushwhackers and had by them been " sent to General Forrest," a phrase which they used to explain the disappearance of prisoners.

Near the mouth of Sugar Creek, on the north, is King's Hollow, settled in 1815 by a man named King. Since that time John E. G. Patton, William Smith, William Clemons, and others have lived in this hollow. Patton and Edmond Miller, his father-in-law, were the pioneer stone masons of this district. Miller lived, in 1820, in a hollow near where the late John Dodd lived. Stone chimneys yet stand in the district as monuments to their skill. But one of the most wonderful pieces of masonry in the county is the still standing stone stack of Lee & Gould's old furnace. The stack was built of roughly dressed stone by a man named Heel. The stack is about forty feet

high and about forty feet square at the base.   Some of
the stones of which it is composed weigh several tons.
It stands to-day, unhurt by the ravages of time, a
monument to the skill and energy of the young Irishman, Heel, who superintended its erection.

At the base of a towering bluff below the mouth
of Sugar Creek, in 1870, Minn and Samuel Easley
found buried three human skeletons.   Two were skeletons of adults; the third, that of a child.   They were
found all in one grave, covered by a flat rock.

Above the mouth of the creek is an island into
which many valuable rafts, property of citizens of
Maury, Bedford, and other up-the-river counties, have
been thrown.   Above this island, in 1835, was the
mill of Richard Wilkins, just below the Wilkins Ford
at the mouth of the Barren Hollow.   Above the mouth
of the Barren Hollow, and on the south side of Duck
River, is the famous bluff known as the " Devil's
Grandmother's Building."   However, neither history
nor tradition asserts that the grandparent of His Sa-
tanic Majesty ever had residence here.   At the upper
end of this long wall of rock is the noted cave in which
was once situated Blackwell's mill.   Tradition has it
that here, too, an Indian chief of renown had his council chamber.

Opposite this bluff, and on the north side of the
river, are the fertile lands of Brown's Bend, which
received its name from Dr. William Brown, who came
from Georgia by the way of East Tennessee to Vernon, and later settled in this bend.   He settled here

when the Indians were yet uncomfortably close to
him, they roaming just across the river. Near the
spring at the mouth of King's Branch, where the
blockhouse was located, Allan P. Kelly, a soldier of
the War of 1812, settled in 1815. He often told of
one of the night attacks which occurred previous to
the battle of New Orleans. During this particular
fight in the dark, he said that the running which he
did was far more dangerous than the fighting. Kelly
died in 1849, as the result of blood poisoning caused
by a tick bite under his arm. Dr. William Brown,
the first physician to locate in the district, came from
Vernon some time between 1811 and 1815. He still,
however, was the family physician of Garrett Lane
and other pioneers of Vernon, riding fifteen miles to
visit them when they were ill. He was the father of
John ("Jack"), Jere, and Richard Brown. The latter, who met a tragic death by his team running away,
was the father of Jesse R. and William H. Brown,
the former of whom is still living in Brown's Bend.
Jere Brown was a man of convivial habits, which he
always made manifest when he visited the stillhouse
of "Uncle Dickey" Wilkins. When ready to start
for home, he would say to his horse, Jawbones: " Now
show me how you act when Becky starts to mill."
The horse would immediately fall to his knees, and
Jere would mount and go on his way rejoicing. Local
wags made him the hero of the story of the inquisitive
owl and the unsophisticated traveler, and many were
the choice bits of profanity which they alleged that

Jere, when going home with his " jag," would hurl at the owl, who asked him impertinent questions.

Daniel Murphree, the father of Stephen, Levi, Caleb, Redden, Benton, Daniel, and David Murphree, settled in 1811 at what is now known as the " Willis Brown place." He was from North Carolina, and came to Hickman County with Garrett Lane, Dr. William Brown, and others.

Samuel Wherry came from North Carolina to Pine River, in the Seventh District, in 1825. In 1830 he came to Brown's Bend and bought land from Richard Wilkins. He died a short time after coming here, but his widow and boys—Cornelius, Irving, James, William C., and John—paid Wilkins for the land. Mrs. Wherry was, prior to her marriage, Elizabeth Shirley, and was a native of South Carolina. Of the sons of Samuel Wherry, only one—William C.—is now alive. He was born in 1828.

At the upper end of Brown's Bend is Bickerstaff Eddy, so called from the fact that Bickerstaff, a boatman, who lived at the mouth of Taylor's Creek, floated into this eddy and experienced much trouble in getting out. This was at an early date.

Just above this eddy, at the Blackwell Ford, a son of Redden Weatherspoon was drowned. He and an older brother were crossing the river here in a wagon, when they missed the ford, and the older brother was almost drowned in an attempt to rescue the younger one.

On the same side of the river and above Brown's

Bend is Cude's Bend, which was settled by John Cude about 1815.

The only cotton gin ever operated in the district was erected in Cude's Bend in 1860 by William H. Carothers, who operated it until 1870.

On Duck River, above Cude's Bend and at the Horseshoe Bend, is a point known to boatmen as the " Hurrah Bush." Here a boat was wrecked, and the boatmen, taking refuge in trees, called loudly for help.

This was the place of a double drowning a few years ago. David Askins, now of Centerville, together with Mrs. Huldah Richardson, her daughter— Miss Sallie Richardson—and Miss Cassie Mayberry, attempted to cross the river near this point in a vehicle. The mules became unmanageable, turned into deep water, and soon all were swept downstream. Askins swam ashore, and rescued Miss Richardson. Mrs. Richardson, whose body was recovered on the same day, and Miss Mayberry, whose body was found some months later near the mouth of Wolf Creek, were drowned.

Some of the magistrates of this district were James McNeilly, Amsel Epperson, Jesse Blackwell, Robinson Coleman, W. H. Brown, R. J. Work, Robert Bingham, O. B. Turner, W. H. Baker, C. Weatherspoon, J. J. Sparks, J. A. Pope, and the late Robert S. Potter. Some of the constables were A. W. Coleman, O. B. Turner, John H. Coleman, John Weatherspoon, R. C. Forrester, W. F. Wherry, and Amos Alexander. W. F. Wherry has several times been a deputy sheriff.

John Grimmitt, of this district, was a deputy under Sheriff Stephenson.   William P. Coleman, of this district, has, since the Civil War, been county surveyor and County Court Clerk.   His uncle, Robinson Coleman, was, before the war, tax collector.   W. J. D. Spence, who was reared in this district, represented Hickman County in the State Legislature from 1891 to 1893.   Some of the physicians of this district, in addition to those already mentioned, were Dr. A. B. Brown, Dr. Joseph Thompson, and Dr. Jones.

The Eighth District furnished its quota of soldiers to the Confederate Army.   Benjamin F. Coleman was a captain in the Forty-second Tennessee Infantry, and was killed in battle; his brother, John H. Coleman, was a lieutenant commanding a company in the Forty-second Tennessee Infantry; J. R. Brown was a lieutenant in the Forty-second Tennessee Infantry; W. J. D. Spence was captain of a company in the Tenth Tennessee Cavalry; and David M. Spence was a lieutenant in the Twelfth Tennessee Cavalry. Many gallant men from the Eighth District went out as privates, and sleep to-day in many graves in many States.

The citizens of the Eighth District were much harassed during the closing days of the Civil War by marauders from Colonel Dorr's Eighth Iowa Cavalry, stationed at Waverly.   A troop from this regiment overtook and captured in the Epperson Hollow, after a sharp skirmish, a detachment of Kentuckians under command of Colonel Brewer.   The Kentuckians were attempting to get through to the Southern army. At another time a troop from this regiment was made to double-quick half the length of Sugar Creek by the fire of one lone bushwhacker. Along the line of their retreat they dropped numerous chickens and other booty.

In 1869 and 1870 there was a reign of terror on Sugar Creek without parallel in the annals of the county. The originator of all the trouble was a man called "James Stevenson," who claimed to have come from Ellis County, Texas. On his arm, however, was tattooed the name "James Hooten," which was generally thought to be his name. In 1869 he and Wyatt J. Chappell killed a negro, "Red Joe" Carothers. They took him from his home and shot him through the head with a rifle ball. "Red Joe's" offense was that he had accused Stevenson and others of having robbed him, a crime of which they were doubtless guilty. During this year Kinchen Batteau was shot down from ambush while plowing in a field near where Lee & Gould had their store when they operated their furnace on Sugar Creek. Bob Wilson, a nonresident, who had escaped from the jail at Centerville, and who was being harbored by parties on the creek, was suspected of this crime. Batteau, who had come to Sugar Creek from Kentucky, recovered from his wounds, and afterwards removed to West Tennessee. Previous to this was the killing of Cody near the juncture of the North and Middle Forks of Sugar Creek. He was killed from ambush by Chappell and

Stevenson, against whom he had made threats on account of their having given him a counterfeit bill. At the time of his death, Cody carried a shotgun, the stock of which was riddled with bullets. Stevenson and Chappell fled to Kentucky, where they were later arrested by Stephen Reeves and Luke L. Bingham, of Sugar Creek. They were carried to Centerville and lodged in jail. Reeves went to Nashville to collect the reward offered by the Governor. After his return he was arrested on complaint of Bingham, who claimed that Reeves had not turned over to him his portion of the reward. While this suit was pending, Reeves and Bingham met at a church on Sugar Creek and exchanged several shots. Neither was wounded. Reeves was sent to the penitentiary for three years, but was almost immediately pardoned by Governor Brownlow. He returned to Sugar Creek, but was waited upon by a vigilance committee and requested to move on, which he did. He went West and never returned. During Reeves' trial one of the prosecuting attorneys, Col. N. N. Cox, made remarks which offended the prisoner, who promptly denounced the attorney as a liar. The attorney just as promptly struck him with a heavy book, and a few minutes later gracefully paid a fine for this act. In the meantime Wyatt Chappell and two other prisoners escaped from the jail at Centerville. Chappell made his way to Cairo, Ill., and no further attempt was made to apprehend him. Stevenson did not escape from the Centerville jail, on account of the smallness of the hole through which Chappell and the others escaped. He was removed for safe-keeping to the jail at Columbia, from which place he soon escaped. He, in company with a Maury County criminal named Hatchel, made his way to the mouth of Sugar Creek. He had hardly reached the neighborhood when he commenced to make threats against prominent citizens. He carried none of these threats into execution, as he and Hatchel were slain by Walker Coleman, Milton Spence, and Hosea Chappell. They were buried without coffin or shroud in a hole made by the uprooting of a tree. The place of their burial is on the ridge between Sugar Creek and the Weatherspoon Hollow, near a dogwood tree which stands near the road in the head of a small hollow. This ended the reign of terror.

On Sugar Creek there now lives a grandson of the celebrated Indian fighter, Capt. John Rains, whose deeds have already been frequently mentioned in these pages. This is Jonathan Hans Rains, a son of Capt. John Rains' youngest son. In addition to the frequent mention of Captain Rains' exploits in the preceding pages, the following additional information is given concerning him: In October, 1779, John Rains started to what is now Kentucky from New River, Va. When he reached Kentucky, he met the party led by James Robertson. This party was going from East Tennessee through Southern Kentucky to the French Lick on the Cumberland River, and Rains, who had with him his family and live stock, was persuaded to join them. When they came to the Cumberland on the side which is now East Nashville, they found the river frozen over. This was in January, 1780, during the winter which is till this day referred to as " the cold winter." Rains and his party and their stock crossed the river on the ice. He was the first man to bring live stock into what is now Middle Tennessee. Rains settled on what has since been known as " Deaderick's Plantations." Here he remained for three months, when the killing of a settler caused him to seek safety in the fort at " The Bluffs." He remained here four years. Rains had a horse, Bowie, which his daughter, Patsy, was one day riding. The Indians fired upon her, killing Betsey Williams, who was riding behind her. The horse, however, carried Patsy Rains away in safety, leaping the stockade surrounding the fort. Rains soon became prominent among the settlers, who were all daring, by his cool bravery, and for years there was seldom a fight with the Indians at Nashville or in the surrounding country in which Rains was not a participant. When the handful of defenders of Buchanan's Fort were surrounded by seven hundred howling Indians, Rains was among the first to enter the fort from the outside and give cheer and assistance to those within. There is scarcely a page of the early history of Tennessee on which the name of " Rains " does not appear in connection with some deed of daring. So great was his energy and persistency when in pursuit of the savages that they soon began to call him " Golong " Rains. In Humphreys County there lives a brother of Jonathan H. Rains who is generally known as " Long " Rains. His real name is John Golong Rains, which perpetuates the name given by the Indians to their unrelenting enemy, Capt. John " Golong " Rains. As a hunter and woodsman, Captain Rains had few equals in the Cumberland settlements. It is said that during one winter he killed thirty-seven bears in the vicinity of Nashville.

CHAPTER XII.

THE NINTH DISTRICT.

T HE Ninth District lies on both sides of Duck River, and includes the mouth of Beaverdam Creek and both sides of this creek up to the line of the Eleventh District. It is bounded on the north by the Seventh and Eighth Districts; east, by the First and Eleventh Districts; south, by the Tenth and Eleventh Districts; and west, by the Eighth District and Perry County.

In 1808 Richard C. Lowe, father of Jesse, Wyley, Aquilla, Anon, and Aden Lowe, located in that portion of the district which lies north of Duck River, and which is known as " Lowe's Bend." Lowe, for whom the bend was named, was a man of wealth and owned a number of slaves. He and his slaves were rebuilding his fence which had been thrown down by the earthquake of 1811, when a neighbor, Shumake, came up and remonstrated with them, saying that the Lord had destroyed the fence and that they should not attempt to rebuild it. Lowe answered that he did not intend that his hogs should get out and run wild, it mattered not who tore down the fence. He continued to rebuild it. Jesse Lowe was a man of great strength, and was able to defend himself in the fistic arguments which frequently occurred in those days. He emigrated to Missouri, to which State his brother,

Wyley, went at a later date. Other members of the family sleep near where their father's remains were interred and near the place where they were born.

Perhaps the first to locate in Lowe's Bend was ———— Sellars, who settled in the upper end of the bend, at the place which has for years been known as the "Lomax place." The house which Sellars built here in 1808 is still standing. It is a log house, twenty by twenty-four feet in size. It stands on a hill, at the foot of which is a fine spring. It was well suited for the purposes for which it was built, it having been built for a residence, and also for a blockhouse into which the settlers could go for protection, should the Indians come across the river to attack them.

Just opposite the lower end of Lowe's Bend the Indians had a camp on Skull Creek, so called by the pioneers on account of the finding there of a human skull. Duck River alone separated the approaching whites from the Indians, who looked with jealousy and hatred upon their encroachments. On Skull Creek John Scott, who lived at the mouth of Taylor's Creek, erected an overshot mill in 1825. This mill was patronized for years by those who had pushed across the river after the treaty of 1818. Panther Branch, so called on account of its having been infested by panthers in the pioneer days, is above Skull Creek.

After the death of Sellars, his widow married Josiah Lomax, who had been employed by her late husband. Mrs. Lomax died in 1832, and Lomax, who had come into possession of the fine lands here, married Susan Southall, who was the mother of Thomas Lomax, of Humphreys County, and William Lomax, who died in 1861.

Stephen Cotham settled at an early date near the Lomax place. He was the father of Pleasant, Harvey, James, and Josiah Cotham, all of whom were good citizens.

Jesse Lovett, for whom Lovett's Island was named; James Walker, and Levi Murphree were prominent men who once lived here.

At the lower end of Lowe's Bend there lived that prominent and industrious citizen, the late Abram Burchard, who bought the lands on which he lived so long, in 1843, from Wyley Lowe. Burchard, who became a man of wealth, made his first money by the hardest of work. When Lee & Gould operated their furnace on Sugar Creek, he chopped wood for them at thirty-one and a half cents per cord. While industrious and attentive to business, he was a great admirer of, and participator in, outdoor sports. In his old age he recounted with much pleasure the story of a wrestling bout which he had in the Lee & Gould "coaling" with the Pace brothers. Burchard was victorious in the wrestling contest, but the fight which followed was a draw. However, in later years, Burchard and Milton Pace, who were the participants, acknowledged that they were both whipped.

At the lower end of Lowe's Bend a county bridge was built in 1891. The material was hauled from

Nunnelly Station, thirteen miles away, by Newton McClanahan, John Fowlkes, and Ollie McClanahan. They were engaged at this for six weeks. The bridge ccst about $6,000. In 1896, the original pillars having proven to be unstable, stone pillars were placed in their stead. The stone was obtained from the quarry of fine building stone between the residences of S. G. and J. C. Carothers.

On the south side of the river, opposite the Burchard farm, is the farm of John A. Jones. This farm lies on Duck River and on both sides of Beaverdam Creek. These lands, as well as those across the river belonging to Samuel G. Carothers, were entered by the pioneer surveyor, John Davis. Davis owned a fine tract of land in Humphreys County below the mouth of Tumbling Creek. This Humphreys County farm Davis sold for $4,000 to Dennis G. Jones, a son of the pioneer, Solomon Jones. Jones concluded that, as the lands were so frequently overflowed by the river, he preferred more elevated lands. He then gave these Humphreys County lands and $1,000 for the valuable body of land now owned by his son, John A. Jones. The farm of Samuel G. Carothers belonged to his father, William Carothers, and, prior to that, to his grandfather, William H. Carothers. Samuel G. Carothers bought the interests of his brothers, J. C. and W. D. Carothers. The former of these lives near by, and the latter is a prosperous farmer of Shipp's Bend, where he married the daughter of Van Buren Shouse, a highly respected citizen of that bend.   When Dennis G. Jones located at the mouth of Beaverdam Creek, he moved to this place the mill which his father had built in the Eighth District, four miles below, on the William A. Jones place, near where Hugh R. Carothers, who married a daughter of William A. Jones, now lives.   The mill, after its removal, was erected at a point where the waters of Beaverdam Creek fall abruptly into a cave, through which they run in a northerly direction under a bluff two hundred feet high, rising in the bed of Duck River, three-fourths of a mile away.   At high tide a portion of the waters of Beaverdam Creek flows through the natural channel west to the river, one mile distant.   The first settler on the Jones place was William Loftis, who married a sister of Solomon Jones.   He leased the lands from John Davis and cleared the first acre.

At the S. A. J. Peeler place, above the Jones place, Levi McCollum, father of James McCollum, and grandfather of Hon. Levi McCollum, built a mill in 1830.   He expected the large volume of water which comes in a sluggish stream from under the high hill here to furnish the power, but in this he was disappointed and the mill was abandoned.

Southwest from the location of McCollum's mill is the Brier Pond, so called on account of the mass of green briers which grew here in the early days. Here Hugh Pinkerton and John Pinkerton, who came from Bedford County and married daughters of John Cooper, lived for many years.

John Cooper lived at what was later known as the "Walker place." He bought this place from John Stoddard, who bought it from Caleb McCord, who had purchased it from the original owner, John Davis.

James Walker, the father of Dr. W. L. Walker, John T. Walker, David N. Walker, and James B. Walker, all worthy sons of a worthy sire, married a daughter of John Cooper. James Walker was in the Mexican War, and participated in the battles which made famous Campbell's "Bloody First."

Near the western portion of the Brier Pond, Valentine Flowers, father of William Flowers, located in 1825. Valentine Flowers was a Primitive Baptist preacher, and in a church house which stood on his lands Liberty Church was organized on June 1, 1827. Two Baptist preachers who signed the minutes of the day's proceedings were Willis Dotson and Elias Deaton. The church was afterwards moved from the Flowers place to the Sulphur Fork of Beaverdam Creek, and in 1853 it was moved to its present site, where, instead of the original round-log cabin, there is now a neat frame building. Here, before the Civil War, preached that humble old servant of the Lord, "Black George." "Black George" was a slave, who showed great ability as a Baptist preacher. So marked was this ability, and so unquestioned was his honesty and devotion, that the members of the Baptist Church purchased his freedom. He died several years after the Civil War. One of the most celebrated of the preachers of the Baptist Church was

E. A. Meadows, who lived on Sulphur Fork prior to
1839, at which time he went to Mississippi.   Dr.
Richard Fain, who, in addition to being a prominent
physician, was a Baptist preacher of note, at one
time lived at the Joseph Cooper place, west of Brier
Pond.

William Flowers reared a large family at the place
settled by his father, Valentine Flowers.   Sons of
William Flowers were Robert, John L., James, Valentine, Dr. David D., and Rev. Gideon Flowers.   His
daughters were Mrs. Nancy Fowlkes, wife of James
H. Fowlkes; and Mrs. Sarah Price Burchard, who,
on November 24, 1841, married Abram C. Burchard.
William Flowers owned a number of slaves.   Near
his home he operated an old-time stillhouse.   After
the death of William Flowers, his son, Dr. David D.
Flowers, lived at the old homestead, where he practiced medicine until the time of his death.

In 1846 the Methodists and Presbyterians erected
a church near the Flowers place, to which they gave
the name " Macedonia."   Here they held several
camp meetings, which were conducted by B. B.
Brown, James Parrish, John Brigham, and others.
Services were held morning, evening, and night, under a large arbor, covered with boards and brush.
The seats were benches made of split poplar logs.
Services were announced by the blowing of a horn or
a conch shell, which was kept hanging on a peg driven
into a post near the pulpit, or " preacher's stand," as
it was called.   When this was sounded the congrega-

tion commenced to assemble from the adjacent woods, the near-by cabins, and the surrounding grounds. For those who came from a distance to attend these meetings, eight log cabins were erected. The cabins were built in pairs—one for the women, the other for the men. Straw was placed on the dirt floor and on the shelf which extended around the cabin, providing upper and lower berths for the lodgers. Fifty people could sleep in each cabin. Provisions were furnished by the citizens of the surrounding country. Part was cooked at home, and part in the camps. This was placed on long board tables, to which all were invited. It is said that upon one occasion one man, during the course of his breakfast, visited four tables and drank four cups of coffee at each. One night after the services a large snake was discovered in the straw near the wall of one of the cabins reserved for the women. There were numerous loud screams and appeals for assistance from the women, most of whom were in deshabille. Gallant men soon rushed to the rescue of the fair ones, and the "snake," which was about three feet in length, was speedily slain. The men held it up in momentary triumph, then dropped it, looked disgusted, and walked out into the night. One, however, called back to the women to pick up the "snake," that it would not bite them. Finally, one of the more courageous of the women picked up the " snake " on a stick to throw it from the cabin. It was a tunic. A tunic was not a species of poisonous reptile, but an article of feminine dress, the predecessor of the bustle of the present day.

While Liberty Church was located at the Flowers place, Mrs. James Pope joined the church, was baptized, and started for home rejoicing. When three miles away, she remembered that she had left her infant with a friend at the church. The terrified mother started to return, but found the little one sleeping complacently in the arms of one of those who were then with her. John Halbrooks was a Primitive Baptist preacher of that period.

Some of those who taught school at Macedonia were William Moore, of Shipp's Bend; J. N. Pace, who now lives in Bedford County; and Professor Haynes, who afterwards went to Lewisburg and established a good school there. Miss Josephine Spence taught school at Macedonia in 1861. Some of those who taught at Liberty were James D. and Robert S. Murphree, sons of Stephen Murphree; and Dr. William L., John T., and David N. Walker, sons of James Walker. During the winter of 1858-59 Dr. Andrew J. Lowe gave instruction in an informal manner to a party of young men at his home in the Ninth District. The young men formulated their own rules, and met and adjourned at their pleasure, their instructor joining them when his business affairs permitted. Some of those who had the benefit of his instruction were Samuel G. Jones, Thomas Lomax, John F. M. Fain, Wesley Morrison, Pleasant Poore, Samuel Woolard, Amsel Murphree, William Burchard, Jared C. Frazier, W. J. D. Spence, " Bud " Woolard, and Henry Lowe. Dr. Lowe, who was a son of Maj. Lewis Lowe, was a good physician, but preferred farming. He was a member of the Forty-Sixth General Assembly, and died during the term.

At the upper end of Brier Pond, on the south side of Beaverdam Creek, is Cow Hollow, so called on account of a large number of cattle having been herded there between 1820 and 1825. The winter range was good here, and stockmen from Davidson and Williamson Counties would bring their cattle here. Tradition says that Henry Gee, from Williamson County, or the eastern portion of Hickman County, during one winter killed one hundred and twenty deer while he was herding cattle here.

At the mouth of Powder Mill Branch, which runs into Sulphur Fork, a primitive powder mill was built in 1823, saltpeter being found near by. William Bates, father of Lewis Bates, was badly burned by an explosion of this mill. He died from the effects of the burns. A man employed about the mills was an enemy of Bates, and he was suspected of having put gravel in the mill, a spark from which caused the explosion. There was, however, no direct proof against him.

On Sulphur Fork, in 1823, Adam Coble erected a pottery, from which he turned out in large numbers jars, crocks, jugs, lamps, churns, etc., of various shapes and sizes. Good potter's clay was found near by. The wares made by Coble for many years found ready sale in Hickman County and adjoining counties. Agents representing him, and accompanied by wagons loaded with his wares, traveled throughout these counties. First they were sold from ox carts, and later from wagons drawn by horses, but still the demand continued and the work went on until the Civil War. After the war, competing firms from other points, with more improved machinery, caused the Coble pottery to suspend, after having been operated, under the management of several proprietors, for half a century. However, many of the products of the Coble pottery may yet be found in a number of Middle Tennessee counties.

Prominent men who located on Sulphur Fork at an early date were Joseph Halbrooks, William Woolard, and William Chandler, all of whom came from North Carolina. Halbrooks, after he came here, became dissatisfied with life in the wilderness and returned to the old State, but there he became dissatisfied when he thought of the good lands which he had left behind him in the West. He returned to Sulphur Fork, and this time he remained.

Above the mouth of Sulphur Fork there runs into Beaverdam Creek from the south a little stream known as "Blue Water," from the fact that in the early days, before the lands were cleared and cultivated, the waters of this stream were very blue. Major McClaren erected a mill on this creek in 1829. At the mouth of Blue Water, Samuel Lancaster laid a land warrant in 1830 on lands claimed by

David Blackfan, a land speculator. Lancaster won the lawsuit which followed. He came from North Carolina, making the journey in an ox cart. Near Lancaster's residence, at the foot of a steep hill, there stood a blacksmith shop, at which an exciting incident occurred in 1864. John Flowers, a much-wanted guerrilla, being a blacksmith, stopped at this shop to shoe his horse. While in the shop about forty Federals came upon him. Not having time to mount his horse, he rushed around the corner of the shop and up the hill in safety, followed by a shower of bullets. Previous to this the Federals had attempted to capture him by surrounding his house at night. When they knocked at the door, he made no answer, and they forced it open. Eleven entered and attempted to strike matches. Three of these he shot, and, with a pistol in either hand, firing as he went, he rushed through the body of Federals in the yard and escaped.

Above Blue Water, and on the same side of Beaverdam Creek, is Joe's Branch, named for Joe McCann, who lived there in 1825. This branch is near the line between the Ninth and Eleventh Districts.

Below Blue Water, in 1830, James McCollum settled where his father, Levi McCollum, had placed a land warrant a few years before. He here erected a gristmill, and, later, a sawmill. This soon became a point of importance, people hauling logs to this mill from a distance of fifteen to twenty miles. James McCollum was the father of Hon. Levi McCollum.

Another good citizen of the Ninth District who lived in the upper portion of the district was Simeon Wright. One of his daughters married John M. Bates.

Although the Baptists were largely in the majority in this district, Samuel Chesser, of the Christian Church, preached on Sulphur Fork as far back as 1836. A prominent preacher in this church to-day is Elder Thomas Cagle, of this district. He is a great-grandson of the pioneer Baptist preacher, Thomas Curb, who lived in the Seventh District and preached throughout the surrounding country as early as 1807. Curb's daughter, Elizabeth, married Charles Cagle, the father of Thomas Cagle, Sr., who was the father of Elder Thomas Cagle. Charles Cagle lived on Mill Creek, in the Seventh District, at the time of the earthquake of 1811. He had a chill, and when th earthquake shook down some venison suspended over his bed, he thought that his ague was severer than usual. The people throughout the country had not recovered from the effects of the " Great Revival " of 1800, and they were much wrought up over the earthquake of 1811, which they understood as a manifestation of the Lord's displeasure. Andrew Carothers, the Baptist preacher, baptized large numbers who sought to flee from the wrath to come.

In 1839 Cyrus W. Russell sold goods in the valley near where his widow, Mrs. Delphia Russell, now lives. Cyrus W. Russell was a rigidly honest man, who wanted all that was his, and nothing more. His wife is a sister of Jared C. and William G. Frazier. James H. Fowlkes, a son-in-law of William Flowers, sold goods at the Flowers place about 1855. John W. Walker & Co. commenced the mercantile business at Whitfield in 1852, and continued until 1860, when they were succeeded by James Walker and James Gray. After the war John T. Walker and —— Petway sold goods here, and were succeeded by the Walker brothers—John T., David N., and James B. Walker. They were succeeded by their cousin, Thomas B. Walker, who is still in business here. One mile southwest of Whitfield, Flowers & Coble now sell goods near the mill of Cagle & Coble. The post office, Whitfield, was established in 1857, and was named in honor of John W. Whitfield, who was perhaps the most famous man who ever lived in Hickman County. He commanded the Hickman County company in Campbell's "Bloody First," and, after the Mexican War, was several times a State Senator. During the Civil War he served in the Confederate Army as a colonel and brigadier general. Before the war he was connected with the Indian Bureau, Department of the Northwest; but at the breaking out of the war he cast his fortunes with his Southern brethren, and brought a regiment of Indians into the Confederate service. He died in Texas on October 27, 1879. His first wife was a daughter of Robert Charter, the Centerville merchant, and his second wife was a sister of Gen. George Dibrell.

The following are the names of some of the magistrates of this district: William Flowers, William Woolard, Cyrus W. Russell, James H. Fowlkes, Josiah Cotham; Samuel Chesser, John A. Jones, D. N. Walker, W. L. Walker, S. G. Carothers, Samuel Chesser, Jr., and D. S. Chandler.

This district has furnished the following deputy sheriffs: S. A. J. Peeler, John T. Walker, and J. A. Cunningham. J. A. Cunningham's father, John Cunningham, was at one time census taker for Hickman County.

Two widely known constables of this district were Lewis Bates and D. T. Pinkerton.

Dennis G. Jones, of this district, was a State Senator in 1837 and 1839. His son, Samuel G. Jones, in 1889 represented Humphreys County in the Lower House, and his grandson, J. Grady Jones, is at present the Representative of the counties of Humphreys, Perry, and Wayne. In 1895 J. Alonzo Bates and W. Valentine Flowers, of Centerville, both of whom were born and reared in this district, were in the Senate and Lower House, respectively. Flowers was succeeded in 1897 by Dr. W. L. Walker, of this district. Dr. A. J. Lowe was Hickman County's Representative in 1889. Levi McCollum, who was born and reared in this district, represented Hickman County in the Legislature in 1871 and 1873.

James D. Murphree, of this district, a gallant soldier who lost a leg while in the Confederate Army, was at one time County Court Clerk of Hickman County.

In the Mexican War, Dennis Jones, James Walker, John S. Pickard, and others were soldiers in Whitfield's company. To the Confederate Army the Ninth District furnished Lieut. William Clinton Jones, who was one of the best-drilled men in the Eleventh Tennessee Infantry, together with a large number of private soldiers, who were as brave as any who donned the gray and as true as any who wore it.

The names of some of the physicians of this district not already mentioned are: Leroy Blackburn (1848), John S. Dickson, James A. Edwards, and Dr. J. C. Flowers.

Stephen Murphree, born in the Eighth District on January 3, 1823, came to this district on January 1, 1846. Between Murphree's house and the mouth of Cow Hollow there occurred, about 1820, a tragedy not altogether traditional, as for more than sixty years there could be seen nailed to two black oak trees two shoes of oak-tanned leather. Between the trees was a grave, and in the grave a stranger who lodged one night in the long ago with a settler near the mouth of Cow Hollow. Just at dawn the stranger was preparing to depart. He was standing in the cabin door, when a man came out of the woods with a gun presented. The stranger attempted to flee, but the man fired and wounded him. The wounded man then rushed at his assailant, wrenched the gun away from him, and was preparing to brain him with it, when a second man came from the woods and shot the stranger, who fell dead. To the terrified settler the slayers of the stranger told the following story: They said that the dead man had, two weeks before this, killed in Kentucky a brother of one of them. He left Kentucky, and they had been on his trail for ten days. They immediately after the killing went away, and as to the truth of their story nobody knows. The identity of the dead man and of his slayers was never discovered. The dead man was buried near the place where he fell, and for over sixty years his shoes remained nailed to the trees which marked his grave.

William Gilbert, a young man of Lowe's Bend, accidentally shot himself while hunting on Lovett's Island, in 1885. In Duck River, at Scott's Ferry, at the mouth of Taylor's Creek, Thornton Scott was drowned in 1856. His body was recovered four miles below. One Sunday in 1850, Edward Wright, a son of George Wright, was drowned at the head of Blakeley's Island. He, with an older brother and a negro boy, were returning from the island, when their canoe was overturned in the swift current. Verses composed by Dr. John L. Spence were sung at the funeral, and were for several years frequently sung in this portion of the county. Blakeley's Island received its name from the fact that a pioneer boatman named Blakeley ran his raft aground here and had to await another rise of the river before going farther. Reece Flowers, a negro, was drowned in Duck River, at the mouth of Beaverdam Creek, in 1892.

About 1835 the wife of Arthur Atkinson was drowned in Beaverdam Creek, just above McCollum's mill, over the dam of which her body floated. She was going to visit the sick wife of John Grimes, and was riding behind him on his horse, when, becoming dizzy, she fell into the slightly swollen stream and was swept away.

On April 24, 1859, a hurricane of violence unparalleled in the county's history swept across the Ninth District from southwest to northeast. Fences, orchards, and outbuildings were destroyed. Maj. Lewis Lowe's residence was unroofed, and a tree falling across the residence of John A. Jones was perhaps what saved it from being blown off the bluff into the river. In Lowe's Bend the walls of Josiah Cotham's house were blown away, together with all of the furniture, except the chair in which Cotham sat. Bedclothes and wearing apparel were found miles away.

In the northern portion of the Ninth District, below the mouth of Rocky Branch, is a fine body of land known as " Whitson's Bend," named for one of its first settlers, William P. Whitson, Sr., who died on February 25, 1892. Major Whitson was a tanner, and here so well plied his trade that he became a man of wealth and prominence. He was a son of George Whitson, of East Tennessee. Other sons of George Whitson were George Whitson, Jr.; Samuel Whitson, of Wartrace, Tenn.; Capt. Robert M. Whitson; and David Whitson, who in 1833 was killed at Shelbyville by the storm which destroyed that place, this storm being known throughout Hickman and Humphreys Counties as the " Bearden storm." In the upper end of Whitson's Bend, years before the Civil War, Robert Wright built a mill. Nancy, a daughter of Wright, married Major Whitson. Robert Wright was the father of Robert, Jr., John, Levin D., and Thomas Wright. The latter was killed in Perry County, near Lobelville, by Dock Leiper, who had married his sister. Leiper claimed to have acted in self-defense. Wright was insane at the time of his death.

The early settlers of Wolf Creek, so named on account of the large number of wolves which infested its hills, were Henry Sawyers, John Duff, the Devineys, the Bakers, the Blackwells, Henry Powell, and —— Ammons, who was the owner of a small water mill. Rans Peppers, of this creek, was one of the principals in the " rough-and-tumble fight " which took place at the Lomax muster grounds in 1858. The other principal was Willie Forrester, who yet lives on Sugar Creek, where he is a highly respected citizen. Other participants were Maj. Lewis Lowe, —— Chambers, Thornton Scott, and a brother of Rans Peppers, on the Peppers side; and Bright Forrester (who was left-handed), Richard Forrester, Stephen Forrester, and Carroll Forrester, on the Forrester side. This was one of the many incidents of a like kind which almost invariably occurred on general muster days.

The Line of 1784 runs through the Ninth District, crossing Beaverdam Creek at the Jack Malugin place, and Sulphur Fork at the James Malugin place. It crosses Cow Hollow near its head. This information was furnished by the late Thomas Cagle, who entered fifty acres of land south of this line, which was his northern boundary. North of this line and north of Cagle's entry was an entry made by Henry Nixon, one of the pioneer lawyers of Centerville. Thomas Cagle, Sr., was born on June 2, 1814, on Taylor's Creek, in the Seventh District. His father, Charles Cagle, was born in North Carolina in 1779, and married a daughter of the pioneer preacher, Thomas Curb. Thomas Cagle settled in the Cow Hollow in 1823, and ten years later saw the thrilling meteoric display which, in pioneer chronology, made the year 1833 known as " the year the stars fell." He married Rachel Chesser, daughter of James Chesser. She was born on October 19, 1818.

CHAPTER XIII.

THE TENTH DISTRICT.

T HE Tenth District is bounded on the north and
west by Perry County; on the east, by the Ninth
and Eleventh Districts; and on the south, by Lewis
County. It includes Cane Creek from the Lewis
County line down to the Perry County line, which
runs near Enon Church, near the mouth of Lower
Sinking. Upper Sinking and Lower Sinking, the
valleys of which enter the valley of Cane Creek, are
so called on account of the waters of each disappear-
ing before Cane Creek is reached. The disappearance of the waters of Lower Sinking is gradual, and
is not so marked as is the disappearance of the waters of Upper Sinking, which drop abruptly into the
mouth of a cavern at the foot of a large and rugged
hill. The place of disappearance is on the farm once
owned by Amos Edwards; the place of reappear-
ance is supposed to be the large, bold spring near the
A. C. McClaren place. Upper Sinking is about three
miles above Lower Sinking. Cane Creek, which is
about twenty miles long, rises in Lewis County, and
empties into Buffalo River in Perry County, near
Beardstown. In the Cane Creek valley are found
some of the most fertile farms and some of the neatest
and best-built farmhouses to be found in the county.

Coming into Cane Creek, just above the Perry

County line, and near where Robert C. Murray now lives, is Salmon Branch, named for —— Salmon, who located here about 1820. Martin's Branch, which runs into Cane Creek above the mouth of Salmon Branch, was named for George Martin, an early settler. Where Mrs. Dudley now lives, William Whitwell and Eli Dyer once lived. James Salmon, a prosperous citizen, at one time lived on Salmon Branch. In his old age he became involved in debt, and, after brooding over this for some time, he went into the woods a few hundred yards west of Robert C. Murray's present residence, and there cut his throat with a razor. His body lay undiscovered in the woods for a week. It was finally found by the searching neighbors and buried on the spot. Salmon's wife and children paid his debts and retained possession of his lands.

One of the earliest and most important settlements in the Tenth District was made on that portion of Cane Creek between the mouth of Upper Sinking and the present site of Farmer's Exchange. The permanent settlement was made immediately after the withdrawal of the Indians, and locations were selected here as early as 1815, while this was yet in the Indian country. The pioneers who settled here were Thomas Whitwell, Alexander Davidson, John D. Murray, John Mitchell, Lewis Dunning, and John Anderson. Whitwell located where " Bud " Joyce now lives; Davidson, just below the present site of

292 HISTORY OF HICKMAN COUNTY, TENN.

Pleasantville; Murray, where Thomas Rodgers now
lives; Mitchell, near the fine spring on the Adolphus
McClaren place; Dunning, on the lands now owned
by James S. Bates; and Anderson, at the Wesley
Jones place. On one of his trips into the Indian
country, John Anderson camped one night in 1815
in Cow Hollow, in the Ninth District. His name,
together with the date, was cut on a tree which stood
near the Line of 1784. John Anderson was a hunter,
a shoemaker, and a cooper. He made and mended
shoes for the pioneers; made barrels, washtubs, water
buckets, churns, etc., for them; and made for himself
the well-earned reputation of being one of the best
hunters in the settlement. His children cleared his
lands, while he worked at his trades. His daughter,
Jennie, who was born on September 4, 1806, married
Samuel Bates, who was born in Maury County on
August 21, 1807.

Samuel Bates was the father of the late William
Bates, who married a daughter of J. R. Sutton.
Sutton, who is the father of Dr. K. I. Sutton, of
Centerville, was at one time a magistrate of this district and a prosperous merchant at Farmer's Exchange, to which place he gave the name. He was
the first postmaster at this point. He now lives at
Dickson, where he is, as he was in Hickman County,
a prominent citizen. Samuel Bates was the father
of James Samuel Bates (born on January 17, 1829),
who yet lives in this district. J. S. Bates married

Phœbe Turner. Their children are Andrew Jackson, John T., Daniel D., Susan J., Delia A., and Nora T. Bates.

James Bates, an old settler, lived at one time where the late Green D. Leiper lived. Green D. Leiper, who was a good and highly respected citizen, came to Hickman County from Maury County, and for several years lived in the Eighth District. About 1870 he came to the Tenth District.

At the mouth of Cave Branch, so called on account of the large cave near its mouth, there lived another good citizen of the district, who came from another county to this—the late James S. Rodgers. Rodgers was born in Williamson County on July 20, 1825, and came in 1881 to the Tenth District, where he died on January 23, 1897. In 1844 he married Elizabeth Hughes, of Williamson County. She was born on October 24, 1828, and is yet living. When he first came to the county, Rodgers lived where W. A. McClaren now lives, and owned the land from the mouth of Cave Branch down to near where Hughes now lives. He later sold a portion of this to W. A. and Adolphus McClaren, who own one hundred and twenty-five acres of fine land. The unsold portion of the Rodgers lands is yet owned by his son, Thomas Rodgers, who was born on February 9, 1860. On May 6, 1894, Thomas Rodgers married Sallie Eastland, daughter of W. C. Eastland, of the Third District.

The Rodgers lands were formerly owned by Shad-

rach Lewis. One of the first settlers on Cane Creek
was John Comer Lewis, who came from North Carolina in an ox cart soon after the removal of the Indians, and settled near the present site of Farmer's
Exchange, on lands entered by Reuben McClaren.
McClaren was a land speculator who entered much
land on Cane Creek and Beaverdam Creek. In
making an entry on Cane Creek, he used the name
of Lewis, who settled on the land, of which, in after
years, by industry and economy, he became the owner.
His first wife was Miss Forrest, a cousin of the Confederate cavalryman, Nathan Bedford Forrest; his
second wife was a daughter of Reuben McClaren.
The sons of John C. Lewis were Shadrach, Fielding,
and Henry Lewis.

One of the first mills built on Cane Creek was built
by Shadrach Lewis. In 1830 he and his brother,
Fielding Lewis, built a carding mill on the lands
entered by John D. Murray. In 1854 this mill was
bought by George S. Stephens, who died one mile
below Pleasantville in 1884. The father of George
S. Stephens was William A. Stephens, who was born
near Henry Courthouse, Va., on March 15, 1802.
A son of George S. Stephens is Sidney Stephens, a
prominent farmer of the Eleventh District.

Col. James Lewis, of the First Tennessee Cavalry,
C. S. A., was a grandson of John C. Lewis, and a
second cousin of Gen. Nathan Bedford Forrest, under
whom he served. At the breaking out of the Civil
War, Colonel Lewis lived at Linden, Perry County.

A number of the young men of Cane Creek were members of Lewis' Regiment, they being under the immediate command of their neighbor, the brave and chivalrous Hartwell F. Barham, captain of Company I. James S. Bates served in this company, as did also his brother, W. C. Bates. In 1864 two of Barham's company, John Cotham and Daniel Kelly, while at home on furloughs, were murdered by Perry County jayhawkers, the leading participants in the murder being Alex. Guthrie and George Shelton. Cotham and Kelly were spending the night with Morris Twomey, where Mrs. Rainey now lives. The jayhawkers surprised them, and, after capturing them, murdered them. The jayhawkers were out after Commodore Cotham, a man by them much wanted and much feared. At the head of Cane Creek they attacked a party at a dance and killed James Peeler, a son of Jesse Peeler, of Beaverdam Creek. Commodore Cotham escaped with a few scratches; but the jayhawkers, coming on down the creek, wreaked their vengeance on his brother, John Cotham, whom they clubbed to death with their pistols. After boasting that they left three dead Rebels behind them, these brave " homemade Yankees," who defended their country's flag by killing unarmed prisoners, went on their way to Linden, varying the monotony of their journey by killing another prisoner whom they had with them. Another attempt was made to capture Commodore Cotham, he being at that time with David Miller, in the Fifteenth District. When surprised by the Federals, Miller and Cotham were engaged in cleaning out a well. Miller was in the well, and Cotham was turning the windlass. Their pistols were in the house near by, and they surrendered. However, they were allowed to go into the house, whereupon they seized their pistols and immediately rescinded their recent action. When armed, so great was the terror of their names that the troop of Federals, during the confusion which followed, allowed them to escape unharmed.

W. H. Whitwell, of the Tenth District, was a captain in the Tenth Tennessee Cavalry, C. S. A., and lost a leg in the service.

In 1840 William Bradley Cook sold goods near where George Williams now lives. He was the first merchant at Pleasantville and the first postmaster at this post office, which was established about this time. Andrew J. Dudley was the first mail carrier who brought the mail here, he carrying the mail from Linden to Franklin. A young man in his employ occasionally carried the mail for him, and on one of his trips the mail was robbed. Suspicion pointed to the young man, whom Dudley discharged. This incident cost Dudley, who was a poor man, about three hundred dollars. At one time Dudley paid a security debt of seven hundred dollars, selling all of his property, except one horse and a pair of oxen, in order to do this. These he offered to sell, too, but the creditor refused to allow him to make the further sacrifice.

In 1820 Pleasant Whitwell, a Primitive Baptist

preacher, taught school near where Beech Grove
Church now stands, near Pleasantville. Whitwell
was not only a good school-teacher, but was a good
preacher and an upright man, who labored long and
well in the Tenth District and surrounding country. In 1838 Silas Record taught school at Beech
Grove. The following year John Nolan, a Methodist preacher, taught here. The Tenth District has
to-day good schools and churches, and some of the
leading school-teachers of the county are to be found
here.

The most extensive enterprise ever conducted in
the Tenth District was the large sawmill operated at
Pleasantville by C. L. Storrs. This mill was placed
here about 1890, and continued in operation for four
years.

In 1817 Aaron Anderson Edwards married Nancy
Moody, this being the first wedding on Cane Creek.
Eleven children resulted from this marriage. Their
names were John Anderson, Andrew Jackson, William Thomas, David L., William J., Nicholas, Elizabeth A., Martha J., Malinda, Margaret, and Amanda.
Aaron Anderson Edwards lived just above the mouth
of Ivy Branch, which flows into Cane Creek from the
north. The first marriage in the county was that of
William Cotham and Sarah Shipp, in 1808.

John Anderson Edwards was born on March 9,
1824. He married Mary Ann Wilburn (born on
December 20, 1822), a daughter of Burrel Wilburn,
who came from Virginia to Perry County. Burrel

Wilburn married Mary Lomax, a daughter of Samuel Lomax, of North Carolina. John A. Edwards, who was a prominent preacher of the Primitive Baptist Church, died on January 9, 1878. His brothers, David L. and Andrew Jackson Edwards, were also preachers of prominence in this church. John Edwards, a son of John A. Edwards, is at present a magistrate of this district. Another son of John A. Edwards is Thomas C. Edwards, who lives near Lobelville, Perry County, and who owns a fine tract of land, bounded on the north by the Line of 1784; another son is Dr. James A. Edwards, of Columbia, a man of whom Hickman County is justly proud. A. J. Pace, a son of Pleasant G. Pace, married a daughter of John A. Edwards and lives near the old Edwards homestead.

At an early date Amos Anderson Edwards lived on Upper Sinking, and the cavern into which the waters of Upper Sinking fall is on the farm on which he lived. He was born on October 27, 1814. He married Elizabeth Wilburn, who was born on May 12, 1826. He was the father of Wilburn Edwards.

John Lancaster and his brother, Gabriel Lancaster, of Beaverdam Creek, were Baptist preachers who preached in the Tenth District in the early days. Their father, Benjamin Lancaster, was probably the first preacher who held services in this district.

Isaac Cotham came from Georgia in 1807 and located on Sugar Creek, in the Eighth District. He located at what is known as the " Coleman place," where, in 1809, Andrew Carothers erected a gristmill, this being the second mill erected in the county. In 1815 Cotham removed from Sugar Creek to near the mouth of Ivy Branch, this then being in the Indian country. Having doubts as to the title of his lands, he returned to Sugar Creek. After the treaty he (in 1818) returned to the Tenth District, and remained here until his death. His son, John Cotham, who was born on Sugar Creek on November 26, 1808, is yet living in the Tenth District, he being the oldest native citizen of Hickman County. The mother of John Cotham was Sallie Depriest, a daughter of Randall Depriest, who came from Georgia to Big Spring Creek, in the Sixth District, in 1812, and to Cane Creek in 1818. John Cotham married Eliza Sanders, who was born in 1812. She was the daughter of Joseph Sanders, who was one of the pioneers of the Tenth District, he settling at an early date above the Walter W. Brown place. The aged John Cotham remembers the bottoms of Cane Creek when he first saw them as a dense canebrake, with here and there a settler between Buffalo River and the head of the creek. One of these settlers was —— Petty, who lived at the Turner Depriest place in 1818, when the people of this section carried their corn to a mill near Vernon. Mr. Cotham's first teacher was Moses Nicks, who taught on Sugar Creek above the point where Lee & Gould later built their furnace. The sons of John Cotham are W. A. and Richard Cotham; his daughters, Martha, Susan, and Mary.

On the north side of Cane Creek, about one mile below the mouth of Ivy Branch, is one of the best mill sites to be found in the county. Here for many years have been run a gristmill and a cotton gin. The lands on which the mill stands have been owned successively by Jones Whitesides, John Sisco, Hiram Campbell, Martin McClaren, Jack McClaren, Adolphus McClaren, James Rodgers, William D. Humphreys, and John E. Sisco, who is the present owner. John E. Sisco was born on July 6, 1842, and is a son of A. J. Sisco. The father of A. J. Sisco was John Sisco, who in 1820 came from North Carolina and settled near the mouth of Cane Creek.

In the territory annexed to Lewis County by the Tennessee Legislature in 1897, lived for many years those two worthy citizens, Johnson Downing and Walter W. Brown, who were brothers-in-law. Downing, who was born in 1813, came to Cane Creek from Lincoln County in 1835. He for many years ran a gristmill and sawmill on his farm, which, prior to 1897, was the last farm on Cane Creek in Hickman County. He died a few years ago.

Walter W. Brown was born in Virginia in 1807, and came to Cane Creek in 1833 and located near Brown's schoolhouse, where he lived until his death, a few years ago. He was for many years a magistrate in the Tenth District. He was the father of John, Isham, and Walter W. Brown, Jr.

Some of the other magistrates of this district were Pleasant Whitwell, J. R. Sutton, Robert C. Murray, and James S. Rodgers. The present incumbents are John Edwards and R. C. Beasley. Harvey Hinson, who lived near Farmer's Exchange, was at one time a constable in this district, as was also Mr. Depriest, who lived on Depriest's Branch. J. D. Whitwell was a deputy under Sheriff Stephenson.

J. N. Pace, a son of Pleasant G. Pace, of Cane Creek, was for two terms Trustee of Hickman County; and his brother-in-law, A. J. McClaren, was serving his second term as County Court Clerk at the time of his death, in 1897.

In the autumn of 1864 the Confederates under Col. Jacob Biffle came upon the Federals under Colonel Murphy near Buffalo post office, in Humphreys County, and a running fight continued, with the Federals retreating, until the final engagement at Centerville. Biffle had under his command the companies of Capts. Robert Anderson, Thomas Easley, and —— Green, and the detached companies of Henon Cross and David Miller. The pursuit continued up Buffalo River to Beardstown, and then up Cane Creek to near Farmer's Exchange. A detachment of Confederates here attempted, by turning to the left, to intercept the Federals at the head of Depriest's Branch. In this they were unsuccessful, the Federals in their wild flight passing this point before the arrival of the Confederates. The Federals continued their retreat through the Eleventh District.

CHAPTER XIV.

THE ELEVENTH DISTRICT.

THE Eleventh District lies on Beaverdam Creek, and includes this creek and its tributaries from the Lewis County line down to the line of the Ninth District, near Joe's Branch, below the Levi McCollum farm. It is bounded on the north by the Ninth and First Districts; on the east, by the First and Twelfth Districts; on the south, by Lewis County; and on the west, by the Tenth District. Beaverdam Creek derives its name from the fact that the first settlers found, near where John Peeler now lives, the remains of a large dam which had been built by beavers. Portions of fallen trees were in the creek here, and the stumps standing near by showed plainly that they had been felled by the beavers. This dam was above the mouth of Milam's Branch and near the present McClaren place.

Milam's Branch was named for Jordan Milam, who settled on this branch in 1819, he having occupant's rights in the lands on this tributary of Beaverdam Creek. Milam had been a soldier in the Revolutionary War.

Above Milam's Branch is Wade's Branch, known originally as "Murray's Branch." James and Joseph Murray settled on this branch in 1819. In 1828 they sold to Robert Wade, whose name the branch has since borne. Wade was born in Virginia. When a young man, he went west into Kentucky, where he married Miss Bearden. From Kentucky he and his young wife came, in 1823, to Hickman County. Wade then owned a black mare, a gun, and a dog. He placed his wife on the mare, shouldered his gun, called his dog, and started on foot for Tennessee, and in this manner they made the entire journey. They settled on Murray's Branch, and in 1828 bought the lands here from the Murrays. When Wade first came here, he traded his mare for a still, his saddle for some corn, and commenced the manufacture of whisky, which he continued for thirty years. During this time he claimed that he drank one quart of whisky each day. When at home his drinks were carefully measured, and when he was on a journey he carried with him that quantity of whisky which his frequent measurements had shown him he would need. Yet Wade was not considered a drunkard, but was an energetic and prosperous citizen, who for a number of years was one of the magistrates of this district. According to his statement, he drank during these years nearly three thousand gallons of whisky. The place where his distillery stood is about one mile below the location of Old Ætna Furnace, at the present George Milam place. Sons of Robert Wade were Robert and George Wade. Robert Wade, Jr., married Harriet, the daughter of Samuel Malugin, and soon after his marriage he died. George Wade married a daughter of Ross Breece. He died

at Fort Donelson in 1862.   Benjamin Harris married
a daughter of George Wade, and now owns the lands
originally owned by Robert Wade, Sr.   At this place
the Federal Colonel, Murphy, was overtaken and surprised, early one morning in 1864, by the Confederate Colonel, Biffle, during the running fight from
Buffalo to Centerville.   The firing was for a time
brisk, but there were no casualties, and the Federals
continued their retreat.

Above Wade's Branch is Brushy Fork of Beaver-
dam Creek, which was settled about 1820 by Levi
Garrett, John Hinson, and —— Halbrooks, all from
North Carolina.   Robert and Thomas Dolison and
Daniel Davidson came here from North Carolina in
1825.   In 1830 John Hinson lived where Joel P.
Morrison now lives, but these lands were entered in
1825 by Robert Thompson.   At the mouth of Brushy
Fork, in 1830, Daniel Davidson taught school, and
his patrons were the Dolisons, Hinson, Garrett, the
Walkers, John Angel, and Joseph Kimmins.

Joseph Kimmins lived just below the site of Old
Ætna Furnace.   Here, in 1830, his son, Robert Kimmins, died.   Daughters of Joseph Kimmins were
Nellie, who married Daniel McClaren; Jennie, who
married Elias Denson Morrison; Keziah, who married Elias Bradshaw; Elizabeth, who married James
Chandler; Theresa, who married James Halbrooks;
Margaret, who married Zerah Shipp; Grace, who
married John Cunningham; and Charity, who married James Garrett.   Four of these sisters held a

'eunion in 1892 at the home of one of them, Mrs.
Jennie Morrison. The youngest was seventy-seven
years of age; the oldest, ninety-four. Major Mc-
Claren was for many years the only slaveholder
in the Eleventh District. After his death his slaves
were being hired publicly, when one of them—Wyley
—announced to a bidder that he need not bid for him,
as he would die before he would go with him. This
bidder made the highest bid, and Wyley was expected
to commence work for him on the following Monday
morning. On that morning, however, Wyley was
found hanging to a rope tied to the " eaves bearer "
of his cabin.

Williamson Poore, who married a Kimmins, was
the father of John M., Joseph C., Pleasant B., Robert, Benjamin, David, Samuel, and James Poore. Of
these, only Samuel and Pleasant are now living.

One of the last bears killed in Hickman County
was killed in 1822 by James Arnold, on the farm
now owned by Joel P. Morrison. Arnold, who settled on Peter Branch of Sulphur Fork in 1820, was
a great hunter, and, although a poor man, he paid his
debts punctually with the skins and meat of the wild
animals he killed. In making trades he would not
promise to pay in money, but would promise so many
deer skins, wolf skins, or deer horns. The last panther killed in the county was killed in 1828 by
Claiborne Berryman, near the place now known as
" Buffalo Switch," on the railroad between Centerville and Ætna. On the day before that on which

the panther was killed it had pursued the wife of Elias Denson Morrison for two miles, she escaping on account of the superior speed of her horse. Berryman settled near the site of Old Ætna Furnace in 1820, and was for several years miller at Spencer Tinsley's mill. While out hunting he found the panther fast asleep on a log, and shot it.

James Lawrence, a pioneer " Baron Munchausen," lived at this time near the Ninth District line, and the unreasonable and humorous stories which he told about his favorite dog are yet recalled by old citizens.

Henry Breece, father of Benajah Breece, settled in 1820 on Beaverdam Creek, seven miles from Centerville. He died here in 1834. Benajah Breece married Mary J. Winters.

Marcus Black in 1820 settled at the Elias Bates place, and cleared some of the land now owned by Bates.

Arthur Atkinson about 1825 settled on Wade's Branch. His son, John F. Atkinson, was shot one night in 1870, the shot being fired through an open window. A young man named Shepherd, whom Atkinson had discharged a few days before this, served a term in the penitentiary for this crime. This occurred near where Wesley Morrison now lives.

William B., Robert, Elijah, and James Hicks, who were brothers, settled near the present site of Ætna Furnace in 1818. Benjamin and William Harris, who removed to Illinois in 1825, also settled here at this time. They moved to Illinois in ox carts, one of which broke down soon after they started, delaying them for several days. A son of one of them, Wooten Harris, had twelve fingers and twelve toes.

Jere Booth, a pioneer of this section, was a hunter and fortune teller, and had great faith in the divining rod. He spent much of his time in pursuit of game and in search of valuable minerals. He claimed to have discovered gold in what is now Lewis County, but died without ever having disclosed the location of his mine.

From North Carolina, Bunis Warren, John Patton, and " Billy " Morrison came to the lower part of the district in 1818. They were brothers-in-law, they having married sisters named Peacock. Patton entered one thousand acres of land, and there are now several fine farms which originally were a part of the " Patton survey." In 1830 Morrison was miller at Arthur Atkinson's mill, and went during the entire winter without shoes. His appearance gained for him the nickname, " The Short and Dirty Miller." Major McClaren made a large entry in this portion of the district in 1820, and during this year Joseph, John, and Cleve McCann—relatives of Warren, Patton, and Morrison—came from North Carolina and settled here. When the wife of Patton failed to make any butter from " a churning," she concluded that " old lady Hamby," who lived near by, had bewitched her cows or had bewitched the milk. She thereupon thrust a piece of heated iron into the milk. Much butter was the result; and

when she went to the house of " old lady Hamby "
and found her suffering from a burn, her suspicions
were confirmed. This occurred about 1825.

In 1825 Sylvanus Walker lived near the present
site of Ætna Furnace, as did also Elijah Blackburn.

Jacob Byler lived where Alex. Prince now lives,
and was Hickman County's first coroner after the
Constitution of 1834 was adopted.

John Lovett in 1830 lived in the Eleventh District, and here was born his son, Jesse Lovett, who
afterwards lived in Lowe's Bend.

Ewel Warren, father of the late Jasper N. Warren and of Hickman County's present register, David
Warren, was for many years a magistrate in the Eleventh District.

Jesse Peeler was born in Rowan County, N. C.,
on May 4, 1788. He married Hannah Smith on
February 14, 1814, and in 1816 he came to Vernon.
Here his wife died, and, returning to North Carolina,
he married Miss Joyce F. Woodson on February 14,
1817. He then returned to Vernon, but later moved
to Lick Creek, where his second wife died. On February 14, 1839, he married Margaret B. Giles. This
was his third and last marriage, and all of them
were on the same date—February 14. He in 1853
moved from Lick Creek to the Eleventh District,
where he died on August 30, 1883, at the advanced
age of ninety-five years, three months, and twenty-
six days. He was the father of David W., George,
Jesse G., Jacob R., Jasper N., James M., and John C.

Peeler. James M. Peeler was killed on Cane Creek by Perry County jayhawkers; Jasper N. Peeler, who was in 1888 tax assessor for Hickman County, now lives in Giles County; Jacob Peeler was at one time constable of the First District; John Calvin Peeler, who has been a magistrate since 1888, is now chairman of the County Court. Frances Cordelia, a daughter of Jesse Peeler, married John Bates. Jesse Peeler lived where his son, John C. Peeler, now lives, and this point has been the voting place of the district for over sixty years.

Spencer Tinsley erected a mill near the site of Old Ætna Furnace in 1824. In 1840 Madison Napier erected a mill one mile below the site of Tinsley's mill. This mill furnished meal for the employees of Napier, who had since 1837 been operating Ætna Furnace. About 1845 Robert Wade built a mill on Wade's Branch, and five years before this Jacob Byler had a mill near this branch. Squire Peeler, a half-brother of Jesse Peeler, at one time owned the Byler mill, and Thomas Warren had a mill at the same time on the opposite side of Beaverdam Creek. Sometimes Beaverdam Creek would not furnish enough water for both mills, and Peeler would prosper in the milling business, but his competitor would not. It is said that upon one occasion Warren, during the night, cut a ditch into Peeler's mill pond and proceeded to appropriate the water thereof to his own use. A lawsuit followed this, but with what result is not known. Elias Bates and Jonathan Arnold now have mills in this district. The mill of the former has been in operation since 1867; the mill of the latter has been in operation for over fifty years.

Even before Tennessee became a State it was known that rich deposits of iron ore were in the hills surrounding the head of Beaverdam Creek, but not until 1830 were steps taken toward the converting of this ore into iron. In this year Madison Napier, who was already interested in mineral lands in Dickson County, bought a large number of acres in this section. In 1836 Napier came with his slaves and many other laborers, built a furnace here, and commenced the mining of ore and the manufacture of iron. The pig iron from this furnace, which was named "Ætna Furnace," was carried to the place on Duck River, opposite Shipp's Bend, which has since been known as the "Metal Landing." Napier continued to operate this furnace until 1848, when he became financially embarrassed. The property was then sold by Sheriff J. W. Huddleston, and was purchased by Dr. Napier, who sold it to W. H. and W. C. Napier, who, in turn, sold it to Dr. Bellfield Carter and Daniel Hillman. Carter and Hillman continued to operate the furnace until 1855, when operations were suspended until 1862. In 1862 they resumed operations, employing a large number of slaves, who were hired from their owners in Dickson and Davidson Counties—points exposed to the Federal Army. However, in the following year the Federals came here, confiscated the stock, carried away the iron, freed the slaves, and hushed forever the hum of

business where Old Ætna stood. In 1884 a company
of which V. K. Stevenson was manager began the
building of a furnace on the railroad, four miles above
the site of Old Ætna. After the death of Stevenson
the Ætna Iron Company pushed the work to completion. The furnace here afterwards passed into the
hands of the Southern Iron Company, which operated
it until 1893, since which time it has not been in
operation.

At a muster at the Cross Roads, above Peeler's, in
1830, Meredith Hinson and Charles Warren, who
had prior to this been friends, engaged in a pugilistic
encounter, from the effects of which both died within
two weeks. In 1886 a negro was killed at Ætna by
another negro, Ben. Humble. In 1892 Martin Hinson and " Dock " Hightower killed Stump Devisor at
Ætna.

In 1828 a man, who later figured as principal in
one of the most celebrated criminal cases of this section of the State, came to the Eleventh District. This
was Joe Bearden, who came with his two brothers
from Kentucky in search of employment. After
stopping here for a short time, he went to Mussel
Shoals, where the government was having work done.
After remaining there for some time, he and a companion left for their respective homes. Bearden
came to the Eleventh District, but his companion,
who lived elsewhere, never reached home, and was
last seen alive with Bearden. The missing man's
relatives instituted a search, and his dead body was

found in the southern portion of Perry County. Suspicion naturally pointed to Bearden; and Thomas Green, who lived in the Eleventh District, said that he recognized a coat which Bearden had as the property of the dead man.   Green arrested Bearden and held him until the relatives of the murdered man could be communicated with.   The coat was identified by a peculiar patch there was on it, a sister of Bearden's victim writing to Green a description of this patch.   Bearden was taken to Centerville and placed in jail.   He was tried at Perryville, and his case was taken to the Superior Court, at Reynoldsburg, where he was finally convicted and hanged in 1832.   Bearden said, while in jail, that if he was hanged, the meeting between him and the devil would be a stormy affair.   During the night following the day on which Bearden was hanged there swept over Tennessee a terrible storm, which in its course almost destroyed the town of Shelbyville.   Remembering Bearden's remark, the people throughout the counties of Hickman, Perry, and Humphreys called this " the Bearden storm."

Thomas Sheppard, Robert Wade, Jacob Byler, Thomas Warren, John F. Atkinson, Ewel Warren, Joel P. Morrison, J. F. M. Fain, Fort George, and G. W. Mathis have been magistrates in this district. The present incumbents are P. R. Lovelace and John C. Peeler.   John Doddy, James Devore, John F. Atkinson, Van Arnold, Will. Black, and James Norman have been constables of this district.   Col. Levi Mc-

Collum, of this district, was twice a member of the State Legislature.

In the autumn of 1861 Sheriff Levi McCollum, who had just been elected after a close race with Elijah Cantrell, resigned and raised a company for the Forty-second Tennessee Infantry. In this regiment he was promoted successively to the positions of major and lieutenant colonel. During the same year Joel P. Morrison raised a company for the Forty-eighth Tennessee Infantry. Captain Morrison was captured at Fort Donelson, and, after having been imprisoned at Camp Chase and Johnson's Island, he was exchanged at Vicksburg in 1862. He was in the battles of Chickamauga and Missionary Ridge, and in January, 1864, he was discharged, he being too old for the service. Captain Morrison served in the Mexican War as a private in John W. Whitfield's company, being present at the battle of Monterey and at the siege and capture of Vera Cruz.

Elias Denson Morrison was born in Mecklenburg County, N. C., on February 20, 1795, and died on Sulphur Fork of Beaverdam Creek on March 30, 1852. His wife, Jennie Kimmins, was born in North Carolina before her father, Joseph Kimmins, came to Tennessee. She was born on November 7, 1798, and died on June 30, 1893, aged ninety-five years. The daughters of Elias D. and Jennie (Kimmins) Morrison were: Jane, who married Dr. William Russell, a brother of Cyrus W. Russell; Margaret, who married Andrew Russell, a brother of Dr. William

Russell; Dorothy, who died unmarried; and Cynthia, who married John Pickard. Their sons were: John Cooper, David Bradshaw, Robert Kimmins, James Wesley, Elias Kirkpatrick, Thomas Brown, and Joel Porter. David B. and Thomas Brown Morrison died while prisoners of war at Camp Douglass. Capt. Joel Porter Morrison, the only surviving son of Elias Denson Morrison, was born near Old Ætna on July 14, 1823.

A portion of Sulphur Fork is in the Eleventh District, and here William Chandler settled in 1825. He married Miss Bates, a sister of Robert, James, William, Jere, Jesse, Josiah, and Samuel Bates. The sons of William Chandler were John, Benjamin, James, William, Isaac, and Willis, all of whom are now dead. Benjamin Chandler had seven sons in the Confederate Army, and a majority, if not all, of them lost their lives during the Civil War.

Jesse Southern lived on Sulphur Fork in 1840, and, while cutting rye in his field, was shot from ambush, the ball striking the index finger of his right hand and shattering the handle of the old-fashioned sickle which he was using. Elconah A. Curry was charged with shooting him, arrested, tried, convicted, and sent to the penitentiary for a term of years. The judge was Edmund Dillahunty (de la Honte) and the attorney-general was Nathaniel Baxter, who afterwards became a judge.

At the head of Sulphur Fork are the celebrated Beaverdam Springs. In 1832 Joseph Jones commenced the erection of a hotel here, and by 1835 he had it completed, together with about forty cabins for the accommodation of guests. He also built a grist-mill and sawmill at a point one mile below the springs, where a cotton gin had stood prior to this. The sons of Joseph Jones were: Allan, George, Abner, Stephen, Joel, Montague, and Dr. William Jones. Joel Jones, the only one of these now living, lives at Palestine, in Lewis County. Joseph Jones sold the springs to Jesse Hart, who, after owning them for a time, sold them to Thomas Walker and —— Armstrong, of Maury County. The springs are now owned by the Beaverdam Springs Company, composed of citizens of Maury County. A serious fight occurred here before the war between some young men from Columbia and some young men from the neighborhood. Lewis Bates, who was using his fists in the most effective Hickman County style, was stabbed with a sword cane in the hands of a young Maury Countian. Bates was not seriously injured, and, despite the difference in the weapons used, he and his party came out of the engagement with colors flying.

James Pope taught school on Sulphur Fork in 1823; Paschal Lancaster, in 1838; and Thomas Smith, in 1840. While teaching here, Lancaster one day at " playtime " became choked on a sweet potato. He called two of his pupils, Isaac and Willis Chandler, to his assistance, instructing the former to rub his neck, while the latter went for water.

While they were doing this he gasped: " Rub, Ike, rub! Run, Willis, run!" These, however, were not the last words of Lancaster, as the rebellious potato was finally overcome.

One of the early preachers of this section was John Lancaster, the Primitive Baptist. Lancaster assisted in the building of the cabins at Beaverdam Springs, working six days and preaching on the seventh. Other pioneer preachers of the Baptist Church were Pleasant Whitwell and —— Ragsdale. Andrew Craig and Isaac Pace were preachers of the Christian Church, who preached here from 1835 to 1840.

Carey Pope, who had settled at Vernon in 1808 and planted a peach orchard there, removed in 1820 to Sulphur Fork and settled at the Adam Coble place. James Pope lived three miles below Beaverdam Springs in 1827. He had here a mill and distillery. Mrs. David Morrison and Mrs. Jack Malugin are daughters of James Pope.

In 1840 a party of hunters from Centerville and Shipp's Bend chased a deer to Beaverdam Creek. On this creek Dr. Bird Moore, Thomas Dansby, and Horatio Clagett were waiting for the deer, which was being pursued through the woods by the hounds belonging to William Shipp. When the deer came to the " stand," Dansby and Moore both fired. Moore shot the deer, and Dansby shot Moore. Moore was badly wounded, and while Clagett, Dansby, and others were trying to relieve his sufferings, William Shipp arrived. He was told of the serious accident and saw the wounded man, but his first words were: " But where's the deer ? " He soon found the wounded deer, cut its throat, and then commenced to render assistance to the sufferer. A messenger was sent for Dr. Samuel B. Moore, who was at Beaverdam Springs, and another went to notify the wife of Dr. Bird Moore, at Centerville. Moore was placed in a coal cart obtained from Ætna Furnace. When, on their return to Centerville, the party was met by the sorrowful wife of the wounded man, Dr. Moore outdid Shipp by replying to his wife's question, "Are you dying, Bird ? " with the statement: " I killed the deer, Evaline; Dansby never touched it." Dr. Moore recovered.

CHAPTER XV.

THE TWELFTH DISTRICT.

THE Twelfth District is bounded on the north by the First and Fourteenth Districts; east, by the Fourteenth District; south, by Lewis County; and west, by the Eleventh District. It includes Swan Creek and its tributaries from the Hiram Prince place, now the William Prince place, up to the Lewis County line, above the Harder place. Swan Creek received its name from the fact that a swan was killed in this creek by hunters prior to 1800. As stated elsewhere, it was called by the party which ran the Line of 1784 " Swan River," and it was probably one of this party who killed the swan.

At Swan Bluff, which is just over the line in the First District, B. M. Hutcheson sold goods for twelve years, Arthur I. Nixon succeeding him at this point. Above Haw Branch, at the mouth of which is Swan Bluff, is Persimmon Branch, on which Peter Condor located as an occupant in 1816. John Burcham lived here in 1820. George Tatom, who lived on this branch years ago, was at one time a magistrate in the Twelfth District. He sold his lands to George Peery about 1820. Elihu Morrison lived here from 1816 to 1820. On this branch a family named Banks lived in 1830. Bartlett Mathis lived on this branch in 1860; ——

Clayton, a wagon maker, wheelwright, and shoemaker, lived here in 1833.

Copperas Branch, so called on account of this mineral being found here and used by the pioneers in dyeing their clothing, was settled by George Berry, an occupant, prior to 1830. An "occupant" was one whose occupancy of a tract of land, supplemented by a small established price per acre, constituted his title; his title was based on no warrant; he merely came, settled on a tract, and later paid a small price for it. Joseph Rossen, a cooper and a faith doctor, married a daughter of George Berry and lived for years on this branch a homeless, inoffensive man.

In 1825 William Beakley returned from Missouri (he had gone there in 1820), and bought lands at the mouth of Copperas Branch from Thomas Bingham, of Cathey's Creek, Maury County.

Coleman's Branch, named for Coleman, an occupant, who settled on it prior to 1830, is above Copperas Branch.

Next is Jenkins' Branch, named for the occupant, Jenkins. This branch was named by the surveyor, George Peery, "Fall Branch West of Swan Creek," and is so called in the early land papers of this section.

The Lewis County line runs near by, and here John Harder has a gristmill, and Mr. Bates a sawmill, both operated by water power, secured by the confining with a dam the waters of a large spring.

The tributaries above named are on the west side of Swan Creek. Going down Swan Creek from the

Lewis County line, the first tributary on the east side is Horse Branch. Tully Gregory lived here as an occupant in 1834. The Tolly family lived here as early as 1824, they being original settlers. Below Horse Branch are Upper and Lower Pine Branches, so called on account of the luxuriant growth of pine trees here. Farther down is Fall Branch, named by the surveyor, George Peery, on account of the falls on this branch.

Early settlers on Fall Branch were Azariah Anderson and James Edwards. Anderson, who lived here in 1825, was the father of Whig Anderson. Azariah Anderson, Jr., also lived on this branch. Martin Condor lived here in 1823.

William Duncan, the father of W. H., James A., David M., Marcenus, and John Duncan, came from Kentucky and bought land at this point from the original owners. The father of William Duncan was killed by Indians. In recent years much phosphate has been mined in this section.

Near the line between the Twelfth and Fourteenth Districts are the places now known as the "Arch Peery place" and the " Gilmore place." They were settled by Robert Peery in 1817. Robert Peery, a son of James Peery, Sr., was born in Virginia in 1796, and in 1814 he enlisted in the American army and went with his three brothers from Leatherwood Creek, in the Thirteenth District, to New Orleans, where they took part in the battle of January 8, 1815. Robert Peery was one of the few American soldiers wounded in this battle. After his return from New Orleans, the Peery lands on Leatherwood Creek were lost as a result of a long and expensive lawsuit; but, undaunted by misfortune, the Peery brothers—Alexander, Robert, William, and George—bought the John Tate lands, five hundred acres. When the land was divided, Robert Peery's portion included the present Arch. Peery and Gilmore lands. In 1820 Robert Peery married Jane Brown, daughter of Charles Brown, of Cathey's Creek The children of this union were Charles Brown Peery and John Luther Peery. Charles Brown Peery, who was born on January 23, 1824, at the R. G. Peery place, married Mary A. Lusk, of Maury County. After her death he married Mrs. McGill, of Swan Creek. Brown Peery's two daughters, Margaret and Mildred, died in their infancy. His sons are Robert Alexander Peery and James Rufus Peery. John Luther Peery, who was born on March 12, 1826, married Elizabeth Wheat, of Maury County. A son of John L. Peery is Hon. Robert L. Peery, who represented Hickman County in the Legislature from 1893 to 1895. He married Sarah C. Holmes, of Maury County, a daughter of Samuel H. Holmes, the Cumberland Presbyterian preacher. The wife of Samuel H. Holmes was Nancy E. Whitesides.

Robert, Alexander, William, George, and James Peery, Jr., were the sons of James Peery, Sr. The first three named were triplets, and all lived to be over fifty years of age, but not one lived to be sixty. The first four named were at the battle of New Orleans. All returned and became leading citizens and the ancestors of a numerous posterity. James Peery, Sr., was born in England and came to Virginia when young. He served in the American Army during the Revolutionary War. He was a soldier under General Morgan at the battle of the Cowpens.

William Peery moved to Mississippi, where he died. His son, W. D. Peery, was a State Senator in Mississippi. The other sons of James Peery, Sr., lived and died in Hickman County, and were buried at " the old camp ground " on Swan Creek. As a family, they were Cumberland Presbyterians.

George Peery was a pioneer school-teacher and surveyor, and lived a long life of usefulness. He was born in Virginia and came to Tennessee at an early date. He married Ann Carson, of East Tennessee, and was the father of Marcenus G. Peery, David C. Peery, and George Peery, Jr. His daughters were: Nellie, who married David B. Warren; Mary, who married William P. Weatherly; Martha, who married Abner F. Aydelott; and Alzenia, who married —— Brown, of Lewis County. George Peery was the second man to hold the position of county surveyor for Hickman County, holding this office from October 28, 1825, to May, 1851. He was succeeded by Samuel C. Aydelott, who served from May, 1851, to 1865. David C. Peery was entry taker for Hickman County from 1836 to May, 1851, when he was succeeded by George Peery, who served until 1856, at which time the office was abolished.

Near the line of the First and Twelfth Districts, in 1816 and 1817, George, Alexander, and William Peery operated saltpeter works. One evening George left for their home on Leatherwood Creek, cautioning his brothers, who were to remain overnight, to be on the lookout for Indians, the works being located in what was still their territory. After going a short distance, George, for the sake of amusement, rushed back, crying: "Indians!" William and Alexander, trained woodsmen, seized their rifles and sprang into the bushes, from which George expected them to soon reappear. In this he was disappointed. Minutes grew into hours, and finally George Peery reached the correct conclusion that he was there alone, ten miles from the settlement on Duck River at Gordon's Ferry. He, however, remained through the night; and next morning as he journeyed through the woods toward Leatherwood Creek, he met his brothers returning cautiously toward the saltpeter works, accompanied by a party of settlers. Explanations followed, but it was difficult to find a place to introduce a laugh.

Samuel C. Aydelott, already referred to as the successor of George Peery, was born in 1802, and was the son of Joseph and Ann Aydelott, who came from North Carolina. He married Adeline McMinn. He was a brother of Abner F. Aydelott, the father of Marcenus P., William D., James D., Luther, and

Samuel D. Aydelott.   The latter died in the Confederate Army while a soldier in the Forty-Eighth Tennessee Infantry.   The daughters of Abner F. Aydelott were: Margaret, who married Beakley; Priscilla, who married Burcham; Frances, who married Whitesides; and Ellen, who married Sharp.

The Sharps were early settlers here, and the old Sharp place was for years the voting place and muster grounds for this section.   Nehemiah Sharp was the original owner of the James Campbell lands, he having entered them prior to 1825.

The lands where David M. Duncan and Jonathan Tolles now live were in 1835 the property of —— Carothers, an early settler.   Jere Harder in 1830 lived where John L. Peery now lives.   Here, before the Civil War, lived J. H. Plummer, the owner of a number of slaves.   He afterwards lived at Palestine, in Lewis County.   He was the father of the late Dr. H. K. Plummer and of O. T., Frank, Lee, William, and T. A. Plummer.

William Harder, Sr., a brother of Jere Harder, was an early settler and lived where Thomas Duncan now lives.   He came from North Carolina and married a daughter of his neighbor, Carothers.   His son, William Harder, was a lieutenant in the Confederate Army, was a school-teacher, and was at one time a magistrate in this district.   Another son, Pleasant Harder, died while a soldier in the Confederate Army.

In 1821 Thomas McMinn became the owner, by soldier's warrant, of five hundred acres of land adjoining the Tate five hundred acres, bought by the Peerys. These lands are now owned by the Meece heirs, John L. Beakley, and others. William Beakley, grandfather of John L. Beakley, became owner of these lands in 1825. Louisa, a daughter of William Beakley, married John L. Flowers.

Richard Meece, who came here from Maury County about 1860, married Margaret Ann, a daughter of William Duncan. He became the owner of a large portion of the McMinn lands and died here.

Robertson Whitesides, who was born in 1800, came from South Carolina to Maury County, and from Maury County to Swan Creek, in 1825. He died here in 1885. He bought land from Brock, the original owner, and afterwards entered and bought land until he owned over six hundred acres. He was for years a magistrate in this district, and was at one time a member of the Legislature. He married Sarah, a sister of Joseph Webb, of Pine River, and was the father of Pleasant, Luther, and Lafayette Whitesides. His daughters were: Mrs. Mary Ann Duncan, Mrs. Peggy Jane Sharp, Mrs. Nancy E. Sharp, and Mrs. Keziah Burcham. One mile below the Robertson Whitesides place, at which Alexander Peery now lives, is the post office, Sunrise. J. L. Beakley has a store here, and Luther Lindsay has a blacksmith shop.

Luther Lindsay is a son of David Lindsay, who was born in North Carolina on May 18, 1818. David Lindsay married Margaret Gresham, of Lawrence County, who was born on March 22, 1822, and died on October 27, 1895. He is a carpenter and wheel-wright, having learned these trades when a boy from W. S. Ricketts, who lived near Mount Pleasant, in Maury County. Since 1837 David Lindsay has been a member of the Cumberland Presbyterian Church. The Cumberland Presbyterian Church at "the old camp ground" was organized in 1826, and at present has a membership of nearly one hundred and fifty. The first elders were Robert Peery and James Peery, Jr. Brown Peery, a son of Robert Peery, is one of the present elders. The present pastor is Wesley Young Lindsay, a son of David Lindsay. He has been pastor here for about twenty years.

Buffalo Switch, the point from which the phosphate of this district is shipped, is on the railroad between the head of Indian Creek and Ætna. It was named a few years ago for "Buffalo Bill" Coleman, a well-known bridge carpenter.

Hiram Prince, who lived for a time in the First District, came from Bedford County to the Twelfth District in 1830. His sons were: Isaac, John, Thomas; H. C., who lived in Kentucky; and James Prince, who died in the Confederate Army. His daughters were: Mrs. Sarah Anderson, Mrs. Louisa Short; Mrs. Malinda Williams, of Perry County; and Mrs. D. W. Peery, of Kentucky.

Pinkney Prince, the father of O. A. Prince, at one time lived where Hon. R. L. Peery now lives. He married a daughter of Alexander Peery, and during his wife's last illness she disclosed to her attendant neighbors four hundred dollars in coin stored away in a stocking between the mattress and the feather bed upon which she lay, this representing the savings of years.

Prior to 1844 the people of this section voted at Palestine, at that time in Hickman County. Musters were held at the Robert Peery place, where Gilmore now lives; and at one of these, in 1835, Thomas Kingston and Edward Anderson, a son of Whig Anderson, had an unusually savage fight. Peery would not after this incident allow musters to be held on his premises.

In 1825 a man named Jones built a mill at the Thomas Bates place, and in 1822 the Peery brothers had a small mill and distillery at the spring near the church at " the old camp ground."

There is a Missionary Baptist Church at Fall Branch called " Pine Grove." The Primitive Baptists have a church at Center, near the county line. This denomination had a church in the pioneer days near the line of the Twelfth, Fourteenth, and First Districts. It was called " Sycamore," it being built of sycamore logs. The preachers here were Benjamin Lancaster, Temple Hicks, and —— Wolverton. This church was a short distance from the present site of Swan Bluff post office. Some of the pioneer Cumberland Presbyterian preachers were Reuben Burrows, —— King, Richard Baird, and James Calhoun. The latter preached here in 1826 at the first camp meeting held in this section,

Hand in hand with the pioneer preacher came the pioneer school-teacher, who taught from a wonderful assortment of readers and spellers. There was then no uniform system of text-books, and for readers the "scholars" used the Bible, "Life of Washington," "Life of Lafayette," "Life of Francis Marion," or, in fact, any book that might be found in the very scantily supplied libraries of their parents. Webster's blue-back speller was used as a reader and speller. The "scholars," in many of the schools, when "getting their lessons," would "spell out loud." For years the question would frequently be asked applicants for schools: "Do you teach a silent school or a spelling-out-loud school?" The noise from the "spelling-out-loud schools," when in session, could be heard for half a mile. The "big scholars"—the privileged class who, on account of their superior knowledge, were allowed to "go outdoors" to "cipher"—studied Walker's Dictionary, in which only one word ("arc") ended with a "c." Arithmetic, spelled "a-r-i-t-h-m-e-t-i-c-k," was taught only to the "big scholars." The text-books were Pike's and Smiley's, and, later, Ray's. Girls seldom studied "arithmetick," and the boy who reached "the single rule of three" or "the double rule of three"—simple and compound proportion— often "stalled the teacher." This does not apply to the early schools of the Twelfth District alone, but to many of the schools of all the districts of the county.

Samuel C. Aydelott, a surveyor and a good mathematician, taught at "the old camp ground" in 1830;

James P. McNutt taught at Pine Branch in 1832; David B. Warren taught in this district years before the Civil War, as did also George and Alexander Peery. The latter taught here in 1842.

Dr. Carroll, of Centerville, practiced medicine on Swan Creek at an early date. He attended James Peery, Sr., during his last illness, in February, 1829. Later Dr. Samuel B. Moore, of Centerville, practiced here. Dr. Pettus and Dr. H. K. Plummer at one time lived on Swan Creek.

Some of the magistrates of the district were Alexander Peery, William Duncan, Jere Harder, Robertson Whitesides, George Peery, Marcenus G. Peery, Pinkney Prince, J. M. Harder, and R. D. Clark. The present incumbents are W. D. Aydelott and Esau Anderson. Some of the constables were George Hardin, T. S. Southall, W. A. Beakley, and J. L. Baker.

One of the natural curiosities of this district is "Bat Cave," near where J. M. Bates and D. M. Duncan now live. Miners in 1896 exhumed, while working in the phosphate mines at Fall Branch, four skeletons, of the identity of which the oldest settlers know nothing.

CHAPTER XVI.

THE THIRTEENTH DISTRICT.

THE Thirteenth District is bounded on the north by the Fourth District; on the east and south, by Maury County; and on the west, by the Second and Fifteenth Districts. It includes within its boundaries Leatherwood Creek, with its tributaries—Gracey's Branch, Webb's Branch, and Adair Branch. It also includes a portion of Dog (or Cedar) Creek and Fort Cooper Hollow, these being tributaries of Lick Creek. This district was formed by the Legislature in 1847, it being taken from the Third District.

The Line of 1784 runs through this district, as stated in preceding pages. Through this district ran the old Chickasaw Trace, near the mouth of Leatherwood Creek was "the old Chickasaw crossing on Duck River," and through this district marched the Coldwater Expedition in 1787. Nearly every man prominent in the pioneer history of Middle Tennessee set foot, before the beginning of the present century, on the soil now included within the limits of this district. Many incidents connected with the early history of this territory are mentioned in the sketch of the Third District, of which it was for years a part.

The derivation of the name "Sugar Creek" in this

district is the same as that of "Sugar Creek" in the Eighth District. On this creek, in 1820, there was located a "sugar camp." It was from this creek, which is a tributary of Dog Creek, that Malugin rushed to the home of Gee, in the Fourth District, running from imaginary Indians. On this creek is the Wild Cat Cave, also known as the "Saltpeter Cave." Its first title comes from the fact that it was for years the den of numerous wild cats; the second title comes from the fact that from 1805 to 1820 saltpeter was procured from this cave and carried to Nashville. It was carried over the Natchez Trace, which runs through one corner of this district. The Natchez Trace has the same general direction as the old Chickasaw Trace, but, when it was being opened, the more easily traveled ridge was followed instead of following the old route down Lick Creek and over to Leatherwood Creek. So, on the south side of Duck River, it followed the ridge to the head of Swan Creek instead of going over to Blue Buck Creek and up Swan Creek to the head.

Fort Cooper Hollow enters the valley of Lick Creek a short distance below the location of the historic lick which gave to the creek its name. David Killough settled near the mouth of this hollow in the Fourth District, and some of his tenants lived from 1810 to 1815 near the spring at which Dr. Warren now lives. The family was named Cooper, and their log cabin was given the name "Fort Cooper" by some pioneer wag. A cabin nearer the head of the hollow was

called " Campbell's Station." The upper portion of
the hollow is now inhabited by a prosperous settlement of negroes. They have a school and a church
here. The patriarch of this tribe is Nathan George,
who was born in Maury County in 1827, and was
brought to Swan Creek in 1829 by his master, Hezekiah George. After the Civil War he came here and
bought two hundred acres of land. He belongs to that
fast-vanishing class, the ante-bellum negro. Some of
the negroes of Hickman County who belong to this
class are: William Phillips, the preacher, of Pinewood; John Johnson, the school-teacher and barber,
of Centerville; and Centerville's two veteran blacksmiths, Charlie Whitesides and Robert Hornbeak.
All of these, with possibly one exception, were born
in slavery.

Along the ridge between the head of Fort Cooper
Hollow and Leatherwood Creek runs an old road
opened in 1815 by Parker Tyler, the man who named
Little Lot. This road was opened from the place
later owned by Tarkington to where it intersects the
road running from the old lick on Lick Creek to
Leatherwood Creek—the route of the old Chickasaw
Trace. Parker Tyler was one of the sons of William
Tyler, who was one of the number of aristocratic
Marylanders who came, between 1810 and 1815, to
Lick Creek, they hoping to repair in this undeveloped
country their somewhat shattered fortunes. William
Tyler bought the Tarkington place from Asa Shute,
who had entered it in 1810. This road opened by

Parker Tyler connected the Maryland colony with the outside world.

On the east side of Lick Creek, just above the mouth of Fort Cooper Hollow, Dr. Charles Smoot, one of the Maryland colony, located. He married Nettie Dent Tyler, a sister of Mrs. Berry, and a daughter of William Tyler. A daughter of Dr. Smoot, Ann Hinson Smoot, married Dr. James Greenfield Smith, who in 1840 owned the Killough place. Dr. Smith, who was born in Maryland in 1799, came to Greenfield's Bend, in Maury County, below Williamsport, in 1812. He was a cousin of Dr. Greenfield, who located in this bend and from whom it received its name. In 1825 he came to Hickman County and settled near Gordon's Ferry. From this place he went to the Killough place, on Lick Creek. His oldest son, Patrick Sims Smith, was born on September 18, 1823. He married Martha, the daughter of Josephus Russell. In 1847 he went with Whitfield's second company to Mexico, and in 1861 he again volunteered, going out with Bateman's company, the first company raised in Hickman County. In 1897 he was still living, although deprived of the use of an arm and a leg by a stroke of paralysis. For his service in the Mexican War he receives a pension.

Gracey's Branch received its name from John C. Gracey, Sr., its first settler. John C. Gracey, Sr., was born on November 25, 1808, and settled here on lands bought by his father, Newell Gracey, on November 24, 1822, from John C. McLemore and John

Davis. On these lands is a fine spring, at which, tradition says, the Indians camped while traveling to and from the crossing at the mouth of Leatherwood Creek. John C. Gracey, Sr., was the father of John C. Gracey, Jr., and of Atlantic Gracey, who married R. W. Shaffer. John C. Gracey, Sr., taught school on Leatherwood Creek in 1834, near the present site of the schoolhouse below Jones' Valley.

Jesse Temple at one time lived on Gracey's Branch. He was born in South Carolina on December 20, 1790, and married Tabitha Tinsley. In 1825 he came to what is now the Thirteenth District, and first located on the line between Hickman and Maury Counties. Here his son, the late John Loyd Temple, of the Sixth District, was born on April 18, 1825. A daughter of Jesse Temple, Mrs. Edith T. Balch, lives in Kansas. John L. Temple's only brother, Jesse Marion Temple, died in June, 1862, while a soldier in the Confederate Army. On May 29, 1846, John L. Temple enlisted in Whitfield's company of the First Tennessee, and at the expiration of his term of service he again enlisted, on September 27, 1847. After his second enlistment he was second lieutenant of Company K, Third Tennessee Regiment. Of this company Ned Fowlkes was first lieutenant, and John W. Whitfield was captain. While a member of the First Tennessee he acted as fifer, and during the Civil War he performed the same service for Hubbard's company in the Forty-second Tennessee Infantry. In the Thirteenth District lives Joshua W. Burnham, who was in Whitfield's first company in the Mexican War, and in Bibb's company of the Ninth Battalion in the Civil War. The soldiers of the First Tennessee in the Mexican War were mustered out of service at New Orleans; the soldiers of the Third Tennessee, at Memphis.

Near the mouth of Gracey's Branch lived for years Berry Jones, the father of James Jones, who lives at this place, and of Thomas Jones, the well-known Nashville drummer.

Above the mouth of Gracey's Branch is the store of James Greenberry Loftin, a son of Matthew Bishop Loftin. He was born in Davidson County on April 7, 1834, but came to this district when young. He has several times been the constable of this district, and was at one time a candidate for sheriff. His father was born in Virginia.

One-half mile farther up the creek William Hassell built a mill in 1836. Near the present site of the church and schoolhouse Thomas Newcomb's mill stood. Near the present location of the store at Jones' Valley, Joe Davie's mill stood in 1830. Leatherwood Creek has had more mills on it since 1810 than any creek of the same length in the county. As many as four mills have been running on this creek at the same time. The names of some of those who have been millers on the creek are: Joe Davie, Thomas Newcomb, William Hassell, Peter Hanes, Vernon F. Bibb, Robert Woody, Thomas Brooks, and Newell Johnson.

At the Newell Johnson mill three fine springs burst

from a cove, and, uniting, form Leatherwood Creek. The waters from these springs, confined by a stone dam, make the power for Johnson's mill. The lands here were first entered in 1811 by —— Branch, who conveyed them to Robert Woody. Woody was born in Orange County, N. C., in 1806. He married Mary Brooks, who was born in Kentucky in 1807. His son, Samuel Thomas Woody, was born on March 30, 1837. He was buried at the V. F. Bibb place.

Two brothers, Joseph and Richard Davie, were among the earliest settlers on Leatherwood Creek. Richard Davie lived where C. S. Johnson now lives. Joseph Davie built the house, later known as the " Wash. Fowlkes place," where Robert and Thomas Woody now live. This house, which is still standing, was in pioneer days used as a blockhouse. Tradition says that at the house of Richard Davie, John A. Murrell was once arrested for horse stealing. He had stopped here overnight, and in the morning he was arrested by the pursuing posse. The Davie brothers bought lands from Asa Shute, who cut his name on a tree in their line in 1811. This tree, which is still standing, is near the mouth of Gracey's Branch and near the Continental Line of 1784. Benjamin Adair, father of Col. Andrew Adair, was an early settler on this creek, as was also Houston Cooper. Robert Woody once owned the mill now owned by Puckett, and the V. F. Bibb lands were once owned by —— Brooks. Here located an early settler, John Griffith, uncle of James O. Griffith, once a prominent newspaper man of Nashville. A daughter of John Griffith married William H. Bratton; another daughter, Hannah, married Joseph Davie.

John Wesley Webb, who was born in North Carolina on January 14, 1812, came to this district in 1840 and settled where his son, Charles S. Webb, now lives. Charles S. Webb was born here on March 9, 1847.

Benjamin Charter and Thomas Jones were the first merchants at Jones' Valley, they selling goods here in 1866.

Col. Vernon F. Bibb, who was for years one of the most prominent citizens of the county, lived on Leatherwood Creek. He was born in Dickson County on August 24, 1816, and died in 1896. He was several times a member of the State Legislature, both as a Senator and a Representative. In 1861 he raised Company C of the Ninth Battalion of Tennessee Cavalry, C. S. A., and was the first captain of this company. The Ninth Battalion was a splendid body of men, who, as fighters and good soldiers, had no superiors in either the Southern or Northern armies. The men from Leatherwood Creek and vicinity, under the leadership of Bibb and Mayberry, did, and did well, whatever they were called upon to do.

A good citizen and prominent man was Granville M. Johnson, who lived on the Dry Fork of Leatherwood Creek. The " captain's company " to which he belonged embraced the citizens of what is now the Thirteenth District as well as those of the Third and

Fifteenth Districts. Each "captain's company" was entitled to two justices of the peace selected by the Legislature. In 1826, at the request of his neighbors and friends, the Legislature selected him as one of the magistrates of the county, and this position he filled long and well. He was the father of Jacob H. Johnson, Granville M. Johnson, Jr.; Dallas Johnson, one of the present magistrates of the Thirteenth District; and C. S. Johnson, a prominent citizen, who has several times been constable of the district. Jacob H. Johnson enlisted as a private in Company H, Eleventh Tennessee Infantry, the first company from Hickman County to join the Confederate Army. At the reorganization in May, 1862, he was elected second lieutenant. A few weeks after this Gen. George W. Gordon, then lieutenant colonel commanding the regiment, was captured. Lieut. "Jake" Johnson, with eighteen men, searching for his superior officer, came upon forty-two Federals and captured them. Some of these were exchanged a few days later for Gordon. When the gallant Capt. P. V. H. (Van) Weems was promoted to be major, Lieutenant Johnson was promoted to the captaincy of Company H. In the battle east of Atlanta on July 22, 1864, Captain Johnson was killed. This was on the same day that Maj. Van Weems was mortally wounded. Of them General Gordon says: "These were popular and daring officers, and in their fall the regiment sustained a great loss." Concerning Granville M. Johnson, Jr., Gen. George W. Gordon writes: "Granville Johnson, killed in battle at Chickamauga, a mere boy, under eighteen years of age, and when shot, said: ' Tell them at home that I died like a soldier.' A grapeshot broke his thigh, one minie ball passed through his breast and another shattered his hand, and the noble boy did die like a soldier." A daughter of Granville M. Johnson, Sr., married Thomas Spencer, a prominent man and a good financier. He loaned money to buyers of live stock, and was the cause of much money being put into circulation. The father of Thomas Spencer was, it is said, killed in the mountains of East Tennessee. He was returning from North Carolina, where he had been to settle some unfinished business, and had with him a large amount of money, of which he was robbed.

On the hill just south of Jones' Valley lived the father of Joseph, James, and Thomas Meadors. He was an old settler of this vicinity. Up the East Fork (or Dry Fork) of Leatherwood Creek lived George W. Bratton, a prominent citizen. He died a few years ago. One of the pioneers of this locality was John R. Charter. Leatherwood Creek was in the pioneer days known as " No B'ar Creek," from the fact that, while found elsewhere in this section, no bears could be found on this creek. This was told to the first settlers by the Indians. This was found to be particularly true concerning the East Fork.

Near where Cave Charter lives, Squire William Anderson, in 1895, fell dead from the mule which he was riding. In 1873 William Charter was drowned

in Duck River near where it is now spanned by the
" Leatherwood Bridge." James Hooten was killed
about 1880 near where C. S. Webb now lives. It was
night, and Hooten was overtaken by a party of young
men, with some of whom he had previously quarreled.

At the mouth of Leatherwood Creek lives Richard
A. Smith, who is a son of John Y. Smith. John Y.
Smith married Polly, a daughter of Richard (" Kettle Dick ") Anderson. She was born on October 17,
1806. After the death of Smith she married Richard ("Big Dick") Anderson, her cousin, and was the
mother of David H., Philander P., and John M. Anderson. Her daughter, Isabella Anderson, married
J. B. Cathey. Philander P. Anderson is a citizen
of the Thirteenth District. He was born on December 22, 1845. The land on which Smith now lives
belonged originally to Jeremiah Harlan, a brother
of Benjamin and Jacob Harlan, of Maury County.
Harlan was one of the early magistrates of the county.
He sold these lands, about 1820, to Joseph Hassell.
Haywood Partee married one of Hassell's daughters
in 1833; and William Hassell, a son of Joseph Hassell, married Clementine Partee, of Maury County.
In 1855 Elias Dotson bought the upper portion of
these lands from William Hassell. The remaining
portion was owned by Kit Hudson, who married the
widow—Mrs. Sanford—to whom it belonged. Hudson was a man of wealth, owning many slaves.

Among the physicians who have practiced their profession in this district are Dr. Richard Fowlkes, son

of Wash. Fowlkes, a highly respected citizen; and Dr. L. G. Hensley.

One of the early school-teachers of the district was Thomas Smith, of Georgia. In later years J. J. Keyes, of the Nashville city schools, and R. S. Ballow, County Superintendent of Public Instruction, have taught here. One of the early preachers was that veteran of the cross, Britton Garner.

CHAPTER XVII.

THE FOURTEENTH DISTRICT.

THE Fourteenth District is bounded on the north by the Third and Fifteenth Districts; on the east, by Lewis County; on the south, by the Twelfth District; and on the west, by the First District. This district was established in 1857, during Hon. J. J. Williams' first term in the Legislature. Prior to that time the voters of this district voted at Shady Grove and Centerville. After the adoption of the Constitution of 1834 twelve districts were established, and the three additional districts—the Thirteenth, Fourteenth, and Fifteenth—were established later by the Legislature. The boundaries of the Fourteenth District, as given in the Act creating it, are as follows: "Beginning one-quarter of a mile from Stanfill's Mills on the Williamsport road, running to nearest point of Swan Creek, leaving Mrs. Stanfill and John McGill in District No. 1; thence up said creek with its meanders and on to the dividing ridge between Short and Fall Branches; thence with said ridge to the old Natchez road, east with same to the Old Well; thence on a line to what is called the ' Robert Totty road ' where the same intersects the Williamsport and Centerville road; thence with same to beginning." Later in the session the line was so changed as to include in this district the residence of William P. Kelley. The

Act creating the district provided that the voting place should be at Wheat's Shop until removed by a vote of the people of the district. Blue Buck Creek, the principal stream of the district, is about seven miles in length, and rises near the Maury and Lewis County line, flowing west into Swan Creek, which it enters near Rawley's Chapel. Long before the early settler came, this creek was known as " Blue Buck Creek," from the fact that on this creek a hunter had killed a buck at that season of the year when its hair was of a bluish color. This creek was probably named by some member of the party running the Line of 1784. Swan Creek was called by this party " Swan River of Duck River." It derived its name, as stated elsewhere, from the killing of a swan in its waters. The derivation of the name " Ugly Creek " the principal tributary of Blue Buck Creek, is unknown Pickett's Branch, which flows into Blue Buck Creek on the north, was named for Tapley Pickett, an early settler.

William Wheat, who came from Maury County to Blue Buck Creek in 1830, lived for years near the voting place of the district. Charles Wheat, his son, lived on an adjoining farm, and was for several years a magistrate of this district. He was also at one time a constable.

Jared Cotton, who was born in North Carolina in 1800, came in 1835 to Blue Buck Creek, where he died in 1879.

Where Will. Whitesides now lives, Isaac Farris

lived in 1839; but George W. McNutt was the original owner of these lands, he having settled here in 1817. In 1837 he removed to Northern Mississippi. His wife was Margaret, the daughter of James Peery, Sr.; and their sons were James P., Robert, Wiley B., Samuel, George H., and the twins—William and Tilford. James P. and George H. McNutt were Cumberland Presbyterian preachers.

The first settler at the place where Samuel Bond lives was —— Searcy. It was later owned by John McGill, who gave it to his daughter, Mary, the wife of Thompson Fowlkes. After the death of Fowlkes she married Mark Mathis. Of this place the late Joseph Bond became the owner in 1869, and here he lived until his removal to the Third District. The old Chickasaw Trace crossed Blue Buck Creek near the Bond place. This trace was originally a path made by buffaloes on their way to the sulphur lick on the John T. Overbey place on Lick Creek. Later it was the trace, used by whites and Indians, connecting Nashville and the Chickasaw country.

An early settler was William Watts, who lived at the Wheat place at the juncture of Ugly Creek and Blue Buck Creek. Other members of the Watts family were early settlers here, and John Gibbs lived above the Wheat place as early as 1830. These families have disappeared from the county, leaving no posterity here.

Jack Devore lived at the upper Wheat place in 1840. He removed to the Eleventh District, where he died. He was at one time constable of the Eleventh District.

Alton McCaleb lived for many years in this district, and died here. He was a son of James McCaleb, whose father was James McCaleb, of North Carolina. Alton McCaleb, who was born in the Third District in 1823, was for years a magistrate of the Fourteenth District, and was a prominent and influential citizen. He was a gallant soldier in the Civil War, being a lieutenant in the famous Ninth Battalion of Tennessee Cavalry, C. S. A. He was the father of the following sons: James P., W. M., J. A., Andrew, M. B., M. M., D. R., and Jasper McCaleb. His only daughter was Alena Belle McCaleb. His oldest son, James P. McCaleb, who was born on December 8, 1847, is one of the magistrates of this district.

John Skipper, the father of Samuel Skipper, settled on Blue Buck Creek in 1830, and erected a gristmill and distillery, two things which seemed to be inseparable and necessary to the comfort and happiness of the pioneers of Hickman County. At that time almost every man kept whisky at his home, stillhouses were in every district and in almost every neighborhood, and whisky was sold by every man who desired, as its sale was unrestricted by law. Occasionally at that time an old man would so far forget himself as to become a drunkard; but young men then seldom ever became intoxicated, as they do in these days of higher civilization. It was then considered disgrace-

ful for them to do so.   John Skipper lived and died
a respected citizen, and his posterity are good citizens
of this district.

The lands upon which James P. McCaleb lives
were entered in 1818 by —— Holston.   George
Peery at the same time entered lands adjoining, and
a portion of these he sold to Ann Watts.

In 1817 James Peery, Jr., a son of the pioneer and
old Revolutionary soldier, James Peery, Sr., entered
lands on Ugly Creek.   On these lands he lived, and
after him lived his son, Andrew Peery, the hermit of
Ugly Creek.   The following stories are not intended
to reflect upon the character or memory of this quiet,
honest, and inoffensive man, who lived and died a
hermit—respected, however, by all who knew him.
After the death of his father, James Peery, Jr., Andrew Peery became the owner of his father's lands,
and soon after commenced the erection of his wonderful rock house.   This house was about sixteen by
eighteen feet in size, and the stone of which it was
built was quarried, dressed, raised, and placed in position by Peery, unaided.   This work occupied his time
for several years, and, as his neighbors never saw him
at work, the secret of how he succeeded in doing this
work without assistance died with him.   After the
completion of his house he built a stone milldam
about one hundred and fifty yards in length, and then
he erected a mill, at which he ground his corn into
meal.   Occasionally, if convenient, he would grind
corn for his neighbors.   The stone for the milldam

was drawn by him to the place in a cart which he had made. The timbers were prepared in the forest and drawn in the same manner to the place where the house was framed. After having framed it satisfactorily, he tore the house down and removed it, piece at a time, to its permanent location near the dam. The mill, which was of the old water-wheel kind, had no " rattle staff " to shake the corn from the " shoe " beneath the hopper; so Peery was forced to drop the corn into the " eye " of the stone—that is, he would feed the mill by hand—a tedious process. Upon one occasion, William, a son of James P. McCaleb, went to the mill and was requested by Peery to feed it. McCaleb commenced to feed it rapidly, and, choking, it soon came to a standstill. Peery, returning, found his mill in this condition, and gave young McCaleb a rebuke which, coming from Peery, was terrible: " William, you are a bad boy; you have choked my mill." This was language as bitter as was ever used by this kind-hearted and sympathetic man, and nothing but the great provocation of having his mill choked by too many grains of corn would have brought from his lips such bitter words of denunciation. Upon one occasion he found a mouse in his clothes chest. Catching it, he carried it to the mouth of Fall Branch, three miles away, and there released it, unharmed, warning it, however, against again being found in his clothes chest. An opossum which he found molesting his chickens was carried beyond Swan Creek and released, and requested not to molest his chickens in the

future.   Peery, before his mill was completed, would
not borrow his neighbor's horses to carry his corn to
mill, but would walk and carry it.   To cross the
creeks, he would carry with him two light benches.
He would place one of these benches in the creek,
and, walking out on it, he would place the other bench
in front of it, repeating this operation until he had
reached the opposite bank.   It was a slow method,
but he successfully carried his corn across in this
manner.   In the yard surrounding his rock house he
built a log house, which he used as a workshop.   Here
he commenced a wagon.   However, when he had finished one wheel he found that it was so large that it
would not pass through the door, and he abandoned
the enterprise, the wheel remaining in the house until
his death.   Preparing his supply of pork, he shot all
of his hogs, and then remembered that he had heated
no water.   Leaving his hogs lying on the ground, he
then proceeded to heat the water.   He at one time
conceived the idea of swimming the Tennessee River,
and started on foot on the journey of forty miles to
the river.   Reaching the river, parties to whom he
told his intentions would not allow him to attempt it
unless one of them accompanied him with a skiff.   To
this he objected, and returned without having carried
into execution his designs.   He was, however, an expert swimmer, and often went to Duck River, five
miles distant, for the purpose of bathing and swimming.   Upon one of these trips he swam to the opposite side, and before he returned some cattle destroyed

his clothing, which he had left on the sand bar, where he entered the river. They left unmolested a sack which he had brought for use as a towel. Opening both ends of this sack, he utilized it as clothing, and in this garb he reached home, going through the woods and along unfrequented paths. Peery was an unceasing worker. He "pieced" two quilts, and then concluded to have a quilting, to which he invited his neighbors. Some of those present were: Mesdames James McCaleb, Alton McCaleb, Joseph Wheat, William Short, —— Rochell, Alex. George, Jones Totty, and Charles Wheat, the daughters of Campbell Peery, and Mr. and Mrs. Winfred Cotton. The best families were present at this quilting, as all respected the peculiar old man. It was a noted quilting, well remembered by many who were children when they were present, but are now heads of families. Some of the older ones present are yet living, and refer to the occasion as one around which pleasant memories cling. Upon this occasion some of the young ladies found his cider in a trough in his smokehouse. They discovered that it was drawn by removing a peg from the bottom of the trough. Drawing some of it, they failed to replace the peg and the remainder was wasted. One of the quilts finished upon this occasion was a silk quilt, made from scraps which he had been collecting for years. This quilt was afterwards entered in the contest at the Centerville Fair for the prize offered for fancy patchwork. It was awarded the prize, but Peery refused to receive it, giving it, instead, to an unsuccessful contestant. At the quilting Peery assisted in preparing the dinner, much of which, however, he had prepared on the previous day. Despite his peculiarities, he was a devout Christian, and as such was recognized. He was a member of the Cumberland Presbyterian Church, and this doctrine he preached at irregular appointments. His congregations were always large, and, despite the fact that the Presbytery would not recognize him and furnish him with the necessary authority, he continued to preach whenever and wherever he desired. He would always walk to the places where he had announced that he would preach. On these journeys he would always wear moccasins, made frequently from boot legs. With him he carried his shoes, and before reaching the church he would remove the moccasins and wear his shoes instead. He studied the Scriptures and knew their contents. He preached stirring discourses, and often during his services shouted the praises of his Maker. He lived to the age of sixty-five, and died on Ugly Creek. Buried at "the old camp ground" on Swan Creek, near the graves of his ancestors, his body has returned to dust and his spirit to his God. Now noise and activity are where once slowly moved the hermit preacher of Ugly Creek. Even the rock house, which so long defied the elements, has fallen into the hands of the phosphate dealer and is, too, numbered among the things that were.

At the William Simmons place Samuel Golden settled in 1825, and lived here for several years. In 1838 Jesse Briggs bought this place. In 1830 William Briggs built a mill at the place now owned by the A. W. Anderson heirs. William Briggs was the father of Jesse, James ("Pap"), William, and John Briggs. The late James Briggs was for years prior to his death a grocer at Centerville. John Briggs, who died recently in the Second District, and his brother, William Briggs, were for years prosperous citizens of the Seventh District. Briggs' Chapel was named either for them or their father, who was a Methodist preacher. In 1840 William Briggs, Sr., sold his lands to Joseph Campbell, who bought them for Alex. ("Biscuit") Baker and Thomas Stuart. Stuart & Baker improved the Briggs sawmill and gristmill and added a carding factory, thus giving to the people of this section a convenience which they had not hitherto possessed. This was for years the most extensive business of the kind in the county. Meal and flour from these mills were carried in wagons to Nashville, Franklin, Columbia, and other Middle Tennessee towns. The location of these mills is now marked by a large barren sand bar. Baker was a Pennsylvanian and was not accustomed to the use of corn bread. His partiality to biscuits gained for him the name "Biscuit" Baker.

The post office, Swan Bluff, named for the bluff north of this place, was established here in 1871. The first postmaster was the late John N. Smith. The post office was moved in 1892 to its present location at the mouth of Haw Branch, which is in the First District. At the latter location B. M. ("Dock") Hutchison sold goods from 1885 to 1896, when his store was purchased by Arthur I. Nixon.

In 1818 there lived on Blue Buck Creek, Spencer Tinsley, who had no fixed place of residence. He was a man of ability, and was here when the land south and west of the Congressional Reservation Line (which from the mouth of Leatherwood Creek was the same as the Continental Line of 1784) was vacant and could have been easily obtained from the United States. This he made no attempt to do, but contented himself with an attempt to discover the secret of perpetual motion. He was an ingenious workman, and this was the only attempt of his ever accompanied by failure. He lived in several districts of the county, and finally died in poverty.

John Williams, who settled at the forks of Blue Buck Creek in 1817, was one of the first settlers of the district. Where he first settled he died at an advanced age. John Davis, his son-in-law, was a pioneer Primitive Baptist preacher, who preached in this section before churches were built. As was the custom in this and other portions of the county, he preached at the residences of the citizens. The pioneer preacher was always a welcome guest, and the house of the pioneer was gladly surrendered to the preacher and his congregation. Upon these occasions young and old would come for miles around. They traveled on foot, as the roads were not well suited for travel on horseback. Wagons were seldom seen then and buggies were unknown. The principal wheeled vehicle was the two-wheeled ox cart and the two-wheeled horse cart. In the summer many of the congregation would travel to church barefooted. Some would carry their shoes, which they would put on their feet just before they arrived at the place where services were to be held. John Davis became insane and was sent to the asylum near Nashville. He later returned to his home on Blue Buck Creek, where he died.

Robert Willey came to Blue Buck Creek in 1817 and located at the Alson Shelby place, where he lived until his death, in 1862. He was drowned in the creek where the water was not more than one foot deep. He was one of the first settlers of this section, settling here when it was still in the Indian country. He assisted in the cutting away of the cane in this valley and in the clearing of the first lands on this creek. This was but a short distance inside the Indian country, as the line, the Natchez Trace, ran along the ridge at the head of the creek. Often friendly Indians would visit the frontier settlements here. Robert Willey was the father of Moses, Andrew, and John Willey. Andrew Willey had a stillhouse from 1861 to 1863 above Crawford's house, in a hollow, north of the Centerville and Columbia road, in the First District.

Large deposits of phosphate, the value of which was not appreciated prior to 1893, are to be found in this section. This phosphate has been mined by different companies, with varying degrees of success.

In the pioneer days Hibbard Moore taught school on upper Blue Buck Creek. Samuel Erwin, who taught a ten-months' school here in the early days, was a Missionary Baptist preacher, and he often preached on this creek. John Golden, a son of Samuel Golden, taught here about 1835. Charles Wheat was at one time a teacher on this creek, and here John Beasley was teaching in 1861. He closed his school and joined the Confederate Army.

A pioneer preacher was the Missionary Baptist, Elijah Hanks; another was Thomas Rasco, a Primitive Baptist. Rev. Roland Hull, of Williamsport, had for years prior to 1897 preached at "Union Church," which stands near the home of James P. McCaleb. The Missionary Baptist Church here has a membership of sixty. Rev. W. T. Ussery, a prominent preacher of the Missionary Baptist Church, has often preached here. The old Methodist church, "Rawley's Chapel," has been replaced by a new and commodious church which bears the same name. The church here was established in 1830.

Since its organization the Fourteenth District has not had its share of county officials. E. Brown Short was an efficient deputy under the late Sheriff J. A. Harvill. John N. Smith, of this district, was at one time a prominent candidate for sheriff, and in 1898 Samuel R. Bond, one of the present magistrates, made a good race against two prominent and popular opponents—Robert Brown and J. W. Russell.

The magistrates of the district have been William Wheat, Charles Wheat, Alton McCaleb, Joseph Bond, Polk Grimes, A. B. George, Samuel Bond, and James P. McCaleb. Some of the constables here have been Charles Wheat, John N. Smith, J. W. Smithson, and J. A. Smith.

From this district, as from every other district of the county, went many brave men to the Southern Army. Joseph Bond and Alton McCaleb, of this district, were lieutenants in the Confederate Army.

CHAPTER XVIII.

THE FIFTEENTH DISTRICT.

THE Fifteenth District is bounded on the north by the Second District, Duck River being the line; on the east, by the Third District; on the south, by the Fourteenth District; and on the west, by the Second and Fourteenth Districts. Until 1859, when it was created by the Legislature, its territory belonged to the Second and Third Districts. Some of the citizens were compelled to go to Little Lot to vote; others, to Shady Grove. The County Court was several times appealed to in vain for the creation of a new district. Finally, when Hon. J. J. Williams was in the Legislature, the advocates of a new district were successful. The boundaries as fixed by the Act are as follows: " Beginning at the mouth of Buck Branch, running up said branch to the line of the Fourteenth Civil District, thence with that line west until it reaches the Totty road, and thence with the same and the old Greene road to the river, thence up the river to the beginning." It was enacted that the voting place should be at or near the house of Nathaniel Young until the voters of the district voted for its removal to another point.

As the Fifteenth District includes Anderson's Bend, a sketch of this district is almost entirely a history of the Anderson family. The pioneer Andersons were four brothers—David, Robert, Richard, and James. Their father came from England, and Robert Anderson had in his possession an old-fashioned clock made in London prior to 1600. David Anderson lived in Bedford County. He was born on December 29, 1772, and was the father of Joseph, William, and Richard ("Big Dick"). Of these, only the latter came to Hickman County. He was born on December 20, 1810, and married Polly, the daughter of his uncle, Richard ("Kettle Dick") Anderson. She, as heretofore stated, was the widow of John Y. Smith. The sons of this marriage were David H., Philander P., and John M. Anderson. A daughter, Isabella W., married J. B. Cathey. William Anderson, a son of Joseph Anderson, of Bedford County, came to Hickman County, and was one of the first two magistrates of the district. This position he held for twenty-eight years.

Robert Anderson was born in Buncombe County, N. C., in 1774, and in 1804 he located on the north side of Duck River in the Little Lot bend, near the river. He afterwards sold these lands to Lawson H. Nunnelly. In 1805 he came across the river and built the house where Mrs. Xantippe Anderson now lives. This is probably the oldest house in Hickman County. Robert Anderson had married Jane Shinn, daughter of Colonel Shinn, of a North Carolina regiment in the Revolutionary War. For this service Colonel Shinn was given by the North Caro-

lina Legislature 2,500 acres of land. These lands
his son-in-law, Robert Anderson, inherited. Robert
Anderson, in partnership with his brother, Richard
(" Kettle Dick ") Anderson, bought other warrants
granted by North Carolina for services in the Revolutionary War, and made their locations in what was,
for them, named "Anderson's Bend." These locations were just north of the Continental Line of 1784
—the southern boundary of the Continental Reservation, which extended north to the Kentucky line. As
heretofore stated, this line ran through the yard surrounding Robert Anderson's house, he having settled
as far south of the river and the cane-covered bottoms
as possible. This was then in the Indian country, as
the Indians did not by treaty relinquish their right to
land in the Continental Reservation south of the river
until 1819. Only a few miles away Duck River
ceased to be the Indian line, as at Gordon's Ferry it
turned and followed the Natchez Trace. Being in
the corner of the Tennessee territory yet claimed by
the Indians, he was probably never molested. In this
bend the brothers, Robert and Richard Anderson,
located the fine body of land extending from Bluff
Point, at the lower end of the bend, up to Boat Branch.
When they divided their lands, Richard's portion was
the lower end of the bend; Robert's, the upper end.
The sons of Robert Anderson were William, Joseph,
and Burton. His daughters were: Jane, who married
—— Hooten; Elizabeth, who married Nathaniel

Young; Matilda, who married William Walker; and Sallie, who married Robert Harrington, father of the late Dr. A. L. Harrington.

Burton Anderson, the youngest son (born on March 28, 1818), on account of some misunderstanding between himself and his father, left home when a young man, stating that he would never return. About thirty years later William Walker and others, on their way to Columbia, met a stranger, who was walking. On their return from Columbia, they overtook the same man. Entering into conversation with him, they discovered that he was on his way to Anderson's Bend, and that he was the long-absent Burton Anderson. He had been in Texas, Missouri, and California, and, although afoot, he did not return empty-handed. At home he found no parents' greetings, as both were dead. Over their hitherto unmarked graves he placed tombstones. He married Xantippe McClanahan (born on February 22, 1836), and lived at his father's old homestead, which had been bequeathed to him by his father, provided he ever returned. He became a good citizen, and at his death was buried in the same graveyard in which rest the remains of the pioneer, Robert Anderson. In this graveyard are buried, also, Joseph Anderson (born on December 18, 1806), and his wife, Roena (Baird) Anderson (born on August 9, 1805).

The first constable of this district was Nathaniel Young, who was born on Greene's Lick Creek, Maury County, on September 16, 1807, and was in 1897

the oldest man living in Hickman County. He was
born on the 25,000-acre tract of land given by North
Carolina to Gen. Nathaniel Greene, and located by the
commissioners who ran the Commissioners' Line of
1783. This land lies south of Williamsport and between Bigby Creek and Duck River. Benjamin Harlan and Edward Littlefield lived on this tract. The
father of Nathaniel Young was also named " Nathaniel," and was born in South Carolina in 1777. He
married his cousin, Jemima Young, who was born in
the same State in the same year. Nathaniel Young,
Jr., married, as above stated, Elizabeth, a daughter
of Robert Anderson. She was born in 1810. Their
daughter, Mary Young, married David Miller. Nathaniel Young, Sr., came to Maury County in 1805,
and to the place where David Miller now lives in 1829.
Since Nathaniel Young, the first constable, some of
the other constables of the district have been Polk
McCaleb, John R. Bates, and William Beasley.

William Walker, who was one of the most successful financiers who ever lived in the county, was born
on April 8, 1806, in Northumberland County, Va.,
and was a son of Thomas Walker. He married Matilda Caroline Anderson, who was born on November
7, 1813. In the possession of his son, Thomas J.
Walker, is his well-worn Bible, printed in 1828. A
son of William Walker, Hon. Leon Walker, was born
on May 15, 1832. He lived several years in Texas,
but returned to his native State and county, where he
died. In the House of Representatives of the Thirty-

ninth General Assembly he represented the counties of Hickman, Perry, and Lewis. Another son of William Walker, Thomas J. Walker (known as " Old Reliable "), was born on April 19, 1838. In 1874 he was elected register for Hickman County, and held this position for eight years. While a private in Company I, Forty-second Tennessee, he lost three fingers from his left hand at the battle of Shiloh, on April 7, 1862. They were shot away after his gun had been discharged, but before he had removed it from his shoulder. He remained in the army, and, although his wound had not entirely healed, he went into the battle of Murfreesboro, and on December 31, 1862, had his left arm so badly shattered that amputation was necessary. He married Sarah C. Gray, who was born on September 21, 1841. She was a daughter of Sherrod Gray, of Gray's Bend. A daughter of William Walker married Dr. A. Norris, who, in partnership with Dr. Rolffe Wilson, is now a physician of Centerville.

Richard Anderson, brother of Robert Anderson, was called " Kettle Dick " on account of his being the owner of the valuable lands in the Kettle Bend of Duck River, just over the line in Maury County. He was a Whig, and his brother, Robert, was a Democrat, and the discussions between these two pioneers would sometimes become very heated. Richard Anderson was the father of John, David, Henry, and Craig Anderson. His daughter, Mary (or Polly), first married John Y. Smith, and then Richard Anderson, son of

David Anderson, of Bedford County. Craig Anderson married a daughter of John Willey, who was with the party that opened the Natchez Trace.

John Anderson, son of Richard (" Kettle Dick ") Anderson, and father of Gill and Richard M. Anderson, was born on February 22, 1805. He married Mary Gill (born on February 27, 1805), a daughter of John Gill, of Dunlap Creek. Gill was one of the pioneers of that section, and it was at his house that the pioneer preacher, —— Nixon, held services.

Richard M. Anderson, son of John and Mary (Gill) Anderson, was born on November 24, 1808. He married Mary Jane Baker, who was born in Philadelphia on March 6, 1834. She was the daughter of Alexander Baker, whose father, Samuel Baker, was a noted gunsmith at Baker's Cross Roads, Pa., during the Revolutionary War. So diligently did he ply his trade, and so destructive were the arms he manufactured when in the hands of the Continentals, that the British made an attempt to capture him. Being warned of their coming, he sent his entire stock of guns to the Continental Army, and was preparing to go himself when the British approached his house. It being too late to attempt an escape, his wife hid him between the ceiling and the floor above, and the British searched for him in vain. Mrs. Baker assured the British that the arms had by this time reached the American camp; but they, believing that Baker was concealed about the house, commenced preparations for burning it. She asked for permission to remove her household goods and children, and said that after this was done they could proceed. This convinced them that Baker was not there, and they went away much disappointed over their failure to capture him. Mrs. Anderson's grandmother was a Burnsides, a sister of James Burnsides, the first clerk of the United States Supreme Court. Jane Burnsides married William Phillips, of Pennsylvania, and became the mother of three daughters, one of whom married John Campbell, father of the prominent lawyer, David Campbell. Richard M. Anderson was one of the first two magistrates of this district, and held this office for eighteen years—as long as he would accept it. He was succeeded by Wash. Young. He is now postmaster at Bluff Point, named from the high point of the bluff which comes abruptly to Duck River at the lower end of Anderson's Bend. This post office was established in 1855, and Isaac Perry was the first postmaster here. In 1847 Richard M. Anderson enlisted as a private in Whitfield's second company from Hickman County—Company K, Third Tennessee. This regiment was commanded by Col. B. F. Cheatham, the brave Gen. Frank Cheatham of the Civil War. The brigade commander was General Lane, of Missouri, who, in an address to the soldiers at Jalapa at the close of the war, told them to remain calm and to not attempt to rush home. He told them the trip home would take time, and that he had as many reasons for wanting to get home as any of them, that he had eleven reasons—a wife and ten children. The return trip was of a month's duration. Anderson's military career did not close here. While a member of Beale's company during the Civil War, he was so seriously wounded at Shiloh that he was discharged. After his discharge he lived on Robertson's Creek above where he now lives. His father lived where Clifford Smith now lives. In the autumn of 1863 a detachment of Michigan mounted infantry came from Centerville and met John Anderson near Willey's stillhouse, on Swan Creek, five miles from Centerville, and took from him some private papers and money to the amount of $1,500. He protested against this, as he had before this taken the oath of allegiance. Among his papers there was no copy of the oath he had taken, but two of the Federals were detailed to go with him to his home in order to see if his claim was true. When he reached home he readily produced the paper, which should have given him the protection of Federal troops. This the Federals took also, and, adding a fine horse to their booty, they started on their return to the command. Richard M. Anderson, learning that his aged father had been robbed, went in pursuit of the two robbers. His father was with him. They came up with the two Federals at Willey's stillhouse and tried to persuade them to return the stolen property. Arguments finally led to anger, and one of the Federals arrested Richard M. Anderson, who was unarmed. The Federals and their prisoner proceeded down the hollow to the spring opposite the house at which —— Crawford lived.

Here one of them dismounted and lay down to drink at the spring. In an instant Richard Anderson was on his back, striking him heavy blows with his fist. Although taken at a disadvantage, the Federal regained his feet, and a struggle for the possession of the gun ensued. The other soldier advanced with his gun presented, seeking an oppprtunity for shooting Anderson without at the same time shooting his comrade. However, at this juncture the aged John Anderson, from behind a near-by tree, commenced to hurl stones at this Federal with so much force and accuracy that he mounted his horse and retreated hastily. In the meantime Richard Anderson had forced his antagonist backward into a hogpen, and there gave him such a pommeling that, deserted by his comrade, he speedily surrendered. From this Federal, who was paroled, they recovered the stolen horse and $900 of the stolen money. With the remaining $600 the other Federal escaped, and in this he did well, as Richard Anderson, armed with his prisoner's gun, was now ready for a more deadly affray. The paroled Federal went on his way on foot, inquiring as to the route to Columbia, stating, however, that he did not want to go by way of Anderson's Bend. John Gill Anderson was a lieutenant in Beale's company of the Twenty-fourth Infantry.

The pioneer, James Anderson, brother of David, Robert, and Richard ("Kettle Dick"), settled on Swan Creek. He was the father of James Anderson, Jr., who was the father of Esau Anderson, who is at

present a member of the Hickman County Court.   So
it will be seen that from the four pioneer brothers—
David, Robert, Richard, and James Anderson—there
has sprung a numerous, prominent, and progressive
posterity.

The Fifteenth District, unlike almost every other
district of the county, consists almost entirely of level,
tillable lands.   Within its boundaries are only a few
small branches.   Boat Branch was so called for two
reasons: At its mouth flatboats from up the river
frequently " tied up " and remained overnight; in
addition to this, at the mouth of this branch numerous flatboats were built.   The fine poplars of this and
the Third District were much in demand by the builders of flatboats farther down the river and by local
builders.   Flatboats built here were floated down the
river to the Metal Landing for Ætna Furnace, opposite Shipp's Bend; to the Oakland Landing, at the
lower end of the Young Mayberry farm; and frequently to Lee & Gould's landing, at the mouth of
Sugar Creek, in the Eighth District.   In addition to
this, corn was shipped in these flatboats from Anderson's Bend to New Orleans.   The boatmen, when they
reached New Orleans, either returned home on foot
or returned to Nashville by steamboat and walked
from Nashville.   Skilled pilots in the old flatboat-
ing days were Joseph Anderson, James Grimes, and
Daniel Smith.   Although several attempts at opening
Duck River for navigation by steamboats have been
made, none of them have been attended with more

than temporary success. Several small steamers have from time to time entered Duck River and plowed its waters near its mouth, and several have come up the river into Hickman County. One in recent years was the Mary Clees, which in 1878 came as high up as Centerville. In the following year the James K. Shields also came to Centerville. Later the J. H. Russell, built by Joseph H. Russell above Centerville, went down the river, but never attempted a return trip.

In 1820 Robert Anderson built a mill on the slough near the Joseph Anderson place. Before he could reach this slough he was compelled to cut his way through the dense canebrake. On the branch near his house he had a mill, probably before 1820. This branch is from this fact called " Mill Branch."

Buck Branch, the line between the Third and Fifteenth Districts, derives its name from the fact that down this branch the hunted deer would run to Duck River. Deer, when weary from a chase, will always seek water, and there are certain routes which they follow. When they reach a stream like Duck River, they quench their thirst, and then, swimming into deeper water, cause the dogs to become confused in their attempt to follow them. Many large bucks have been killed on Buck Branch in their attempts to reach Duck River. On this branch B. B. Bates was found dead a few years ago. He was plowing, and it is supposed he fell dead from his plow. As he lived alone, sometimes spending the night at home and sometimes with his sons, his absence was not noted for several days.

Hen Island, in Duck River at the mouth of Buck Branch, is so named on account of a boat loaded with chickens having run aground here. While the boat was aground the chickens were turned out of their coops on the island.

In the upper portion of the Fifteenth District lived the Binghams, Rays, Grimeses, and some others already mentioned in the sketch of the Third District. At the Robert Anderson place Capt. " Lam " Kelley would in the days before the war often drill his company. Kelley afterwards stabbed and killed Tom Ollison on Love's Branch, in Maury County. He then left Hickman County and never returned.

In the lower end of Anderson's Bend, just above the high bluff which gives to the post office the name " Bluff Point," is the mouth of a small creek, or branch, known in the pioneer days as " Robertson's Creek." At the spring on the west side of this creek, about two hundred yards from Polk McCaleb's residence, is where Mark Robertson, a brother of Gen. James Robertson, was killed in 1787. This was near the Line of 1784, and Mark Robertson was probably at this time locating land here. The commissioners who laid off General Greene's land in what is now Maury County passed through this district as they went several miles farther to the north to run, fifty-five miles from the southern boundary of the State, the Commissioners' Line of 1783. After the laying

off of Greene's land, the members of the party, the
names of a number of whom are given in preceding
pages, made numerous entries for themselves, relatives, and friends, throughout the surrounding country. A large number of these entries call for certain
points in the boundaries of General Greene's land—
for Greene's Lick, for Greene's Lick Creek (Lick
Creek of Hickman County being known as "Lick
Creek of Duck River"), and other points made notorious by this survey. The larger portion of these entries were within the present limits of Maury County.
Others called for points no longer points of notoriety
and which cannot now be easily identified. Several,
however, were within the present limits of Hickman
County. In these entries the Bigby Creeks, of Maury
County, are called by a variety of names, some of
which are: "Tombigbee Creek," "Big Tombigby,"
"Big Tom Bigby's Creek," "Don Bigby Creek,"
and "Dun Bigby's Creek." One of the entries made
at this time (1783) was as follows: "John Provine,
Thomas Elliott, and Samuel Hensley—In Greene
County on the north side of Duck River at the mouth
of No Bare Creek." This was the pioneer name of
Leatherwood Creek, and this entry was made while
the commissioners and guards were going north from
Greene's land. Another entry was as follows: "Anthony Bledsoe—In Greene County on the south side
of Duck River, beginning on the bank of the river a
small distance below the mouth of No Bear Creek and
above the mouth of Lick Creek, both of which empties

[*sic*] in on the north side, and running down the river to include a bottom viewed by Col. James Robertson and said Bledsoe the second day after they left General Greene's land." Another entry is as follows: "Joseph Shinn—On the south side of Duck River to begin on bank of river one-quarter of a mile below the place where a southern corner from the lower lick intersects the same." Probably it was while surveying these and other entries made in this section in 1783 and 1784 that Mark Robertson, in 1787, lost his life. Another entry made at this time was as follows: "James White—In Greene County on Duck River, beginning about the mouth of Lick Creek and running up both sides of the creek, including two large licks up said creek." Another was: " Thomas Hardin Perkins—In Greene County on a creek of Duck River, beginning about fifty yards or more from a large lick formerly called ' Lewis' Lick,' but of late it is called ' Duck River Lick.' " Farther down the river this entry was made: "John Gray Blount—In Greene County, beginning four miles above the mouth of Pine River at the mouth of a big branch." An entry in the name of Nicholas Rochester called for Duck River and both sides of Beaverdam Creek. As stated elsewhere, the location of the Commissioners' Line of 1783 cannot now be discovered, as the report of the commissioners running it was not accepted by the North Carolina Legislature, and it, therefore, never had any legal existence. However, the party running it passed through Hickman County. This

was but three years after the commencement of the settlement at "The Bluffs" on the Cumberland River, and these men were beyond doubt the first explorers of what is now Hickman County. They named No B'ar Creek, Pine River, and other streams of the county. Lick Creek was probably named by Robertson's party in 1780, and possibly received its name as early as did Duck River.

At the head of Robertson's Creek, where Orten and Pruett now live, a woman named Sallie Brady was buried in 1833. The first person buried here was the grandfather of John H. Anderson, in 1830. Zebulon Tarkington was one of the first settlers on this creek; and where Richard M. Anderson now lives, one-half mile from the spring at which Robertson was killed, Joshua Tarkington lived in 1825. He lived on the Polk entry. The Polk entry, which included several hundred acres, joined the lands of " Kettle Dick " Anderson at the lower end of Anderson's Bend and included much of the land on Robertson's Creek. John Willey, the father-in-law of Craig Anderson, lived on Robertson's Creek in 1830, and on this account it came to be known as " Willey's Branch."

In 1862, back of Anderson's Bend and opposite the mouth of Short Creek, which runs into Duck River between the mouths of Leatherwood and Lick Creeks, Caleb McGraw was drowned by unknown parties. He was a Federal sympathizer, and, it being alleged that he had reported to the Federals the presence of

Confederate soldiers at home on furloughs, he was taken to the river and told to choose between drowning and taking the oath of allegiance to the Confederate States of America.   He refused to take the oath, a rock was tied around his neck, and he was carried in a canoe to the middle of the river.   He was again told to choose.   He replied: " Drown and be damned! " He was drowned.

In Anderson's Bend, years before the Civil War, Clark D. Fowler and Lawson H. Nunnelly had a " rough - and - tumble, old - fashioned fight " of such fierceness that the occurrence is yet readily recalled by old citizens.   Nunnelly did not swim the river in order to reach Fowler, but deliberately crossed it in a canoe, he having made an engagement with Fowler to meet him for the purpose of fighting him.   Odium did not then attach to affairs of this kind.   This was the manner in which pioneer gentlemen settled minor differences.

CHAPTER XIX.

OUR LEGISLATORS.

I N the Sixth General Assembly, which met at Knoxville in 1805 and again in 1806, Duncan Stewart represented, in the Senate, Montgomery, Robertson, Dickson, and Stewart Counties; and Dickson and Robertson Counties were represented in the House of Representatives by Anderson Cheatham, of Robertson County. On September 3, 1806, Senator Sampson Williams introduced a bill granting to John Gordon preëmption rights in 640 acres of land on Duck River, the bill, which became a law, reciting that Gordon, "under the sanction of the United States, did make an establishment at the crossing of Duck River for the purpose of affording necessary convenience to travelers on the route from Nashville to Natchez." Gordon had, prior to 1795, been engaged in furnishing supplies to the soldiers of the government on duty in Tennessee, he furnishing supplies to the party, under Captain Butler and Lieutenant Gaines, engaged in opening the Natchez Trace. After this party had completed their work, Gordon, with the consent of the government, opened a trading post at the place where the trace crossed Duck River. Here he had a ferry and stand—that is, an inn. He wisely selected as his partner the Chickasaw chief, Gen. William Colbert.

Colbert, in return for his friendly attitude toward the whites, bore a major general's commission. The contract between Gordon and Colbert was made on February 14, 1804, and was witnessed by James Robertson, Andrew Jackson, John McNairy, and William T. Lewis. Colbert agreed to place in the possession of Gordon all of the property left at this point by the United States troops and to protect all property brought from Nashville by Gordon. Gordon was given the privilege of clearing and cultivating as much land as he thought necessary, and this privilege was to be his during his lifetime, and was to descend to his son, John, who was to continue the partnership with Colbert's son, Jamison. In return for these concessions, Gordon was to furnish all necessary supplies and was to employ a bookkeeper and manager. The net profits were to be equally divided. This contract was read to Colbert by an interpreter. Gordon's bookkeepers and managers, under this contract, were: Smith Ogilvee, from February 15 to June 16, 1804; —— Dromgoole, from June 17 to December 1, 1804; and Thomas H. Benton ("Old Bullion"), from December 1, 1804, to May 20, 1805. In 1806, as above stated, Gordon was granted preëmption rights in the lands around Gordon's Ferry. At this time, in each county the Court of Pleas and Quarter Sessions, composed of the justices of the peace of the county, had criminal and civil jurisdiction to about the extent of the Circuit Courts and Chancery Courts of the present day. In addition to this, the Court of

Pleas and Quarter Sessions had about the same functions as the County Court of to-day. Appeals from this court were taken to the Superior Court of Law and Equity for the district, this court differing from the Supreme Court of to-day to the extent that trials were had by judge and jury. The jurors for this court were selected by the courts of the several counties composing the district. In 1806 the counties of Stewart, Dickson, Robertson, and Montgomery were formed into the Robertson District, the court for which was held at Clarksville. At Clarksville was erected the jail for the district.

The Seventh General Assembly met at Knoxville in 1807. Parry W. Humphreys was Senator from the counties of Robertson, Dickson, Montgomery, and Stewart; and Anderson Cheatham was again in the House of Representatives. On Wednesday, November 11, 1807, there was presented " the petition of a number of citizens of Duck River praying to have a new county laid off." This petition was referred to the " Committee on Propositions and Grievances." Senator Nicholas T. Perkins, of Williamson County, chairman of this committee, reported on Saturday, November 14, that " the petition of sundry inhabitants of Duck River to the south part of Dickson, praying to have a new county laid off, is reasonable." This report was read, concurred in, and sent to the House. On Monday, November 23, Senator Humphreys introduced a bill, entitled "An Act to reduce the present limits of Dickson County, and to form a new county to the south of the same." This bill was on this date read the first time, passed, and sent to the House. On Wednesday, November 25, it was received from the House, read, and, on motion of Senator Robert Weakley, of Davidson County, withdrawn by him for amendment. On the following day it was returned with amendments and was read, passed as amended, and sent to the House. On Monday, November 30, it was again received from the House, read the third time, passed, and returned to the House. On Thursday, December 3, 1807, it was reported as being correctly engrossed by Hugh Lawson White, chairman of the " Committee on Engrossed Bills." On this day Senator Humphreys was elected by the Legislature as one of the judges of the Superior Court. The Act creating Hickman County, after giving its boundaries, provided that the Court of Pleas and Quarter Sessions should meet on the first Mondays of January, April, July, and October, at the house of William Joslin, on Pine River. The justices of the peace for Hickman County, they to compose this court, were appointed by the Legislature, and were: Thomas Petty, William Wilson, James Miller, Robert Dunning, and Alexander Gray. This court at its first session elected William Wilson chairman. Wilson was the father of the first white child born within the limits of what is now Hickman County. This was Jane Wilson (born on December 27, 1806). This court elected William Phillips sheriff; John Easley, trustee; Bartholomew G. Stewart, register; Joseph Lynn, ranger; and William Stone, clerk of the court. The lands upon which Jackson, West Tennessee, now stands were originally owned by B. G. Stewart and Joseph Lynn. It was provided in the Act that the elections for Governor, members of Congress, members of the Legislature, and presidential electors should be held at the place for holding court, and that the sheriff of Hickman County should on the following day meet the sheriff of Dickson County at Charlotte and canvass the returns with him. The vote for Representative was to be added to the vote of the counties of Robertson and Dickson. Hickman County was made a part of the Robertson District, and was entitled to send two jurors to the Superior Court, held at Clarksville. Before the adjournment of the Legislature the time for holding courts in Hickman County was changed from the first Mondays to the third Mondays of January, April, July, and October. It was also provided that there should be held in Hickman County, in the following May, an election for regimental officers, the county being entitled to one regiment of militia with one colonel and two majors. At this election John Holland was elected lieutenant colonel; Joseph Wilson and Joseph Inman, majors. Hickman County was made a part of the Fifth Electoral District.

The Eighth General Assembly met at Knoxville in 1809. John Shelby, of Montgomery County, was Senator for the district composed of the counties of Stewart, Dickson, Hickman, Robertson, and Montgomery. John Coleman, of Dickson County, represented in the House of Representatives the counties of Robertson, Dickson, and Hickman. Thomas H. Benton was chairman of the Senate " Committee of Engrossed Bills." The place for holding regimental musters in Hickman County was fixed at the place for holding court. By this Legislature, Circuit Courts were established, and the State was divided into five judicial circuits, the counties of Montgomery, Dickson, Hickman, Humphreys, Stewart, and Robertson composing the Fifth District. For this circuit Parry W. Humphreys was elected judge by the Legislature, and George W. L. Marr was elected solicitor general. A Supreme Court of Errors and Appeals was created, and this system took the place of that which had hitherto existed. On October 5, 1809, Senator Shelby presented the tax aggregate of Hickman County for 1808. This statement, made and signed by " William Stone, Clerk Hickman County Court," was as follows: "An Aggregate Amount of the Taxable Property of Hickman County, 1808—36,807 acres of Land, 71 dolls.; 167 white polls, 20 dolls. and 87 cts. and 5 mills; 72 black polls, 18 dolls.; 7 stud horses, 18 dolls.; 1 tavern license, 5 dolls.; 1 lawsuit, 67 cts. and 5 mills; Tax on Registration of 3,665 acres of Land, 3 dolls. and 36 cts. and 5 mills." The lawsuit was the case of Compton vs. Peery, referred to in preceding pages. On October 18 a bill establishing a permanent seat of justice for Hickman County was reported as correctly engrossed. The town selected as the seat of justice

was to bear the name " Vernon." The Act provided
that an election should be held in the county of Hickman on the first Monday of March, 1810, for the purpose of naming five commissioners who were to fix
the location of the county seat. A record of this election is not now in existence, but the commissioners
were chosen and they selected the present site of
Vernon. On November 22 a county academy for
Hickman County was established, with the following
trustees: James Barr, Hugh Ross, William Wilson,
John Holland, John McCaleb, Alexander Gray, and
William Ward. This was Johnson Academy. The
teacher was John Y. Peyton, Vernon's first school-
teacher. For a seat in the Senate of this Legislature, the veteran Sampson Williams was defeated
by Thomas K. Harris, from the counties of Smith,
Jackson, Overton, White, Warren, and Franklin.
Williams contested and many depositions were filed,
but Harris was given the seat.

The first session of the Ninth General Assembly
met at Knoxville in 1811. Robertson, Montgomery,
Stewart, Dickson, Hickman, and Humphreys Counties were represented in the Senate by James B.
Reynolds, of Clarksville; and the county seat of
Humphreys County, established during this session,
was named " Reynoldsburg " in his honor. Robertson, Dickson, and Hickman Counties were represented in the House by Sterling Brewer, of Dickson.
In the Senate were Newton Cannon and Robert C.
Foster; also Sampson Williams, who had been vindi-

cated by an appeal to the people. Land warrants were ordered issued to John Rains, Thomas Brandon, and the heirs of Richard Shaffer. Rains had been a hunter; Shaffer, a chain carrier; and Brandon, a guard, in running the Continental Line of 1784. While these men were with one of the parties running this line, it is not known whether they were with the party that went west from Mount Pisgah and through Hickman County, or with the party that went east from that point. Shaffer was one of the men with Hickman at the time of the latter's death, and was himself later slain by Indians. Rains was the celebrated Capt. John Rains, grandfather of J. H. Rains, of the Eighth District of Hickman County. The second session of this Assembly met at Nashville on September 7, 1812, this being the first session to meet at Nashville. By a communication from the clerk of the Hickman County Court, giving the number of captain's companies in the county, the attention of the Legislature was directed to the fact that Hickman County had not its quota of justices of the peace. The Legislature, therefore, appointed two additional magistrates—Thomas Porter and Jesse G. Christian. Since 1803 the State had been divided into three congressional districts. One of these, the Mero District—a perpetuation of the old name " Miro "—included Dickson County, and later Hickman County. It had been represented by William Dickson (two terms), Jesse Wharton, Robert Weakley, and Felix Grundy. The State by this Legislature was divided into six congressional districts, the Sixth District being composed of the counties of Robertson, Montgomery, Dickson, Humphreys, Hickman, Stewart, Maury, and Giles. Its first representative in Congress was Judge Parry W. Humphreys, of Montgomery County.

The Tenth General Assembly met at Nashville on September 21, 1813. No journals of this General Assembly can be found in the archives of the State, and it is, therefore, impossible to give the names of Hickman County's Senator and Representative. Prior to this time the voting place for the county had been at the house of Robert Joslin, near the present site of Pinewood, and later at Vernon. By this Legislature a second voting place was established " at the house of Zebulon Hassell on Lick Creek of Duck River." The penalty for voting at both places during the same election was a fine of ten dollars. Alexander Gray and Garrett Lane, of Hickman County; and Robert Hill, William Cathey, and William Stockard, of Maury County, were made a commission to open Duck River for navigation from Gordon's Ferry to the mouth. They were to receive as funds for the carrying on of this work $1,050 from the commissioners of the town of Columbia. This was to be supplemented by the County Court of Hickman County raising by taxation $110 during the years 1814 and 1815. The time for holding court in Hickman County was changed to the second Mondays of February, May, August, and November.

The Eleventh General Assembly met at Nashville on September 18, 1815. The Senator for Robertson, Hickman, and Dickson Counties was Robert West; the Representative from Dickson and Hickman Counties, William Easley. Easley was the first Hickman Countian to hold a seat in the State Legislature. In the Senate was Adam Huntsman, of Overton County, who emigrated to West Tennessee in after years and defeated David Crockett in a race for Congress. Another voting place was established in Hickman County at the house of Crawford Goodwin, on Tumbling Creek. This territory was then a part of Hickman County, and here lived B. G. Stewart, Hickman County's first register. Several of the early magistrates of the county were also from this section. Voters who presented themselves at the house of Goodwin were to swear that they had not already voted at either of the other voting places. Failing to swear this, they were not to be permitted to vote. This law also governed the election at the other two places. David Rolling, of Humphreys County, who, while going up the Tennessee River in a boat in 1808, had been shot by Indians "through both thighs and in the left knee, through both arms and in several places in the body, hitting him with eleven bullets, some of which remain," was allowed to conduct "an ordinary or house of entertainment" in Humphreys County without paying license therefor. He was also allowed to "hawk and peddle spirituous liquors" in the counties of Humphreys, Stewart, and Hickman.

Public inspections of tobacco, hemp, flour, lard, butter, and other articles intended for exportation were established for Hickman County. The warehouses at which they were to be deposited to be examined by the inspector were authorized established " at or near the mouth of Lick Creek" and "at Joseph Ship's [Josiah Shipp's] in Ship's Bend." Here in 1811 the pioneer, Josiah Shipp, had erected the first cotton gin in the county. The militia of Hickman County was constituted the Thirty-sixth Regiment and attached to the Sixth Brigade.

The Twelfth General Assembly met at Knoxville on September 15, 1817. Senator Sterling Brewer, of Dickson County, represented Robertson, Dickson, and Hickman Counties. In the House was William Easley, who represented the counties of Dickson and Hickman. In the Senate were John Bell and Hugh Lawson White. Ten solicitorial districts were established, the Ninth District being composed of Giles, Maury, Lawrence, and Hickman Counties. For this district Robert L. Cobbs was elected solicitor-general. Lawrence and Wayne Counties were established, they being composed, in part, of territory taken from Hickman County. The Supreme Court for the Fifth Circuit was removed from Clarksville to Charlotte. The commissioners already appointed by the Circuit Court of Hickman County to divide the lands in this county of Asa Shute, deceased, were empowered to divide all of his lands in the State. The ranger of Hickman County was authorized to publish notices of estrays in

newspapers of either Columbia or Nashville.   It was
made lawful for the justices of Hickman County, if
a majority so desired, to levy a tax to provide for
additional compensation of jurors.   This compensation, however, was not to exceed fifty cents per day.
The time for holding the Circuit Court of Hickman
County was fixed as follows: First Mondays in March
and September.   The County Court was required to
meet on the second Mondays in January, April, July,
and October, and to remain in session for one week.
An election place was established " at David Williams' on Beaver Dam Creek."   Robert Murray and
John Brown were appointed notaries public for Hickman County.

The Thirteenth General Assembly convened at Murfreesboro on September 20, 1819.   The senatorial district, composed of Robertson, Dickson, and Hickman
Counties, was represented by Sterling Brewer, who
resigned and was succeeded by James R. McMeans.
McMeans was a lawyer who lived at Vernon, and later
at Centerville.   He married the widow of Captain
Porter, of Vernon.   He removed from Centerville to
Paris, West Tennessee.   Mrs. Porter was the sister
of the wife of John G. Easley, who for several years
conducted a hotel at Centerville.   She was the mother
of Mrs. Paralee Haskell, who from 1871 to 1881 was
State Librarian.   Dickson and Hickman Counties
were represented in the House of Representatives
by Robert E. C. Dougherty.   Robert Weakley was
speaker of the Senate; and James K. Polk, clerk.

Felix Grundy represented Davidson County in the House. An Act was passed for the relief of Robert Murray, who had obtained retail merchants' license in Williamson County and had removed to Vernon before the expiration of the license. He was allowed to continue selling in Hickman County under his Williamson County license. Perry County was established at this session. David Lowe, Joel Walker, John T. Primm, and Joseph Lynn were appointed commissioners to have run and marked the lines of the county of Hickman for the purpose of reducing it to its constitutional limits of 625 square miles. After having had the line run as prescribed in the Act of 1807, they were to ascertain the center of the county, and, if the place proved to be a suitable location, they were to buy not less than fifty acres for the purpose of laying out a town thereon; this to be the seat of justice for the county. If the exact center proved to be an unsuitable location, they were to select a suitable location near the center. It was provided that nothing in the Act should be construed as preventing the commissioners from selecting Vernon as the seat of justice, if, in their opinion, it was the nearest and most convenient place to the center. The compensation of the commissioners was to be fixed by the County Court. The compensation of the surveyor was fixed by the Act at two dollars and fifty cents per day. It was further enacted that the line between Hickman and Dickson Counties, run by William B. Ross, remain unchanged. The town directed to be

laid off was to be named " Canton." Provisions were
made for the removal of records and public business
from Vernon to Canton whenever the completion of
the public buildings in the latter town were certified
to by the commissioners. In the event that the commissioners could not agree as to the location of the
seat of justice, Col. Robert Weakley, of Davidson
County; Maj. James Fentress, of Montgomery County; and Col. Archer Cheatham, of Robertson County,
were appointed as umpires. An Act was passed for
the relief of Amos Johnston, who had laid his land
warrant on both sides of Duck River at the mouth of
Pine River, a portion of this land being within the
Indian boundary. Eli B. Hornbeak and Garrett Lane
were appointed notaries public for Hickman County.
The time for holding the courts of Hickman County
was fixed as follows: Circuit Court—Second Mondays in March and September; County Court—Third
Mondays in January, April, July, and October. On
November 25, 1819, Robert E. C. Dougherty was
elected surveyor general of the Twelfth Surveyor's
District, and on the following day he resigned his seat
in the Legislature. His bondsmen were Hugh Hill,
W. Malugin, James Hicks, John Stockard, John K.
Campbell, Felix Grundy, and George Kinzer. The
second session of this General Assembly convened on
May 15, 1820, with William Easley as the successor
of Robert E. C. Dougherty. Representative Easley
introduced a bill to divorce John Hulett and wife,
and to divorce Sarah Capps from her husband. At

that time the Legislature alone had the power to grant divorces.

The Fourteenth General Assembly convened at Murfreesboro on September 17, 1821. James K. Polk was again clerk of the Senate. Hickman, Lawrence, Wayne, and Hardin Counties were represented in the Senate by Dr. Joel Walker. In the House of Representatives, Hickman and Lawrence Counties were represented by David Crockett, the famous bear hunter and pioneer politician, who afterwards lost his life at the Alamo. It is related that during this session Crockett engaged in a heated debate with a colleague. He was being worsted in the war of words, when he rushed at his antagonist. He grasped his collar, when the entire false front of his shirt came loose. Crockett then seemed satisfied, and carried this token of victory back with him to his seat. William Hall, Aaron V. Brown, and Felix Grundy were members of this Assembly. It appearing that Richard Campbell, of Hickman County, had exhausted his funds in the building of a gristmill, and was, therefore, unable to buy the land upon which it was erected, it was made unlawful for any person, save Campbell, to enter or obtain a title to the fifty acres of land, having the mill for a center, for one year. Henry Hardin, Edward Nunnellee, David Curry, and James McNeilly were appointed commissioners for the purpose of running the county lines of Hickman County, finding the center of the county, etc., having practically the same duties to perform and the same powers as the commissioners appointed at the previous session of the Legislature. The town which they were to lay out was, however, given the name " Centerville." Provisions were made for the removal of the public business, records, etc., to Centerville. William Easley, William Phillips, and Charles Bowen, of Hickman County, were appointed umpires to aid in the selection of a location for the seat of justice for Perry County. The musty records of the second session of this General Assembly, which met in 1822, convey a faint idea of the bitter fight which was then being waged in Hickman County over the removal of the county seat. The commissioners appointed at the previous session, or a part of them, had selected the present site of Centerville as the place for the permanent seat of justice for the county, and the town was already being built on the forty-six acres donated by John C. McLemore and the fifteen acres donated by Charles Stewart. The Centerville faction of the Court of Pleas and Quarter Sessions held court at Centerville on the second Monday in July, 1822; while the Vernon faction held court at Vernon on the same day. On July 31 Representative David Crockett presented a petition to the Legislature from members of the Hickman County Court praying that the seat of justice remain at Vernon. This was supplemented by " a petition from citizens living north of the Hickman County line asking to be annexed to said County." This was an attempt to throw the center of the county farther north; but this was counter-

acted by a like petition from citizens living south of
the line, presented on August 5 by Senator Walker.
One week later Representative Crockett presented a
" petition of sundry citizens of Vernon asking that
said town may continue the seat of justice." On
August 17 an Act was passed to the effect that " all
the tract of country lying north of the following
described bounds shall remain a part of Hickman
County: Beginning on the southeast corner of the
Hickman County line on the old Natchez Road, running with this road to Griner's Old Stand, thence
eastwardly on top of ridge between head waters of
Swan and Buffalo, extending on with said ridge between the head waters of Cane Creek and Trace Creek
(of Lawrence County), so as to include Raccoon
Creek in Hickman County, to the east boundary line
of Perry County, thence north with Perry County
line to the northwest corner of Hickman County."
This fixed beyond controversy the true boundaries of
the county, and James Young and William Carothers,
Sr. (uncle of William H. Carothers), were added to
the commission, appointed at the previous session, to
determine the center of the county and establish a permanent seat of justice. It was provided that, in the
event of a tie vote, the County Court was to elect
another member to give the casting vote. The loss of
county records by fire during the Civil War leaves no
records showing whether the commission agreed, or
whether the battle was finished at a session of the
Court of Pleas and Quarter Sessions. Vernon, how-

ever, gained a temporary victory by the Act of August 22, which, while it legalized the acts of both the court held at Centerville during July and that held at Vernon, provided that processes from the court at Centerville should be returnable to Vernon, which was to remain the county seat pending the action of the commissioners. Senator Walker presented the petition of James Peery. It stated that he had placed his warrant on lands already entered, and at the end of a long lawsuit had lost them too late to make application to the commissioners of West Tennessee for another location. He asked that provision be made for him to have other lands. Hickman, Humphreys, Stewart, Dickson, Montgomery, and Robertson Counties were constituted the Eighth Congressional District.

In the Fifteenth General Assembly, which convened at Murfreesboro on September 15, 1823, Hickman County was represented in the Senate by Thomas Williamson, this county then being in a senatorial district with Lawrence, Wayne, Hardin, Madison, and Shelby Counties. In the House of Representatives it was represented by William Crisp, of Lawrence County. William B. Carter, Aaron V. Brown, William Hall, Felix Grundy, and James K. Polk were members of this General Assembly, as was also David Crockett, who at this time represented Humphreys, Perry, and eight West Tennessee counties. Robert Weakley, who was with Edwin Hickman at the time of the latter's death near Centerville, was speaker of the Senate. Robert L. Caruthers, who in 1863 was elected Governor of Tennessee, was clerk of the House of Representatives. Andrew Jackson was elected United States Senator. The counties of Montgomery, Robertson, Stewart, Dickson, Humphreys, and Hickman were formed into the Tenth Electoral District. Richard (" Kettle Dick ") Anderson was authorized to build a fish dam and trap across Duck River. The commissioners for establishing a seat of justice for the county of Hickman were authorized to sell the jail and courthouse at Vernon to the highest bidder, on a credit of twelve months. Edward Nunnellee, James Young, Jonathan J. Stanfill, Robert Anderson, and Eli Hornbeak were appointed permanent commissioners of the town of Centerville, and were authorized to sell the unsold lots of the town, the proceeds of these sales to be used in paying for the building of a courthouse, prison, and stocks. In the deed made by McLemore and Stewart to the commissioners of the town of Centerville the name of Hornbeak does not appear, and the following are added to this list: Henry Hardin, Benjamin Coleman, William Carothers, and Joel Smith. They were further authorized to let contracts for the building of a courthouse, prison, and stocks, and to superintend the erection thereof. Should the sales of the lots not produce an amount sufficient for their erection, the County Court was authorized to raise the remainder by taxation. It was further enacted that the County Court and Circuit Court of Hickman County be in the future held at Centerville.   All Acts incorporating the town of Vernon were repealed, and it was provided that thereafter owners of lots in Vernon should " pay taxes as for other lands, and not as for town lots." Centerville had won! Dr. Samuel Sebastian, who had succeeded William Stone as clerk of the County Court, came to Centerville and was its first physician.   Canty Nixon was Centerville's first school-teacher, he teaching here in 1824.   Dr. Joel Walker was the first postmaster.   By this Legislature Robert Sheegog was made entry taker for Hickman County; and James Weatherspoon, surveyor.   Lawrence County was authorized to pay George Peery for surveying that county.   A bill to incorporate Centerville was laid on the table.   Robert E. C. Dougherty was appointed one of the commissioners of the town of Christmasville, which was to be laid off on the bank of the Tennessee River opposite Perryville.   The second session of this General Assembly met in 1824. Montgomery, Robertson, Stewart, Dickson, Humphreys, and Hickman Counties were constituted the Tenth Electoral District, and the returning officers of this district were required to meet at Charlotte to canvass the vote for President and Vice President.   Permission was given for an independent militia company to be raised at Centerville.   This company was the Centerville Domestic Blues, and its first officers were: Henry Nixon, captain; Samuel D. McLaughlin, lieutenant; and Davis H. Morgan, ensign.   The sheriff and ranger of Hickman County were required to pub-

lish their official notices in some Columbia newspaper.
At this session the bill to incorporate Centerville became a law. J. D. Easley was Centerville's first
mayor.

The Sixteenth General Assembly met at Murfreesboro on September 19, 1825. The second session met
at Nashville on October 16, 1826. Hickman, Lawrence, Wayne, Hardin, McNairy, Hardeman, Fay-
ette, Shelby, Dyer, Tipton, Haywood, and Madison
Counties were represented in the Senate by Dr. Joel
Walker. Dr. Walker had been an ardent worker for
the removal of the county seat to Centerville, and was,
therefore, opposed by Robert Murray, of Vernon, who
was a candidate for Senator. Murray was probably
assisted in his race by David Crockett, who now lived
in West Tennessee, and who had opposed Walker in
the county-seat-removal fight. Murray was an Irishman, and was a merchant and the postmaster at Vernon at the time of the removal of the county seat.
His brother, Francis P. Murray, also lived at Vernon;
and a brother-in-law, Alfred Rutherford, was buried
in 1819 on the farm owned by the late W. F. Mays.
So close was the race between Walker and Murray
and so large the district—extending to Alabama and
Mississippi on the south, and to the Mississippi River
on the west—that it was many weeks after the election
before the final result was known. Returns from one
West Tennessee county would place Murray in the
lead; returns from another would give the lead to
Walker. Dr. Walker won, and learned of his elec-

tion just in time to take his seat. In the House of
Representatives, Hickman and Lawrence Counties
were represented by William M. Crisp, of the latter
county. On October 26, 1825, the resignation ,of
James Weatherspoon, county surveyor of Hickman
County, was read and accepted, and on October 28
George Peery was elected to succeed him. The report
of Samuel Sebastian, clerk of the Hickman County
Court, for the years 1821, 1822, 1823, and 1825, was
presented. The third Saturday in September was
fixed as the muster day for the Hickman County militia—Thirty-sixth Regiment. Eli Hornbeak, Samuel
Sebastian, James Scott, Henry Nixon, and Alexander Gray were appointed trustees of Centerville
Academy. The second session of this General Assembly met in 1826. A fifty-acre tract of land entered
by Horatio Clagett and donated to the Methodist
Church, including " Mount Pleasant church house,"
was exempted from taxation. William Phillips, late
sheriff of the county, was allowed the further time of
two years to collect arrearages of taxes due him. Acts
were passed providing for the adjudication of land
claims of Robert E. C. Dougherty, Reuben McClaren,
Daniel McClaren, and Joseph Porter. William Onstot was " allowed to make void an entry for twenty
acres lying on *Blew* Buck Creek in Hickman County,"
and to reënter same on any vacant land in surveyor's
district. In the proceedings of the Senate for November 22, 1826, is the following entry: " Received
from the House of Representatives: A Bill to ascer-

tain at what age a man becomes a bachelor and to in-
crease the revenue of the State. Mr. Walker moved
to lay said bill on the table for the same number of
years that a man must live to be denominated a bachelor under the provisions of the bill—to-wit, thirty
years. And the question thereon was taken and determined in the affirmative unanimously. And so
said bill was ordered to lie on the table for thirty
years." In 1826 Jesse Sparks, elected by the Hickman County Court, was commissioned as coroner for
Hickman County.

The Seventeenth General Assembly met at Nashville on September 17, 1827. William Hall, who before the expiration of his term became Governor by
the resignation of Gov. Samuel Houston, was speaker
of the Senate, of which Dr. Joel Walker, of Hickman
County, was again a member. The record does not contain the name of Hickman County's Representative.
Hugh Lawson White was reëlected United States Senator. Bedford, Maury, and Hickman Counties were
constituted the Ninth Electoral District. The sheriff
of Hickman County was authorized to advertise sales
in newspapers published either in Nashville or Columbia. It appearing that Sheriff Gabriel Faulx
(Fowlkes) had advertised a tax sale on Sunday, and
was thereby prevented from collecting delinquent
taxes for the years 1824 and 1825, he was authorized
to readvertise. Spencer Tinsley was given the right
of occupancy where he lived and where he had built a
mill " in Hickman County on Indian Creek." He

was to continue in possession of not more than 160 acres until these lands were finally disposed of by the United States. William Beakley, who had established a tannery (location not given), and Robert Wright, who had built a mill " on Cane Creek," were given the same privileges. Robert E. C. Dougherty, of Carroll County, was allowed to lay off a town on his lands. This town was to be named " Carrollton." Dougherty, after his election as surveyor general, had removed from Lick Creek to West Tennessee.

The Eighteenth General Assembly met at Nashville on September 21, 1829. Dr. Joel Walker, Senator from the counties of Hickman, Lawrence, Wayne, Hardin, and Perry, was elected speaker of the Senate without a dissenting vote. This was just five months after Hall, by virtue of his holding this office, had become Governor, and the fact that they might be selecting a Governor of Tennessee was plainly before the Senators when they voted unanimously for Hickman County's distinguished citizen. Son of the pioneer, Allan Walker, Joel Walker was the first and only Hickman Countian who was ever speaker of the Senate. A brother, Pleasant Walker, was for four years the sheriff of Hickman County, and relinquished this office for that of Representative, which he filled for five consecutive terms, he being the only man whom Hickman Countians ever so honored. Another brother was that legal giant—a great lawyer among great lawyers—Elijah Walker, who was for fifteen years a circuit judge. In the House of Representatives of this General Assembly was Bolling Gordon, representing Hickman and Dickson Counties. This Assembly passed an Act providing for the establishment of a penitentiary, and another providing for the establishment of a uniform system of public schools. Articles of impeachment were presented against Judge Joshua Haskell. One of the charges was that during the trial of George W. Garrett at Centerville in September, 1828, Judge Haskell was " sometimes out of the courthouse, out of sight and out of hearing of the same."

The Nineteenth General Assembly met at Nashville on September 19, 1831. William Davis represented in the Senate the counties of Hickman, Lawrence, Wayne, Hardin, and McNairy. In the House of Representatives was Bolling Gordon, who represented Hickman and Dickson Counties. Aaron V. Brown represented Giles County in the House. Judge Joshua Haskell, against whom articles of impeachment had been presented in 1829, was tried during the session of this Assembly. Dr. Samuel Sebastian, Sheriff Gabriel Fowlkes, Henry Nixon, Dr. Joel Walker, and Robert E. C. Dougherty were witnesses. Nixon testified that during the Circuit Court of Hardin County, while the case of Thompson vs. Sloan was being tried, the Judge left the courthouse while the first witness was being examined and remained away until the argument of counsel had closed. Returning at this time, he was informed by Nixon that they were ready for the charge. He stood at the end of the bar and gave a very good charge, considering that he had not heard the testimony. Nixon's client, Thompson, won; but after the departure of Nixon a new trial was granted, and at a subsequent term Nixon's client lost the suit. During the trial a. question arose as to the admissibility of testimony. The Judge being absent, Austin Miller, a disinterested attorney who was present, decided the question and the trial proceeded. Dr. Sebastian testified that in the trial of Garrett, at Centerville, the Judge remained until the jury was impaneled; then he absented himself and remained away much during the trial. Henry Nixon was solicitor-general, and was compelled to send for the Judge to hear a part of his argument addressed to the court. At one time a dispute arose between counsel, but the matter was finally satisfactorily arranged by them without their having to interrupt the Judge, who, according to Fowlkes, was either eating a watermelon in the courtyard or was at a show near by. According to the testimony of Nixon, the Judge was at that time at the tavern, seventy yards away, engaged in conversation with Judge Nathan Green. Finally, in despair, Nixon announced that they could proceed no further on account of the continued absence of the Judge, whereupon Congressman Cave Johnson, who was present, remarked that they could do as well without the Judge as with him. Nicholas T. Perkins, who defended Garrett, testified that the prosecution of his client was so manifestly frivolous that the Judge did no wrong in ignoring the entire proceedings. This

was only a small portion of the evidence against Judge
Haskell, but he was acquitted. John R. Charter was
released from the judgment against him in the Circuit
Court of Hickman County. He was on the appearance bond of Franklin and Addison Weaver, who
failed to appear for trial at the September (1830)
term of the court. An Act was passed for the relief of Gabriel Fowlkes, who had made incorrectly a
land entry. Robertson, Montgomery, Stewart, Humphreys, Hickman, and Dickson Counties were constituted the Eleventh Congressional District.

In the Twentieth General Assembly, which met on
September 16, 1833, the senatorial district of which
Hickman County formed a part was represented by
John Rayburn. In the House of Representatives,
Dickson and Hickman Counties were again represented by Bolling Gordon. John Netherland, Spen-
cer Jarnagin, Joseph C. Guild, Robert C. Foster, and
A. O. P. Nicholson were members of this Assembly.
Stephen C. Pavatt represented Humphreys County.
An Act was passed calling a constitutional convention to meet at Nashville in the following May. The
counties of Hickman, Lawrence, and Wayne were to
compose one district, which would be entitled to two
delegates to this convention, the returning officers to
meet at Catron's iron works, in Lawrence County.
An election was held in March, 1834, and Bolling
Gordon and Henry Sharp were selected as delegates
from this district. Another Act passed provided for
the removal of the Supreme Court of the Fifth Judi-

cial Circuit from Reynoldsburg, Humphreys County, to Centerville. Of this court Stephen C. Pavatt had been the clerk since 1832. One of his bondsmen was Henry Nixon. It was further provided that all appealed cases from the counties of Lawrence, Wayne, Hardin, Humphreys, Hickman, and Perry should be tried in the Supreme Court at Centerville. The Constitution of 1834 provided that the Supreme Court should be held " at one place, and at one place only, in each of the three grand divisions of the State." Nashville was selected as the place for Middle Tennessee, and, therefore, but few sessions of the court were held at Centerville. There is no record of the Supreme Court ever having been held here, but, according to that old and well-informed citizen, Horatio Clagett, the court met at Centerville several times. Persons desiring to build mills in Hickman and other counties named in the Act were granted any quantity of acres, not exceeding twenty-five, for this purpose. Robert Charter, Henry Nixon, Robert Sheegog, Eli B. Hornbeak, John Phillips, and Millington Easley were appointed to solicit subscriptions for the purpose of establishing the Planters' Bank of Tennessee, to be located at Nashville. The State was redistricted this year, but Hickman County remained with the counties that it was then with. The returning officers of the senatorial district were to meet at Waynesboro; of the " representative district," at " the house of the late Thomas Petty on Piney."

The Twenty-first General Assembly met at Nashville on October 5, 1835. Senator Bolling Gordon represented the counties of Lawrence, Wayne, and Hickman. In the House of Representatives was Gabriel Fowlkes, of Hickman County, who had relinquished the office of sheriff to accept this position. Prominent members of this General Assembly were: William Trousdale, Andrew Johnson, Hopkins L. Turney, Robert L. Caruthers, Joe C. Guild, A. O. P. Nicholson, and Meredith P. Gentry. The first-named was in the Senate; the others, in the House. The State was divided into three chancery divisions and eleven judicial circuits. Dickson, Hickman, Humphreys, Stewart, Montgomery, and Robertson constituted the Seventh. The Middle and East Tennessee Railroad Company was incorporated, and books for subscription of stock were opened at Centerville. These books were placed in the hands of John G. Easley, E. B. Hornbeak, and Samuel H. Williams. Tumbling Creek and that portion of the present county of Humphreys which had previous to this been a portion of Hickman County were annexed to Humphreys County.

The Twenty-second General Assembly met on October 2, 1837. Lawrence, Wayne, and Hickman Counties were represented in the Senate by Dennis G. Jones, of Hickman County. Hickman County's member of the House of Representatives was Pleasant Walker. Joseph C. Guild, Meredith P. Gentry, and A. O. P. Nicholson were members of this Assembly, the two latter being members of the House. Hickman County was added to the Eighth Judicial Circuit, and the time for holding courts at Centerville fixed as follows: On the second Mondays of March, July, and November. A " chancery district," composed of the counties of Dickson, Humphreys, Hickman, Stewart, Montgomery, and Cumberland (afterwards organized under the name " Cheatham "), was established, the court for the same to be held at Charlotte on the fourth Mondays of March and September. James D. Freeland, of Maury County, was granted the privilege of navigating Duck River with steamboats from Columbia to the mouth. An Act was passed incorporating the Penitentiary Turnpike Company, which was to make a turnpike from the city limits of Nashville to a point beyond John Harding's, by the way of the penitentiary and Cockrill's Spring. They were further authorized to make it, if they desired, five miles farther in the direction of Centerville, Hickman County. This was the first step toward the making of what is now known as the " Harding turnpike," which has been used as a thoroughfare by thousands of Hickman Countians. The Vernon Academy was incorporated, Robert Sheegog, William N. Holt, Millington Easley, Thomas W. Easley, William H. Carothers, Basil B. Satterfield, and Jacob Humble being named as trustees. The Centerville Academy was also incorporated, with the following trustees: William Bird, Samuel Whitson, David B. Warren, James D. Easley, John G. Easley, and Samuel Sebastian. The time fixed for the county drill for Hickman County, Seventeenth Brigade, was the first Friday and Saturday in September; the time for the regimental muster, the first Friday and Saturday in October. P. M. Hornbeak was allowed " thirty dollars for fitting up the hall at the commencement of the session." The line between Maury and Hickman Counties was changed so as to place in Hickman County the territory embraced in the triangle formed by Duck River, Fall Branch, and the Natchez Trace. Vernon was again incorporated. Robert Sheegog, Basil B. Satterfield, Dr. W. B. Douglass, G. Lane, and Howell Huddleston were appointed commissioners to lay off and establish the corporate limits. Provisions were made for the election of five aldermen by the voters of the town. The aldermen, when elected, were to elect one of their number mayor. Pleasant M. Hornbeak was allowed $480 for services as assistant doorkeeper of the House of Representatives.

Both Jones and Walker were reëlected and were members of the Twenty-third General Assembly, which convened on October 7, 1839. Andrew Johnson and James C. Jones were members of the House of Representatives. A joint resolution was adopted on November 14, 1839, instructing the Senators from Tennessee, Hugh Lawson White and Ephraim H. Foster, to vote against chartering national banks by Congress, in favor of the subtreasury bill, and against a bill to prevent the interference of Federal officers in elections. White and Foster, feeling that they could not conscientiously carry out these instructions, resigned, and Alex. Anderson and A. O. P. Nicholson were named as their successors by Governor Cannon. Felix Grundy had been elected by the Legislature to succeed Foster, but he died on December 19, 1840. During this session of the Assembly, Williamsport Academy was incorporated, with the following trustees: Gerard T. Greenfield, William W. Coleman, John O. Cook, Bolling Gordon, Troy S. Broome, Thomas P. Johnson, and John B. Hamilton. The militia regiments of Hickman County were made No. 97 and No. 98, and were attached to the Seventeenth Brigade, composed of the militia of Hickman, Hardin, Wayne, and Lawrence Counties. The time for holding regimental musters in Hickman County was fixed as follows: First Friday and Saturday in October. The Duck River Steam Navigation Company was incorporated, and the following were appointed to open books for subscriptions to the stock at Centerville: Bolling Gordon, Samuel B. Moore, David B. Warren, Edwin M. Baird, and John Studdart. The Centerville Academy was designated as the county academy of Hickman County, and the Act of 1838, constituting William Bird and others a body corporate under the style of the " Centerville Academy," was repealed.

Pleasant Walker was again elected a member of the House of Representatives and represented Hickman County in the Twenty-fourth General Assembly. Thomas J. Matthews represented the senatorial district of which Hickman County was a part. The appointments of Nicholson and Anderson as United States Senators having expired upon the day the Legislature convened—October 4, 1841—it devolved upon this Assembly to name their successors. It was found that in a joint ballot the Whigs would have a majority and elect the Senators. In the Senate, however, the Democrats had a majority, and this majority refused to allow the Senate to meet the House for the purpose of electing a United States Senator. These Democrats were called the " Immortal Thirteen." Andrew Johnson was the leader of the Democrats, and one of the thirteen was Thomas J. Matthews. Governor Jones did not make any appointments, and Tennessee was without a United States Senator until 1843. An Act was passed fixing the time for holding Circuit Court at Centerville as follows: " The third Monday in August, December, and April." Pleasant M. Hornbeak was allowed $508 for services as assistant doorkeeper of the House. The Penitentiary Turnpike Company was again incorporated for the purpose of making a turnpike from Nashville in the direction of Centerville. The length of this turnpike was to be fifteen miles, and John Davis was appointed one of the commissioners to locate it.

In the Twenty-fifth General Assembly, which convened on October 2, 1843, the senatorial district composed of the counties of Hickman, Lawrence, Wayne, and Hardin was represented by Bolling Gordon, of Hickman County. The veteran Legislator, Pleasant Walker, again represented Hickman County in the

House of Representatives. A. O. P. Nicholson, the ex-United States Senator, represented Maury and Giles Counties in the Senate. Powhattan Gordon, a brother of Bolling Gordon, was one of the Representatives from Maury County; and Dr. Joel Walker, a brother of Pleasant Walker, was one of the Representatives from Williamson County, he having removed from Hickman County to Williamson County. Spencer Jarnagin and Ephraim H. Foster (whose resignation has been previously referred to) were elected United States Senators. Foster served two years, when he again resigned, this time to make the race for Governor against Aaron V. Brown. Lewis County, named in honor of Meriwether Lewis, was established, taking a portion of the territory of Hickman County. Samuel B. Moore, Robert Sheegog, and Bolling Gordon were appointed commissioners to open books at Centerville to receive subscriptions to stock of Duck River Steam Navigation Company. The corporate limits of Centerville were so changed as to include the residence of Samuel H. Williams and the Centerville Academy. P. M. Hornbeak was allowed $488 for services as assistant doorkeeper of the House of Representatives.

In the Twenty-sixth General Assembly, which met on October 6, 1845, Pleasant Walker represented Hickman County in the House of Representatives for the fifth and last time. Archibald G. McDougal represented the senatorial district of which Hickman County formed a part. Harvey M. Watterson (father of Henry Watterson, of the Louisville Courier-Journal) was speaker of the Senate. Landon C. Haynes, Joseph C. Guild, and Emerson Etheridge were members of this Assembly. The Democrats now had a majority and hoped to elect a Democratic successor to Foster. A. O. P. Nicholson was nominated by a Democratic caucus. Hopkins L. Turney, father of ex-Gov. Peter Turney, secured the support of the Whigs, who, with the assistance of six Democrats, elected him. The fourth Mondays of March, July, and November were fixed as the times for holding the Circuit Courts of Hickman County. Dr. Samuel B. Moore, William G. Clagett, A. M. Williams, William H. Foster, and John B. Gray were appointed trustees of the Centerville Female Academy. Friday and Saturday after the first Monday in October were designated as the time for holding the regimental musters of Hickman County. The Duck River Slackwater Navigation Company was incorporated and was granted the exclusive right to navigate Duck River, from Columbia to the mouth, with steamboats, barges, and keels for a period of fifty years. This company was to erect a series of locks and dams, and was given the right to fix the tolls. Rafts and flatboats were, however, to be allowed to descend free when the water was such that they could have descended without the aid of the locks and dams. The incorporators were: Robert Campbell, Jr., Christopher Todd, R. B. Mayes, James Smizer, Gideon J. Pillow, George W. Gordon, Robert T. Webster, Will-

iam F. Rankin, Meredith Helm, Abraham Church,
Edwin Baird, M. C. Napier, John Montgomery, Dennis G. Jones, John B. Gray, Joseph Blackwell, and
Henry G. Cummins.   This scheme for the navigation of Duck River failed to materialize.   The settlements on Brush Creek and Raccoon Creek were annexed to Perry County.

In the Twenty-seventh General Assembly, which
met on October 4, 1847, the Senator from Wayne,
Hardin, Hickman, and Lawrence Counties was William P. Rowles.   Hickman County's member of the
House of Representatives was Dr. Samuel Bowen
Moore.   Landon C. Haynes, Return J. Meigs, Isham
G. Harris, and John Bell were members of this Assembly.   Bell was elected United States Senator to
succeed Jarnagin.   An Act was passed providing for
the appointment of three Commissioners of the Poor
by the County Court of Hickman County, the appointment to be made at the term next preceding January 1.
These commissioners were to serve for three years.
They were to appoint a superintendent, to serve
until his successor was appointed.   The Tennessee
Central Railroad Company was incorporated, and the
subscription books for Hickman County were placed
in the hands of the following commissioners: William
Bird, A. M. Williams, Horatio Clagett, James D.
Easley, and David B. Warren.   The time for holding Circuit Courts in Hickman County was fixed
as follows: The third Mondays in April, August, and
December.   The Third Civil District of Hickman

County was divided, with Duck River the line, thereby forming the Thirteenth District. The house of John Bibb was made " the election ground." Provision was made for the appointment of a Hickman County director of the Bank of Tennessee. P. M. Hornbeak was appointed as an additional commissioner to solicit subscriptions to stock of Duck River Slack-water Navigation Company.

In the Twenty-eighth General Assembly, John W. Whitfield, of Hickman County, was in the Senate, he being elected as a reward for his services in the Mexican War, which had just closed. Samuel B. Moore was again in the House of Representatives, of which Landon C. Haynes was speaker. In this Assembly, which convened on October 1, 1849, Sumner County was represented by William B. Bate. Although a half century has intervened, Senator Bate yet remembers Dr. Moore, of Hickman County, as a genial, intelligent gentleman, who was much more than the ordinary Representative. Other members were: Felix K. Zollicoffer, George H. Nixon, and J. D. C. Atkins, a brother-in-law of Dennis G. Jones, and afterwards Congressman from the Eighth District. The time for holding the Circuit Courts of Hickman County was fixed as follows: Third Mondays in March, July, and November. Hickman County was attached to the Fourteenth Judicial Circuit, and Elijah Walker was elected judge by the Legislature. It was provided that the attorney-general for the Eighth Circuit should continue to attend the court at Centerville. The Centerville Male Academy was divided into two branches—one for the education of boys, the other for the education of girls. A. M. Williams, Samuel B. Moore, C. Johnson, R. E. Griner, and P. Walker were appointed additional trustees for this academy. Bolling Gordon was made one of the trustees of Lawrence College.

The Twenty-ninth General Assembly met on October 6, 1851, with Whitfield again in the Senate. He was this year appointed major general of the Third Division of the State militia. In the House of Representatives was William Phillips, of Hickman County. The following were members of this Assembly: Francis B. Fogg, Joseph C. Stark, J. D. C. Atkins, David Campbell, Gustavus A. Henry, Stephen C. Pavatt, and John Netherland. Since 1843 Hickman County had been in the Sixth Congressional District, with Hardin, Maury, Giles, Lawrence, and Wayne Counties. These counties, with the exception of Maury County, were now, with McNairy, Perry, Decatur, Benton, Humphreys, and Lewis Counties, formed into the Seventh Congressional District. James C. Jones was elected United States Senator to succeed Hopkins L. Turney. Hickman County was made exempt from the general law imposing the duties of entry taker upon the registers of the several counties. An Act was passed establishing Taylor County, which was to be composed of portions of Hardin and Wayne Counties. The county seat was to be Whitfield, named in honor of Gen. John W. Whitfield. This county was never organized. The line between Hickman and Perry Counties was again changed. The time for holding Chancery Court at Centerville was fixed as follows: First Mondays in March and September. The Duck River Slack-water Navigation Company was empowered to transfer or donate its stock to any company that would run a railroad through Williamson and Maury Counties, or from Columbia to the Alabama line or the Tennessee River. Hickman County stockholders were made exempt and not liable for any stock subscribed.

The Thirtieth General Assembly—the first held in the present State Capitol—met on October 3, 1853. The Senator from the counties of Maury, Lewis, Hickman, and Dickson was Dr. Samuel B. Moore. The Representative from Hickman County was William Phillips. In this General Assembly were George H. Nixon and John F. House. An Act incorporating Centerville was passed. The Sixth Chancery Division was established. It was composed of the counties of Carroll, Benton, Humphreys, Dickson, Hickman, Perry, Decatur, Henderson, McNairy, Hardin, Wayne, and Lawrence. Previous to this time judges and attorneys-general had been elected by the Legislature. In this year an amendment to the Constitution was adopted providing for the election of these officials by the people. The first chancellor of the Sixth Division was Stephen C. Pavatt, of Humphreys County, a brother-in-law of Henry Nixon. The farm and residence of Philip Hoover, of Maury County, were annexed to Hickman County, and the line between Hickman and Perry Counties was so changed that William Watson, Abisha Curl, Owen Morgan, John Sutherland, and David Carrys became citizens of the latter county. James D. Easley, Troy S. Broome, S. H. Williams, Charles Johnston, and W. G. Clagett were appointed trustees of the Centerville Male and Female Academy. The Western Central Turnpike Company was authorized to extend its turnpike to Centerville and a branch to Vernon. William Clagett, Levin Goodrich, and S. H. Williams were appointed commissioners of this company.

The Thirty-first General Assembly met on October 1, 1855. Edward S. Cheatham, of Robertson County, was speaker of the Senate, and Neil S. Brown was speaker of the House. The senatorial district composed of the counties of Maury, Lewis, Hickman, and Dickson was represented by W. C. Whitthorne. Hickman County was represented in the House of Representatives by Robertson Whiteside. J. D. C. Atkins, F. C. Dunnington, George H. Nixon, and Robert Hatton were members of this Assembly. The lands of Jesse G. Thompson, of Hickman County, were annexed to Lewis County. The time for holding the Chancery Court of Hickman County was fixed as follows: Second Mondays in March and September. The Hickman County Iron Company was incorporated, the incorporators being: Aaron V. Brown, Anthony W. Vanleer, Samuel B. Moore, B. L. Goodrich, and Bellfield S. Carter. They were

authorized to engage in the mining of ore, the manufacture of iron, and to build a turnpike from Centerville to the Tennessee River. The office of entry
taker for Hickman County was abolished and the duties of this office made a part of the duties of the
county surveyor. The Comptroller of the State was
authorized to issue a warrant to John W. Lane, jailer
of Hickman County, for the board of a prisoner sent
from Perry County to the jail at Centerville. The
town of Centerville was constituted the forty-fifth
school district of Hickman County.

The Thirty-second General Assembly met on October 5, 1857, with W. C. Whitthorne again in the Senate. John J. Williams represented Hickman County
in the House of Representatives, and C. W. Beale represented Williamson County. The lands of Philip
Hoover lying in Maury County were annexed to Hickman County. The Fourteenth District of Hickman
County was created. The filing of bills for or against
citizens of Lewis County in the Chancery Court at
Centerville was made lawful.

The first session of the Thirty-third General Assembly met on October 3, 1859. The senatorial district
of which Hickman County formed a part was represented by Thomas McNeilly, of Dickson County.
John J. ("Jack") Williams was again in the House
of Representatives. W. C. Whitthorne, who now represented Maury, Lewis, and Williamson Counties in
the House, was made speaker of that branch. The
citizens of Russell's Creek were annexed to Perry

County, and a slight change was made in the line between Lewis and Hickman Counties. Pleasant Walker, Horatio Clagett, P. M. Hornbeak, George W. Stanfill, T. P. Bateman, William Grigsby, H. A. Shouse, J. P. Baird, S. J. George, James D. Easley, Stephen Worley, George Kennedy, together with such other parties as they in their own judgment might select, were authorized to solicit subscriptions to the stock of the Centerville and Columbia turnpike. It was provided that this turnpike should run from Centerville to some convenient point on the Columbia and Hampshire turnpike. The Fifteenth District of Hickman County was established. Provisions were made for selling any unnecessary streets in the town of Centerville and using the proceeds in the erection of a bridge across Duck River at Centerville. The Columbia, Centerville, and Pine River Railroad Company was incorporated. The proposed route of this railroad was from Columbia, Mount Pleasant, or some point between these places, by the way of Centerville, to the Northwestern Railroad. The incorporators were: Geo. Lipscomb, Geo. Webster, Ben. Harlan, Jas. H. Webster, Henry C. Sowell, A. M. Williams, William Biffle, L. D. Myers, B. Gordon, Theodric Erwin, William Walker, G. W. Stanfill, S. B. Moore, W. G. Clagett, P. Walker, W. H. Carothers, L. H. Nunnelly, P. N. Meroney, W. B. Easley, J. Graham, Robt. McNeilly, J. W. Huddleston, J. D. Easley, and John W. Walker. The Nashville and Centerville Turnpike Company was incorporated, the incorporators being: W. G. Clagett, S. J. George, G. W. Stanfill, J. R. Eason, L. P. Totty, J. M. Baird, Z. Hassell, G. W. Bratton, N. C. Weems, Wm. Walker, B. Gordon, V. F. Bibb, J. G. Tarkington, John Reeves, and G. Mayberry. The proposed route of this turnpike was as follows: To cross Duck River along the most suitable route so as to strike Lick Creek at or below E. Killough's, thence up to William Hicks', thence the most suitable route to intersect the Nashville and Hillsboro turnpike. The completion of this and other enterprises of this and preceding years was retarded by the presidential election of 1860, full, as it was, of alarming possibilities, and was entirely prevented by the stirring events of 1861 and by the Civil War which followed. This General Assembly was called upon to deal with questions of more importance than the granting of charters. The election of Lincoln was the culmination of the series of events, extending over a period of years, which caused the Civil War. The attempt upon the part of the Southern States to take advantage of their constitutional right to withdraw peacefully from the Union was not successful. Coercion was the unfortunate plan of procedure adopted by the general government. Tennessee, loyal as long as the honor of her citizens permitted it, was forced out of the Union. An invasion of this, a sovereign State, was made necessary by the secession of other Southern States, and Tennessee preferred that, when this invasion came, she should be a part of the Confederacy, and not a part of the United States.   And Tennessee became a " wreck in the warpath of might."   Gov. Isham G. Harris called a special session of the Legislature, which met on January 7, 1861.   A resolution providing for the holding of a convention which should determine Tennessee's attitude toward the Union was overwhelmingly defeated.   A bill was passed submitting this question to a vote of the people at an election to be held on February 9, 1861. At this election the people decided by a large majority against the holding of a convention for this purpose. A bill providing for the reorganization of the militia, which for four years had been out of existence, became a law.   After the adjournment of this session came the attack on Fort Sumter, and the Tennessee troops were soon after mobilized at Nashville and Memphis. Another session of the Legislature was called, and met at Nashville on April 25.   The action of the Governor in refusing to furnish troops to the Union was approved, commissioners were appointed to meet a representative of the Confederate Government, and numerous other significant and necessary steps were taken.   One of these was the incorporation of the Hickman County Saltpeter Company.   On May 7 an ordinance of secession was passed, subject to the approval of the people.   Senator McNeilly voted for this; and although Representative Williams was absent when the vote was taken, he showed his approval by raising, a few months later, a company for the Twenty-fourth Infantry, of which he later became a

major. The action of the Legislature was approved
by the people in an election held on June 8. The vote
of Hickman County was: For, 1,400; against, 3. One
of those voting against secession was Andrew Peery,
the hermit of Ugly Creek; another was Caleb Mc-
Graw; the third was his son-in-law, John Baker, who,
after the Civil War, was sheriff of Hickman County.

At this critical time the people of Hickman County
called upon that oft-tried and faithful public servant,
James D. Easley, who represented Hickman County
in the House of Representatives of the Thirty-fourth
General Assembly, which met on October 7, 1861.
In the Senate was Thomas McNeilly, representing
the counties of Maury, Lewis, Hickman, and Dickson.
John M. Fleming and Thomas H. Paine, each of
whom afterwards became State Superintendent of
Public Instruction, were members of this Assembly.
Hickman County was placed in the Eighth Congressional District, which, during the life of the Confederacy, was represented in the Confederate Congress
by Dr. Thomas Menees, of Robertson County. A bill
providing for the holding of Circuit Courts but twice
a year became a law, and the time for holding this
court in Hickman County was fixed as follows: Second Mondays of April and October. The second session of this Assembly met at Memphis on February
20, 1862, and on March 20 it adjourned *sine die*.
Eight days before this Andrew Johnson, military
Governor, had assumed charge of State affairs, and
from that time until 1869 a majority of the white citi-

zens of Hickman County had but little to do with the
management of State affairs through their duly elected
representatives.

The " Brownlow Legislature," which has no number in the series of the State's Assemblies, met at
Nashville on April 3, 1865.   Joshua B. Frierson,
of Maury County, and J. N. Puckett represented
Hickman County in the Senate and House of Representatives, respectively.   They were appointed by
Governor Brownlow, or else elected in elections held
outside of the counties which they were supposed to
represent.   Frierson was made speaker of the Senate.
One of the Representatives appointed by Brownlow
was Elder Absalom D. Nicks, of Dickson County.
Elder Nicks did not approve of the bitterly partisan
acts of his Radical Republican associates, and resigned before the expiration of his term.   One of the
Acts passed by this Legislature was "to limit the electoral franchise to unconditional Union men and soldiers of the Union Army."

Therefore, Hickman County was again represented
by Frierson and Puckett, who were members of the
Thirty-fifth General Assembly, which met on October 7, 1867.   By the preceding Legislature the Ætna
Iron, Manufacturing, and Oil Company had been incorporated, with Daniel Hillman, Levin S. Goodrich,
and George W. Goodrich as directors.   The Act incorporating this company was now so amended as to
make the name of the company " The Ætna Branch
of the Northwestern Railroad Company."   The names

of Hillman and Goodrich were stricken out and the names of S. L. Graham, W. G. Clagett, Wm. Maxwell, L. S. Goodrich, and A. Hicks inserted therefor. This was a step toward the erection of a railroad from Ætna to the Northwestern Railroad.

The Thirty-sixth General Assembly met on October 4, 1869. De Witt C. Senter, Conservative Republican, had become Governor by virtue of his being speaker of the Senate at the time of the election of Governor Brownlow to the United States Senate. He became a candidate for Governor, and, by virtue of the position to which he had succeeded, he had, under the Brownlow laws, complete control of the election machinery. A large number of Hickman County's citizens, who preferred Senter to his opponent, Stokes, Radical Republican, were permitted to vote by Senter's election officers. The result was that for the first time since the Civil War they sent to the Legislature representatives of their own choosing. These representatives were Jesse R. Eason in the Senate, and W. B. Russell in the House of Representatives. Dorsey B. Thomas, of Humphreys County, was speaker of the Senate. Balie Peyton, Emerson Ethridge, B. A. Enloe, and John M. Fleming were members of this Assembly. The citizens of Dickson County were also allowed to send a Representative of their own choosing, and they, remembering the fidelity of A. D. Nicks in 1865, sent him to the Legislature. An Act was passed providing for the assembling of the constitutional convention of the following year. Lewis County was reëstablished by the repealing of a bill which had been passed by the preceding Legislature. The line between Perry and Hickman Counties was changed for perhaps the one thousand and first time, this being a matter which has often engaged the minds of Tennessee Legislators. The Centerville Female Academy was incorporated, the incorporators being S. H. Williams, O. A. Nixon, W. M. Johnson, H. Clagett, and Leonidas Walker. The second session of this Assembly met after the ratification of the new Constitution and enacted numerous necessary laws. Hickman County was placed in the Eleventh Judicial Circuit, with Hardin, Wayne, Decatur, Lewis, Perry, Henderson, and McNairy Counties. It was placed in the Ninth Chancery Division.

In the House of Representatives of the Thirty-seventh General Assembly, which met on October 1, 1871, was Col. Levi McCollum, of Hickman County. The Senator for the district of which Hickman County formed a part was Albert G. Cooper, of Maury County. James D. Richardson was speaker of the House. B. A. Enloe, Jacob Leech, Thomas H. Paine, and J. A. Trousdale were members of this Assembly. The State was redistricted. Hickman, Perry, and Lewis Counties were constituted a Representative District; and Hickman, Perry, Humphreys, Dickson, Cheatham, and Houston Counties were constituted the Sixteenth Senatorial District. Mrs. Paralee Haskell, who was born in Hickman County, was made State Librarian.

In the Thirty-eighth General Assembly, which met in January, 1873, the senatorial district of which Hickman County formed a part was represented by W. A. Moody, of Humphreys County. Colonel Mc-Collum was again in the House. James D. Richardson, J. A. Trousdale, L. C. Houk, Jacob Leech, H. M. McAdoo, and John R. Bond were members of this Assembly. The present public school system was established. The counties of Wayne, Lawrence, Giles, Lewis, Maury, Hickman, and Williamson were constituted the Seventh Congressional District.

In the Thirty-ninth General Assembly, which met in January, 1875, Mitchell Trotter, of Humphreys County, represented the senatorial district of which Hickman County formed a part. In the House of Representatives was Leon. Walker, of Hickman County, he representing two other counties—Perry and Lewis. Thomas H. Paine was speaker of the Senate. The venerable president of the Tennessee Historical Society, Judge John M. Lea, was a member of this Assembly, as was also Tennessee's present Governor, Hon. Benton McMillin. No Act of a local nature, affecting Hickman County, was passed by this Assembly.

The Fortieth General Assembly met in January, 1877. Hugh Montgomery McAdoo, of Humphreys County, Senator for the counties of Hickman, Perry, Humphreys, Dickson, Cheatham, and Houston, was made speaker of the Senate. C. B. Dotson represented in the House the counties of Hickman, Perry, and Lewis. Joseph E. Washington, S. F. Wilson, and John H. Savage were members of this Assembly. This Assembly passed the Act known as the " four-mile law," and as a result numerous schools were incorporated in Hickman County and throughout the State. Resolutions of regret at the death of Judge Alfred Osborne Pope Nicholson were adopted by this Assembly.

The Forty-first General Assembly met in January, 1879. In the Senate the counties of Hickman, Humphreys, Perry, Dickson, Houston, and Cheatham were represented by Col. V. F. Bibb. In the House, representing the counties of Hickman, Perry, and Lewis, was the late Orville A. Nixon, a courteous gentleman and a lawyer of ability, who as a Legislator was much more than the ordinary. Hon. Henry P. Fowlkes, of Williamson County, a descendant of two prominent pioneer families of Hickman County—the Fowlkes and Mayberry families—was speaker of the House, he being the only native of Hickman County who was ever speaker of the House of Representatives. John R. Neal, John H. Savage, S. F. Wilson, and David L. Snodgrass were members of this Assembly. An Act was passed " to settle the debt of the State at ' 50-4,' and to submit said settlement to the people." It was enacted "that the State revenues collected and to be collected in the county of Hickman for the years 1878 and 1879 be, and the same are hereby, remitted to the people of that county, for the purpose of enabling them to complete the Nashville and Tuscaloosa

OUR LEGISLATORS. 423

Railroad to Centerville." This railroad was incorporated on June 6, 1877.

In the Forty-second General Assembly, which met in 1881, Colonel Bibb was again in the Senate. In the House the counties of Hickman, Perry, and Lewis were represented by the late Dr. H. K. Plummer. The Act incorporating Centerville, passed on October 14, 1824, was repealed. Hickman, Humphreys, Dickson, and Houston Counties were constituted the Twenty-second Senatorial District, and in this redistricting Act Hickman County was declared entitled to one Representative. The counties of Williamson, Maury, Giles, Lawrence, Wayne, Lewis, Hickman, and Dickson were constituted the Seventh Congressional District. The settlement of the State debt was the all-absorbing question, and three extraordinary sessions of this Assembly were called by Governor Hawkins.

In the Forty-third General Assembly, which met on January 1, 1883, Col. Vernon F. Bibb was again in the Senate; in the House was Orville A. Nixon. E. D. Patterson, Dorsey B. Thomas, and James M. Head were members of this Assembly. Two important Acts passed were " to settle the State debt in conformity with the platform on which Governor Bate was elected, called the ' fifty-and-three ' settlement," and one providing for a railroad commission. The line between Maury and Hickman Counties near Gordon's Ferry was changed, as was also the line between Dickson and Hickman Counties on Plunder's Creek.

In the Forty-fourth General Assembly, which convened in January, 1885, the counties of Hickman,
Humphreys, Dickson, and Houston were represented
in the Senate by Dorsey B. Thomas, of Humphreys
County.   In the House, representing Hickman County, was the veteran Joseph Weems.   C. R. Berry, of
Williamson County, was speaker of the Senate.   N.
B. Sugg, of Dickson County, was a member of the
House.   E. W. Carmack, of Maury County, was a
member of this Assembly.   The Act creating a railroad commission, passed in 1883, was repealed.

In the Forty-fifth General Assembly, which met in
January, 1887, Hickman, Humphreys, Dickson, and
Houston Counties were represented in the Senate by
the late Jacob Leech, of Dickson County, an able
lawyer.   His nephew, Hardin Leech, of Dickson
County, was a member of the House.   Colonel Bibb
represented Hickman County in the House.   John P.
Buchanan was a member of this Assembly.   The late
Dr. A. B. Brown, a physician well known in Hick-
man County, represented Humphreys County in the
House.

In the Forty-sixth General Assembly, which met in
January, 1889, J. D. Sensing, of Dickson County,
represented the senatorial district of which Hickman
County formed a part.   In the House was the late
Dr. A. J. Lowe.   Resigning on account of ill health,
he was succeeded by Dr. E. G. Thompson.   The late
Samuel G. Jones, son of Col. Dennis G. Jones, repre-
sented Humphreys County in the House.   The ven-

erable Judge J. J. Williams, who in his younger days had represented Hickman County in legislative halls and on the field of battle, was a member of this Assembly, he representing Franklin County.

In the Forty-seventh General Assembly, Hickman County was represented in the Senate by George M. Tubb, of Humphreys County, and in the House by W. J. D. Spence. R. C. Gordon, of Maury County, and R. J. Work, of Dickson County, former citizens of Hickman County, were members of the House. Maj. J. H. Aiken, of Williamson County, who commanded the fighting Ninth Battalion during a portion of the Civil War, was a member of the House. George Hash, of Warren County, father of Victor Hash, who married Miss Weems, of Bon Aqua, was a member of the House. Resolutions concerning the death of Judge J. J. Williams were adopted. The Nineteenth Judicial Circuit, composed of the counties of Hickman, Williamson, Dickson, and Cheatham, was established. Governor Buchanan appointed as judge of this circuit William Lafayette Grigsby, of Dickson County, a son of the late Col. Thomas K. Grigsby, of Charlotte, and a nephew of William H. Grigsby, of Centerville. At the next general election Judge Grigsby was a candidate for this position, being opposed by a native of Hickman County, at present a prominent citizen of Williamson County— Hon. Henry P. Fowlkes. Judge Grigsby was elected and held this position until the abolishment of this circuit by the Legislature in 1899. He was recently

appointed a Special Judge of the Supreme Court by
Governor McMillin.   After the establishment of the
Nineteenth Judicial Circuit, John L. Jones continued
as attorney-general until 1894, when W. Blake Leech,
of Dickson County, was elected to fill this position,
which he held until 1899, when the circuit was abolished.

In the Forty-eighth General Assembly, which met
at Nashville in January, 1893, Hickman County was
represented in the House by R. L. Peery.   The counties of Williamson and Hickman were represented in
the Senate by Park Marshall, of Williamson County.
W. Blake Leech represented Dickson County in the
House.   B. R. Thomas, a son of the late Dorsey B.
Thomas, of Humphreys County, was a member of the
House.   Hardin Leech, of Dickson County, was a
member of the Senate.   All laws declaring Duck
River navigable above Paint Rock, in Humphreys
County, were repealed.   Permission was given, by
resolution, for the removal to the Capitol grounds of
the remains of President James K. Polk and his wife,
Sarah Childress Polk.

In the Forty-ninth General Assembly, which convened in January, 1895, Hickman County was represented in the House by W. V. Flowers, and the counties of Williamson and Hickman were represented in
the Senate by J. A. Bates, of Hickman County.   R.
H. Gordon, of Davidson County, and R. C. Gordon,
of Maury County, descendants of the pioneer, John
Gordon, were members of the House, as was also the

veteran Maj. J. H. Aiken. Duncan B. Cooper, Maj. W. J. Whitthorne, and J. R. Winbourn (who at one time conducted Bon Aqua Springs) were members of the Senate. Hon. Peter Turney was declared Governor instead of H. Clay Evans, who was elected on the face of the returns, Senator Bates and Representative Flowers being among those who opposed this action.

In the Fiftieth General Assembly, which met at Nashville in January, 1897, Hickman County was represented in the House by Dr. W. L. Walker; and Hickman and Williamson Counties, in the Senate, by Samuel B. Lee, Jr., of Williamson County, a son of Samuel B. Lee, Sr., who was one of the operators of Lee & Gould's Furnace on Sugar Creek. In the House, representing Dickson County, was W. L. Cook, a grandson of Nathaniel Weems. John Thompson, of Davidson County, was elected speaker of the Senate; and Morgan C. Fitzpatrick, of Trousdale County, was made speaker of the House, the latter being the youngest man ever elected to this position by a Tennessee Legislature. The line between the counties of Lewis and Hickman was changed by this Legislature.

In the Fifty-first General Assembly, which met at Nashville in 1899, the counties of Hickman and Williamson were represented in the Senate by John M. Graham, of Hickman County. In the House, Hickman County was represented by Y. F. Harvill. Joseph W. Byrns, of Davidson County, was elected speaker of the House. J. C. Hobbs, of Hous-

ton County, a grandson of Col. Alfred Darden; and
M. H. Meeks, of Davidson County, who married
Miss Annie Nunnelly, of Vernon, were members of
the Senate. A member of the House was J. Grady
Jones, of Humphreys County, a grandson of Col.
Dennis G. Jones. Maj. J. H. Aiken, of Williamson
County, was a member of the House. The Nine-
teenth Judicial Circuit was abolished and Hickman
County was attached to the Seventh Judicial Circuit.
By an Act which is to take effect on August 1, 1902,
Hickman County is to be a part of the Eleventh Ju-
dicial Circuit, composed of the counties of Maury,
Giles, Lawrence, Wayne, Lewis, Perry, and Hick-
man. The sixth Chancery Division is to be com-
posed of the counties of Wilson, Sumner, Robertson,
Montgomery, Cheatham, Stewart, Houston, Dickson,
Humphreys, and Hickman.

Congressmen.—Jesse Wharton (1807-09), Robert
Weakley (1809-11), Felix Grundy (1811-13), Parry W. Humphreys (1813-15), James B. Reynolds
(1815-17), Geo. W. L. Marr (1817-19), Henry H.
Bryan (1819-23), James T. Sanford (1823-25), John
H. Marrable (1825-29), Cave Johnson (1829-43),
Aaron V. Brown (1843-45), Barclay Martin (1845-
47), James H. Thomas (1847-51), William H. Polk
1851-53), R. M. Bugg (1853-55), John V. Wright
(1855-57), G. W. Jones (1857-59), James H. Thomas
(1859-61), John F. House (member of Provisional
Confederate Congress), Thomas Menees (member of
First and Second Permanent Confederate Congress),

Dorsey B. Thomas (elected in 1865, but "counted out"), S. M. Arnell (1867-71—Confederate sympathizers disfranchised), Washington C. Whitthorne (1871-83), John G. Ballentine (1883-87), W. C. Whitthorne (1887-91), N. N. Cox (1891—).

Elections.—The earliest records now in existence of an election held in Hickman County are of the election held on August 7 and 8, 1817. Sheriff William Phillips certified that Joseph McMinn, candidate for Governor, received 527 votes; and his opponent, R. C. Foster, 174. In Hickman County, in 1832, Andrew Jackson received 764 votes; Henry Clay, 1. In 1836 Bolling Gordon, elector for Van Buren, received 621 votes; the Hugh L. White elector, 149. In 1840 Gordon, who was again elector for Van Buren, received 952 votes; the Harrison elector, Gustavus A. Henry, 293. In 1844 James K. Polk received 1,034 votes in Hickman County; Henry Clay, 255. In 1848 Solon E. Rose, the Taylor elector, received 301 votes; the Cass elector, 988. In 1852 E. R. Osborne, the Scott elector, received 241 votes; the Pierce elector, 839. In 1856 Thomas J. Brown, the Buchanan elector, received 1,086 votes; the Fillmore elector received 238. Tennessee went Democratic in this presidential election for the first time since the election of Jackson in 1832, but during all of these years Hickman County remained a Democratic county. In 1860 the vote of the county was as follows: Breckinridge, 1,067; Bell, 273; Douglas, 16. John C. Brown was elector for John Bell in the district of which Hickman County formed a part. In 1868, despite the election laws of Governor Brownlow, Hickman County remained Democratic, Seymour receiving 104 votes; Grant, 97. In 1872 Col. N. N. Cox, the Greeley elector, received 891 votes; Joshua B. Frierson, the Grant elector, 235. In 1876 Col. John H. ("Jack") Moore, of Hickman County, the Tilden elector, received 1,273 votes; A. M. Hughes, the Hayes elector, 179. In 1880 E. T. Taliaferro, the Hancock elector, received 1,157 votes; T. J. Cypert, the Garfield elector, 392; the Weaver elector, 62. In 1884 L. P. Padgett, the Cleveland elector, received 1,135 votes; T. J. Cypert, the Blaine elector, 709. In 1888 Flournoy Rivers, the Cleveland elector, received 1,509 votes; J. H. Morris, the Harrison elector, 1,137. In 1892 Frank Boyd, the Cleveland elector, received 1,179 votes; H. S. Thompson, the Harrison elector, 963. In 1896 E. E. Eslick, the Bryan elector, received 1,523 votes; T. F. McCreary, the McKinley elector, 988; W. B. McClanahan, the Bryan and Watson elector, 30; the Prohibition elector, 13; and J. A. Cunningham, the Palmer and Buckner elector, 12.

Population of Hickman County.—Census of 1810, 2,583; 1820, 6,080; 1830, 8,119; 1840, 8,618; 1850, 9,397; 1860, 9,312; 1870, 9,856; 1880, 12,095; 1890, 14,476.

CHAPTER XX.

HICKMAN COUNTY MAGISTRATES.

F ROM 1808 to 1834 the justices of the peace were selected by the Legislature of the State. They formed the Court of Pleas and Quarter Sessions, and elected all of the county officers. In the following list the date preceding the names is the year in which commissions were issued.

1808: Thomas Petty, William Wilson, James Miller, Robert Dunning, Alexander Gray.

1809: Hugh Ross, Robert Dean, Ezekiel Thomas, William Curl, Josiah McConnell, William Higginbotham, Robert Anderson, James Peery, James Morrison, Isaac Shull.

1811: Jonas Messer, James Wilson, Robert Bowen, Jr., George Reeves, Samuel Spencer.

1812: Thomas Porter, Jesse Christian.

1813: John Hewlett, William Higginbotham, Morgan Gess, Anderson Nunnelly, William Charter, David Kilough.

1815: Crawford Goodwin, Edward Stringer, Benjamin Holland, Jacob Dansby, Jesse Sparks, Daniel Smith, Gabriel Fowlkes.

1817: William Flemmings, Joseph Lynn, James Laxon, Richard Lowe, William Cash, Hugh Hill, Robert E. C. Dougherty, Carter Eason, Edward Nunnellee, James Young, Zedediah Aydelott, Abraham Lann.

1819: Andrew Stewart, Henry Muirhead, Sr., Nimrod Murphree, David Curry, Robert Anderson, Reuben Elliott, Thomas Jones.

1820: Benjamin Coleman, Robert Murray, Charles Bowen, John Hayes, Jeremiah Harlan.

1821: Eli B. Hornbeak.

1822: Joseph Halbrooks, Josiah Thornton, James Rhodes, Robert Thompson (commissioned on February 25), William Lancaster, Alexander Gray, George H. Erwin, Joel Smith, Archibald Ray.

1823: Joseph Jones, Edward Sharp, Robert Sheegog, Jacob Humble, Culton Pace, John Hewlett.

1824: Thompson Wood, John Gregory.

1825: Hugh B. Venable, George Peery, David Duncan, Silas Thompson (or Silas Tompkins), William B. Craig, Samuel C. Aydelott, Elias Deaton.

1826: Till. McCaleb, Granville M. Johnson, Edward Stringer, Daniel Shouse, William Donnelly, John C. Lewis, Hiram Campbell.

1827: Samuel A. Baker, Aaron B. Wilson, John H. Christian, Joseph Halbrooks, Clement Wilkins, Joseph Blackwell, Ephraim McCaleb, John Scott, Garrett Lane, Thompson Wright.

1829: George Hicks, Josiah Thornton, Henry Golightly.

1831: John Depriest, Isaac Lowe, James Rhodes, Robert Wade, Thomas Shepherd, David S. Hobbs, Cornelius D. White, Jacob Peeler, George Sheegog, Hardy Sparks.

1833: Alexander Goodman, William H. Foster,

Jared Curl, Willis Weatherspoon, William I. Nacly (?).

The Constitution of 1834 provided for the establishment of civil districts and the election of justices of the peace by the voters of the several districts. The sheriff, trustee, and register were after this elected by the people.

1836: Eli B. Hornbeak, John McGill, Samuel Whitson, William D. Willey, Zill McCaleb, Samuel A. Baker, Granville M. Johnson, Jacob Peeler, John T. Primm, James M. Ponder, Moses Thornton, Jacob Humble, Eli White, Garrett Lane, Jared Curl, Amsel Epperson, Willis Weatherspoon, Joseph Blackwell, Joseph Halbrooks, John Depriest, William B. Cook, Thomas Shepherd, Robert Wade, James Rhodes, William Duncan.

1837: William Bird, Samuel B. Lee.

1839: Elijah Murphree, Jno. B. Gray, Robert Totty.

1840: Eli Dyer, John Christian, Robinson (Buck) Coleman.

1841: Jacob Bylor.

1842: William Bird, John B. Gray, John McGill, Robert Totty, William D. Willey, G. M. Johnson, S. A. Baker, E. Murphy, D. K. McCord, Moses Thornton, John H. Christian, H. Dudley, Jared Curl, A. Walker, A. Epperson, R. Coleman, D. G. Jones, G. Pickard, William B. Cook, Robert Wade, Nathan W. Springer, A. B. Edwards, William Duncan, John G. Nixon, Jacob Bylor.

1844: Richard H. Campbell.

1845: Jacob Humble.

1846: E. Warren, Ezekiel W. Hassell, Felix Badger, James N. Bingham, John M. Anderson.

1848: William G. Clagett, William Wilson, Pleasant Walker, Jared Curl, Benjamin Grimmitt, Allen C. Deshazo, George W. Martin, Jr., Robinson Coleman, Nathaniel Young, Amsel Epperson, James N. Bingham, Dennis G. Jones, Young J. Harvill, Green Pickard, Christopher C. Hudson, John P. A. Parks, Granville M. Johnson, Eli Dyer, John T. Primm, Jacob Bylor, Noah H. Randall, Thomas Warren, John P. Beasley, Alexander Peery, John L. Griffin, Jeremiah Harlan, Jacob Humble (all on March 30), Isaac Depriest (June 5), P. A. Dudley (August 7).

1849: Isaac Lancaster.

1850: Miles Patton, Francis M. Easley.

1851: Joseph Reeves, John Reeves, William Gravitt, James McCollum, F. D. Leathers, Walter W. Brown.

1852: John McNeiley, Robertson Whiteside, B. F. Brown, Robert Totty.

1853: Isaac M. Goin, Ewel C. Warren, William Brown.

1854: Pleasant Walker, William G. Clagett, Benjamin Grimmitt, Troy S. Broome, Robert Totty, James H. Martin, Young J. Harvill, William T. Leiper, John Reeves, Isaac Goin, Jesse K. McMinn, John P. Beasley, William Wilson, Elijah W. Christian, William Gravitt, Jared Curl, Robinson Coleman, William H. Brown, James McCollum, Cyrus W. Russell, William Whitwell, Isaac Depriest, Ewel C. Warren, Robertson Whiteside, William Duncan, Vernon F. Bibb, Joseph A. Reeves (all on March 20), A. J. Peeler (April 12).

1855: W. W. W. Fowlkes.

1856: Walter W. Brown, Thomas Henry.

1857: Johnson H. Totty, A. J. Nixon.

1858: J. C. Golden, Arthur J. Nixon, William Wheat, James G. Briggs, George W. Tatum.

1859: John C. Gracey.

1860: William G. Clagett, Troy S. Broome, S. J. George, J. H. Martin, Y. J. Harvill, G. T. Overbey, John D. Cooper, William Allen, William Wilson, Hardy Petty, L. D. Wright, William Gravitt, Calvin Weatherspoon, M. Forrester, C. W. Russell, Luke Bates, J. R. Sutton, G. W. Tatum, E. C. Warren, R. Whiteside, Samuel Bartley, R. C. Gordon, J. C. Gracey, R. M. Anderson, William Anderson (all on March 19), W. Overbey (April 2), D. D. Smith (May 30).

1862: Thomas T. Henry.

1865: The following were appointed by Governor Brownlow: J. N. Puckett, J. P. Beasley, D. Caldwell. Following their names is this memorandum: "Blanks to Dr. Puckett for justices." The names of the following justices are to be found in another commission book, under date of January 1, 1865: James N. Puckett, Sr., chairman; Wm. M. C. Thompson, James H. Hinds, Henry G. Nichols, Myatt Mobley, David A. Caldwell, Levi Tidwell, Jno. P. Beasley,

Wm. T. Allen, Hardy Petty, Wm. Martin, Wm. Dodson, P. N. Maroney, Robt. S. Bingham, Stephen Reaves, Josiah Cotham, Jas. H. Fowlkes, Walter W. Brown, Thomas Bastian. On May 3, 1865, commissions were issued to the following: Wm. M. C. Thompson, Geo. W. Gray, Jas. D. Easley, Edmond W. Nunnellee, Chas. Capps, James Martin, H. G. Nichols, M. Mobley, D. A. Caldwell, Levi J. Tidwell, Wm. T. Allen, John Pitts Beasley, Hardy Petty, E. Y. Andrews, W. C. Dodson, Solomon George, Stephen Forrester, W. H. Brown, Jas. Fowlkes, John A. Jones, Walter W. Brown, Thos. W. Bastian, Jno. F. Atkinson, Jno. W. M. Fain, Marcenus G. Peery, Pinkney Prince, M. P. Puckett, J. A. Reeves, Alton McCaleb, Wm. Wheat, G. W. Young, William Anderson. On July 1—Ben. A. Huddleston, Stephen F. Halbrooks, John C. Gracey, Jesse Briggs.

1869: W. F. Meacham, R. S. Johnson, J. B. Dean.

1870: On April 7—J. R. Sutton, Jas. Rogers, R. Coleman, L. D. Wright, H. Petty, E. Y. Andrews, Joseph Weems, T. S. Broome, Jno. W. Hornbeak. On September 1—Geo. W. Gray, Stephen G. Warren, Jas. H. Martin, Sr., Ephraim A. Dean, H. G. Nichols, Wm. B. Erwin, H. G. Primm, J. P. Beasley, W. B. Russell, Jesse James, Wm. H. Brown, J. A. Jones, Samuel Chesser, Lewis Bates, Joel P. Morrison, E. C. Warren, Geo. G. Tatum, Wm. Harder, Jr., M. P. Puckett, R. A. Smith, Wm. Wheat, Joseph M. Bond, Geo. W. Young, William Anderson.

1871: Walter W. Brown.

1872: J. P. Clark, James D. Easley, J. W. Duncan, Jno. H. Hines, R. M. Anderson.

1873: Daniel Dean, M. M. Petty, O. B. Turner (*vice* R. J. Work, resigned).

1874: S. T. Broome, Luther Whiteside, W. G. Clagett, W. H. Dean.

1875: J. T. Jones.

1876: W. G. Clagett, Thos. S. Easley, Thompson Fleming, G. W. Gray, J. H. Martin, Archie Young, M. H. Puckett, W. B. Erwin, Milton Haskins, H. Primm, Wm. Donegan, Taylor Jones, W. B. Russell, W. H. Beasley, Jesse James, Jared Curl, W. H. Brown, O. B. Turner, J. A. Jones, D. N. Walker, A. B. Edwards, R. C. Murray, J. G. Anderson, R. Breece, Luther Whiteside, J. M. Harder, M. P. Puckett, B. C. Charter, Chas. Wheat, Alton McCaleb, William Anderson, R. M. Anderson.

1877: T. P. Litton.

1878: W. S. Beasley, Thos. Cagle, J. A. Jones, Jr., V. B. Shouse, E. C. Warren, R. A. Smith.

1879: T. L. Grimes.

1880: L. J. Tidwell, Ford George, J. W. Taylor.

1882: G. W. Gray, V. B. Shouse, J. A. Bates, Jno. W. Cummins, James Harrington, W. J. Thornton, T. L. Grimes, L. J. Tidwell, J. M. Fly, J. O. Rice, T. S. Bartlett, Hardy Petty, W. H. Beasley, Jesse James, Josiah Bastian, W. H. Brown, W. H. Baker, Thomas Cagle, Samuel Chesser, R. C. Murray, A. B. Edwards, E. C. Warren, John C. Peeler, Pinkney Prince, W. D. Aydelott, J. W. Taylor, M. P. Puckett, Charles

Wheat, J. P. Grimes, William Anderson, R. M. Anderson.

1883: Richard A. Smith, G. W. Mathis, C. C. Cany, L. B. Beasley, Henry Gray.

1884: W. J. Thornton.

1885: J. M. Grimmitt, Marshall Sanders, John A. Jones.

1886: W. J. Brown, E. W. Easley.

1887: E. M. Hinson, G. D. Johnson, J. T. Jones, W. A. J. McDonough, J. E. Still.

1888: W. G. Clagett, G. Fowlkes, Joseph Adair, John Cummins, James Martin, T. L. Grimes, S. M. Cummins, E. K. Cooper, H. G. Primm, Thomas Patton, J. T. Jones, W. A. J. McDonough, W. B. Russell, W. C. Thompson, E. W. Easley, W. H. Baker, W. M. Sanders, Thomas Cagle, W. K. Chandler, R. C. Murray, E. M. Hinson, S. C. Heath, Joel P. Morrison, R. D. Clark, Esau Anderson, G. D. Johnson, R. A. Smith, J. M. Bond, J. N. Smith, S. Anderson, F. P. McCaleb.

1890: J. E. Still, J. J. Sparks, J. J. McGill, P. R. Lovelace.

1891: A. B. George.

1892: G. W. Hedge.

1893: G. M. Ferguson, W. P. Russell.

1894: G. Fowlkes, Jno. B. Gardner, E. A. Dean, Y. F. Harvill, W. M. Hunter, S. M. Cummins, J. M. Thornton, Johnson Tidwell, R. A. Smith, J. T. Jones, L. R. Cochran, J. V. McDonough, W. G. Brown, E. W. Easley, J. T. Webb, J. J. Sparks, R.

S. Potter, W. L. Walker, S. G. Carothers, R. C. Beasley, A. J. Depriest, P. R. Lovelace, J. C. Peeler, W. D. Aydelott, Esau Anderson, R. A. Smith, G. D. Johnson, A. B. George, James McCaleb, J. R. Grimes, T. J. Walker.

    1895: S. R. Bond.

    1896: T. H. Duncan.

    1898: A. J. Pope.

    1899: Thomas Cagle, J. H. C. Tarkington.

CHAPTER XXI.

MILITIA OFFICERS.

MUSTER days were red-letter days in the calendar of the ante-bellum citizen of the county. Attendance upon musters was made compulsory by law, and all citizens of the State between the regulation ages were members of the State militia. The militia of Hickman County constituted the Thirty-sixth Regiment. Militia officers were elected by the militia of the county, and the men who held these offices were men of local prominence. They were commissioned by the Governor, and from records in the Secretary of State's office the following names and dates were obtained. The date preceding the names is the year in which commissions were issued:

1808: Lieutenant colonel—John Holland. Majors—Joseph Wilson and Joseph Inman.

1809: Captains—James Alston, Jones (or Jonas) Messer, William Carrethers (Carothers), William Phillips, William Haley, Jr., Samuel Snoddy, Charles B. Harvey, Ephraim McCaleb. Lieutenants—John Mitchell, William Mynett, John Owens, John Copeland, Aaron Parker, Frederick Mayberry, John Peery, Samuel Faught. Ensigns—Jacob Humble, Silverney (probably Sylvanus) Hassell, Benjamin Hawkins, John Harris, John Walker, Joab Haile.

1810: Captain—Pleasant Easley. Lieutenant—

George Read. Ensigns—John Lomaks, John Hart. In a cavalry regiment: Captain—Millington Easley. Lieutenant—Tristram Thomas. Cornet—William Stewart.

1811: Lieutenant colonel—William Phillips. Major—William Carrethers. Captains—George Reid, Peter Searcy, Daniel Obar (or Daniel O. Barr), Samuel M. Carrethers, Pleasant Easley. Lieutenants— Henry M. Truett, James Clark, William Briggs, Aaron Raynor, Josiah Hanna, Jacob Humble. Ensigns—Silvanus Hassell, William Holland, William Muirhead, Obadiah Lewis, Henry Mayberry, Chas. Spencer, Jr.

1812: Captains—Nathaniel Simpson, Ephraim McCaleb, James Alston, Harvey Jones. Lieutenants —Thomas Gatlin, Edmond Gee, John Scott, Eliot Hornback (Hornbeak), Tristram B. Thomas. Ensigns—William Rice, John Gregory, Edmund Gee, Elisha Walker, Warham Easley, Drury Easley, John Flinn.

1813: Captains—Alexander W. Swinney, Alexander Higginbotham. Lieutenants—Richard Walker, Robert G. Bowen, Bernard Totty. Ensigns—Stephen Easley, Ripley Copeland.

1814: Captain—Thomas Gatlin. Lieutenants— Henry Lieuten (Luten), Jonathan Shelton, William Reeves, James Bailey, Elisha Walker. Ensigns— Isaiah Cates, George Goodwin, Warren Mason, James Wilkins.

1815: Major—John Nunnelly. Captains—Jonathan Shelton, Barney A. Flinn, Andrew Jones. Lieutenant—Jacob Deen (or Dun). Ensigns—William Wright, James Mullen, William Fisher.

1816: Lieutenant colonel—B. G. Stewart. Major—Joseph Lynn. Captains—John B. Willey, Samuel Harrison, Real Williams. Lieutenants—Jordan Anderson, Willis Davis, William Thompson, Joshua Lewis, Abraham Land, Real Williams. Ensigns—Miles Goodwin, William Tubbs, William Gordon. Cornet in cavalry—Joseph Hanna.

1817· Captains—Hardy Sparks, George Grant (or Gannt), Alexander Anguish (?), Younger McCaslin, William L. Carter, Thomas Dean, Elias R. Walker, Kinchen Pace. Lieutenants—Elijah Dansby, Charles Muirhead, Jesse Hanna, James McClanahan, Archibald Ponder. Ensigns—Labomen Kelly, Andrew Elliott. In cavalry: Captain—Josiah Hanna. Lieutenant—William Bird.

1818: Captains—John P. Rushing, Thomas Jones, Andrew Moody, Thomas J. Martin, William Reeves. Lieutenants—Conrad Shaw, Hugh McCrory, John McCaslin, Alexander Peery, Noel Tony, John Lewis. Ensigns—John Yarbrough, William Hornberger, Aaron B. Edwards, Jonathan Toland, Jesse Laxton, Barnet Donalson.

1819: Major—Josiah Hannah.

1820: Surgeon—Joel Walker. Adjutant—William' L. Carter. Judge advocate—Garrett Lane. Quartermaster—Stephen Lacy, Jr. Captains—John Lewis, John G. Anderson, Jesse Laxton. Lieutenants

-–David Warren, David Meredith, Robert Hughes, James Andrews. Ensigns—William Bates, Samuel Griffin, James Pigg.

1821: Major—Robert Totty.

1822: Captains—Thomas Warren, James Few, Elijah Walker. Lieutenants—Charles Warren, Elijah Cantrell, Thomas Roberts, John Balton. Ensign —Joseph Baird.

1823: Captain—Edwin M. Baird. Lieutenant— John Murray. Ensigns—John Mitchell, Solomon Tucker.

1824: Captains—John Davis, Levi McCollum, George Gannt. Lieutenants—John Neighbors, Joseph Webb, Jonathan Jones, Alfred McCaslin, Patrick D. Lafferty. Ensigns—Jonathan Reeves, John Christian, Isha C. Kelly, Edmond Jones.

1825: Captain—David B. Warren.

1826: Lieutenant colonel—Samuel D. McLaughlin. Major—Basil B. Satterfield. Captains—John H. Gatlin, John T. Primm, John L. Anderson, James Capoor (or James K. Poor), Henry Ammons, John Campbell, Jacob Riley, Charles Warren. Lieutenants—James McCaleb, Alfred Sanders, John Duncan, Ambrose Blackburn, Thomas Grantham, Daniel Shouse, Martin Seawell, David Lancaster, Dennis Jones. Ensigns—Andy Fergusson, Willis Lowe.

1827: Captain—Millington Easley. Lieutenants --Henry R. Fowlkes, John McGill, Cornelius Matthews. Ensign—Thomas Cannon. Officers of the " Houston Guards " commissioned were: David B.

Warren, first lieutenant; Davis H. Morgan, second lieutenant; Jacob Shouse, ensign. At another time during this year the following were commissioned in this company: Pleasant M. Hornbeak, captain; Jas. D. Easley, lieutenant.

1828: (36th Regiment) Colonel—B. B. Satterfield. Captain—John McCaleb. Lieutenants—Robert Harrington, Henry Golden. Ensign—Dempsey Harrington. (106th Regiment) Colonel—James Bailey. Lieutenant colonel—Jacob Riley. Majors—Jesse Lowe, Lewis Denning. Captains—William Sutton, Elias Rogers. Lieutenants—Lewis Rogers, William Burchard, Richard Brown, William Phillips, Samuel Scott, Abner Coleman, Andrew Walker. Ensigns—William B. Murphree, Jesse Lowe.

1829: (36th) Major—Alfred Darden. Captains —Robert Charter (Houston Guards), Lewis P. Totty, John Harrison, Newton Forrester, Benjamin B. Wilson. Lieutenants—James Prewett (or Trewitt), William F. Twilla, Owen Edwards, Joseph Patterson, James M. Ponder. Ensigns—James Baird, John M. Fielder, Abraham Stillts, Mitchell Anderson. (106th) Major—William Sutton. Captains—James McCollum, John Smith, William Whitwell. Lieutenants—Drury Brock, Terrell Goodman, Jackson Patton, Paschal Lancaster, William Tatum, James Laxson. Ensigns—Simpson Depriest, Patton McCollum, William Murray, James Jones.

1830: (36th) Captain—John McGill. Lieutenants—Newell K. Poore (Houston Guards), William

Lewis, James Spraddlin, Sterling Carroll, Benjamin Adair, William Poore, Abel Overton, Allen D. Montgomery, Jacob Jenkins. Ensigns—Josiah Reed, William Dickey, Joseph Willey, Levi G. Murphree. (106th) Captain—Samuel Scott. Lieutenant—Robert Haile. Ensigns—Thomas Price, John Scott.

1831: (36th) Colonel—Robert Charter. Captains —Edward Carnes, John Burcham, Richard H. Allison. Lieutenants—Benjamin Adair, Asa Pipkin, James M. Baird, John Gray, William Smith. Ensigns—Harbert Totty, Wiliam H. Willey.

1832: (36th) Major—Pleasant M. Hornbeak. Captains—Solomon Tucker, Reuben F. White, Thos. Dotson. (106th) Majors—James E. Sheegog, William Whitwell. Captain—Joel C. Hobbs. Lieutenants—Thomas P. Kimbro, Nudam Briant, Benjamin Wells, Jefferson Daniel. Ensigns—John W. Petty, Lawson Smith.

1833: (36th) Captain—Reuben I. White. Lieutenant—James H. Giles. (106th) Major—Dennis G. Jones. Captains—William Wilson, James Moore, Terence Bates, Robert Easley, James Jones, Isham West. Lieutenants—Jackson Deaton, Viach Light, J. Reeves. Ensigns—Henry Milam, Isaac Sparks.

1834: (36th) Colonel—Alfred Darden. Lieutenant colonel—Lewis P. Totty. Majors—James D. Easley, Newton M. Nicks. Captains—Robert E. Griner, Wiliam Wheat, Benjamin Adair, James M. Ponder, Bailey G. Wilson, Henry G. Nichols. Lieutenants—Neverson Perritt, Jesse Temple, John Grif-

fin, Christopher Nichols, Green Regions, Alfred A.
Lanly.   Ensigns—Silas Wheat, John Griffin, Edward O. Totty, Asa Savage.   (106th) Captains—Anderson Tate, D. A. Walker.   Lieutenants—A. Bruce,
W. Grant, A. Barr, E. Anderson.   Ensigns—William Harmon, William Milam.

1835: (106th) Colonel—Dennis G. Jones.   [The
Legislature of 1835, following the constitutional convention of 1834, reorganized the militia of the State,
the two Hickman County regiments being numbered
Ninety-seven and Ninety-eight.]

1836: (97th) Colonel—Lewis P. Totty.   Lieutenant colonel—Neverson Perritt.   Majors—Thomas
Dodson, Edward Cavenor.   Captains—Benjamin
Grimmitt, Jacob Jenkins, William Hicks, Lemuel
P. Kelley, William Adair, George McCrary, John
Parker, Jeremiah Harder.   (98th) Colonel—Dennis G. Jones.   Lieutenant colonel—William Wilson.
Majors—Joel C. Hobbs, David A. Walker.   Captains—Patrick Coleman, Lewis D. Lowe, Jacob Bylor, Nicholas Davis, Thornton Scott, Reuben Thornton.

1837: (97th) Captains—John Oliver, Albert S.
Griner.   (98th) Major—Samuel Scott.

1838: (97th) Major—John Whitfield.   Captains
—Charles Dougherty, Minor B. Hanes, Miles Harrington.   Lieutenants—Andrew Morgan, John Litton, William Thornton, Joseph Alexander, Thomas
Rogers.   Ensigns—John L. Tarkington, George Adcock, Calvin Harrington.

1839: (97th) Lieutenant colonel—Albert S. Griner, John A. Oliver. (98th) Lieutenant colonel—Thornton Scott.

1840: (97th) Colonel—Albert S. Griner. (98th) Lieutenant colonel—Thornton Scott.

1841: (97th) Major—William Neal. (98th) Captains—S. Lewis, I. Lancaster. Lieutenants—W. Quillen, Jno. McNeilly, B. Brown (or Breece), M. Reeves, Wm. Brown (or Breece). Ensigns—Daniel Brown (or Breece), Daniel Winters.

1842: (98th) Colonel—W. A. Calvert. Captain—B. F. Brown. Lieutenant—W. Brown. Ensign—J. Petty.

1843: (97th) Major — Nathaniel Le Duff (?). (98th) Colonel—David Walker.

1844: (97th) Captains—M. G. Peery, Jno. Baker, W. C. Barnes, W. L. Bateman, J. C. Bradley. Lieutenants—Hiram Baird, G. W. Fowlkes, E. C. Willey, M. W. Davidson, Alpheus Truett. Ensigns—Calvin Shouse, David Darden, James W. McMinn. Benj. Hassell. (98th) Colonel—D. A. Walker. Captains—W. Gravett, G. W. Car (?). Lieutenants—J. Parham, W. Breece (or Brown), J. —— (?), W. Quillen, J. C. Cavendor, T. W. Easley. Ensigns—W. Holt, J. H. —— (?), J. Barber, Lewis Bates.

1845: Brigadier general (Seventeenth Brigade)—Thos. J. Whitfield. (97th) Colonel—J. A. Oliver. Major—A. A. Alexander. Captains—Jesse Briggs, Noah K. Randall, Wm. H. Miller, Jno. Young, Jno. P. Beasley, Henry C. Campbell. Lieutenants—B.

Liggins, Francis M. Totty (or Tolly), James H. Devore, Henry R. Raymond, H. Church, John Worley, James Gwin, Josiah Jones, Pinkney Prince, P. Savage, Horatio Clagett. Ensigns—Nathan Hickman, Andrew Clymer, Rufus Coleman. (98th) Lieutenant Colonel—T. Thompson. Major—Jno. Shepard.

1848: (97th) Colonel—Andrew M. Adair. Majors—Thomas Brooks, Jas. Devore. Captains—Thos. O. Smith, Wm. H. Bratton, Jno. C. Anderson, Robt. Newsom, A. W. Weatherly, Stephen Reeves, Ira H. Barnhill, Wm. P. Kelly. Lieutenants—Thomas Massey, Jesse C. Hicks, J. W. McMinn, Jno. G. Turman, Henry Lyle, Jesse P. Bates, Jno. W. Jones, Stephen S. Rogers, Jno. Worley, Jno. Nicks, Wm. Cockrum. Ensigns—Jno. A. Randall, Chas. A. Nash, Sir Winfred Cotton, Henry Darden, Jno. L. Clymer, Jonathan Hardwick.

1849: (97th) Captains—Jno. Haile, Turner Tyler, Whitman W. W. Fowlkes. Lieutenants—Chas. W. Gracey, M. L. Giles, Jno. Williams, Wm. T. Hagins, Wilson Overbey. Ensign—Abram Groves.

1850: (98th) Captains—E. W. Christian, B. M. Harris, Wm. Collier. Lieutenants—James Blackburn, Z. M. Garner, Wm. Phillips, J. G. Anderson, Wm. Foster, James B. Wright. Ensigns—A. J. Bates, Wm. Leathers.

1851: (97th) Lieutenant colonel — Edward A. Fowlkes. (98th) Colonel—Aden Lowe. Majors—Alfred Forrester, James M. Davidson.

1853: (97th) Colonel—Jno. A. R. Fogge. Lieutenant colonel—Patrick Smith. Major—James Miller.

1861: On May 1, under the Act reëstablishing the State militia, the following were commissioned: (97th) Colonel—Edward A. Fowlkes. Lieutenant colonel—E. W. Nunnellee. Majors—Howell A. Shouse, Jesse K. McMinn. Captains—James D. Easley, H. C. Campbell, William Anderson, Wilson Overbey, A. J. Lovell, G. H. Andrews, J. A. Nunnellee, Wm. H. Brown, Jno. A. Jones, Marshall Twomey. (98th) Colonel—John Morris (?). Lieutenant colonel—S. J. Easley. Majors—D. J. Easley, D. L. Bastian. A few weeks later the enlistment of men for the Confederate Army commenced in Hickman County.

CHAPTER XXII.

COUNTY AND COURT OFFICIALS.

THE destruction of records by the fire which destroyed the Hickman County courthouse during the latter days of the Civil War caused the task of compiling lists of county and court officials to be a difficult one. Some of the following lists are complete and accurate; while others are only partially so, despite strenuous efforts to make them both complete and accurate:

Judges of Circuit Court.—Parry W. Humphreys (1809-13), Bennet Searcy (1813-18), Parry W. Humphreys (1818-36) [Judge Joshua Haskell presided at Centerville by interchange with him in 1828], Mortimer A. Martin (1836-38), Edmond Dillahunty (1838-49), Elijah Walker (1849-61), Fielding Hurst (1865), Hilary Ward (1365-67), A. M. Hughes (1867-70), Elijah Walker (1870-73), Thomas P. Bateman (1873-86), E. D. Patterson (1886-91), W. L. Grigsby (1891-99), John W. Childress (1899—).

Solicitors-general.—G. W. L. Marr (1809-13), Bennet Searcy (1813—in June of which year he became judge), E. T. Paine (1813—June to November), Henry Minor (1813-14), James L. Brown (1814-15), Samuel Chapman (1815-17), Robert L. Cobb (1817-19), James R. McMeans (1819-21), James Scott (1821-26), Henry Nixon (1826-31),

Alex. M. Hardin (1831-36). *Attorneys-general.*—
William K. Turner (1836-39), Willie B. Johnson
(1839-41), Nathaniel Baxter (1841-47), . . .
John M. Taylor (1870-78), M. H. Meeks (1878-86),
John L. Jones (1886-94), W. Blake Leech (1894-99),
H. Clay Carter (1899—).

Circuit Court Clerks.—Robert Estes (1809—?),
Millington Easley (made bond on March 14, 1820),
David B. Warren (1836-48), Samuel Whitson (1848-
50), A. Z. Deshazo (1850-54), Robt. C. Huddleston
(1854-59), E. W. Easley (1859-60), John L. Griffin (1860-63), Frank Puckett (1865—appointed by
Brownlow),Wm. G. Clagett (1865-74), E. G. Thompson (1874-82), J. D. Flowers (1882-86), J. W. Atkinson (1886-94), William A. Adair (1894—).

Sheriffs.—William Phillips (1808-24), Gabriel
Fowlkes (1824-32), Pleasant Walker (1832-36),
William H. Carothers (1836-42), Reeves A. Huddle-
ston (1842-43—died), William Phillips (1843-48),
John W. Huddleston (1848-54), Solomon J. George
(1854-60), Levi McCollum (1860-62), Daniel D.
Smith (1862-65), Joseph Beasley (1865-67), John
Baker (1867-72), E. A. Dean (1872-78), Horatio C.
Hunter (1878-80), J. A. Harvill (1880-84), W. H.
Phillips (1884-90), J. A. Harvill (1890-92), W. J.
McEwen (1892-96), John V. Stephenson (1896-98),
J. C. Yates (1898—).

Chancellors.—Stephen C. Pavatt (1854-61), : . .
J. C. Walker (1868-70), George H. Nixon (1870-86),
A. J. Abernathy (1886—).   Prior to 1854 Chancery

Courts for Hickman County were held at Charlotte. Some of the Chancellors who presided there were: William E. Anderson, Nathan Green, Wm. A. Cork, Lunsford M. Bramlett, Andrew McCampbell, Terre H. Cahal, A. O. P. Nicholson, John S. Brien, and Samuel D. Frierson.

Clerks and Masters (at Centerville).—S. H. Williams (1854-56), Orville A. Nixon (1856-61), Pleasant M. Hornbeak (1865-67—died and was succeeded for a short time by his son, F. B. Hornbeak), W. M. Johnson (1867-83), O. A. Nixon (1883-90—died), E. G. Thompson (1890-93), Samuel T. Broome (1893—).

County Court Clerks.—William Stone (1808-18), Samuel Sebastian (1818-1835), James D. Easley (1835-58), J. W. Hornbeak (1858-61), M. H. Puckett (1865-70—appointed by Brownlow), J. D. Murphree (1870-73), J. D. Easley (1873-74), A. M. Reaves (1874-82), W. P. Coleman (1882-90), A. J. McClaren (1890-97—died), Robert Brown (1897-98), J. W. Russell (1898—).

Tax Collectors.—James H. Fowlkes (1847-48), Green Pickard (1849-50), D. McCord (1851), J. A. Bizwell (1852), Isaac Lancaster (1853), R. Coleman (1854), Geo. W. Martin (1855), Cyrus W. Russell (1856), A. J. Nixon (1857), Wm. F. Shipp (1858), J. K. McMinn (1859), Z. F. Beasley (1860), J. N. Puckett, Jr. (1865-70—appointed by Brownlow), Robt. F. Green (1870-72), H. C. Campbell (1872-74), J. C. Frazier (1874-76).

Trustees.—S. McE. Wilson (1876-82), A. W. Warren (1882-88), J. N. Pace (1888-92), J. H. Brown (1892-96), W. M. Baxter (1896—).

County Surveyors.—James Weatherspoon (1824-25), George Peery (1825-51), Samuel C. Aydelott (1851-65). Since the Civil War the following have held this office: Andrew J. Stanfield, W. H. Burchard, W. P. Coleman, John M. Anderson, and Isaac A. Hunter.

Registers.—Bartholomew Grayson Stewart (1808 to as late as 1817, and probably later), Eli B. Hornbeak (1822—terminal dates not known), Samuel B. Moore (filled out Hornbeak's unexpired term), Pleasant Hornbeak, N. T. Fowlkes (1851—terminal dates not known), John C. Gracey (1854—terminal dates not known), —— Grimes, of Beaverdam Creek (1854-58), E. W. Lawson (1858 to Civil War), J. H. Hines (appointed by Governor Brownlow), E. W. Lawson (1870-74), Thos. J. Walker (1874-82), W. D. Thompson (1882-90), J. D. Flowers (1890-98), W. D. Warren (1898—).

County Superintendents of Public Instruction.—A. J. Stanfield (1867-69—office abolished), Orville A. Nixon (1872 to September 4, 1874—resigned), J. A. Cunningham (September 4, 1874, to January 1, 1876), S. H. Holmes (January 1 to October 1, 1876—resigned), W. P. Clarke (October 1, 1876 to 1886), I. A. Hunter (1886-90), R. E. Arnall (1890—resigned), W. V. Jarrett (1890-91), I. A. Hunter (1891-96), R. S. Ballow (1896—).

CHAPTER XXIII.

HICKMAN COUNTY SOLDIERS.

REVOLUTIONARY WAR.

ALL of that portion of Hickman County north of the Continental Line of 1784 (known locally as the " Military Line ") was embraced in the territory given to her soldiers in the Revolutionary War by North Carolina; therefore, the larger portion of this territory was granted to holders of North Carolina military warrants. Many of these warrants were bought from the soldiers by land speculators; some became the property of soldiers' heirs. Several old soldiers came here in person, laid their land warrants here, and spent their last days in Hickman County. Some of these were: Josiah Davidson, —— Hardin, Abner Ponder, and James Peery. On June 1, 1840, there were living within the limits of Hickman County the following old Revolutionary soldiers: Elijah Mayfield, Josiah Grimmitt, Jordan Milam, John Tucker, Richard Campbell, and Richard Nolls.

WAR OF 1812.

In the War of 1812 Hickman County furnished a number of soldiers. Some of them were: Capt. —— Porter, Capt. John Gordon, William Shipp, John Gainer, Matthew Totty, William Totty, Drury Harrington, Dempsey Harrington, Robert Harrington,

William Harrington, Epps Bishop, James Birden, Jared Curl, Thomas Uslam, John Richardson, Dr. ——— Schmittou, William Bird, William Carter (orderly sergeant in 1814), Allan P. Kelley, Robert Peery (wounded at New Orleans on January 8, 1815), Alexander Peery, William Peery, and George Peery.

FIRST SEMINOLE WAR.

Of the Hickman County participants in the First Seminole War, only the names of William Bird and William Carter have been preserved. With a well-organized militia in the county and with the military spirit of the people alive, Hickman County doubtless furnished more soldiers in the War of 1812 and in the two Seminole Wars than are here named, and it is to be regretted that the absence of records prevents the naming of all those who participated in these wars.

SECOND SEMINOLE WAR.

The following names of Hickman Countians who participated in the Second Seminole War have been preserved: Maj. Powhattan Gordon, William Mc-Cutcheon, Zach. Totty (wounded), and Barnett Totty. Felix K. Zollicoffer, son-in-law of Capt. John Gordon and brother-in-law of Maj. Powhattan Gordon, was in this war.

MEXICAN WAR.

When Gov. Aaron V. Brown made the call for volunteers in 1846, John W. Whitfield's company, " Hickory Guards," was one of the first to respond.

It became Company A of the First Tennessee Regiment, commanded by Col. William Bowen Campbell, who afterwards became Governor of Tennessee. Colonel Campbell was a relative of Dr. Samuel Bowen Moore, Dr. J. C. Ward, and other citizens of Hickman County. This regiment, after its baptism of blood at Monterey, was known as "The Bloody First." The deeds of this regiment have gone into the brightest pages of Tennessee history; but the tattered and faded diary of Dr. William D. Dorris, who succeeded Dr. McPhail as surgeon of the regiment, tells of the hardships encountered by this regiment—the stern realities which were associated with the glamour of glory. The regiment was organized at the race course below Nashville on June 3, 1846, and spent this and the succeeding day in drilling. On June 5 it started on its long journey by water to New Orleans. One of the steamboats was the Tallerand, on board of which a Bible class was organized on June 7. This class had about 150 members, but the list of their names was lost before Mexico was reached. Dr. Dorris, in his diary, says: "June 13 and 15, inclusive, we landed at New Orleans and encamped in the lower part of the city, at Williams' Mills, a most filthy place." On the night of June 17 the regiment embarked on three sailing vessels for Brazos Santiago, an island about nine miles from the mouth of the Rio Grande. Two companies were placed on the schooner Orleans, and five companies on the ship Charleston, of Boston. Five companies were placed on the third vessel, although the captain had contracted for but four. Dr. Dorris says: "We suffered like African slaves from the jam being so great as to cause difficult breathing, sickness, etc. We anchored off the island on the fifth morning, and some five companies were taken off five or six days after, and the balance, with our poor bruised horses, were taken off after weathering out a storm of forty hours at anchor. We were miserably neglected by Major Thomas at Point Isabel." They were "then placed in a miserable flat, where we had to sink barrels to get the natural red soda water, which, with the malaria, has given the surgeons more than they were able to do." Captains Whitfield and Walton (the latter of whom is still living) erected the first two hospital tents. Dr. Dorris says: "The first report I made of bowel complaints was 230 cases. One case died, belonging to Captain Whitfield's company, since we landed here." This was Nimrod Hartzogg. Dr. Dorris expresses surprise that there were no more deaths. From the sick roll of Whitfield's company, kept by Dr. Dorris, it seems that nearly every man in the company was seriously ill before they reached Monterey. Two entries on the sick roll are as follows: "George W. Banks, mosquito bite; Owen Edwards, homesick." In this season of distress the Bible class was reorganized on July 4, 1846. The following names are signed on the roll of this class: Joseph Weems, R. H. Smith, James E. Burchard, William E. Whitson, William Walker, Henry G. Darden, Robert Harrington, Lewis

P. Totty, Joseph S. Anderson, Owen Edwards, John
C. Lewis, John Duncan, George W. Banks, Ira H.
Barnhill, R. J. Newsom, Samuel Weatherly, James
B. Harder, Edmond Harder, Abner Weatherly; "J.
W. Whitfield, Capt. H. Guards." This memorandum was made on this roll: "Our Bible class has
generally been neglected more on account of sickness
than anything else, and dividing our regiment into
detachments in transporting us from place to place
on steamboats. This the 13th Sept., 1846. (Signed)
Joseph Weems, Sec." Under date of "July 5 & 6,
1846," is this entry in Dr. Dorris' diary: "Camp
Brazos Santiago—a flat, low, nasty place." Concerning the illness of Dr. McPhail, the surgeon of the
regiment, Dr. Dorris says: "Dr. Starnes went with
him, the doctor's boy, and Joseph Weems to nurse
him. George Martin nursed him on the beach at
Brazos Santiago. Both good nurses." Dr. McPhail
died on July 12, 1846, and was buried on the following day with military honors. He was a brother-in-
law of Captain Whitfield, and was a physician in the
Third District before the breaking out of the Mexican
War. On July 8 the regiment marched from the
island of Brazos Santiago to the mouth of the Rio
Grande. This march of nine miles consumed three
hours. For one-fourth of a mile they marched across
a bar which was covered by water from the gulf. The
average depth of the water was two feet. They were
transported by steamboats fifteen miles up the Rio
Grande. "The water of the Rio Grande, the only

kind we now use, is rather muddier than the Mississippi, but easily settles and has a good taste; and is far better than any which we have had since we left New Orleans," says Dr. Dorris. Dr. Dorris, Lieutenant Lewis P. Totty, and eighteen others were sent to General Taylor to warn him of a contemplated attack on his wagon train, which had with it $200,000. By July 23 the regiment had reached Camargo, farther up the Rio Grande, at the mouth of one of its tributries. Here a number of Whitfield's company were discharged on account of sickness and sent home. When a call came, on August 29, for men to move up this tributary of the Rio Grande to attack Monterey, less than half the regiment responded. The march to Monterey commenced on September 7, and they came in sight of the city on September 19. Under date of September 13, 1846, is this entry in the diary of Dr. Dorris: " The sickness that has prevailed in this regiment has never been excelled by any I ever heard of or read of in my campaigns. (Signed) William D. Dorris, M.D., Surgeon First Tennessee. By Joseph Weems, secretary." Dr. Dorris had gone through the Second Seminole War as a surgeon. Company A was, on account of orders, not under direct fire during the attack on Monterey on September 21. Dr. Dorris says: " Tennesseans made the best charge ever made by Americans against fortress and batteries. The flag that was presented by the ladies of the Nashville Academy was the first placed on the walls of Monterey." Along with the Tennesseans in this charge was the First Mississippi Rifles, commanded by Jefferson Davis. At Camp Allen, near Monterey, on October 25, 1846, Whitfield's company had but thirty-nine privates and nine officers. Nine had died and the remainder had been discharged on account of sickness. On the sick roll is this entry: " Z. Hassell has not done duty for more than fifteen days since we left New Orleans, two of which were in battle in Monterey." In Dr. Dorris' diary is a roll of Whitfield's company, which bears the following indorsements: " I do hereby certify that this is a correct copy of the names of the officers and privates of Capt. Jno. W. Whitfield's company. (Signed) Wm. E. Whitson." " I do hereby certify that the above is a correct list of the Hickory Guards. (Signed) Jno. W. Whitfield, Capt. H. G. of Hickman Cty." The roll is as follows: Jno. W. Whitfield, captain; James D. Easley, first lieutenant; Lewis P. Totty, second lieutenant; Abraham C. Dansby, first sergeant; Thomas E. Dansby, second sergeant; Albert Griner, third sergeant; Edward W. Nunnellee, fourth sergeant; (Dr.) Francis M. Easley, first corporal; Alfred Darden, second corporal (promoted to be third lieutenant); Richard H. Smith, third corporal; William D. Willey, fourth corporal; Joseph S. Anderson, John S. Browning, James E. Burchard, Alexander Barnhill, Ira H. Barnhill, Joshua Burnham, George W. Banks, Joseph B. Campbell, Henry C. Campbell, John L. Clymer, Ransom Dean (color bearer), Adley Davidson, Henry G. Darden, Benjamin G. Darden,

George A. Duncan, James Devore, Elisha Dotson, John H. Davidson, James M. Davidson, John C. Duncan, Joseph Ellis, William Easley, Owen Edwards, William H. Easley, William A. Farlow, Edward A. Fowlkes, Willis Fergusson, George C. Gordon, Zachariah Hubbs, ALEXANDER HARVILL (died of measles, on September 7, 1846, at camp below Camargo, Mexico), Zebulon Hassell, Robert Harrington, Edmond Harder, James Harder, Beverly R. Holt, Eben House, NIMROD HARTZOGG (died on June 23, 1846, at Brazos Santiago), Benson M. Harris, Josiah Jones, Joshua Jones, William Jones, John C. Lewis, William Lewis, Isaac Ledbetter, Melford M. Leonard, Socrates Martin, (Dr.) William Montgomery, William McClanahan, Reuben McClaren, Joel P. Morrison, Miles Milam, Dudley Milam, GEORGE W. MARTIN (died on June 5, 1847), Ebenezer Morrison, Robert Newsom, Hezekiah Ragsdale, Thomas E. Ragsdale, JAMES P. SHOUSE (died at camp above Camargo, Mexico, on September 17, 1846), Andrew J. Sullivan, Leroy Stuart, Richard Smith, Green W. Sullivan, Barnett Totty, John L. Temple (fifer), James Truett (drummer), ANDREW J. TOTTY (died on August 19, 1846, of dysentery and fever), PEMBERTON TOTTY (died on August 24, 1846, of dysentery), Francis M. Totty, Zachariah Totty, (Dr.) John C. Ward, Samuel W. Weatherly, Abner Weatherly, Wiley A. Wheat, William B. Watts, Joseph Weems, William E. Whitson, Robert M. Whitson, Thomas S. Warren, James Walker, Ephraim N.

Willey, Albert Wray, and William Walker. From this roll is omitted the name of William Holt, who in an official report is marked " recruit." The following names, not included in this roll, have been furnished by survivors of Whitfield's company: Campbell Baird, David Duncan, George W. Gordon, John Jones, Wash. Martin, G. W. Nunnelly, Asa Totty, Thomas Campbell (name by which H. C. Campbell was known), Thomas Fielder, Mitchell Leonard, Armistead Martin, Edward Owens (probably transposition of name " Owen Edwards "), and Jack Totty (probably Zach. Totty). Some of these names are evidently repetitions; but this is preferred by the authors, rather than omissions. The First Tennessee Regiment later joined General Scott's army and participated in the capture of Vera Cruz and in the engagements at Madeline Bridge and Cerro Gordo. The latter affair was on April 18, 1847, the twenty-second birthday of the late John L. Temple, who, as a member of Whitfield's company, participated in this battle. The First Tennessee then went to Jalapa, from which place it was ordered to return to Vera Cruz. Here it embarked for New Orleans, where it was mustered out of service.

At Pueblo, General Scott awaited reinforcements. When a second call was made for troops, Hickman County again furnished a company, composed in part of discharged soldiers of Whitfield's first company. It became Company K of the Third Tennessee Regiment, commanded by Col. B. F. Cheatham.

This regiment was mustered into service on October 8, 1847. They went to New Orleans by boat, and from that point sailed to Vera Cruz. Although never engaged in battle, this regiment was well drilled and saw much hard service in an unhealthy climate. The regiment did not reach the City of Mexico until after the fall of that city. At the close of the war it was mustered out of service at Memphis. Through the kindness of Mrs. John L. Temple, the following copy of the official roll of Company K has been secured: John W. Whitfield, captain; Dennis G. Jones, first lieutenant (promoted to be captain); John L. Temple, second lieutenant; John C. Duncan, third lieutenant; Edward (Ned) Fowlkes, promoted to be first lieutenant; John P. Nixon, first sergeant; John N. Nunnelly, second sergeant; Wm. R. Hogwood, third sergeant; John Crudup, fourth sergeant; Elias Dotson, first corporal; James E. Burchard, second corporal; Thos. E. Ragsdale, third corporal; Henry Skaggs (or Staggs), fifer; John Hardin, drummer; Richard M. Anderson, Aaron P. Baird, G. F. P. Baird, William J. Baird, Thomas P. Bateman, Thomas L. Berry, HUMPHREY BIBB (died in the service), John H. Blackburn, Willis Booker, Jefferson C. Bradley, William L. Brown, William Bugg (?), Robert C. Chester, David C. Coble, H. Chambers, Anderson (or Henderson) Chappell, George C. Coble, ANDERSON CRAIG (died in the service), Frederick Davis, James Deviney, BARNET B. DEPRIEST (died in the service), Morgan Dorton, James C. Downey, Morgan

Elmore, David C. Fielder, John W. Forehand, G. W. Garrett, Anderson Gray, Zach. Green, James P. Green, James B. Guinn, H. P. Haley, Thos. Harbison, JAMES M. HARVISON (died in the service), Thomas Harvill, JOHN HASELETT (died in the service), Benj. (or Ren) Hassell, Thomas L. Holt, William J. Hendricks, Jacob W. Haggins, W. Hogan, Jas. M. Horton, Wiley Horton, THOS. HUTSON (died in the service), John J. Johnson, John W. Jones, John W. Land, Isaac Lancaster, James H. Ledbetter, John C. Ledbetter, William A. Ledbetter, James A. Lovell, John Moore, Daniel B. Murphree, James A. C. McFall, William E. Mays, Levi McComb, Hiram McComb, Jordan Milam, Elisha McCann, Jesse K. McMinn, Joseph Morris, Franklin Morrison, Timothy J. Nunnelly, David C. Nichols, William C. Nichols, John H. Nichols, Patterson Norris, John Pickard, Geo. W. Patton, S. REEVES (died in the service), Hiram G. Rossin, James Roberts, Jas. G. W. Rogers, Peter Sanders, L. P. Shepherd, John S. Smith, Patrick S. Smith, Samuel Skaggs, William H. Turman, George W. Tidwell, Samuel W. Thompson, Johnson S. Vaughn, W. A. VINYARD (died in the service), SAMUEL D. A. WADKINS (died in the service), E. S. WHITE (died in the service), JOHN B. WILSON (died in the service), James M. Woolard, Willis H. Whitwell, Ephraim N. Willey, James B. Wright, Richard T. Winn, William N. Worley, and William H. Willis (or Wills).

FEDERAL SOLDIERS.

The following is a partial list of Hickman Countians who, during the Civil War, served in the Federal Army: Capt. A. J. Sullivan (killed at Little Lot), James A. Sullivan, Frank Lewis (died in the service), Wid Duncan (died in the service), John McCalpin (died in the service), Isaac Ragan (died in the service), Henry Golden (died in the service), James Dunn, J. D. Harbin, W. B. Hendricks, Wm. Cochran, Edward Fowlkes, Wm. T. Easley, A. J. McDonough, J. W. McDonough, Jas. A. McDonough, James Puckett, David Puckett, Alex. Puckett, Johnson Totty, John A. Totty, Richard Totty, John Thomas, Thomas Ferguson, Philip Cland, James Stephenson.

OUR BOYS.

Hickman County closed the century, as she began it, with gallant soldiers in the service of the general government. The following Hickman County boys were members of the First Tennessee Regiment, U. S. V., lately returned from the Philippine Islands: Crocia Anderson, Jno. Darden (discharged at San Francisco), Jno. F. Dean, Wm. Fly, Ed. Green, Thos. Green, Benj. Haskins, Robt. McCord (reënlisted), Robt. McDonald (reënlisted), Ed. Milam, W. L. Morrison (discharged at San Francisco), Thos. Nixon (discharged at San Francisco), Nathan Parish (discharged at San Francisco), Pleasant Russell (reënlisted), F. Vickers (reënlisted), Alex. Warren, Wm. Williams, Thos. Wilson, J. W. Woods, and Claude Woolard.

CHAPTER XXIV.

HICKMAN COUNTY CONFEDERATES.

" The foeman need not frown,
    They are all powerless now—
We gather them here, and we lay them down,
And tears and prayers are the only crown
    We bring to wreathe each brow."

COMPANY H, ELEVENTH TENNESSEE.

THE following circular, immediately after its issuance, was circulated throughout Hickman County by Thos. P. Bateman, a veteran of the Mexican War, at that time a lawyer of Centerville:

TO ARMS!

We are now in a state of revolution, and Southern soil must be defended, and we should not stop to ask, Who brought about the War? or, Who is in fault? but let us go and do battle for our native, or adopted soil, and then settle the question as to who is to blame.

I have the acceptance of a company to go to the South and fight for Tennessee and the South, provided it can be mustered into service between the 1st and 10th of May next. Come forward and enroll yourselves immediately at my office in the town of Centerville.

April 23d, 1861.   T. P. BATEMAN.

One of the original circulars, neatly framed, now hangs in the office of the Centerville Hotel. In this frame is a card on which are these words: " Many of the braves who answered my roll call have answered the last call, and I will soon be with them over there. E. A. Dean, Sergeant, Co. H, 11th Tenn. Inf."

In his office Bateman had the following, to which numerous signatures were placed: " We, the undersigned, agree to volunteer for the term of twelve months to serve in the military service of the State of Tennessee, subject to the order of I. G. Harris, Governor of the State of Tennessee, to serve in any part of the South that we may be needed, or on the borders thereof to defend the State of Tennessee and the rights of the South. April 23d, 1861."

The organization of Bateman's company was completed at Centerville on May 1, 1861, and it then commenced the march to Nashville, the fifer playing, as the company left Centerville, " The Girl I Left Behind Me." On May 14 the company was mustered into the service of the Confederate States of America and became Company H of the Eleventh Tennessee Infantry. This regiment participated in the following battles: Wild Cat (or Rock Castle River), Ky.; Walden's Ridge, Murfreesboro, Chickamauga, Missionary Ridge, Rocky Face Ridge, Resaca, Calhoun, New Hope Church, Kennesaw Mountain, Peachtree Creek, Sugar Creek (east of Atlanta), Jonesboro, Franklin, Nashville, and Bentonville, N. C. It was surrendered with General Johnston's army at Greensboro, N. C., on April 26, 1865. The battle flag of the regiment was, however, brought away in safety from the place of surrender. The following is the roll of Company H: T. P. Bateman, captain (elected lieu-

tenant colonel at organization; resigned on April 1,
1862); P. V. H. WEEMS, first lieutenant (elected
captain to succeed Bateman; promoted to be major;
killed at Atlanta on July 22, 1864); R. C. Gordon, second lieutenant; ALEX. H. VAUGHN, third
lieutenant (killed at Tazewell, East Tennessee, by
drunken soldiers of Brazzleton's Confederate Cavalry); W. C. Jones, first sergeant (subsequently lieutenant, then captain; wounded); E. A. Dean, second
sergeant (subsequently first sergeant; first lieutenant
at reorganization; wounded at Murfreesboro); Thos.
D. Thompson, third sergeant (subsequently aid-de-
camp to Gen. James E. Raines); W. J. D. Spence,
fourth sergeant (later a captain in Napier's Battalion
of cavalry); James A. Brown, first corporal; W. H.
White, second corporal; J. H. (" Tack ") Carothers,
third corporal (later wagon master); W. G. Frazier,
fourth corporal (afterwards a lieutenant in the Tenth
Tennessee Cavalry); James H. Anderson (of David-
son County), WILLIAM ALLEN (died on October
16, 1861), W. A. Baker (wounded), Wm. Burchard,
S. H. BALLARD (killed in battle at Jonesboro, Ga.),
J. C. Bradley, W. S. Brown, W. M. Baxter, Thos.
Burch (frequently regimental color bearer), E. Bibb,
James Barr (wounded at Murfreesboro), Jno. H.
Barr (wounded at Peachtree Creek), A. V. Burchard,
A. N. CHAMBERLAIN (died at Camp Cheatham
on May 20, 1861), JAMES CHANDLER (died at
Camp Cheatham on July 1, 1861), JOHN CHAN-
DLER (killed in battle at Murfreesboro), Jesse Co-

ble, Charles Cagle, Samuel Cochran, Jno. T. Cochran, Jones Collins, JOSEPH CHANDLER (killed in battle at Jonesboro, Ga.), Henry G. Darden, J. G. Darden, Alfred B. Darden, H. A. DUDLEY (died at Camp Cheatham on June 4, 1861), W. D. EASLEY (died at Bean's Station, East Tennessee), John A. Easley, Gabriel Fowlkes (corporal; commissary sergeant), HARRIS FLOYD (killed on skirmish line near Jonesboro, Ga.), J. Polk Fielder, SAMUEL W. GARNER (killed by Federals in Humphreys County), J. M. GODWIN (killed in battle at Nashville), G. W. F. Garner, Thos. Grimes (transferred to regimental band), SAMUEL B. GRAY (killed in battle at Missionary Ridge), L. P. GRINER (died at Bean's Station), ANDREW GRAVITT (died at Camp Cheatham in June, 1862), J. CALVIN GOSSETT (died at Bean's Station on June 28, 1862), A. W. GRENILL (died on July 14, 1862), Joseph Gray (of Perry County), Wash. Gill, James George, RICHARD GREER (died at Newnan, Ga., in 1863), HARRY GORDON (transferred from Eighth Texas Cavalry; killed on skirmish line near New Hope Church), Arten Hassell, Brit. Hassell, F. B. Hornbeak (transferred), Wm. Hooper, James H. Huddleston, Zebulon Hassell, S. M. Hornbeak (transferred), E. A. Hornbeak (transferred), W. H. Huddleston, Andrew Hunt (transferred to regimental band), J. M. Harbison, Thos. Henley, Samuel G. Jones (wounded at Murfreesboro), GRANVILLE M. JOHNSON (killed in battle of Chickamauga),

Harris Jones, JACOB H. JOHNSON (second lieutenant at reorganization; promoted to be captain; killed in battle at Atlanta on July 22, 1864), Fred. Jones, John Kemp, James Lunsford, Jno. H. Leeper, J. S. J. LANCASTER (killed in battle of Chickamauga), G. W. Lancaster, Dr. A. J. Lowe (assistant surgeon), N. H. LEEK (died on April 13, 1863), WILLIAM E. LOMAX (died in 1862), HENRY LOWE (died at Camp Cheatham on July 10, 1861), Thomas Loftin, Alfred Leek, David D. Murphree, J. S. MARTIN (died on April 2, 1863), ARMISTEAD MARTIN (killed in battle at Atlanta on July 20, 1864), M. B. McClanahan, L. B. McClanahan, H. H. Mumford, W. G. Malugin, B. B. Mobley, W. H. Maroney, DANIEL MONTGOMERY (killed in battle at Jonesboro, Ga.), George W. Martin, Albert Morrison, Luther Miller, " Tip " Mumford, Griff. Nichols, John Plunkett, Jno. M. Poore, THOS. BENTON PETTY (killed in battle at Atlanta on July 22, 1864), D. M. Parker, JOSEPH PATTERSON (killed in battle at Murfreesboro), David A. Randall (said to have deserted), T. J. Rochell (transferred), W. N. Ratliff, JASPER ROCHELL (killed on skirmish line near New Hope Church), Cephus Reeves, William Reeves, F. J. Reeves, James Rhodes, G. M. Rhodes, Wilburn Ragsdale, J. SHIPP (killed near Dalton, Ga.), Nat. Suggs, Patrick S. Smith, Thos. S. Smith, JAMES SHIPP (joined Tenth Tennessee Cavalry; killed in battle at Nashville), John S. Satterfield, Wm. B. Sutherland, Jno. P. Sutherland, J.

W. Shouse (sergeant), David Moore Spence (hospital steward), WHITE TUCKER (died on July 8, 1861), J. H. C. Tarkington, STEWART THOMPSON (mortally wounded in battle of Missionary Ridge), WILLIAM C. WEBB (killed in battle at Murfreesboro), R. J. Work (third lieutenant at reorganization; wounded at Murfreesboro), M. M. WRIGHT (killed in battle at Murfreesboro), James Yates.

TWENTY-FOURTH INFANTRY.

Hickman County furnished two companies to the Twenty-fourth Tennessee Infantry, which was organized at Camp Anderson, three miles south of Murfreesboro, on August 6, 1861. This regiment first encountered the enemy at Camp Joe Underwood (Kentucky) on the night of October 22, 1861, when six companies of the regiment, together with Captain Lewis' cavalry company, surprised and captured this Federal camp of instruction. This regiment took part in the bloody battles of Shiloh, Perryville (Ky.), Murfreesboro, and Franklin; and the death rolls of the two Hickman County companies show only too well the gallantry of their members.

The following roll of Company H, Twenty-fourth Tennessee Infantry, is a copy of that sent by Capt. J. A. Holmes to W. C. Whitthorne, adjutant general, State of Tennessee, on May 14, 1863. Entries on this roll concerning events of dates subsequent to this are based on information obtained from survivors of this company: CHARLES WESLEY BEALE, captain (died at Bowling Green, Ky., on December 7, 1861); J. G. Anderson, first lieutenant; (Dr.) R. K. Dawson, second lieutenant; G. W. Young, brevet second (third) lieutenant; H. C. Campbell, first sergeant (promoted to captain on December 10, 1861; wounded at Shiloh on April 6, 1862); R. F. Bratton, second sergeant; W. C. McCord, third sergeant; J. N. Anderson, fourth sergeant (promoted to second lieutenant on November 2, 1861); J. W. Tyler, first corporal; W. D. BAKER, second corporal (killed at Shiloh on April 6, 1862); L. E. Reeves, third corporal; W. H. H. Hunter, fourth corporal; Allan Adcock, R. M. Anderson (wounded at Shiloh), D. C. Anderson (wounded at Shiloh), —— Alexander, W. S. Anderson, F. M. Anglin, W. D. Arnold, N. J. Anglin (wounded at Franklin; leg amputated), M. M. Bradley, F. M. Ballard (promoted to lieutenant in December, 1861), B. Bates, J. A. Brickle (third corporal), E. R. BEASLEY (killed at Shiloh on April 6, 1862), W. C. Beard, W. B. Beard, W. C. Baird, A. G. BAIRD (died on March 8, 1862), R. H. BATES (died in November, 1862), B. B. Bates, Thos. Cunningham (wounded at Shiloh), G. B. Cavendor, W. W. Campbell, J. H. Clark (wounded at Perryville), J. D. Clymer (fourth corporal), G. W. COOPER (died at Tupelo, Miss., on June 30, 1862), W. M. Deal, R. A. Dean (wounded at Murfreesboro; right arm amputated; mentioned in official Roll of Honor for gallantry in this battle), Patrick Dwyer, James Dunlap, L. H. Dawson, FRANK EMLER

(died at Shelbyville on April 20, 1863), Henderson
Emler, J. M. Fly, Frank Fergusson, W. C. J. Giles
(wounded at Shiloh), J. R. Goins, J. H. Greer (promoted to second lieutenant on April 14, 1863), J. T.
Garrett, G. W. Groves, HENRY GROVES (died at
Bowling Green, Ky., in January, 1862), J. B. Hooten
(wounded at Shiloh), W. W. Harrington, S. G. Hendricks, F. M. Hassell, J. D. Hensley, James Hooper
(second sergeant), J. A. Holmes (promoted to cap-
tain on August 26, 1862), Thos. Holmes (promoted
to second lieutenant on April 14, 1863), J. H. Hutchi-
son, J. H. Harris, J. T. Kennedy, J. G. Killough,
Elias Lane, J. H. McCord (wounded at Perryville,
Ky.), W. C. McCord, N. F. Moss, Robt. McCoy, F.
P. McCaleb, T. F. Moss (wounded at Perryville), J.
P. Morrison, G. W. Malugin (fourth sergeant), Robt.
McClanahan, R. G. Moore, Chas. Milam, R. C. Nutte,
Alexander Overbey (wounded at Franklin), Wilson
Overbey, W. E. Oliver, S. P. Parker, W. A. PAR-
KER (killed in battle of Shiloh on April 6, 1862),
J. A. Pickard, Alex. Plunkett, Samuel Pace, JAMES
PINKERTON (died at Camp Trousdale in August,
1861), B. H. PENDERGRASS (died at Frank-
lin on September 25, 1861), M. P. Poplin, G. H.
PRITCHARD (killed at Shiloh on April 6, 1862),
H. G. Primm, J. P. Ragsdale, A. Rogers, W. N.
RAGSDALE (killed at Perryville on October 8,
1862), S. J. Reeves (wounded at Shiloh), J. J.
Reeves, Wiley Richardson, David Reeves, J. A. Rob-
erts, Zach. Simms, M. M. Shaw, Albert Stephens,

Chas. Stephens, J. K. Stephens, J. P. Stephens, A. J. Slayden, J. N. Smith, Walter Smith, W. G.' Smith, M. W. Tolley, Kearney Turman (wounded at Perryville), B. B. Turman, THOS. TURMAN (died at Bowling Green, Ky., in November, 1861), James Truett, J. H. Tucker, D. M. Underhill, R. J. Warren, W. C. Warren, Ralph Warren (wounded at Murfreesboro), Elijah Warren, W. T. Warff, B. L. Warff, E. D. WARFF (died at Tullahoma on November 24, 1862), N. Young (promoted to first lieutenant in December, 1861). In addition to these, the following names are furnished by survivors of this company: Wiley Rickman, T. S. J. Scruggs, Daniel Underhill, G. W. Cavenor, A. D. Easley. W. A. Neely, and W. Pinkerton. On what purports to be a death roll of this company are the following additional names: W. D. Parker (killed at Shiloh), A. T. Bird (died on March 7, 1862), B. S. Cornwell (killed at Shiloh), Alex. P. Cleveland (died on April 26, 1862), Wm. R. Beasley (killed at Shiloh), Dixon Dyer (killed at Shiloh), Rufus Davis (killed on March 10, 1862), P. W. Lawrence (died on March 24, 1862), Benj. Matthews (died on April 4, 1862), Thos. M. Haynie (killed at Shiloh), W. H. Pate (died on April 6, 1862), Jesse Powell (killed at Shiloh), John Payne (died on April 24, 1862), John D. Taylor (killed at Shiloh), Henderson W. Winkler (killed at Shiloh).

The following roll of Company I is a copy of that sent by Captain Holmes along with the roll of Company H. These companies were consolidated, and

Captain Holmes, therefore, reported concerning the two original companies: J. J. Williams, captain (promoted to major; elected lieutenant colonel, but declined; wounded at Shiloh); Edward W. Easley, first lieutenant (promoted to captain; wounded at Shiloh); P. S. Mayberry, second lieutenant; T. S. Beaty, third lieutenant; Samuel Dunbar, first sergeant; J. G. PEELER, second sergeant (promoted to third lieutenant on August 26, 1862; died on February 26, 1863); Henry Mayberry, third sergeant; R. F. Green, fourth sergeant (wounded at Shiloh; arm amputated); D. R. Rivers, first corporal; W. Z. Curl, second corporal; Willis Turner, third corporal (wounded at Perryville, Ky.); F. C. CHAPPEL, fourth corporal (joined Tenth Tennessee Cavalry; killed in battle of Nashville); A. I. White, fifer; Thomas Alexander, N. W. Armstrong, B. F. Arnold, Alonzo Askins, MOSES BATES (died at Nashville on September 17, 1861), W. A. Barber, DENNIS BATES (died at Bowling Green on November 11, 1861), Elijah Baker, ADOLPHUS BATES (died at Nashville in September, 1861), Milo Baker, ELIAS BUCHANAN (died at Camp Trousdale on September 10, 1861), H. Beatty, S. C. Brown, J. F. M. Campbell, D. M'CLURE COOPER (died at Nashville on September 20, 1861), W. D. Campbell, W. J. Campbell (wounded at Shiloh), William Cook, John Cox, W. S. Cotham, Harvey Cross, William Cash, J. M. DUKE (killed at Shiloh on April 6, 1862), A. J. Depriest, FRANK DEPRIEST (died at Nashville on January 19, 1863), A. D. Easley (wounded at Perryville), FRANK EMERSON (died at Columbia on January 4, 1862), T. S. Easley (promoted to second lieutenant in December, 1861; wounded at Shiloh; subsequently captain in Tenth Tennessee Cavalry), JAMES FENTRESS (killed at Perryville on October 8, 1862), W. C. GARNER (wounded at Shiloh; died in prison), T. J. Groves, E. H. GARRETT (died at Columbia on January 10, 1862), L. J. Griffin, A. S. GARRETT (killed at Shiloh on April 6, 1862), Samuel Gentry, W. C. GRIFFIN (killed at Shiloh on April 6, 1862), PERRY GUNTER (killed at Shiloh on April 6, 1862), NATHAN GRIFFIN (died at Nashville on September 17, 1861), R. C. Halbrooks, W. F. Hale, B. F. Harris, J. M. Hamock, T. B. Henry (promoted to first lieutenant on August 26, 1862), F. M. Hutchison, J. C. Hutchison, Elijah Hutchison (transferred from Forty-second Regiment), James Hutchison, William Jenkins (wounded at Shiloh), J. A. Kunkle, W. J. Lancaster, J. C. LAWSON (mortally wounded at Perryville, Ky.), S. S. Lawson, William Lovelace, J. S. Mayberry, Robert Malugin, Adolphus McClaren, ROBERT M'CLAREN (died at Bowling Green on November 11, 1861), B. M. Milam, G. W. Milam, W. N. MILAM (transferred from Forty-second Regiment; mortally wounded at Shiloh), J. (or A.) N. McClanahan, J. L. McClanahan, J. D. L. Nunnellee (promoted to first lieutenant), J. A. Nunnellee, JAMES PARKER (died at home in September,

1862), P. G. Pace, WILSON PACE (killed at Shiloh on April 6, 1862), Ethelbert Parker, John Pickard, William Pinkerton, W. T. Peeler, ANDREW PARKER (died at Camp Trousdale on September 15, 1861), William Pinkerton, Jr. (wounded at Shiloh), DAVID C. PINKERTON (died at Bowling Green on November 30, 1861), D. R. Rivers, Joel Rivers, J. M. REECE (killed at Shiloh on April 6, 1862), M. M. Rivers, J. M. Rivers, W. M. Sanders, (wounded at Shiloh), John Sisco, John E. Sisco, F. H. SISCO (died on July 8, 1862, at Tupelo, Miss.), W. H. Stoops, Wiley Stuart (wounded at Shiloh), S. A. Tatum, W. A. Tibbs, Elias Turner, W. B. Thornton, A. J. Turner, E. P. Twilley, J. T. WARREN (died in the service), George Wright, F. B. Wright, Robert Wright, W. P. Wofford (wounded at Shiloh), T. J. Walker (wounded at Shiloh and at Murfreesboro), Richard Wilkins. The following additional names are given by survivors of this company: Jack Wright, James Jenkins, "Babe" Sisco (wounded at Shiloh), William Curl, THOMAS CURL (killed at Shiloh), William H. Thornton, Abe Bentley, George Groves, Jack Sims, John W. Nunnellee, John Climer, Charles Milam. On the death roll of this company are found these additional names: J. B. WOOTEN (or HOOTEN), died in the service on February 27, 1864; J. A. TURNBOW, died in the service on March 5, 1863.

FORTY-SECOND TENNESSEE INFANTRY.

The Forty-second Tennessee Infantry was organized about October 1, 1861, it responding to the second call for troops.   Hickman County furnished two companies to this regiment.   This regiment participated in the engagements at Fort Donelson and was surrendered at this place on February 16, 1862.   The officers were carried as prisoners to Johnson's Island; the privates, to Camp Douglas, Ill.   At the latter place many Hickman County soldiers died, far from home and unattended by sorrowful and sympathizing relatives.   The officers were exchanged in Virginia; and the privates were exchanged at Vicksburg, Miss., on September 17, 1862.   The regiment was reorganized at Clinton, Miss., on September 27, 1862.   At Port Hudson, La., the regiment was exposed to a heavy fire on March 14, 1863, when Commodore Farragut passed up the Mississippi River. The Forty-second was on its way to the relief of General Pemberton when Vicksburg fell.   It then retreated to Jackson, Miss., where it was engaged, holding the enemy in check.   Transferred to the Army of Tennessee, it participated in the battles of New Hope Church, Pine Mountain, Kennesaw Mountain, Smyrna Depot, Peachtree Creek, Atlanta, Lick-skillet Road, Jonesboro, Big Shanty, the second battle at Dalton; the bloodiest of them all—Franklin, and Nashville.

The following roll of Company B, Forty-second Tennessee Infantry, is based upon information fur-

nished by survivors of this company and the death
roll of the regiment: Josiah R. Hubbard, captain
(promoted to major in March, 1863); John Nunnellee, first lieutenant; GEORGE A. LOWE,* second
lieutenant (mortally wounded at Atlanta; died at
Forsyth, Ga.); William Carothers, third lieutenant
(wounded at New Hope Church and at Franklin);
William W. Lyell, first sergeant (escaped from Fort
Donelson, and joined Morgan's Cavalry); Richard
Wills, second sergeant; Jack Christian, third sergeant; William Clark, first corporal; Samuel M.
Carothers, second corporal (elected second lieutenant at reorganization; wounded at Kennesaw Mountain and at Franklin); W. W. ASKINS (died in
prison at Camp Douglas, Ill., on February 9, 1863),
Thomas Armstrong, Samuel Armstrong, Nathaniel
Armstrong, Riley Beasley, James Barnhill, Robert
Booker, James Burch (wounded), WESLEY BOYD
(died on February 9, 1863), James Booker, Alexander Barnhill, John Briggs, James Bryant, Hugh R.
Carothers (wounded at Franklin), Stephen E. Carothers (wounded at Kennesaw Mountain—eye shot
out), James T. Carter, James Chappell, Wyatt J.
Chappell, Jack Chappell, Hosea Chappell, DAVID
CUFF (died in the service), FRANK CARTER
(killed at Perryville, Ky.), Van Dougherty, Thomas

---

*Lowe, at the time he received his death-wound (July 28,
1864), was captain of his company, and was exposed to the
enemy's fire while remonstrating with a private for exposing
himself unnecessarily.

Duncan, Dennis J. Easley (sharpshooter; quartermaster), GEORGE FOX (died on October 27, 1863), T. Fergusson, Tillman Gray (wounded at Franklin), James Gossett, J. K. P. Gravitt, WEBSTER GILBERT (died in prison at Camp Douglas, Ill.), Spivey Gossett, Hiram W. Hassell (wounded at Perryville, Ky., and at Franklin), James Hubbs (wounded at New Hope Church), J. B. Hassell, Gustavus Hamer, James Hutson, THOMAS J. HASSELL (died at Columbus, Miss.), Carroll Hubbs, GEORGE W. HOWELL (died in prison), John Hudgens, William Hudgens, Dennis Jones, CARTER JEANES (died in prison), David Lowe, William Luther, William Lynn (wounded at Kennesaw Mountain), Robert Lyell, John Lewis, James Lewis, John W. Martin, E. Morrison, Oliver McMinn, Calvin McCord, Daniel K. McCord, OLIVER P. MILBURN (died in prison), B. Moore, John Moore, William Moore, Marshall Nicks, Douglass Nicks, FRANK OWENS (killed at Fort Donelson), Samuel Owens, George Petty, Tim. Petty, David Potter, Richard Phillips, Robert Redden, James Richardson, JOHN G. W. ROCHELL (died in March, 1862), Robert Reeves, Newton Reeves, John L. Temple (fifer), David Thornton (at one time first sergeant), Asa Totty, Zachariah Totty (veteran of both Seminole Wars and Mexican War), Benjamin Thornton, Thomas Vinyard, Reuben Wills, Epps Wills, James W. Warren, Neal Warren, C. Warren, FRANCIS M. WOODS (died in the service), MAJOR J. YATES (died on May 6, 1863), James Yates, John Yates, Thomas Yates. This roll, as well as all other rolls where the information has been obtained almost solely from the survivors, is necessarily incomplete and may contain errors. While errors and omissions are regretted, they are unavoidable. After the lapse of over one-third of a century, it is impossible to obtain all of the names and to secure the correct initials. The difficulty of this task shows its importance. Had it been left undone for another third of a century, many gallant soldiers whose names are here recorded would have been by that time forgotten.

The following comparatively correct roll of Company F, Forty-second Tennessee Infantry, was furnished by Lieut. J. R. Brown: Levi McCollum, captain (elected major; promoted to lieutenant colonel); John W. Walker (elected captain at organization); Lewis Bates, first lieutenant; John H. Coleman, second lieutenant (wounded); Stephen Forrester, third lieutenant; BENJAMIN F. COLEMAN, first sergeant (elected captain at reorganization at Clinton, Miss., on September 27, 1862; killed at New Hope Church on May 27, 1864—struck by a grapeshot); T. J. LANDERS, second sergeant (died in prison at Camp Douglas, Ill.); J. S. Forrester, third sergeant; A. C. Dunagan, fourth sergeant (third lieutenant at reorganization; wounded at Franklin); William Peeler, first corporal; OSCAR M. SUTTON, second corporal (died in prison at Camp Douglas, Ill., on April 4, 1862); L. L. Bingham, third corporal; JAMES CAGLE, fourth corporal (killed in battle of Franklin); Gideon Arnold, David Arnold, LEWIS ASKINS (died at Trenton, Miss., on October 7, 1862), J. J. BAKER (second sergeant at reorganization; died at Mobile, Ala.), J. R. Brown (second lieutenant at reorganization; wounded at Atlanta on June 28, 1864), W. C. Bates (promoted to lieutenant), SEABORNE BLACKWELL (killed at Nashville on March 10, 1864), H. R. Barnhill, W. H. BASTIAN (died in prison at Camp Douglas on June 12, 1862), D. L. BASTIAN (died in prison at Camp Douglas on March 23, 1862), W. C. BASTIAN (died on June 12, 1862), James Blackwell (wounded at Atlanta on June 28, 1864), WILLIAM BLACKWELL (died on November 12, 1861), Thomas Bates, GEORGE W. BAKER (died on April 14, 1862), RICHARD CUDE (killed at Atlanta on June 28, 1864), Duncan Campbell, Jesse Chesser, JOHN CUNNINGHAM (died in 1863), James Claiborne, Frank Claiborne, Benjamin Chandler (third sergeant at reorganization), J. N. CHANDLER (died in prison at Camp Douglas on March 9, 1862), J. M. CHANDLER (died in prison at Camp Douglas on March 17, 1862), J. G. CHANDLER (died in prison at Camp Douglas on April 12, 1862), ADAM CAGLE (died on April 7, 1863), S. M. CUNNINGHAM (died on June 14, 1863), L. C. Dunaway, S. W. Dunaway, F. M. Forrester, J. F. GRAY (first lieutenant at reorganization; died at St. Louis, Mo., in 1864), DAVID GROVES (died on October 22, 1863), WILLIAM A. HUGHES (died on September 13, 1863), J. M. HUTCHISON (died in prison at Camp Douglas on August 25, 1862), E. Hutchison, JACK HINSON (killed in Hickman County), William Hinson, (Rev.) James Johnson, H. W. Jones, JOHN JONES (died at Camp Cheatham on November 18, 1861), THOMAS JOHNSON (died in Georgia), Anon Lowe, CYRUS LOWE (died in prison at Camp Douglas on June 30, 1862), Thomas Lucas, James Lancaster, MILTON LANCASTER (died at Atlanta on June 28, 1864), George Morrison, T. B. MORRISON (died in prison at Camp Douglas on August 17, 1862), A. J. MORRISON (died in prison at Camp Douglas on May 15, 1862), Joseph Morrison, William McClanahan, James D. Murphree (fourth sergeant at reorganization; wounded at Atlanta on June 28, 1864; leg amputated), AMSEL MURPHREE (died at Camp Cheatham on November 3, 1861), Jesse Matthews, WILLIAM MITCHELL (died on May 15, 1862), J. E. McCollum, J. C. POORE (first sergeant at reorganization; died at home), Samuel Poore, ASA PELL (killed at Atlanta in July, 1864), D. S. Potter (wounded at Fort Donelson), D. T. Pinkerton (wounded at Perryville, Ky.), RUFUS RICHARD-SON (died in October, 1862), JAMES SAWYERS (died at Port Hudson, La., on March 14, 1862), James Singleton, Frank Shipp, G. C. Sibley, JESSE SPARKS (died at St. Louis, Mo., on March 1, 1862), T. G. SANDERS (died on May 11, 1862), Willis

Turner (wounded at Fort Donelson), JAMES VER-
NON (died in some Northern prison), J. D. VER-
NON (died in prison at Camp Douglas on April 11,
1862), THOMAS VICK (died in prison at Camp
Douglas on June 2, 1862), J. T. Woolard, W. F.
Woolard, James Wherry (sharpshooter; wounded
twice at Atlanta), JAMES S. WALKER (died in
Alabama in 1865), Pleasant Walker (wounded at
Franklin on November 30, 1864), William Womack,
JOHN WILKINS (wounded at Atlanta; killed on
November 30, 1864), R. C. Wilkins, Mark Williams,
Nathan L. Williams, Albert Weatherspoon.

FORTY-EIGHTH TENNESSEE INFANTRY.

The Forty-eighth Tennessee Infantry was organized about December 15, 1861, one mile from Nashville on the Gallatin turnpike. Milton Voorhees, of
Maury County, was elected colonel. This regiment
was first engaged with the enemy at Fort Henry.
From this place it retreated to Fort Donelson, losing
most of its baggage on the retreat. This caused a
large number to be detailed to return home and collect
clothing. Then the measles and mumps broke out
and a large number were sent to the hospitals. So,
as a result, when Fort Donelson fell, less than half
the regiment was captured. The captured field officers were sent to Fort Warren, Mass.; the line officers,
to Camp Chase, O., from which place they were transferred on May 1, 1862, to Johnson's Island, in Lake
Erie; and the privates were sent to Camp Douglas,

Ill. While the official death roll of this regiment
(which is the most incomplete and unintelligible of
those examined in connection with the writing of this
history) is silent as to this point, the dates indicate
that many Hickman Countians, members of this regiment, died in Northern prisons. The uncaptured
portion of the regiment made its way south, and,
uniting with similar fragments from the Third and
Forty-second, which had escaped capture at Fort
Donelson, organized the new Forty-eighth Tennessee Infantry. Of this regiment the late Chancellor
George H. Nixon was elected colonel. About August
15, 1862, the privates of the original Forty-eighth in
prison were sent to Vicksburg, Miss., and exchanged.
The officers were exchanged at Akin's Landing, on
the James River, in Virginia. The regiment was reorganized at Jackson, Miss., Milton Voorhees being
again elected colonel. Members of Nixon's Forty-
eighth, then at Shelbyville, nearly all returned to
their original regiments. The existence of two Forty-
eighth Regiments, one of them composed of fragments
of several regiments, in addition to the obstacles already mentioned, makes the task of compiling a roll
of the Hickman County companies in the Forty-
eighth Regiment one of particular difficulty. In the
compilation of the following rolls the source of information was almost solely the survivors of the
companies; and although they readily gave whatever
assistance in their power, the following rolls are,
however much it may be regretted, incomplete, and

probably in some respects inaccurate. It is, however, believed that they are as nearly accurate as they can now be made. After the reorganization this regiment was exposed to a heavy fire at Port Hudson, La., on March 14, 1863; was in the engagements around Jackson, Miss., from July 10 to July 16, 1863; and, then being transferred to the Army of Tennessee, was in the battles of New Hope Church, Pine Mountain, Kennesaw Mountain, Peachtree Creek, Atlanta, Lickskillet Road, Lovejoy's Station, Nashville, Anthony's Hill (near Pulaski, Tenn.); Kingston, N. C., and Bentonville, N. C. It surrendered on March 19, 1865.

Company D: Solomon J. George, captain; Elijah Cantrell, first lieutenant (elected captain at reorganization at Jackson, Miss., in 1862); John L. Griffin, second lieutenant (promoted to captain); Van Buren Shouse, third lieutenant; Richard Kendrick, first sergeant; Z. J. Waters, corporal (elected first lieutenant at reorganization); Armistead Allison, William Anderson, Washington Anderson, Ed. Anderson, Joseph Anderson, John Anderson, Samuel Anderson, Newton Anderson, Elijah Arnold, M. P. Aydelott, SAMUEL D. AYDELOTT (died in the service), William Bartley, Robert Bayles, William Baynes, WILLIAM BURCHAM (died on April 8, 1862), GREEN BURCHAM (died in the service), William Biddle, Joseph M. Bond (promoted to lieutenant), C. C. BARNES (died on August 1, 1862), R. Barnes, Wesley Burcham, M. Briggs, John Briggs,

"Shanghai" Bates, Alvin Breece, Samuel Canada, Jesse Coble, William Cash, B. Cooper, Joseph Cooper, Alexander Coates, Griffin Coates, Green Clayton, HENRY DENTON (died on February 20, 1862), GEORGE W. EASLEY (died in the service), Jo. Easley, Thomas ("Green Tom") Easley, Thomas Easley, J. T. EASLEY (killed at Richmond, Ky.), Ford George (elected second lieutenant at reorganization), John V. Gray, John F. Gray, Pleasant Griffin, Sevier Griffin, T. J. GILL (died on May 14, 1862), Carroll Hubbs, Wiley Harper, Wiley Hopper, PLEASANT HARDER (died in the service), William Johnson, Samuel Johnson, James Johnson, James King, Bliss Lewis, James Lewis, Pleasant Lewis, Richard Love (first sergeant), C. Meece, Mark Matthews, M. M'CALEB (died on February 20, 1862), D. M. M'COLLUM (killed at Perryville, Ky.), O. A. Nixon, Felix Nicks, John Oakley, Luther Peery, Henry Porter, Cave J. Peery, J. W. PEERY (died on February 2, 1862), Henry Pell, William Pell, Allan Plunkett, S. A. Plunkett, Isaac Prince, J. S. Prince, JAMES PRINCE (died in the service), Joseph Pruett, Tapley Rochell, "Tobe" Rodgers, Jack Rodgers, JOHN RATLIFF (corporal; died on July 1, 1862), J. H. Shipp, John Sharp, Clarendon Shouse, Marion Sullivan, Green Sharp, George Sharp, Henry Simmons, Levi Simmons, John Smithson, F. C. SHOUSE (died on June 16, 1862), William Short (elected third lieutenant at reorganization), Asa Totty, William Totty, William Thornton,

G. M. TATUM (died on February 4, 1862), "Sub." Tatum, John Thompson, William Thompson, Luther Whiteside, Lafayette Whiteside, Joseph Wheat, Elijah Watts, Robert Wright, John Warren, John Willis.

Company G: J. A. OLIVER, captain (died at St. Louis, Mo., on February 25, 1862); S. J. Easley, first lieutenant; Wilson Overbey, second lieutenant; J. Wilson Pritchard, first sergeant; John A. Petty, second sergeant; Elijah Rushton, third sergeant; FRANCIS PETTY, fourth sergeant (died at Port Hudson, La., in 1863); Charles Allen, W. C. Anglin, SAMUEL BROWN (died at St. Louis on February 25, 1862), J. E. Brown (corporal), T. J. Brown, George Beale, John Beale, James Birch, —— Betty, CALVIN BALLARD (killed at Lovejoy Station, Ga., on August 19, 1864), "Bale" Cooper, Frank Carter, Wesley Carter, Newton Carter, "General" Claiborne, EDWARD CAMPBELL (killed at Richmond, Ky.), B. E. Cooper, William Duke, (Dr.) J. G. Dinwiddie, Gabriel Davidson, John Dougherty, Wiley Erwin, Lytle Erwin, George Erwin, W. B. W. Easley (elected third lieutenant at reorganization at Jackson, Miss., in 1862), "Top" Easley, James Easley, J. C. Frazier (first lieutenant at reorganization), MALFORD ("BRIGHT") FORRESTER (died in prison at Camp Douglas, Ill., in 1862), James Madison Forrester, WILLIAM FRIZZELL (died on January 31, 1862), G. W. FINCH (died on May 13, 1862), "Bud" Forrester, William Forrester,

Richard Forrester, S. F. FORRESTER (died on
May 14, 1862), John Goins, J. G. Goins, W. Gossett,
Lafayette Gossett, W. E. GRIMES (died in the
service), L. C. GRIMES (died in the service), Polk
Gravitt, S. George, Johnson Howell (wounded in
Georgia in 1863), JOSEPH HERNDON (died in
the service), A. J. HALE (died on April 24, 1862),
JOHN T. HENDERSON (killed at Richmond,
Ky.), Hiram Hassell, J. D. Hicks, T. J. HASSELL
(died on July 13, 1862), A. J. HALL (died on April
12, 1862), M. M. Harbinson (second lieutenant at re-
organization; wounded on August 19, 1864), Thomas
M. Hogan (first sergeant at reorganization), J. C.
JENKINS (died on February 14, 1862), A. Jen-
kins, J. M. Jenkins, William Lambert, George Lyell,
John Lyell, Fielding D. Leathers, JOHN LINTZ
(died on January 30, 1862), John McCoy (wounded
in Georgia in 1863), J. J. McCoy, Calvin McCord,
CALVIN MORRIS (died on March 5, 1862), N.
McCord, Benjamin Martin, John Martin, Andrew
Martin, N. J. Martin, T. G. N. McCord, Alexander
Nash, C. A. Nash, DRURY OVERBEY (died on
February 5, 1862), Edmond Overbey, G. T. Overbey,
Clagett Primm, Columbus Potter, William Pruett,
William Phillips, T. B. PRITCHARD (died on
May 20, 1862), G. W. POPE (died on May 29,
1862), John Porter, B. Piland, Robert Reeves, H.
Reeves, N. Reeves, B. Reeves, George Rial, John
Rial, A. J. Rodgers, John Rainey, Robert Steele (ser-
geant; wounded in Georgia in 1864), Dorey Smith,

LEWIS SMITH (died in prison at Camp Douglas in 1862), T. B. Smith, W. T. STEELE (died on January 8, 1862), Mark A. Spence, Jack Thornton, Jonathan Tatum, A. J. Turbeville, ANDREW J. THOMPSON (died in the service), W. C. Thompson, JASPER TURNER (died on May 17, 1862), ABNER TURNER (died on May 30, 1862), J. W. A. Vaughn, Monroe Worley, M. J. Worley, (Rev.) H. Rutherford Walker (captain at reorganization), ENOCH WARREN (died on February 20, 1862), John ("Bull") Warren, B. F. WYNN (died on February 6, 1862), "Dock" Wynn, T. J. WOOD (died on January 25, 1862), M. Woods, G. Washington Walker. One of the original companies of the Forty-eighth Regiment was commanded by Capt. Joel P. Morrison. Numerous attempts to obtain a roll of this company have been fruitless.

MISCELLANEOUS

John H. Moore, a cadet at West Point at the breaking out of the Civil War, was commissioned as third lieutenant in Company B, Seventh Tennessee Infantry, and was promoted to second lieutenant. He served in the Virginia campaigns with distinction.

Capt. John W. Cates, now of Obion County, was a gallant soldier in the Twentieth Tennessee Infantry. The following names appear upon the death roll of Company G (Shy's company), Twentieth Tennessee Infantry: J. M. Dean, William Rial, Green Woods, H. N. Lancaster, John Rossen, William H. Harris,

John W. Cuff, John C. Bates, John Cook, Dallas Davidson, John Carothers, J. B. Forrest, James Gray, George Murray, and Daniel Murphree.

The following names appear upon the roll of Company H, Third Tennessee Infantry: O. T. Plummer (first lieutenant), Robert T. Cooper (second lieutenant; promoted to captain; killed), W. J. Harder (promoted to first lieutenant; promoted to captain), R. M. Plummer (promoted to second lieutenant), James A. Doyel (third lieutenant). The following names appear upon the death roll of this company: T. M. Cooper, A. D. Cooper, C. H. Goodman, J. C. Griner, E. B. Hensley, D. R. Pope, Alexander Pope, J. F. Sharp, W. F. Sims, George Sims, Samuel Langford, Samuel G. Cooper, and Samuel Turner.

E. Kelley, of the Twelfth District, was a member of a Maury County company; W. G. W. Rochell, of this district, a member of Company C, Thirty-second Tennessee Infantry.

FIRST TENNESSEE CAVALRY.

A condensed account of the services of a Confederate cavalry command is almost impossible. Controlled by circumstances, rather than by strict orders from superiors, their movements were not outlined by a clear-cut plan, as were the movements of infantry. Making long and seemingly almost impossible marches, engaging in fighting at close quarters with the enemy, some of their most serious engagements were often affairs which, as they did not mate-

rially affect the general trend of events, are hardly
dignified in histories of the Civil War by the title of
" battle." That the First Tennessee Cavalry fought
the invaders of Southern soil over all the territory
embraced in the Southern Confederacy east of the
Mississippi River is almost literally true. In May,
1861, the Second Battalion was mustered into service,
the First Battalion having been mustered in one day
earlier. A company for the Second Battalion, composed of citizens of Perry County and Cane Creek of
Hickman County, was raised by N. N. Cox, who had
married Miss Slayden, of Cane Creek. At the organization Captain Cox was elected major, Lieut.
James H. Lewis, a grandson of the pioneer, John C.
Lewis, and a relative of General Forrest, succeeding
him as captain. In October, 1861, in an engagement
with the enemy near Hopkinsville, Ky., George W.
Barham, of Lewis' company, was killed, he being the
first soldier killed in the army later commanded by
Gen. Albert Sidney Johnston. During the winter of
1861-62 the Second Battalion repeatedly engaged the
enemy in Southern Kentucky, withdrawing, by way
of Fort Donelson, Nashville, and Columbia, to Alabama. It participated in the battle of Shiloh, remaining on the field for three days after the battle,
at which time it voluntarily withdrew. At Corinth,
Miss., it consolidated with the Eleventh Tennessee
Battalion, forming the First Tennessee Cavalry.
Here Major Cox resigned and proceeded to raise a
battalion, which consolidated with Napier's battalion,

forming the Tenth Tennessee Cavalry. In July, 1862, at the reorganization at Tupelo, Miss., Capt. James H. Lewis was elected lieutenant colonel. The First Cavalry was in the battle at Iuka, Miss., and in the stubbornly contested affair at Corinth on October 5 and 6, 1862. The regiment, which was with General Van Dorn's forces, retreated in front of General Grant. In the engagement at Holly Springs in December, 1862, Colonel Wheeler was wounded, and Lieutenant Colonel Lewis assumed command of the regiment. Connected with the command of General Forrest, it participated in the engagements at Spring Hill, Thompson's Station, in and around Franklin, and at Brentwood. It then drove in every picket around Nashville, between the Franklin turnpike and the Cumberland River. It then crossed the Cumberland Mountains, and, after much service here, took part in the battle of Chickamauga. After pursuing a large detachment of Federal cavalry as far north as Philadelphia, in Rhea County, it went with the raid around McMinnville, Murfreesboro, and Wartrace. Returning by way of Decatur, Ala., it rejoined the army in time to take part in the battle of Missionary Ridge. It participated in the battles of Resaca, New Hope Church, Pine Mountain, Kennesaw Mountain, and the battles around Atlanta. At New Hope Church this regiment and the Ninth Battalion opposed successfully for over an hour a much larger force of the enemy. These commands served as cavalry, and, in addition to this. repeatedly dismounted and fought as infantry. Lieutenant Colonel Lewis is authority for this statement: " We invariably whipped the enemy's cavalry, and then engaged their infantry." Near Newnan, Ga., one hundred and sixty men from Lewis' regiment and Major Aiken's Ninth Battalion held in check McCook's entire force, estimated at 4,500 men, until the arrival of reinforcements. Then, sometimes with Wheeler, sometimes with Forrest, sometimes with Wade Hampton, the First Regiment marched and fought through Tennessee, Alabama, Mississippi, Georgia, North Carolina, and South Carolina. After the battle of Fayetteville, N. C., the command of the cavalry brigade, of which the First Cavalry was a part, devolved upon Lieutenant Colonel Lewis. This brigade took part in the battle of Bentonville, N. C., on March 19 and 20, 1865, and later in the affair near Chapel Hill, N. C. It then " quit fighting." The First Tennessee Cavalry was paroled on May 3, 1865. On the following day, however, a detachment from this regiment, returning from Tennessee with recruits, encountered a brigade of Federal cavalry at Henry Courthouse, Va. Neither party knew of the surrender. In this affair Private Samuel Walker ("Cap.") Edwards, of Barham's company (formerly Cox's, then Lewis', company), was killed. " So that the singular circumstance occurs that this company lost the first and last man killed in the Army of Tennessee—George W. Barham, near Hopkinsville, Ky., early in October, 1861; and Edwards, at Henry

Courthouse, Va., on May 4, 1865." Lieutenant
Colonel Lewis is authority for this statement, which
is taken from Lindsley's " Military Annals of Tennessee."

In the following incomplete roll of Company I,
First Tennessee Cavalry, those names known to be of
Perry County soldiers are marked (*): N. N. Cox,*
captain (elected major); JOHN C. SLAYDEN,
lieutenant (killed in a personal encounter in Perry
County on October 25, 1863); James H. Lewis, lieutenant (captain; lieutenant colonel; commanded regiment and later a brigade); John Aschcraft,* Henry
Ashraft,* Hartwell F. Barham (promoted to captain; wounded), GEORGE W. BARHAM* (killed
near Hopkinsville, Ky., in October, 1861), John Barham,* W. L. BLACKBURN (killed at Shiloh),
James S. Bates, W. C. Bates, T. B. Bates, Moses Bal-
cum,* JAMES COTHAM (killed on Cane Creek by
Perry County jayhawkers), —— Cotham, Commodore Cotham, C. CHAUNCEY* (killed at Corinth,
Miss.), John Cook, Robert Cowan,* Frank Craig
(first sergeant), James Craig,* Joshua Cates,* William Cates,* Monroe Campbell, John Dikas,* L.
Dikas,* Polk Dikas,* Herod Dean,* Lucius Dean*
(promoted to second lieutenant), Andrew Downing,
John Edwards, SAMUEL WALKER (" CAP.")
EDWARDS (killed at Henry Courthouse, Va., on
May 4, 1865), Thomas Edwards, JOHN FRIEL
(killed at Thompson's Station), James Forrest, John
Forrest, John Field, John Flowers, William Greene,*

GRANVILLE GOODMAN (killed at Brentwood), Hugh Guthrie,* Nathaniel Goodman,* William Humphreys,* James A. Hughes, William Hilburn,* Albert Irwin, Mark Jones, William Johnson,* Abram Kelley, DANIEL KELLEY (killed on Cane Creek by Perry County jayhawkers), Thomas Kelley, Hiram Kelley, Benjamin Kitrell, Rufus Kitrell (third lieutenant), Robert Kitrell, Patrick Kelley,* Nick Kirk, Jack Lewis,* W. H. Lewis,* Thomas Lewis,* John Murray, William Marcum,* —— POWDER (killed), Thomas Qualls,* G. W. STALLINGS* (lieutenant; killed at New Hope Church), NEHEMIAH SHARP (killed at Aiken, S. C.), FOUNTAIN P. SHARP (killed), C. C. Sutton, Thomas Sutton, MIKE SIBLAY (killed), Abner Shelton,* G. W. Shelton,* Joseph M. Sutton, Sidney Stephens, William Stephens, James Stephens, Samuel Scott,* R. A. Twomey, Thomas Twomey, BENTON WHITWELL (killed at Triune), JACK WHITWELL (killed at Columbia, S. C.), Allan Whitwell, Pleasant Whitwell, J. N. Wall (promoted to first lieutenant), Richard Wall, Clement Wall, Bart. Walker, John Wall, Wesley Welch.

TENTH TENNESSEE CAVALRY.

In the summer of 1862, Alonzo Napier, of Humphreys County, raised the company which, as Company G, became a part of the Tenth Tennessee Cavalry. The original officers were: Alonzo Napier, captain; W. J. D. Spence, first lieutenant; Leroy

Traylor, second lieutenant; William Davidson, third lieutenant. This company, together with four others, in the autumn of 1862, organized near Ross' Landing, above Johnsonville, the battalion which came to be known as " Napier's Battalion." Captain Napier was elected lieutenant colonel, which was the rank of the commanding officer of a battalion. At this time the following officers of Napier's company were elected: W. J. D. Spence, captain; Thomas S. Easley, first lieutenant; William D. King, second lieutenant; William Wyatt, third lieutenant. Previous to this the men of Napier's command had been several times under fire in their operations through Hickman, Humphreys, Perry, Maury, Wayne, and Dickson Counties. The battalion now crossed the Tennessee River and joined General Forrest's command. At the battle of Parker's Cross Roads, which occurred soon after, Colonel Napier was killed while leading his men in a charge. The battalion was now sent on a raid along the Cumberland River. It was later joined by the entire commands of Generals Wheeler and Forrest, and participated in the attack made on Fort Donelson. Returning to Columbia, Napier's Battalion was consolidated with Cox's Battalion, commanded by Col. N. N. Cox, forming the Tenth Tennessee Cavalry. Napier's original company became Company I of this regiment. Thos. S. Easley was elected captain, and commanded it until the close of the war. The following are some of the engagements in which the regiment participated: Thompson's Station, Brentwood, Tullahoma, Chickamauga, Philadelphia, Maryville, Knoxville, Mossy Creek, Dalton, Resaca, New Hope Church, around Atlanta, Franklin, and Nashville.   This bare enumeration of battles conveys no idea of the marches of hundreds of miles it made through Tennessee, Mississippi, Alabama, Georgia, North Carolina, and South Carolina.   Of this and its accompaniment, fighting, the Tenth Tennessee Cavalry did perhaps as much as any Tennessee regiment, save, possibly, the First Tennessee Cavalry and the Ninth Battalion.

The following roll of Company I, Tenth Tennessee Cavalry, is compiled from information furnished by survivors.   Many names found in the following roll are of soldiers from other counties.   In many cases they are so designated.   All names here found, however, are names of men who belonged to this company at some time during its existence: ALONZO NAPIER, of Humphreys County, captain (elected lieutenant colonel; killed at Parker's Cross Roads on December 9, 1862); W. J. D. Spence, first lieutenant (elected captain to succeed Napier); Leroy Traylor, of Humphreys County, second lieutenant; William Davidson, of Benton County, third lieutenant; Thos. S. Easley (elected first lieutenant to succeed Spence; elected captain at organization of Tenth Tennessee Cavalry; served until close of war); Thomas Alexander, Daniel Atkinson, George W. Ashley (of Humphreys County), Ned Arnold, Thomas Arnold, A. V. Burchard, Monroe Bateman, J. A. Bates, Francis M.

Ballard, Henry Box (of Humphreys County), John Bates, Jacob Beasley, John Beasley, Stephen E. Carothers, William Cash, F. C. CHAPPELL (mortally wounded in battle at Nashville), Joseph Coleman, JAMES COTHAM (killed on Cane Creek by Perry County jayhawkers), Commodore Cotham, Wesley Caughron, Joseph W. Cooper, Samuel Conn, J. F. Crowe, F. E. Cummins, M. L. Dean, William Dean, Andrew Depriest, James Darden, Henry Dozier, N. J. Donegan, —— Dillon, John F. Eason, John A. Easley, Robert M. Easley, Stephen Easley, James D. Easley, Jr. (adjutant), J. H. Easley (third sergeant), W. G. Frazier (elected lieutenant at organization of regiment; horse killed in battle at Nashville), Alston Fowlkes, G. W. Florence, —— Fullerton, William Fullerton, Lewis George, John B. Gray, Jack George, James George, J. D. Garner, B. Garner, W. H. Huddleston, Reeves Huddleston, James Hall (elected second lieutenant at organization of regiment), William Hicks, William Humphreys, William Hurt, David Hicks, Thomas Hartley, William Hilham, Horatio Hunter, W. S. Helms, J. C. Heel (of Humphreys County), William Hutchison, Thomas Jones, W. D. King (elected second lieutenant at organization of battalion), D. R. King, Andrew Lowe, David Lowe, W. H. Lancaster, A. L. Lowe, "Doc" Leiper, D. M. McClanahan, James E. McCollum. Andrew McClerkin, H. McClerkin, M. McClanahan, Joel G. McClaren, H. D. McClanahan, John Mayberry, George Mayberry, Owens Morgan, Richard Milam, G. W.

M'CAULAY (first lieutenant; killed at Sevierville, East Tennessee), J. A. M'CAULAY (killed in battle of Blanch Hill on January 27, 1864), W. W. Mayberry, W. H. McClanahan, George Milam, Curtis Oakley, William Oakley, Jasper N. Peeler, JAMES PEELER (killed on Cane Creek by Perry County jayhawkers), James Porch, John Pickard, Isaac Pickard, William Pinkerton, —— Priestly (first sergeant), John Priest, Henry Richie (sergeant), Newton Rickman (commissary), William Rosson, J. L. Reagan, J. L. Rinehart, John S. Satterfield, JAMES SHIPP (lieutenant; killed in battle), Van Buren Shouse (orderly sergeant), Frank Shipp, Spivey Stanfield, " Pap " Stewart, William Spencer (of Humphreys County), William Shaw, James Stewart, James J. Sparks, James Shirley, G. D. Stokey, W. A. Stewart, John Stewart, Joseph Shipp, Ira Shipp, (Dr.) T. D. Thompson (sergeant major), G. W. Tarkington, Felix L. Totty, Jack Thornton, O. B. Turner, J. H. C. Tarkington, William Thornton, Richard Tatum, A. J. Turner, Samuel Tubbs, Polk Weatherspoon, (Dr.) L. D. Wright, (Dr.) A. C. Wilkins, (Dr.) W. L. Walker, R. C. Wilkins, William Wyatt (of Humphreys County; elected third lieutenant at organization of battalion), Harris Wiley (of Humphreys County; killed), James Watts (of Humphreys County), F. B. Wright, Coleman Williams, Thomas Warren, Richard Weatherspoon, J. R. Weatherspoon, J. M. Weatherspoon, W. C.

Wherry, Irving Wherry, Frank Wherry, Benjamin Wills, Nathaniel Young, G. W. Young.

One of the companies of the Tenth Cavalry— Company C—was commanded by Capt. W. H. Whitwell, of Cane Creek. It was composed principally of Perry Countians. Only the following names of members of this company could be obtained: Willis H. Whitwell, captain (wounded; leg amputated); Thomas Whitwell, second lieutenant; W. W. LAIN (died on March 12, 1863), THOMAS N. BARHAM (died on March 29, 1863), JESSE GOODMAN (died on March 2, 1863), DAVID MORRISON (died on March 27, 1863). It is probable that a number of those who were originally members of this company are named in the roll of Company G.

NINTH BATTALION.

The Ninth Battalion, Tennessee Cavalry, was organized near Nashville in December, 1861. Two of its six companies were from Hickman County. Its first service was around Fort Henry, from which place it retreated to Fort Donelson. Here, under Forrest, it took a prominent part in the defense until the surrender on February 16, 1862. The field officers were sent to Fort Warren, Mass.; the line officers, to Camp Chase, O., from which point they were removed to Johnson's Island; the privates, to Camp Morton. They were exchanged, along with other Southern troops, at Vicksburg, and the battalion was reorganized at Jackson, Miss. Until March, 1864, the Ninth Battalion operated throughout Mississippi and Louisiana, and was under fire upon numerous occasions. At this time it was transferred to the command of General Wheeler. After the Confederate retreat commenced from Dalton, Ga., this battalion was engaged almost daily, and acquitted itself so well upon all occasions that it was uniformly praised. Its conduct at New Hope Church and Newnan Station, Ga., has already been referred to. At the latter place less than two hundred Confederates captured four hundred and fifty Federals, and killed thirty-seven, all without loss to themselves. Coming into Tennessee, the Ninth Battalion had a sharp engagement with Federals at Tracy City. Prevented from rejoining General Wheeler, the battalion became a part of General Forrest's command, and was with him in one raid into Tennessee. Rejoining General Wheeler, the battalion was engaged almost continuously with some portion of Sherman's army during the " march to the sea." At all times encountering overwhelming odds, it was the unceasing annoyance which General Wheeler gave the Federals, without serious loss to himself, that marked him as a great general. Following Sherman into North Carolina, the " Old Ninth Battalion " took part in the battle of Bentonville. A portion of this battalion was with General Hood when he marched into Tennessee, and, going north, with a like detachment from the First Tennessee Cavalry, was in the engagement at Henry Courthouse, Va. No attempt has here been made to enumerate all of the battles in which this battalion was engaged. During its service under General Van Dorn in Mississippi, and under General Wheeler during the retreat through Georgia, and during Sherman's " march to the sea." life with its members was one long, hot fight with Federals. Refusing to consolidate with any other battalion and form a regiment, it was organized, fought long and well, and finally surrendered because its members, though not conquered, were tired of fighting, under the name " Ninth Battalion, Tennessee Cavalry." During the most eventful part of its career it was commanded by Maj. James H. Aiken, who succeeded Lieut. Col. George Gannt, who was wounded during the spring of 1863. Gannt was a descendant of the Gannt family that came from Maryland to Hickman County early in the present century.

The following partial roll of Company C, Ninth Battalion, is compiled from information given by survivors of the company: Vernon F. Bibb, captain; W. B. Erwin, first lieutenant (wounded near Newnan, Ga., in 1864) ; G. L. Grimes, second lieutenant; T. H. Church, third lieutenant; DAVID C. ANDERSON (killed during the raid into Tennessee in September, 1862), Thomas Alderson, Marion Bryant (elected second lieutenant at reorganization at Jackson, Miss., in September, 1862), J. K. P. Baker, S. H. Bratton (promoted to second lieutenant in Company G; wounded at Bentonville in 1865), Jack Bratton, V. F. Bibb, Jr., E. Bibb, LEONIDAS

BIBB (died at Camp Maury on January 17, 1862), William Beard, T. S. BRYAN (died in prison at Terre Haute, Ind., on March 10, 1862), WILLIAM F. BINGHAM (died on February 24, 1863), Joshua W. Burnham, John Clendenning, John Cummins, Samuel Cummins, J. L. Chamberlain, B. F. Chamberlain, D. P. Chamberlain, William Charter, Benjamin Charter, Cave Charter, Richard Grimes (promoted to third lieutenant), Nathan Greer, William Greer, Lee Greer, Milton Greer, W. L. Gracey, J. S. Gracey, R. Gracey, Francis Houser, Felix G. Harrison, Green Harrison, Joseph Hoover, B. C. Hanes, E. Head (third corporal), Francis Ingram, A. M. Jones, G. D. Johnson, D. S. Johnson (third lieutenant at reorganization; promoted to first lieutenant of Company G), Joseph Kelly, Arch. Lipscomb (second lieutenant), J. G. Loftin (first corporal), Mike Luckett, George W. Mayberry (commissary at organization; captain at reorganization; wounded at Fort Donelson in February, 1862), R. F. Moore, Robert Moore, WILLIAM E. MOORE (died at Oxford, Miss., on November 20, 1862), Joseph Meadors (first sergeant), George Meadors, Thomas Meadors, Mortimer Mumford, Frank Meacham, Robert Nichols, —— Nichols, —— Nichols, T. S. Newcombe, R. P. Oakley, R. C. Puckett, Joseph Puckett, John Puckett, James Pollard (second corporal), William Richards, Ira Richards, Henry Ragsdale, JOHN SHELBY (killed on the raid into Tennessee in September, 1862), Frank Sims, William Tyler, Richard Wray,

Hal Wray (promoted to second lieutenant), C. S. Webb, W. T. WEBB (died at Camp Maury on January 13, 1862), S. T. Woody.

The following roll of Company D, Ninth Battalion, has been compiled from information ·furnished by survivors of the company: Robert M. Whitson, captain; Eli A. Hornbeak, first lieutenant (promoted to captain; wounded at Kennesaw Mountain); L. B. McClanahan, second lieutenant; Alton McCaleb, third lieutenant; J. S. Wheat, first sergeant; D. L. Brown, sergeant; Wiley Bastian, sergeant; John Anglin, E. C. Anderson, John P. Broome (on staff of Gen. Albert Sidney Johnston), George Broome (third lieutenant at reorganization), WILLIAM BROOME (killed at Fayetteville, N. C.), William Briggs, Jesse F. Briggs (wounded at Waynesboro, Ga.; leg amputated), James Brown, JOSEPH BARNHILL (died at Vicksburg, Miss.), O. M. Bass, Beverley Beasley, L. Bass, George W. Cude, Cave Charter, Sir Winfred Cotton, DAVID EASLEY (died at Vicksburg, Miss., on September 14, 1862), William Easley, Marshall Foster (of Humphreys County; elected second lieutenant at reorganization at Jackson, Miss., in 1862; wounded at Clinton, La.), Brown Fowlkes, Robert E. Griner (promoted to lieutenant), William Gibbons, W. P. Gentry, Wiley Gentry, W. T. GILMORE (died at Vicksburg, Miss., on September 15, 1862), JEREMIAH GREENE (elected captain at reorganization; killed at Atlanta, Ga., on July 26, 1864), James (" Big Shiny ") George, J. P. George,

W. E. GILL (died in prison at Indianapolis, Ind., on June 20, 1862), James Gill, SAMUEL GARNER (killed on July 2, 1863), W. P. (" Wid ") Griner, Polk Griner, (REV.) B. F. HUMPHREYS (died at Jackson, Miss.), John L. Huddleston, PLEAS-ANT M. HORNBEAK (died on March 19, 1863), Samuel Hornbeak, Frank Hornbeak, Amos Jenkins, G. D. Johnson, JAMES ("STONEWALL") JACK-SON (killed near Tunnel Hill, Ga.), Joseph Jaggers, Simpson Kelley, John Kelley, Adam Killick, ALLAN KELLEY (died in prison at Camp Morton, O.), JOHN KNIGHT (died at Jackson, Miss., on September 18, 1862), John F. Lawson (wounded at Waynesboro, Ga.), J. C. LAWSON (killed, while in the infantry, at Perryville, Ky.), JOHN LANE (killed at Bentonville, N. C.; volunteered to do service instead of his brother, who had received the orders; while performing this service, he lost his life), Pink Lane, Elijah Lankford, William T. Mayberry, Henry Mayberry, James P. McCaleb, Francis Miller, James Miller, JOHN M'CLANAHAN (first corporal; killed by Federal guards while a prisoner at Rock Island), W. T. McClanahan, W. W. McClanahan (third corporal), Richard McClanahan, James Meadors, Joseph Meadors, Thomas Nicks, John Nicks, Samuel Pruett, W. R. Pace (lieutenant), B. F. Parker, Samuel Porter, Pleasant Reeves (sergeant), William Roberts (fourth corporal), James Roberts, John Ratliff, William Ratliff, Samuel Skipper, JO-SEPH SMITHSON (died at Jackson, Miss.),

HARDIN SMITH (died on January 20, 1862), ANDREW SMITH (died on January 25, 1862), James Starnes (second corporal), Henderson Smith, William Sisco, Allan Smithson, Benjamin Turbeville, Moses Twomey, John Totty, W. H. Totty, J. W. Totty, B. F. Tanner, R. H. Tanner, Marion Underhill, Valentine Wiss (bugler), John Woods, Reuben White, Andrew Wiley, William Wiley, Robert Watts, John Ware (sergeant).

NICKS' COMPANY.

This company was raised in 1863 by Capt. John Nicks and Lieut. David Moore Spence, regularly commissioned officers of the Confederate States. It was composed of members of different commands at home on furloughs and discharged on account of disabilities, together with a few recruits. Had it been successful in its attempts to get through the Federal lines to the Southern Army, it would have been attached to the regiment being raised by the gallant and gifted Col. William S. Hawkins. Lieutenant Spence was captured during a fight on the Northwestern Railroad, but escaped from the Federals at Nashville. The company, in September, 1863, engaged in the disastrous affair at Centerville, and was, with the exception of Benjamin Turbeville (who cut his way through the Federal forces) and a few others, captured and sent to Northern prisons. The following roll was furnished by a survivor of this unfortunate command: (Elder) John Nicks, captain; David M.

Spence, first lieutenant; John H. Coleman (wounded while a prisoner by Federals), S. B. (Dock) Easley, WILLIAM EASON (died a prisoner at Rock Island, Ill.), BENJAMIN FEW (died at Rock Island, Ill.), GEORGE FEW (killed in Kentucky), Jack George, HENRY GUNN (died at Rock Island, Ill.), SAMUEL GARNER (killed in an attack on a Federal stockade on Hurricane Creek, in Humphreys County), George Hale (of Cheatham County), General Lewis, John F. Lawson, JOHN M'CLANAHAN (killed by guards at Rock Island, Ill.), William McClanahan, R. L. M'CLANAHAN (died at Rock Island, Ill.), JOHN NASH (killed on South Harpeth), W. L. NUNNELLEE (killed on South Harpeth), John Plunkett, ALLAN PLUNKETT (died at Rock Island, Ill.), Nat. Sugg, JOHN SUGG (died at Rock Island, Ill.), JOHN SHARP (killed at Centerville), Benjamin F. Turbeville, Lafayette Turbeville, David Thomas (a Primitive Baptist preacher), John Ware, John Willis (wounded at Centerville).

ROLL OF CROSS' COMPANY.

Albert Henon Cross, of Davidson County, captain; (Dr.) James W. McLaughlin, of Maryland, first lieutenant; Brownlee Cross, second lieutenant (wounded near Centerville), Duval McNairy, of Nashville, third lieutenant, John Beasley (killed on Tumbling Creek), James Bird, Thomas Cates, E. C. Cates, James Dinwiddie, Stewart Dorton, Alfonso Hunt, John Hammonds, Green Hammonds, General

Lewis, William Murphree, John J. Priest, David Potter, John Riggs, James Riggs, Jonathan H. Rains, William Rice, Bartlett Rice, Thomas O. Smith, John S. Satterfield, James Smith (of Humphreys County), Howell Smith (of Humphreys County), B. F. Turner, Lafayette Turbeville, Benjamin F. Turbeville, John B. Thompson, John Wright.

Prepared by
Beverly Nelms
Ft. Worth, TX

Griner, J. C. 491
   L. P. 469
   R. E. 410
   W. P. ("Wid") 506
     389
   Albert 51,86,460
   Albert S. 446,447
   Bethenia 48
   Eliza 48
   Hulett 51,64
   John 51
   Lewis P. 86
   Noble 51
   Robert E. 445,505
   Robert, Jr. 51,59
   Robert, Sr. 47,48,51
   William 51,86
Groves, A. 168
   G. W. 473
   T. J. 476
   Abram 448
   David 482
   George 477
   Henry 473
   John 95,149,150
Grundy, Felix 230,380,385,
   386,387,390,404,428
Guild, Jo. C. 73
   Joe C. 401
   Joseph C. 399,407
Gunn, Henry 508
Gunter, Perry 476
Guthrie, Alex 295
   Hugh 496
   Kate 232
Guinn, James 464
Gwin, James 448

H_____, ...447
Haggins, Jacob W. 464
Haile, Jno. 448
   Joab 440
   Robert 445
Hailey, Dr. 220
Halbrooks, ...304
   R. C. 476
   James 304
   John 278
   Joseph 280,432,433
   Stephen F. 436
Hale, ...194
   A. J. 489
   W. F. 476
   George 508
   William 223,226
Haley, H. P. 464
   Andrew 195
   Charlie 163
   Dr. 180
   Lytle 195
   William, Jr. 440
Hall, ...95,396
   A. J. 489
   Dr. 220
   James 499
   William 387,390,395
Halton, Robert 78
Ham, ...194
Hamby, ...307,308
Hamer, Gustavus 480
Hamilton, John B. 404
Hammonds, Green 508
   John 508
Hamock, J. M. 476
Hampton, Wade 494
Hancock, ...430
Hanes, C. 504
   Minor B. 446
   Peter 335
Hanks, Elijah 354
Hanna, Jesse 442
   Josiah 441,442
   Joseph 442
Hannah, Josiah 442

Harbinson, M. M. 489
Harbison, J. M. 469
   Thomas 66
   Thos. 464
   William 204
Hardee, ...251
Harder, ...318
   J. M. 329,437
   W. J. 491
   Edmond 458,461
   James 461
   James B. 458
   Jere 324,329
   Jeremiah 446
   John 319
   Pleasant 324,487
   William 324
   William, Jr. 434
   William, Sr. 324
Hardin, ...154,454
   Alex. M. 451
   George 329
   Henry 387,391
   John 24,463
Harding, Joe 402
Hardwick, Dillard 172
   Jonathan 448
   Jonathan P. 172
Harbin, J. D. 465
Harlan, Ben 414
   Benjamin 340,360
   Jeremiah 340,432,434
   Jacob 340
Harmon, William 446
Harold, Ernest 186
Harper, ...220
   Stephen (Jesse) 159
   Wiley 105,487
Harrington, A. L. 359
   W. W. 473
   Calvin 446
   Dempsey 98,444,454
   Drury 98,104,454
   Fannie 98
   James 94,98,437
   Jane 98
   Miles 98,446
   Philip 98
   Robert 98,359,444,454,
   457,461
   Sallie 98
   William 98,455
Harris, B. F. 476
   B. M. 448
   I. G. 467
   J. H. 473
   Benjamin 304,306
   Benson M. 461
   Isham G. 408,416
   John 440
   Thomas K. 379
   William 306
   William H. 490
   Wooten 307
Harrison, ...429,430
   Felix G. 504
   Green 504
   John 444
   Samuel 442
   William 245
   William Henry 103
Hart, Jesse 315
   John 441
Hartley, Thomas 499
Hartzogg, George 172,173
   Mrs. 168
   Nimrod 457,461
Harvey, Charles B. 440
Harvill, J. A. 171,233,354,
   451
   Y. F. 427,438
   Y. J. 147,435
   Alexander 461
   Fletcher 85

Harvill, cont'd:
   George 147
   James 105
   Moses 105
   Thomas 464
   Young J. 86,255,434
   Young James 105
Harvison, James M. 464
Haselett, John 464
Hash, Victor 425
Haskell, ...399
   Joshua 170,171,397,450
   Paralee 384,420
Haskins, Milton 437
Hassell, ...216.239
   F. M. 473
   H. H. 236
   J. B. 480
   T. J. 489
   Z. 415,460
   Arten 469
   Artin 92,143
   Benj. (Ren) 464
   Benj. 447,465
   Brit. 469
   Ezekiel W. 434
   Hardeman 216
   Hiram 216,489
   Hiram W. 480
   James 92
   John 216
   Joseph 92,216,340
   Nancy 92
   Silvanus 441
   Silverney (Sylvanus)440
   Thomas J. 480
   William 335,340
   Zebulon 106,381,461,469
   Zebulon,I. 91,149
   Zebulon,II 91,92,95
   Zebulon,III 91,92
Hatchel, ...267
Hatton, Robert 412
Hawkins, Benjamin 440
   William S. 507
Hay, David 22,34
Hayes, ...430
   John 432
Haynes, Landon C. 407,408,
   409
   Professor 278
Haynie, Thos. M. 474
Hays, Lt. Col. 31
   Robert 30
Haywood, ...29
   Judge 120,124
Head, E. 504
   James M. 423
Headstream, Peter 70
Heath, S. C. 438
Hedge, G. W. 438
   W. D. 233
   Vernon 234
Heel, ...259,260
   J. C. 499
Helm, Meredith 408
Helms, ...161
   W. S. 499
Hemsley, Samuel 369
Henderson, John T. 489
Hendricks, W. B. 465
   Mrs. 89,90
   S. G. 473
   William J. 464
Henley, Thos. 469
Henry, T. B. 476
   Gustavus A. 410,429
   Thomas 435
   Thomas T. 435
Hensley, E. B. 491
   J. D. 473
   L. G. 341
Herndon, Elizabeth 225
   Joseph 225,489